From Clients to Citizens

Praise for the book ...

'This is a terrific book. It brings together the rich diversity of thirteen case studies across the world to illustrate how communities organize and mobilize around their own assets – rather than simply relying on external support. Its critical contribution to all concerned with the realities of development practice makes it essential reading for academics, policymakers and practitioners alike.'

Caroline Moser Professor of Urban Development,
University of Manchester

'*From Clients to Citizens* is a unique guide to discovering the power of mobilized local community assets. Its special significance is in the case studies that demonstrate how effective community building depends upon first developing local resources before outside assistance can be useful.'

John McKnight CoDirector, Asset Based Community
Development Institute, Northwestern University

'In a world where there is often a great deal of scepticism about the impact of development practice, the 13 examples of citizen action described in this book bring hope.'

Betty Plewes Former President and CEO,
Canadian Council for International Cooperation

'This is a thoroughly enjoyable, original and readable book.'

Jethro Pettit Institute of Development Studies,
University of Sussex

'In *From Clients to Citizens*, Mathie and Cunningham have masterfully threaded together a group of inspiring community development stories with the vexed issues of empowerment and citizens' rights. This integrated set of cases persuasively argues for a non-romanticized appreciation of both the potentialities of communities to determine their futures, the importance of suitable leadership, and governments' clear responsibilities.'

Davydd J. Greenwood Goldwin Smith Professor of Anthropology,
Cornell University, USA

'A wonderfully insightful exploration of the new frontiers of community development, this book is a must-read for students, teachers, activists and policy-makers alike.'

Michael Edwards Director, Governance and Civil Society,
Ford Foundation

'This volume is an essential antidote to expert-dominated views about how communities are "developed" through external initiatives. A rich combination of analysis, geographic variety and diversity of cases show where, why and how people's own capabilities, resources and efforts make an enduring difference to their lives and to society.'

Alan Fowler Former President, International Society for
Third Sector Research (ISTR)

From Clients to Citizens
Communities Changing the Course of their Own Development

Edited by
Alison Mathie and Gordon Cunningham

PRACTICAL ACTION
Publishing

Intermediate Technology Publications Ltd
trading as Practical Action Publishing
Schumacher Centre for Technology and Development
Bourton on Dunsmore, Rugby,
Warwickshire CV23 9QZ, UK
www.practicalactionpublishing.org

First published 2008

ISBN 978 1 85339 673 1

Since 1974, Practical Action Publishing has published and disseminated
books and information in support of international development work
throughout the world. Practical Action Publishing (formerly ITDG
Publishing) is a trading name of Intermediate Technology Publications Ltd
(Company Reg. No. 1159018), the wholly owned publishing company of
Intermediate Technology Development Group Ltd (working name Practical
Action). Practical Action Publishing trades only in support of its parent
charity objectives and any profits are covenanted back to Practical Action
(Charity Reg. No. 247257, Group VAT Registration No. 880 9924 76).

Cover design by Mercer Design
Indexed by Indexing Specialists (UK) Ltd
Typeset by SJI Services

Contents

Foreword

'They will use what they have to secure what they have not'

This is perhaps the most famous observation offered by the Rev. Dr Moses Coady, the inspirational leader of the Antigonish Movement, which led to the creation of the Coady International Institute at St Francis Xavier University in Antigonish, Nova Scotia. It could also serve as a wonderfully concise summary of the community development approaches captured under the rubric of 'asset-based community development.' For nearly half a century, the Coady Institute has spread this community empowerment idea, affecting thousands of community development leaders and practitioners throughout the world.

This volume presents thirteen remarkable community development cases from twelve different countries (not surprisingly, India contributes two), each of which amplifies Dr Coady's insights into the potential power of local residents and local resources. These are stories about courageous local leaders who rejected the dominant community development strategy, which can be summarized as the opposite of Dr Coady's dictum: 'Communicate what you don't have – your needs, problems and deficiencies – to secure help from the outside.' Instead these leaders have captured the power of local history, culture, skills, knowledge and relationships to rediscover and to mobilize for building the road toward hopeful futures.

As a step toward preparing this volume, the Coady Institute convened most of the principal architects of these diverse efforts for a week-long set of discussions in Thailand. What a rich and energized teaching/learning experience unfolded there! The entire group absorbed and analyzed each case individually, working all the time to identify common themes, lessons learned, shared challenges, and successful strategies. The comparisons and contrasts among the 13 stories were immensely instructive. Some built stronger communities and economies by rediscovering and activating overlooked, historic skills and knowledge, like the indigenous Ecuadorians who discovered a market for traditional herbs and medicines, and the Vietnamese entrepreneurs who built a successful cooperative business from ancient experience working with bamboo. Many, such as India's Self Employed Women's Association, recognized the underappreciated strengths and contributions of local women. And virtually all of these stories emphasized the critical importance of local relationships, or 'social capital', as the central ingredient which leads to community regeneration. There were struggles as well. Nearly all of these leaders have dealt with the tension between development strategies which focus on 'empowerment' and those which emphasize 'rights'. How can local communities recognize and grow the capacities of local residents to define and accomplish development goals themselves, while still recognizing that support from governments, larger NGOs and funders is essential, and in fact an obligation? In other words, how do local residents expand their capacity to act as 'citizens', and avoid being identified as 'clients' of outside institutions which 'know better' and have the resources to press their own approaches. Leaders reached a powerful agreement – that strategies which combined the two approaches were clearly the most effective – and that 'citizens' must remain at the centre of the action.

Another feature of this volume is worth underlining. The editors at the Coady Institute decided that the stories and lessons from the Global South were clearly the central focus of the book, but that it made sense to include a couple of cases from the 'developed' countries. Hence they explore rich community building experiences involving a powerfully self-activating small town in Nova Scotia along with the work of community organizers in Minneapolis to uncover and develop the economic potential of newly arrived Hispanic immigrants, building the Mercado Central. Including these North American examples – and many more could be added from Europe and Australia – makes it clear that there are parallels and intersections between community development experience across the globe, that common experiences and struggles abound, and that conversations which cross the borders are critically important for our future.

Finally, this volume signals the increasing significance of the Coady Institute's impact on international community development understandings and practice. A half-century of faithful and creative commitment to the well-being of 'ordinary' people in the developing world, and in North America – and in their capacity to 'use what they have to secure what they have not' – has placed the Coady Institute at the centre of the discussions about what works, what does not, and where we go in the next half-century. All of us affiliated with the Asset Based Development Institute are proud and grateful to be part of those discussions. We invite all who read these accounts to join us.

John P. Kretzmann
2008

Acknowledgements

In keeping with the central message of this book, our acknowledgements first go to the communities whose accomplishments attracted the attention of the chapter authors and who so graciously gave of their time to tell their stories. Providing access to these communities are the individuals and organizations that have generously shared resources and insights throughout the research and writing process. Each of the case studies in this book is followed by more detailed acknowledgements of these contributions, but it goes without saying that these studies would not have been possible without this enthusiastic cooperation.

Providing the financial support for the case study research are three donors. The Comart Foundation, our key partner, provided a grant to cover the research and documentation for an initial 10 cases, as well as a one-week forum with the authors and representatives of some of the organizations featured in the collection, held in Thailand in June 2007. An anonymous donor with a special interest in the Canadian context sponsored the research for the St Andrews case, and we were able to stretch and spill over our initial funding to include two additional cases, thanks to our funding support from the Canadian International Development Agency (CIDA).

Financial support, while essential, is not the only way in which donors have been supportive. David Martin of the Comart Foundation, in particular, has taken a keen interest in this work and has pushed us into another round of action-research in East Africa to link communities that are driving their own development with research and technology-based institutions to help these initiatives reach scale and sustainability.

Support has also been extended in different ways by the ABCD Institute, Northwestern University, from which we have drawn inspiration since the mid-1990s. Jody Kretzmann generously gave his time to participate in the forum, read each of the cases, and provided encouragement and inspiration for the lively discussions that ensued. The task of sorting through the particular details to find the general principles emerging from the cases was all the smoother for his insights. John McKnight has also lent his support and encouragement, advising at strategic intervals throughout this project. Both he and Jody have quietly but firmly insisted on language that illuminates rather than obscures, and have taught us much about the power of stories. Finally, the ABCD Institute also kindly agreed to let us adapt Geralyn Sheehan's case study about the Mercado Central in Minneapolis for inclusion in this collection.

Contributing to lively discussion about each of the cases at the forum in Thailand were Lucie Goulet (Oxfam Canada), Samuel Molla (Oxfam Canada),

Rachel Polestico (SEARSOLIN), Jyoti Macwan (SEWA), Bernie Dolley (Ikhala Trust), William D'Souza (Myrada), Gladys Nabiswa (CREADIS), Dixon Yasay (Municipality of Opol, Philippines), Mary Coyle (Coady Institute), and Rewa Misra (Coady Institute). They lent their considerable experience as community members, practitioners, donors, adult educators, local government representatives, and intermediary organizations to make helpful suggestions to the authors.

At the Coady Institute, our colleagues have provided support in many different ways. Megan Foster and Brie MacMahon have at different times been involved in organizing and assisting with field work and helping to organize the forum in Thailand. The latter task was finally pulled off with panache by Kate Fiander who has since been honing her already accomplished editing and writing skills on the final versions of the case studies. Mary Coyle and Rewa Misra have offered suggestions on all the case studies, while Catherine Irving has lent her critical eye to the Introduction and Conclusion. Our thanks also go to Susan Hawkes who has transformed untidy sketches into publishable illustrations.

Writing for a development practitioner audience requires communication skills that have regrettably sometimes been abandoned in the jargon-filled world of development discourse. Ann Simpson has been a writing coach for many of the writers in this volume, reading through early drafts, and making recommendations for rewording and reorganizing so that the cases tell a coherent, engaging story while not losing their credibility or legitimacy as the author's interpretation of community events based on primary and secondary research. Participating in the forum in Thailand, she worked closely with the authors to encourage them to succeed as communicators.

A note of thanks must go to John Bastin for developing the maps included in this collection and to those who have supplied us with photographs, including Patricia Brown, John Berridge, Jacqualyn Dowling, Megan Foster, Waad El Hadidy, Kalachary, Andy Lewke, Leah MacEachern, Migrations et Développement, Rogerio Arns Neumann, Angus Ross, Jay Ross, Nguyen Duc Vinh, and Tom Walsh.

Finally, we acknowledge the helpful suggestions of Jethro Pettit, of the Institute of Development Studies (IDS), Sussex, who reviewed an earlier version of this book.

Boxes

Figures

Tables

Acronyms

AAO	Area Agricultural Officer
ABCD	Asset Based Community Development
AB-SLUM	Asset Base and Sustainable Land Use in Marginal Upland
ADEME	Agence de l'Environnement et de la Maitrise de l'Energie
AFME	Agence Française pour la Maitrise de l'Energie
AMA	Ahmedabad Mill Owners' Association
ANC	African National Congress
ASMOCONP	Residents' Association of Conjunto Palmeira
BEC	Basic Ecclesial Community
BJP	Bharatiya Janata Party
BPL	Below Poverty Line
CARP	Comprehensive Agrarian Reform Programme
CBFM	Community Based Forest Management
CBO	Community Based Organization
CCE	Community Conversation and Enhancement
CCF	Christian Children's Fund
CDA	Community Development Agency
CDF	Constituency Development Fund
CEA	Community Emergency Assistance
CECI	Canadian Centre for International Studies and Cooperation
CESE	Coordenadoria Ecumenica de Serviços
CESO	Canadian Executive Service Overseas
CETCA	Compañia Ecuatoriana del Te CA
CFDT	Confédération Française Démocratique du Travail
CGSI	Community Grantmaking and Social Investment Programme
CIDA	Canadian International Development Agency
CMRC	Community Managed Resource Centre
COMBASE	Community Based Sustainable Agriculture
COMESA	Common Market for Eastern and Southern Africa
CONAIE	Confederation of Indigenous Nationalities of Ecuador
CORPEI	*Corporación de Promoción de Exportaciones e Inversiones*
CREADIS	Community Research in Environment and Development Initiatives
CSI	Centre de Solidarité Internationale
CSO	Civil Society Organization
CTI	Community Talent Inventory
DCBA	Deficit Community Based Approach
DFID	Department for International Development
DGSP	Democratic Governance Support Program
ECLOF	Ecumenical Church Loan Fund

ECNGOC	East Coast NGO Association
EDF	Electricité de France
FEI	Federation of Ecuadorian Indians
FLO	Fair Trade Labelling Organization
FOMRENA	Latin American Network of Rural Producers
GDP	Gross Domestic Product
GEM	Global Entrepreneurship Monitor
GMO	Genetically Modified Organism
GNP	Gross National Product
GTZ	Deutsche Gesellschaft für Technische Zusammenarbeit
HPI	Heifer Project International
HUNDEE	Oromo Grassroots Development Organization
ICCO	Interchurch Organization for Development Co-operation
ICI	Inter-American Cooperative Institute
IDP	Integrated Development Plan
IDRC	International Development Research Centre
IERAC	Ecuadorian Institute for Agrarian Reform and Colonization
ILO	International Labour Organization
INS	Immigration and Naturalization Service
IP	Indigenous Peoples
JDF	Jansenville Development Forum
KACE	Kenya Agricultural Commodity Exchange
KARI	Kenya Agricultural Research Institute
KIPPRA	Kenya Institute of Public Policy Research and Analysis
KMG	Kembatti Mentti Gezzima
LATF	Local Authority Transfer Fund
LED	Local Economic Development
MICODA	Midkiwan Community Development Association
MSAI	Migrant Savings for Alternative Investments
NABARD	National Bank for Agriculture and Rural Development
NALEP	National Agriculture and Livestock Extension Programme
NARC	National Rainbow Coalition
NDA	National Development Agency
NDC	Neighbourhood Development Centre
NDP	New Democratic Party
NGO	Non Governmental Organization
OAS	Organization of American States
ONE	Office Nationale de L'Electricité
PfC	Philanthropy for Community
PLWHAs	People Living with HIV/AIDS
PoC	Philanthropy of Community
PPL	Project for Pride in Living
REST	Relief Society of Tigray
RPPMMN	Red de Productores de Plantas Medicinales Mashi Numi
SAC	Sustainable Agriculture Center

SACRED Africa	Sustainable Agriculture Centre for Research and Development in Africa
SAG	Self-help Affinity Group
SASHA	St Andrews Seniors' Housing Association
SC	Scheduled Caste
SCAPE	Strengthening Capacities for Transforming Relationships and Exercising Rights
SEARSOLIN	South East Asia Rural Social Leadership Institute
SENDAS	Services for an Alternative Development in the South
SEWA	Self-Employed Women's Association
SHG	Self-Help Group
SME	Small and Medium Enterprises
ST	Scheduled Tribe
TEA	Total Early-Stage Entrepreneurial Activity
TFO	Task Force Organic
TLA	Textile Labour Association
TOFSSA	Tongantongan Organic Farmers Society for Sustainable Agriculture
UAGOCONP	Union of Associations and Organized Groups in Conjunto Palmeira
UNDP	United Nations Development Programme
UNIFEM	United Nations Develoment Fund for Women
UWHR	United Way of Halifax Region
VDA	Village Development Association
VDC	Village Development Committee
VDF	Village Development Facilitator
VFCV	Vietnam Federation of Craft Villages
WDA	Watershed Development Association
WIEGO	Women in Informal Employment: Globalizing and Organizing
WIND	Western Initiative for Neighbourhood Development
WTO	World Trade Organization

Contributors

Nadia Bentaleb-Maes

Nadia Bentaleb-Maes is director of Migrations et Développement, based in France. Born in Morocco, she has a wide range of development experience working in various African nations. She is also an associate researcher with the *Centre d'Economie et d'Ethique pour l'Environnement et le Développement*. A specialist in rural development, Nadia is also author of the 2006 publication *Energie Rurale pour le Développement: Etude de Cas Africains*.

Martha Chen

Martha Chen is the coordinator of the global research policy network Women in Informal Employment: Globalizing and Organizing (WIEGO) and a lecturer in public policy at Harvard University. An experienced development practitioner and scholar, her areas of specialization are gender and poverty alleviation with a focus on issues of employment and livelihoods. Before joining Harvard University in 1987, she lived for 15 years in Bangladesh where she worked with BRAC, one of the world's largest NGOs, and in India where she served as field representative of Oxfam America for India and Bangladesh. Martha Chen is the author of numerous books including, most recently, *Mainstreaming Informal Employment and Gender in Poverty Reduction* (co-authored with Joann Vanek and Marilyn Carr), *Women and Men in the Informal Economy: A Statistical Picture* (co-authored with Joann Vanek), and *Perpetual Mourning: Widowhood in Rural India*.

Gordon Cunningham

Gordon Cunningham has more than 20 years of experience in community economic development and community-based microfinance. At the Coady Institute, he is involved in several collaborative action research initiatives in Africa and South East Asia exploring the application of asset-based and citizen-driven approaches to community development. Gordon also teaches courses in Community Economic Analysis, Capacity Building for Community Driven Planning, and Mobilizing Assets for Community Driven Development. Gordon has co-authored several articles relating to these topics in *The Canadian Journal of Development Studies* and *Development and Practice*.

Jim Delaney

Jim Delaney has more than a decade of experience in regional and community development, including over six years based in Vietnam. He has worked for the World University Service Canada, CHF, the Centre for Human Settlements at the University of British Columbia, and the Coady International Institute. Jim's experience lies in rural community economic development, programme planning and evaluation, and agricultural extension and agroforestry, primarily in ethnic minority areas in Vietnam's uplands. He spent a number of years working with the Localized Poverty Reduction in Vietnam Program, which forged links between regional Vietnamese universities and poor communities. Jim is currently enrolled in a Ph.D. at the University of Toronto, where his work focuses on rural enterprises and global commodity chains, as well as the institutional and cultural foundations of economic development and change.

Waad El Hadidy

Waad El Hadidy is a researcher with New York University's Research Center for Leadership in Action at the Wagner School for Public Administration, where her work focuses on collective leadership among social justice organizations in the US. Her prior experience includes work with the Ford Foundation and the Near East Foundation in Cairo, where she managed participatory research projects on asset-based development, collaboration and leadership, and civil society. Previously, Waad worked with Booz Allen and Hamilton, and the European Union Delegation in Egypt on projects dealing with the national accounts system and private sector development, respectively. Waad's interests lie at the intersections of international development and US-based social justice, as well as civil society and corporate governance/social responsibility.

Kate Fiander

Kate Fiander joined the Coady Institute's Asset Based Community Development team in 2007, following prior exposure to the Coady Institute through a work placement in Rwanda with the Youth in Partnership Program and the Xtending Hope Partnership. Before joining the Coady Institute, Kate worked with the Pearson Peacekeeping Centre and the New Democratic Party (NDP) in Ottawa. She is currently a member of Oxfam Canada's Board of Directors.

Natasha Iskander

Natasha Iskander is an Assistant Professor of Public Policy at New York University's International Center for Advanced Studies. Her recent work includes a study comparing the processes by which the governments of Mexico and Morocco elaborated policies to build a link between labour emigration and local economic development, and a study on undocumented immigrant labour protests in France during the late 1990s. She is currently working on a project on Mexican immigrants in the construction industry, investigating how tacit skill moves across national borders. Natasha has worked with non-profit organizations in Egypt and the United States on issues of urban development, micro credit and community health planning. She has also worked as a community activist and migrant labour organizer.

John P. Kretzmann

John (Jody) Kretzmann is co-director of the Asset Based Community Development (ABCD) Institute, a research project of the Institute for Policy Research at Northwestern University. Jody is co-author, along with John McKnight, of the seminal publication *Building Communities from the Inside Out: A Path Toward Finding and Mobilizing a Community's Assets.* Jody has worked to develop community-oriented public policy at national, state and local levels. In Chicago, he served as chair of the Neighborhood Planning Committee for Mayor Harold Washington, and was an active policy consultant through Washington's four and a half years in office. He serves on a wide range of civic, community, and foundation boards.

Joanne Linzey

Joanne Linzey is Vice President of Community Impact for United Way of Canada – Centraide Canada, reflecting the organization's commitment to creating lasting, measurable change in community conditions. Prior to assuming a national role, Joanne was Chief Executive Officer of United Way of Halifax Region for 11 years, where she fostered an asset-based approach to the organization's work. With more than 30 years of diverse experience in the voluntary sector, Joanne is also the founding director of ABC Canada Literacy Foundation in Toronto, and has worked on a CIDA-funded community development project in southern Brazil to support the development of effective asset-based community collaborations.

Alison Mathie

Alison Mathie has over 30 years experience in the international development field and has been teaching at the Coady International Institute and St Francis Xavier University for the last 10 years. Building on 10 years working in education (formal and non-formal) and local community development in Papua New Guinea and Nigeria, her main interest has been in promoting asset-based and community-driven approaches to community development, and using monitoring and evaluation as a means to strengthening practice by communities, NGOs, and multi-lateral agencies. Alison has co-authored articles on these topics with Gordon Cunningham in *Development and Practice* and *The Canadian Journal of Development and Practice,* and has published several manuals for development practitioners on qualitative research, poverty targeting, asset-based community development and participatory monitoring and evaluation.

Rogerio Arns Neumann

With 15 years of community development experience in Brazil, Rogerio Arns Neumann is currently based in Bahia, Brazil where he works for the Odebrecht Foundation. Previously, Rogerio served as senior staff member with Pastoral da Crianca, a non-profit community-based organization that has been recognized internationally for its work to reduce child mortality in Brazil. In this capacity, Rogerio introduced the concept of ABCD to his community and was instrumental in the creation of a CIDA-funded project that helped increase Brazilian capacity to create ABCD collaborations. He is author of *Desenvolvimento Comunitário baseado em Talentos e Recursos Locais – ABCD* [Community Development Based on Local Talents and Skills – ABCD] and *Repensando o Investimento Social – a Importância do Protagonismo Comunitário* [Rethinking Social Investments – the Value of Community Driven Development].

Vinh Nguyen Duc

Nguyen Duc Vinh is a researcher at the Rural Community Development Center of National Institute of Agricultural Planning and Projection in Hanoi, Vietnam. He is currently working with a pilot project which examines the asset-based community development approach relative to other approaches to rural development in the Vietnamese context. Vinh has more than 10 years of experience in the development sector and has worked with various programmes focusing on agriculture and reforestation, microcredit and livelihoods, and education.

Anne Simpson

Anne Simpson is the primary copy-editor of this publication. Anne teaches part-time at St Francis Xavier University, where she also coordinates the Great Blue Heron Writing Workshop. Her most recent book of poetry, *Quick,* was recently published by McClelland and Stewart. She has written several other books of poetry, of which *Loop* (2003) won the Griffin Poetry Prize and was nominated for the Governor General's Award. Her first novel, *Canterbury Beach* (2001), is followed by another, *Falling,* published by McCelland and Stewart in 2008.

Geralyn Sheehan

Geralyn Sheehan is Director of Opportunity International in Nicaragua, where she works with community groups on local development projects in the area of microfinance, blending asset-based community development principles into her work. She is a faculty member at the Asset Based Community Development Institute at Northwestern University, and authored several ABCD publications, including *A Guide to Capacity Inventories: Mobilizing the Community Skills of Local Residents.* Geralyn began her career as a refugee resettlement worker, and later practised law in St Paul and became a Vice-President with the United Ways of St Paul and Atlanta. Through her work she designed a number of new models for how institutions can begin to be inclusive of citizen-directed decision-making. She also designed investment systems that incorporated community and economic development strategies with existing social service programmes. Geralyn was awarded a Fellowship in International Development through Partners of the Americas in 1992, to conduct a community development project between Minnesota and Uruguayan women farmers.

Susan Wilkinson-Maposa

Susan Wilkinson-Maposa is Director of the Community Grantmaking and Social Investment Programme at the Centre for Leadership and Public Values at the Graduate School of Business, University of Cape Town in South Africa. She has a background in small enterprise development and gender equality promotion and is the primary author of the 2005 publication *The Poor Philanthropist: How and Why the Poor Help Each Other.* She has lived and worked extensively in Southern Africa as well as in India, Pakistan and Bangaldesh, working for multilateral, bilateral and private sector agencies. These include the United Nations Develoment Fund for Women (UNIFEM), German Development Cooperation (GTZ), and the International Development Research Centre (IDRC).

Introduction

Alison Mathie and Gordon Cunningham

Abstract

Human history is a history not only of cruelty, but also of compassion, sacrifice, courage, kindness. What we choose to emphasize in this complex history will determine our lives. If we see only the worst, it destroys our capacity to do something. If we remember those times and places – and there are so many – where people have behaved magnificently, this gives us the energy to act, and at least the possibility of sending this spinning top of a world in a different direction. (Zinn, 2004)

Consider two communities, located in the same general area. Over time, one begins to prosper, the other has stagnated. The one that has prospered sees itself as the engine of its own success; the one that has stagnated holds the view that the cause of, and the solution to, its predicament is in the external environment. Both, of course, hold a partial truth. But without detracting from the very real structural constraints on the livelihood options of both of these communities, what can we learn from the community that sees itself achieving success in its own right and on its own terms?

This collection of 13 case studies profiles communities where people have been able to organize to achieve this kind of success. They have designed, built and managed rural electrification systems, recreational facilities, community centres, and water reservoirs. They have secured basic services from government and the private sector. They have organized to improve their local economies through diversified agricultural production or through the development of new cooperatives, new social enterprises, or member-owned financial institutions. Their stories have much to teach us, not only about particular strategies to improve livelihood options at the community level, but also about the motivation behind active communities and the leadership that feeds that action. They offer insights into the dynamic of genuine citizen-driven development and the role played by organizations working with them. Most importantly, as windows on success, the cases challenge us to reconstruct the way we think and talk about development, and see what may be hidden from view in other places.

Prompting us to look at these successes have been critiques of development practice coming from various quarters, aimed at different levels of development practice. At its most sweeping, the critique challenges the development enterprise on a global level as another mechanism of control by affluent and powerful interests (Escobar, 1995; McMichael, 2004) and negligible in its impact (Easterly, 2002). At a more localized level, the critique has challenged practitioners to deliberately 'put the last first' (and the first last), rather than continuously reinforce power relations that limit the opportunities available to the most disadvantaged (Chambers, 1983; 1997; Gujit and Shah, 1998; Cooke and Kothari, 2001). Yet another strand of the critique comes from people working closely with communities who report how well-intentioned external agencies (NGOs, government social workers, donors, for example) have often inadvertently disabled rather than catalysed communities, converting potentially active citizens, or livelihood producers, into clients in the process (Kretzmann and McKnight, 1993; Kaplan, 1997).

In two earlier papers (Mathie and Cunningham, 2003, 2005) we have added our own voice to this critique, agreeing that much of the prevailing development discourse has indeed led to a demeaning view of the 'developing' world. A responsibility to enable the less privileged to live with dignity and opportunity has often been translated into the language of 'victims' and 'saviours' in an arrangement that is at best condescending, but is ultimately self-serving on the part of organizations offering development assistance. Providing an alternative to this tendency, we have joined others in pushing for a shift in the practice of development. We advocate nothing so radical as an end to external assistance, but suggest that some elements critical to community survival and prosperity have been lost in the process of development practice, and these need to be reclaimed.

An important element of that reclamation is to shift the focus away from deficits and problems and on to people's assets and strengths. At the community level, this means recognizing what works, identifying how people have successfully organized in the past and in the present, and the particular strengths and resources people can mobilize themselves to improve their quality of life. It does not mean ignoring problems – to the contrary, that these exist is taken for granted – but an exclusive focus on what is lacking or absent often drains away energy for change. In other words, it means finding the right balance between stimulating or supporting local capacity to act while improving access to basic services as an entitlement of citizenship. At the policy level, the task of finding this balance is being explored in discussions about how to balance social protection policies that help people to minimize risk with policies that provide sufficient political space and incentives for people to take calculated risks aimed at building assets (Moser, 2007). These cases provide vivid illustrations of people organizing to build that base of security from which they can then take advantage of opportunity. In some cases, they have shaped policy, in other cases they have responded to it, and in still others they have taken action in the absence of government policy. At the heart of their action has been a confidence in their own capacities, and a belief in the possibilities that flow from collaboration.

It is now generally accepted that this 'heart' of community action may not be fully grasped in the language of 'asset-based policy', rooted as it is in economic and financial concepts, and typically with the household as its unit of analysis. As social, spiritual, and cultural assets gain wider acceptance as contributors to the production of livelihoods, so too are the ways people organize in associational life, and in the community as a whole. The values that people share, the extent and quality of their relationships with others, and the social constructions of history expressed in their stories, are all significant markers of community identity and reputation. Together, these tangible and intangible assets are more than just a means to an improved livelihood, but also a source of meaning in people's lives (Bebbington, 2004; Brent, 2004) because they provide people with the capacity to act as well as the motivation to do so.

Assets (broadly defined) as a source of identity are therefore linked to 'agency' or capacity to act. Assets (what we have or perceive we have) and agency (our capacity to act with what we have) converge and mutually reinforce each other, whether at individual, household or community levels, and express themselves in the power of individual action and community organizing. In many of the case studies presented here, the power of community organizing – collective agency – has been a signature strategy shaped and reshaped over the course of the community's history. For example, the Brazil case follows a self-described slum community, from the time when it organized to confront the authorities to establish basic infrastructure, through to the now long-standing Residents' Association's efforts to stimulate and sustain the local economy. The power of collective agency is also reflected in a community's ability to use its assets as leverage. To varying degrees, all of these cases are about communities demonstrating unity, organizational capacity, local innovation, and the ability to mobilize assets. With these strengths as leverage, they attract external actors seeking a worthwhile investment.

Many of the cases also illustrate individual agency as it relates to collective agency. One example is the Ethiopian woman whose reputation is bound up in her leadership of a church group. With this 'asset' she is able to organize her group to make and sell ropes, mats and baskets, enhancing her own status and identity in the household as well as in the community. Over time, she becomes a spokesperson for the women and a leader of a burial society, which she subsequently transforms into a multi-purpose cooperative – further increasing her own and her community's assets.

For citizens of communities everywhere we hope these stories will be inspiring. For the practitioner, donor, or policy-maker the challenge is how to support and encourage communities in their quest to live better lives and build their asset base, without stripping them of the 'agency' to do that. These cases help to show what can be done.

Background and overview

In the background of this collection is our involvement over the last 10 years with the Coady International Institute. Rev. Dr Moses Coady, after whom the Institute is named, is known in the Canadian Maritimes and around the world for his work promoting producer cooperatives and credit unions from the 1920s to the 1940s, during and after the Depression. Known as 'The Antigonish Movement', farmers, fishers, and miners organized, mobilizing their local savings, skills, labour and materials into cooperative endeavour, in the spirit of Coady's oft quoted remark: 'They will use what they have to secure what they have not' (Coady, 1939: 163).

The Antigonish Movement was a product of unique historical and cultural circumstance, and so it seemed to us that to do justice to the heritage of the Coady Institute, and to equip us in our educational role with a new generation of development practitioners from around the world, we needed to cast the net wide to understand contemporary expressions of organizing for community development.

To do this, we borrowed an idea from John McKnight and Jody Kretzmann who, in the late 1980s, documented successful community development initiatives in struggling urban neighbourhoods in 25 cities in the US. They analyzed these successes, concluding that a unique combination of assets residing in these communities made the difference in each case, hence their book *Building Communities From the Inside Out* (Kretzmann and McKnight, 1993). We decided to identify communities around the world that would illustrate a similar journey through struggle to relative security and prosperity. Through these cases we would try to explain the distinguishing features of these successes, and see what common threads could be drawn across them. In partnership with the Centre for Development Services (Egypt), assisted by the Ford Foundation, we were able to explore success stories in Egypt; one of which Waad El Hadidy explored in greater depth for this collection. Subsequently, the Comart Foundation provided funding for us to document the Jambi Kiwa cooperative in Ecuador, an initiative by a small group of indigenous women to sell local medicinal plants that eventually grew into a producer cooperative with a membership of more than 400 producer families that is now processing and exporting medicinal and aromatic plants to Europe and North America. Subsequently, with further support from the Comart Foundation, the Canadian International Development Agency, and an anonymous donor, communities were identified in Morocco, Vietnam, Brazil, India, South Africa, Canada, and the US. What these communities had in common was that they first looked to their own assets and organized around those before seeking external assistance.

In several of the cases, the initial impetus for organizing is to secure basic infrastructure and service delivery. The case of Boghada, Egypt, for example, traces the way in which a community disrupted by war was able to organize to establish one public service institution after another, illustrating the ingenuity of both young and established leadership in mobilizing local resources, resolving internal conflict, and negotiating with government.

Covering a similar time period, the Morocco case tells the story of villages in a mountainous area once neglected by government, and how they secured essential infrastructure for electricity through collaboration with migrants who had moved to France, but who now returned to help their villages of origin.

A further example of the initial impetus to organize to secure basic infrastructure, the Brazil chapter offers inspiration with the account of a 30-year-period in the history of an urban neighbourhood where forced resettlement took place under the military regime. Mustering the strength to fight for basic services, the residents eventually established a community-owned financial institution that, in addition to making loans, issued local currency to stimulate the local economy.

Migration is a common thread running through all the cases, whether the energy and determination of new migrants, or the reliance on the skills and resources of people who have moved away, or the legacy of cooperation during earlier periods of migrant settlement reflected in a community-wide volunteer spirit. This is one reason why a rural community in Canada is featured, showing how time and time again volunteers from all walks of life have rallied to establish community facilities that continue to attract new residents in a province where rural out-migration and dependence on government for provision of infrastructure have been the norm.

In the US case, the story is about embracing immigration, and the confidence of recently arrived immigrants and their potential contribution to their new country. Latino immigrants built a retail business incubator and cooperative in downtown Minneapolis, their religious faith overriding internal tensions inherent in collaborative effort. Contrary to the view that there is a general trend for social linkages to decline as local residents 'hunker down' in the face of new waves of immigration (Putnam, 2007), this case reveals the possibility for leapfrogging to social integration when there is a deliberate effort by local residents to help new immigrants forge an identity as contributors to the larger community.

In other cases, preventing out-migration is a motivating factor for community organizing. In Vietnam, a social enterprise illustrates how people can reclaim a traditional skill and build a successful business to offer job opportunities to young people. This unique cooperative shows no desire to expand beyond serving local needs for employment despite the fact that the market is beating a path to its door.

The case of the Self Employed Women's Association (SEWA) in India illustrates associational life at another level. With SEWA's membership now at 500,000 in Gujarat (one million India-wide), the case traces the story of how and why women organized as a community of identity and what they have been able to achieve, both as an association and as individual members in their communities of place.

All of these cases fit the description of citizen-led development in which people have organized to mobilize existing assets, often before securing outside resources from external agencies. Our interest in what could be learned from such communities inevitably drew us into the orbit of those organizations with whom they had worked collaboratively in later stages. Much could be learned from these relationships, shedding light on the questions posed by earlier authors about how collective action as a single event (in response to a crisis, for example) is sustained or institutionalized (Meinzen-Dick, DiGregorio and McCarthy, 2004). In the Brazil case, the NGO *Deutsche Gesellschaft für Technische Zusammenarbeit* (GTZ) recognized what the residents of Conjunto Palmeira had achieved through protest and agitation, and the strong sense of community identity forged in the process, but saw the need for strengthened management and organizational capacities if citizen-led development was to continue. The SEWA case illustrates how a social movement sustains itself as an institution. Guided by Gandhian principles, it is nevertheless pragmatic in its partnerships: 'SEWA is willing to work with government, international donors, and the World Bank: so long as they listen to its perspective and that of its members' (Chen, this volume).

In addition, however, we were interested in finding out how external institutions (NGOs, local government, and donors) could catalyse citizen-led community development where it was not already happening. This led us to take a closer look at Myrada in India and its work stimulating Self Help Groups, and at an example of an umbrella community development organization incubating Community Based Organizations in a small South African town, and its relationship with a community foundation and local government.

Since 2003, the Coady Institute has also been working with a handful of partners to develop a methodology, guided by a set of principles, for external organizations to use at the community level to build both local assets and agency. We have described this methodology as Asset Based Community Development (ABCD) because of the heavy influence of McKnight and Kretzmann (and their US colleagues) on our collective thinking. The final three case studies in this book follow the work of SEARSOLIN in the Philippines, Oxfam Canada in Ethiopia, and CREADIS in Kenya in applying an ABCD approach.

All the cases, even those exploring the innovative practice of external agencies, look at change from a community standpoint, as far as this is possible given the obvious constraints of being outside researchers attempting to reflect this perspective. However, at minimum, this means removing communities from the 'project' domain and understanding them in their proper historical context.

The idea of community

We use the term 'community' intentionally since it implies relationships that give identity and meaning to its members. While the term usually denotes identity with a particular place, the communities explored in this collection often go beyond the confines of place. Members of SEWA, for example, as well as identifying with a village or an urban settlement, also belong to a community of women working in a particular trade, and to the community of members of the association as a whole. As Jyoti Macwan makes clear when she reflects on her life as a daughter of a SEWA member, and as a member herself: 'What is SEWA? I am SEWA!' In other words, the association is both an expression and a representation of community.

The Morocco case illustrates other possibilities for community identity. Here migrants have a strong sense of identity with their place of origin whether they return there or get involved from a distance. Are they 'insiders or outsiders' or is the distinction, as Iskander and Bentaleb-Maes argue, irrelevant?

Woven through the ambiguities of 'community' are the possibilities that the idea of it presents. Far from being harmonious and homogeneous, all communities are riven by differences in power and privilege, from the household level up. Communities are also typically fluid and dynamic, both in terms of social mobility and physical mobility. Many of the cases here reveal that people have had to, or chosen to, move within the last two generations, or have incorporated new migrants in the same time period.

The idea of community, however, presents an opportunity to channel energy towards a common purpose. Whether the construction of a soccer field for passionate young soccer players, as in Boghada, Egypt, the building of 'a home away from home' by Latino immigrants in Minneapolis, USA, or the recognition of the joint interests of merchants and consumers in a local economy as in the Brazil case, there are reasons to collaborate. Collaboration may be temporary, but relationships change in the process, and the old ground of mistrust or disrespect subsides (Elliott, 1999). In the cases of 'community' presented here, the degree of inclusiveness varies. Some are about consistent community-wide involvement – as in the Canada, Egypt, Morocco and US cases. Other 'communities' began as small groups – such as the relatively marginalized self-help affinity groups in the South India case that are pushing their way into mainstream society, or the social enterprise in Vietnam, the producers in the Jambi Kiwa cooperative in Ecuador, or the community activists in Conjunto Palmeira's Residents' Association in the Brazil case. Yet over time, with the ebb and flow of community life, the numbers affected by these groups increases; they identify with a larger community and the larger community identifies with them.

Running through all the cases, therefore, are the myriad ways in which relationships of trust (the glue of the community) are brokered, extended, reinforced, and expanded (or contracted) over time as the reasons to collaborate change. The people who participate actively during the history of the community will also change, as will the reasons that compel particular people to cooperate – activity is more inclusive at times, tapering off at others until the energy and passion for organizing is renewed. The important point, as Brent has argued, is that however illusory 'community' is, however imperfect in its social expression, it remains 'a desire, continuously replenishing itself as people seek voice and connectedness' (Brent, 2004, 213).

From clients to citizens

While different schools of thought on the nature of civil society tend to place emphasis either on associational life or on the role played by citizens in the public sphere (Edwards, 2004), several of the cases illustrate a blending of citizenship roles; cultural or faith-based norms are invoked to encourage mutual support and cooperative behaviour in associational life, while the language of rights and responsibilities is used in deliberations about how to work effectively with different levels of government. Solidarity in one can be the springboard for the other. Many of the cases also illustrate a basic tension between these two views of agency by citizens within civil society, namely the importance of preserving an associational base where people can rely on mutual support and 'produce' community, while at the same time claiming government services as the rights of citizenship. Active citizens in both these contexts see themselves as 'agents' rather than beneficiaries, consumers, or clients in the 'induced' and 'invited' participation of mainstream development practice critiqued by Cornwall (2003).

Because every community resides in (and also identifies with) the larger village, city, or society as a whole, the social norms that bind people together in associations for mutual support intersect with the norms and practices expected of government institutions acting in the 'the public interest', and the norms and practices of the market. Sometimes, as can be said of progressive changes in the constitution in India, the 'public interest' (such as those guaranteeing caste and gender-based rights) can be a powerful tool for community groups pushing for fairer treatment, and an indirect influence on more conservative associations and private sector institutions. In the other direction, citizens, often supported at strategic intervals by NGOs, may be pushing to influence the norms and practices of the state. Their stories are illustrated in this book.

Using this book

Each of the 13 case studies in the following pages is self-contained, providing a detailed account and analysis of the unique events that have taken place. Readers may choose to dip into the book and select those that are of particular interest. However, the book is designed so that the whole is greater than the sum of its parts – reading all the cases and the introductory and concluding chapters provides a greater understanding of the role of communities as agents of their own development and the role outside agencies can play to support this. Learning from communities around the world, in countries classified as 'rich' as well as 'poor', in communities of place as well as of identity, the reader is invited to consider common themes, perhaps unlearn some misconceptions, and find some principles to go by when contributing to the field of development.

The book is designed for development practitioners, including those aspiring to work in this field who are now in universities, wrestling with an academic field that is often heavier on critique than on strategies for making a genuine contribution. To enhance the utility of the book, there is an accompanying website, providing summaries of the cases, photographs of the communities, and questions for discussion.

References

Bebbington, A. (2004) 'Movements and modernizations, markets and municipalities', in R. Peet and M. Watts (eds), *Liberation ecologies: Environment, development and social movements* 2nd edn, Routledge, London.

Brent, J. (2004) 'The desire for community: Illusion, confusion and paradox', *Community Development Journal*, 39(3): 213–223.

Chambers, R. (1983) *Rural development: Putting the last first*, Wiley, New York.

Chambers, R. (1997) *Whose reality counts? Putting the first last*, Intermediate Technology Publications, London.

Coady, M. (1939) *Masters of their own destiny*, Harper and Row, New York.

Cooke, B. and Kothari, U. (2001) *Participation: The new tyranny?*, Zed Books, London.

Cornwall, A. (2003) 'Whose voices? Whose choices? Reflections on gender and participatory development', *World Development*, 31(8): 1325–1342.

Easterly, W. (2002) *The elusive quest for growth: Economists' adventures and misadventures in the tropics*, MIT Press, Cambridge, MA.

Edwards, M. (2004) *Civil society*, Polity Press, Cambridge, UK.

Elliott, C. (1999) *Locating the energy for change: An introduction to appreciative inquiry*, International Institute for Sustainable Development, Winnipeg, Manitoba, Canada.

Escobar, A. (1995) *Encountering development: The making and unmaking of the third world*, Princeton University Press, Princeton, NJ.

Gujit, I. and Shah, M.K. (eds) (1998) *The myth of community: Gender issues in participatory development*, Intermediate Technology Publications, London.

Kaplan, A. (1997) *Capacity building: Shifting the paradigms of practice*, Community Development Resource Association, Cape Town, South Africa. Available from: http://www.cdra.org.za/articles/Capacity%20Building%20%20by%20Allan%20Kaplan.htm [Accessed 10 October 2007].

Kretzmann, J. and McKnight, J. (1993) *Building communities from the inside out: A path toward finding and mobilizing a community's assets*, Institute for Policy Research, Northwestern University, Evanston, IL.

Mathie, A. and Cunningham, G. (2003) 'From clients to citizens: Asset-based community development as a strategy for community-driven development', *Development in Practice*, 13(5): 474–486.

Mathie, A., and Cunningham, G. (2005) 'Who is driving development? Reflections on the transformative potential of asset-based community development', *Canadian Journal of Development Studies*, 26(1): 175–187.

McMichael, P. (2004) *Development and social change: A global perspective* 3rd edn, Sage/Pine Forge Press, Thousand Oaks, CA.

Meinzen-Dick, R., DiGregorio, M. and McCarthy, N. (2004) 'Methods for studying collective action in rural development', *Agricultural Systems, 82*: 197–214.

Moser, C. (ed) (2007) Reducing global poverty: The case for asset accumulation, Brookings Institution Press, Washington, DC.

Putnam, R. (2007) 'E pluribus unum: Diversity and community in the twenty-first century: The 2006 Johan Dkytte Prize Lecture' *Scandinavian Political Studies*, 30(2): 137–174.

Zinn, H. (2004) 'The optimism of uncertainty' *The Nation*, September 2004.

Communities mobilizing assets and driving their own development

CHAPTER 1

Possibilities for income-deprived but capability-rich communities in Egypt

Waad El Hadidy

Abstract

The community of Boghada, near Ismailia, Egypt, is a community that is relatively income poor, yet is 'capability rich,' demonstrating this by building and attracting basic services and institutions. The leadership of two young men, encouraged by village elders, first encouraged young people to build a soccer field, using innovative and ingenious techniques. Building on this success, the leadership and the community that stood behind them were able to effectively advocate for the creation of key institutions – an early childhood education centre, and a local government service unit, for example. Traditions of volunteerism, the capacity to mediate conflict, and astute powers of negotiation with the authorities are blended with deeply held values promoting a strong sense of responsibility to others in the community.

Introduction

The village of Boghada in Egypt may well be the quintessential example of an income-poor, yet certainly not capability-poor community. This chapter shows how Boghada's own assets and capabilities, rather than those of external development agents, provided the real impetus for its transformation into a community equipped with infrastructure and basic services. As such, the case engages with Amartya Sen's (1987) argument that the poor are those whose capabilities are so limited that the way they function is not the result of choice. Income poverty undoubtedly constrains capabilities and functionings, as does political repression, yet despite the odds against them, resilient individuals and communities are still able to carve out space in which to exercise choice, summoning the other resources and assets that they have to lever the resources that they need. Here, the possibilities for an income-deprived community affluent in capabilities are explored in the case of Boghada. Shedding light on how assets, choice, and agency intersect, the case helps to deepen the practice of asset-based community development approaches that have been influenced by Sen's work.

To the people of Boghada, the term 'development' is not associated with the traditional language of development researchers and practitioners, such as 'participation,' 'resource mobilization,' 'donor agencies,' etc. To members of this community, what matters most is the availability of services made possible through an institutional infrastructure largely created through their own efforts. The mantra of 'moving forward' is inscribed in their memories in a do-it-yourself attitude characterized by collectivism, philanthropy and perseverance: values that community elders insist on passing on to future generations. When the people of Boghada talk about development, it is generally within the rubric of 'active citizenry', or 'public spiritedness', a result of internal rather than external agency.

These efforts could be interpreted as convenient for a national development strategy that has been described as *laissez faire* when compared to previous eras. Therefore, some may argue that the community of Boghada is inadvertently relieving the state of its responsibility towards the disadvantaged. However, community members in Boghada would argue to the contrary. Rather, the community sees that its own efforts have been the means to access more government services and leverage more state funds than would otherwise have been possible. Boghada exhibits a strong sense of pragmatism, which translates into an astute use of assets, and an exercise of choice or agency.

Situating Boghada within Egypt's development and welfare strategies

Egypt has a rich history of philanthropy, especially prior to the neo-liberal economic development era. From the mercantile era to the advent of industrialization and agricultural expansion, charitable investments and activities constituted the main forms of wealth redistribution. The members of royalty, who were organically linked to the state and probably safe in both their rent-incomes (i.e. from agricultural lands) and in their relation to those in power, spearheaded charity work. This period saw the thriving of the *awqaf* (*waqf* –singular/*awqaf* plural) system, a form of institutionalized philanthropy (endowments) that donated profit to a social cause selected by the donor (El Daly, 2006).

With the rise of liberalism, the adoption of the 1923 constitution, and the emergence of a thriving civil society, charity moved from individual acts of piety and generosity to organized and collective action. Endowments became institutionalized in the non-governmental organization sector, and the freedom that Civil Society Organizations, or CSOs, enjoyed prior to 1952 made their activities and numbers multiply. What was particularly striking about CSOs[1] in this era was their diversity of interests. Many organizations were active on several fronts, advocating national independence, as well as the rights of particular groups, while simultaneously playing an active role in providing social services to deprived groups.

The populist regime of 1952 made it the responsibility of the state to look after the disadvantaged. A ministry for *awqaf* was established, confiscating all privately owned *awaqf* and putting them under ministry control. The new government sought to co-opt all autonomous CSOs and movements, and establish, in their place, community-level organizations (community development associations or CDAs) which worked closely with the government, essentially as instruments of the state implementing its national development agenda.

During the 1970s, the economy was liberalized under President Sadat's popular *infitah* (open door) policy; however, the state's ability, let alone willingness, to cater to those in need dwindled. In the meantime, the police state remained healthy and powerful, placing heavy restrictions on civil society organizations. Only business associations grew during this time, as their mandates coincided with Sadat's open door economic policy. In recent years, particularly since the 1990s, development-oriented CSO activities have expanded, due to pressure from the international donor community, but their activities are still highly regulated (Infonex and CDS, 2005).

In summary, the poor were looked after by the state during the 1950s and 1960s, but after 1974, economic reforms began to squash them. Now they have neither the care of the state nor the freedom needed to mobilize to secure their needs. While members of royalty prior to 1952 capitalized on their deeds of charity, and President Nasser provided services to the poor through the state apparatus, 'now it seems that poverty is left to, miraculously, sort itself out under an oppressive political situation' (El Karanshawy, 2005). This situation is reflected in socio-economic indicators such as those of the World Bank Development Report (2005), which estimates that 43.9 per cent of Egyptians live on less than US$2 a day. Income disparity is a harsh reality as the poorest fifth of Egyptians share only 8.6 per cent of the country's income or consumption levels, while the richest fifth share more than one third of the country's income or consumption levels (Infonex and CDS, 2005).

What is interesting about Boghada is that it seems to exhibit features of each of the different eras. The community's well-being depends on those acts of charity and volunteerism most common pre-1952, yet here it is not the royalty who act as philanthropists. The ordinary citizens of the community donate money whenever they can, and make non-monetary contributions in the form of land and other resources even when their main livelihood is derived from it. Charity in the form of time or money is guided by both religious norms and a keenness to maintain Boghada's reputation, as will be discussed in the next section 'About Boghada'. The village currently exists within a political climate that Sen might describe as severely limiting capabilities. In spite of this, Boghada enjoys an abundance of capabilities that enables it to move forward. This apparent paradox will be tackled throughout the chapter.

About Boghada

Boghada is a small village[2] of 5,300 inhabitants, located 40 km west of Ismailia governorate and 120 km east of Cairo. Considered 'rural,' according to the

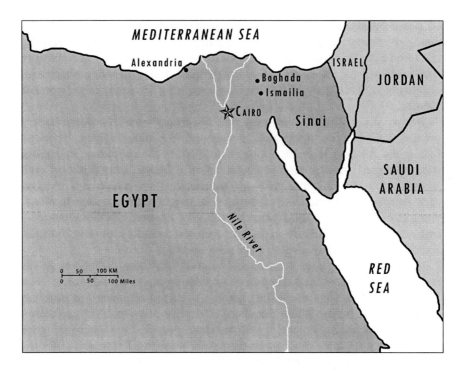

government's zoning and administrative regulations, Boghada, like other rural communities but unlike urban ones, has been neglected in terms of basic services and institutional infrastructure. According to local government officials, about half of the population engages in farming activity on an aggregate of 125 *feddans,* with each farmer typically owning one *feddan*[3] or less. Twenty per cent are employed in local administration offices, 10 per cent work in small vocational businesses, and 20 per cent are unemployed. The village dates back 300 years, or six generations, and is named after the ancestor who first served as *shaykh el-balad,* the government-appointed head of the village.

Situated on the west bank of the Suez Canal, Ismailia suffered an aerial attack by Israel during the 1967 war which virtually wiped out the governorate. In 1969, Egypt intended to exhaust Israel into surrendering the Sinai Peninsula, and again in 1973 on Yom Kippur. For this reason, in 1973, the Egyptian military undertook a rapid migration programme to relocate people to Cairo and relatively safer areas. The people of Boghada proudly recount that the programme stopped at their village, because in their words the community was deemed 'impenetrable by the enemy' (personal communication, 2007). They convinced the military that the community's kinship ties and determination would withstand any impending attack. Following 1973, and later with the signing of the 1979 peace treaty, farmers worked to reclaim and own agricultural lands that were once military property. These efforts added 40 *feddans* to Boghada's original land mass of 85 *feddans*, and can be referred to as another phase in the community's 'development.' Meanwhile, to maintain its reputation for solidarity, a small group of respected elders took responsibility for settling any conflicts that arose, such as those over land or irrigation water, preventing 'scandals' from reaching the outside world, and eliminating the need to resort to the civil justice system. Thanks to its strong kinship ties, the entire community has worked with this older generation of village leaders to overcome tensions and maintain a climate of relative harmony.

Boghada's most recent expression of endogenous development dates back to the 1980s, when the community, led by two young visionaries, began to organize itself around the establishment of various institutions: a school, a day care, a youth centre, a CDA, a veterinary unit, and a local administrative unit. What prompted the current phase was the recognition that institutional infrastructure would guarantee certain services for the community. To the community, this phase represents a continuation of the legacy of collective work: withstanding war conditions, land reclamation, and conflict mediation. Such collective work in effect marks Boghada's 'endogenous development' and is described by the community as active citizenry or public-spiritedness.

Boghada has thus earned a reputation for being self-made – its resilience, solidarity, and activism mark a solid community in the eyes of rural dwellers. It is this legacy of tenacity and unity that enables the community to continue coming up with ingenious solutions and allows it to tap into excellent opportunities. To maintain this reputation is vital, for not to do so would be both shameful and contrary to the spirit of Islam that emphasizes volunteerism, philanthropy, and collective work. This reputation is constantly reaffirmed through action, with community members engaging in highly visible initiatives, such as building the soccer field as outlined in 'Youth centre and soccer field' below, and through communication by making sure that Boghada's 'news' reaches nearby communities, government officials, and the general public. For instance, the community strategically makes use of its location alongside the local train tracks. The train is considered an important 'news-carrier' as passengers witness the latest events in Boghada and circulate the news among their communities and social networks. To engage in action and then communicate such work to others have become Boghada's specialities – two essential capabilities in Amartya Sen's argument.

A series of uplifting events

The most recent phase of Boghada's development – the building of institutions and securing of services – was recounted by the community as a series of victories that gained momentum over time, feeding a voracious desire on the part of local change agents to proceed to the next challenge. The change agents can be described as an active core of young men and women and an older group of adult men guided by two visionaries, Saad Boghdady and

Abdel Mohsen Boghdady (referred to as Saad and Mohsen). This core group is supported by the wider community through philanthropic acts, political influence, and overall solidarity.

Youth centre and soccer field

The development activity in Boghada that is of interest to this case study can be traced back to the time when two local residents, Saad and Mohsen, decided to organize a group of their friends to make use of a vacant piece of land in 1984. These young people, fanatical about soccer, as are many inhabitants of Ismailia, reclaimed the land and converted it into a soccer field where they could practise their favourite sport. Four years later, however, this land was seized by more experienced people registered the land in their own names. This was a painful lesson for the group and from this point on Saad and Mohsen were adamant about taking the proper steps to guarantee communal or public ownership of future initiatives.

It is no coincidence that the start of Boghada's development activity (in terms of institutional infrastructure) coincides with Saad and Mohsen's beginnings as community leaders. At the time when the soccer field was seized from these friends, they were in their twenties and relatively unknown in the community. This failed attempt to create communal space had the effect of galvanizing them to take on subsequent initiatives. It also shifted their thinking from merely patching up available resources to strategically and legally securing facilities that would provide services to the community.

When Saad and Mohsen's energy was noticed by an older generation known for settling community disputes, they received their blessing and moral support. From then on, the two young leaders started to gain a reputation for being pivotal actors who made things happen. With each initiative discussed below, especially with each visible success, their leadership was solidified, enabling them to garner more voluntary support for community projects. Saad and Mohsen emphasized the importance of visible and tangible progress, so that the community would remain motivated to take on more challenges.

The first formal project the two young leaders undertook was the creation of a youth centre. A youth centre is a type of civil society organization overseen by the Ministry of Youth that provides services to youth over 12 years of age. Typically, a youth centre consists of a small library, a tiled gymnasium for sports, and a space for gathering together and holding seminars. In 1989, a fellow villager, Sayed Baqary, offered a small section of his house to temporarily host the youth centre. Yet this space was insufficient to meet the criteria for the ministry to grant official youth centre status, which is accompanied by a disbursement of funds. It took another nine years of temporary status until Saad and Mohsen managed to convince a neighbouring villager to donate half a *feddan* to serve as the official site for the youth centre. The late Hassan Dawood, resident of a nearby village and a farmer relying solely on his land for income, agreed to donate this land, and the ministry in turn fulfilled its obligation by providing LE250,000 (approximately US$45,000 – at 3 March 2008) for the building and facilities. Saad was later appointed manager of the youth centre by the ministry, while Mohsen was elected head of the youth centre's board.

It was not until 2000 that discussions took place over a vacant tract of land, located at the village entrance. It had been used as a waste site by local industry, and community members were ashamed of the state of this abandoned land, especially as it was visible to commuters on the adjacent road and railway line. People felt that this land projected a negative image of Boghada and that the time was ripe for putting it to good use. So, ideas and interests were shared at a series of village meetings. Some people wanted to register the land as personal farm land, provoking disputes that were ultimately resolved by an agreement that the benefits of a communal space would far outweigh those of personal interests.

Meanwhile, the young men advocated for allocating a portion of the land for a new grass soccer field. The tiled gymnasium at the youth centre caused injuries, and the youth wanted to emulate the conditions for professional soccer championships held in Ismailia. The story goes that once those elders who had been in favour of personal land registration heard the youths' wishes, they conceded, since it would ultimately be their sons and daughters who would be benefiting. It can also be inferred that the youths' voices were heeded because their enthusiasm touched Saad and Mohsen, who had never given up on the dream of creating a proper soccer field.

The six-*feddan* portion of land was sectioned into smaller pieces: three *feddans* were allocated for the field and the remainder distributed for various uses: a veterinary unit, a health unit, a religious institute, and a children's playground. Making use of their contacts in local government, Saad and Mohsen painstakingly registered each piece of the land with the ministry in charge: the field with the Ministry of Youth, the health unit with the Ministry of Health, and so on. Such registration is the means by which the land becomes government property – a public good – with usufruct rights held by the community.

The land was in no condition for playing soccer. It was uneven, with deep puddles of sewage water. The youths contacted the head of the nearby Tel El Kebir city council to borrow a bulldozer that could be used for levelling the ground. Thanks to Saad and Mohsen's adeptness in inspiring government officials to take a personal interest in the young people of Boghada, the head of the city council became instrumental in encouraging the youth to lead the work. In fact, the story of the villagers' encounter with the city council has become almost folkloric. It is recounted that when the older villagers asked to meet the head of the city council at the start of the soccer field initiative, he asked 'Who is actually going to do the work?' When told that it was the youth, he said 'well then, tell the youth to come and ask for what they need' (personal communication, 2007).

After partially levelling the ground using the borrowed bulldozer, the youth played in the field for almost two years before an idea for improvement was sparked. The field consisted of sand, which made it easy for unwanted weeds to grow and these scratched and cut the youths' legs as they played. Growing grass to cover the field would solve the problem. A youth camp was organized to clear the area of weeds and prepare it for planting. However, covering the entire area by spreading sod for a lawn would cost LE42,000. One of the older farmers then ingeniously thought of buying a much smaller sod lawn and picking out grass seedlings one by one. The seedlings were planted intermittently so that the patches would join together to cover the entire area. The idea was successful. While the grass was growing, the youth did not play in the field. In order to irrigate the grass, a plumber designed a system based on water pipes with openings at 12-metre intervals. The youth dug a pit for a well, and a water pump was borrowed from one of the villagers.

The field was still too uneven and so it was decided to improve previous levelling efforts. Sand was used to fill the pits and the sandy patches were replanted with grass. Small boulders left over from restoration efforts in a nearby municipality were donated by the city council to place around the field as a border. Trees were then planted as a windbreak. At one point, the governor of Ismailia was passing by and stopped to observe what was going on. He commended the effort, and since then he too has taken a personal interest in Boghada.

Yet the effort was not devoid of obstacles. Without fencing, the field was unprotected from trespassers, and Bedouin shepherds and their livestock eventually intruded. Rather than dismiss the Bedouin, another farmer suggested letting the livestock graze and collecting their manure as organic fertilizer for the field. The suggestion worked, but the task of coordination was overwhelming, and so Saad and Mohsen wrote to the Minister of Youth requesting additional funding to build a fence around the field that would prevent trespassing. Their letter went unnoticed until a ministry-organized celebration of volunteerism took place in Ismailia, and the two friends – Saad and Mohsen – seized the opportunity to speak with the minister. The governor praised the work that had gone into the reconstruction of the field. On the spot, the minister approved a disbursement for LE210,000 to build a fence, a changing room and refreshment facilities, and to turn the field into a state-of-the art soccer field similar to that used by the official Ismailia soccer team.

In addition, at the suggestion of the governor, a portion of the six *feddans* was allocated to build housing for the underprivileged in 2006. As Saad commented, 'the governor wants the rural population to benefit – this is a new way of thinking. It is unprecedented for the governorate to build low-income housing in a rural area' (personal communication, 2007). From the governorate's perspective the vacant land, in a land-scarce region, constituted an opportunity since it was already serviced with water, electricity, waste collection utilities, and even a children's playground. Construction for two buildings – of 92 housing units each – started in March 2007.

The school

By now, the community had gained some experience in taking the legal route to secure communal facilities, such as registering land, taking the initiative in construction, and then leveraging government resources. This experience went back several years. For example, there had been no primary school in Boghada, which meant that children had to cross two busy roads and a canal before reaching the nearest school. So, in 1986, the same team of youth, who were at that time mostly children, together with some adult villagers – all encouraged by Saad and Mohsen – took on the task of building three classrooms out of mud, supported by wooden slabs. This time it was mostly men who took on the construction work. The team recounted the story with bittersweet nostalgia as they pointed at pictures of their first rudimentary school: 'We almost forgot the ordeal of creating this initial school. That is why pictures are so important,' commented Mohsen (personal communication, 2007). Mona, a young woman who frequented the mud classroom scoffed, jokingly, 'I don't want to remember those terrible days' (personal communication, 2007).

As would be true of the soccer field initiative, a critical mass of concerned citizens was mobilized to build the school because of the commonality of purpose. Collectivism and religious norms of piety and philanthropy inspire people to contribute manual labour, time, money, and other resources if they are convinced that the project will serve a wide range of people.

The makeshift classrooms were in a remote location, where stray dogs wandered. Some of the youth remembered the situation: 'we had to run into class and close the shabby metal door behind us. Otherwise our uninvited friends (dogs) would join us,' (personal communication, 2007). Wind would tear through the classroom and water would seep through the roof during rainstorms. It was barely tolerable, but it was all they could afford. Seven years later, and at the prodding of many parents, it became evident that the classrooms were no longer sufficient, so Saad and Mohsen went from door to door to collect donations for building three additional elementary classrooms and two primary classrooms. Those who did not have money donated ducks, geese, and other in-kind contributions to be sold at an auction to raise funds for the school.

The idea of donating to a community cause is intended to foster an open-ended sense of reciprocity among community members, so that contributors may expect some future rewards not necessarily from those they have helped, but from the entire group (White, 1994). This sentiment is reflected in statements such as the following: 'the community genuinely feels that its well-being has been enhanced and so village members never hesitate to contribute when needed' (Saad, personal communication, 2007).

The Ministry of Education assigns teachers from a national pool, so teachers are typically foreign to the communities in which they are placed. Teachers who were assigned to the Boghada school by the ministry were perceived to be unlucky by their colleagues. However, because the people of Boghada were keen on maintaining a certain standard of education for their children, various community members were intent on embracing the teachers and making them feel at home. The people of the community realized how difficult it was for a newcomer to fulfil his or her duties in a remote mud and wood-thatched classroom, so some men and women volunteered to provide supplementary lessons for the students in the evening.

It was not until 2000 that the Ministry of Education supplemented Boghada's efforts by granting funds for the building of a new school, which has come to be known in the community as the 'luxury hotel'. Standing tall in the centre of Boghada, the concrete building serves as a constant reminder that hard work always bears good results – a popular saying in Boghada.

The Community Development Association

The idea of having a Community Development Association (CDA) in Boghada arose initially out of a need for a day-care centre which would fall under the mandate of this type of civil society organization. In 1996, a villager had donated his house for this purpose. The team hired a childcare worker from the community and collected money from each child's family as a nominal contribution. Meanwhile, the core group was adamant about registering the CDA with the Ministry of Social Affairs, to avail itself of annual funds and other services, such as training for the childcare worker and the provision of primary health care. Unfortunately, the donor reclaimed the house for his son, who was about to get married.

Despite this setback, the team was able to find another donor, Hassan El Sayed Khalil, who provided a one-storey house, which at the time was used as a hall for such events as funerals, weddings, and other community gatherings. Meanwhile, the team was undertaking the arduous bureaucratic process of officially registering the CDA, which was successfully completed in 1997.

Then an opportunity presented itself. As part of a strategy that was launched in the late 1990s, the Ministry of Social Affairs sought qualified CDAs to host a new project – the Centre for the Rural Child. The governorate recommended three CDAs, one of which was Boghada. At this time, Boghada's day-care centre had been put on hold since the hall had yet to be converted into a space suitable for children. Yet the team did not want to miss out on the opportunity to host the project. So they devised an ingenious plan. They borrowed a swing from the adjacent municipality to attract the children, and then they gathered the adults, and awaited the visit of the ministry staff. As Mohsen recounted, 'the [ministry] staff members were urbanites from Cairo so they did not know that what they saw was, in fact, a hall and not a day-care centre. What they saw was a bunch of kids playing' (personal communication, 2007). With this little white lie, the team, together with the ministry staff members, planned the space in a way that would comply with project guidelines. The elders waited anxiously during this process, worrying about the prospect of replacing the popular hall – that they so often frequented – with a day-care centre.

That same evening, Saad and Mohsen called for a village meeting at the hall and explained: 'There is *kheir* (prosperity or good deeds) coming to the village, but we must work together to build another storey. We are going to implement the plans agreed with the ministry staff, but not as a replacement to the hall, rather as an extra space that we must create' (personal communication, 2007). Another fundraising campaign was organized, with people donating whatever they could, including livestock. Luckily for Boghada, this happened during the elections of the People's Assembly in parliament. Affluent candidates eager to win votes provided generous donations.

Six months after that meeting, the roof to the events hall was enclosed and three rooms added. The ministry staff members arrived for their second visit to assess progress and were surprised to find the plans indeed implemented, but on another floor. According to Saad and Mohsen, the staff members realized the trick, but they conceded: 'Yes, you did lie to us. But you have proven that you deserve to host this project' (personal communication, 2006). Implementation of the Rural Child Project meant that childcare workers' salaries would be paid by the ministry, and that basic furnishings and equipment would be purchased.

A new element of the Government of Egypt's development strategy has been to enable CDAs to manage micro-loan programmes rather than local banks. The implementing agency of the office of the prime minister announced that four villages would be chosen in each governorate to implement this micro-loan programme. The Ismailia governor, Gen. Abdel Galil Al Fakharany, being familiar with Boghada's efforts had recommended the Boghada CDA, along with three other local CDAs. Loans were used for purchasing livestock and sewing machines; they were also used as start-up funds for small handicraft workshops. Saad and Mohsen were keen on involving the youth in this initiative, and as a result the younger generation of men and women currently participate in sending notices to loan recipients, in bookkeeping, and in various other tasks.

Box 1.1: Timeline of CSO laws

- Laws 91 of 1959 and 62 of 1964: These severely curbed the autonomy of CSOs and imposed numerous bureaucratic shackles. Unions were brought under heavy government control and property belonging to NGOs was sequestered.
- Proposed reforms of 1998: After recurrent lobbying, the government appeared to have intentions to reform Law 62 of 1964. In 1999, a draft considerably relaxing CSO regulation was developed. However, proposed reform legislation was ruled unconstitutional on procedural grounds and was never passed into law.
- Law 84 of 2002: This is the current law passed in June 2002. While some CSO activists praised the law for reducing the bureaucratic obstacles present in previous NGO legislation, others believe that the law is restrictive especially as regards an advocacy role for NGOs. The manner in which the new law has been implemented has come under fire from some civil society actors for being either too repressive or imposing the same bureaucratic shackles on civil society activism.

Source: Civil Society Index Report for Egypt, 2005.

For a local CDA to receive LE1.25 million in loan funds, not to mention further annual funds from the Ministry of Social Affairs, is significant. When word spread of the funds flowing through Boghada, 27 CDAs were established in the vicinity. Yet the team in Boghada was not complacent and continued to seek every possible avenue for funding. A challenge was posed by the Illiteracy Eradication Unit of the Ministry of Education: if the Boghada CDA were to succeed in motivating 100 students to continue attending classes, they would receive LE25,000 in funds for equipment and office supplies. The Ministry had always faced the challenge of sustaining students' commitment to literacy programmes, a national priority given that 44.4 per cent of adult Egyptians are illiterate (UNDP, 2004). Saad and Mohsen once again took it upon themselves to encourage 100 elderly men and women to regularly attend class, explaining that if they were to pass the literacy test, *kheir* would accrue in the form of funds. They also convinced the elders by noting the various capabilities they would acquire by being literate. They collected in-kind donations, such as cooking oil and sugar from private businessmen and storeowners, to distribute to the elders as incentives. On the day of the Ministry literacy test, the two friends were surprised to see an additional 20 villagers show up. These villagers had been studying independently for the test, and the success rate was therefore 120 per cent. The funds were used to purchase a desk, computer, and fax machine for the CDA. As a special gesture to the elderly students who passed the test, the CDA used some of the funds to purchase 100 velvet-covered chairs for use in the hall.

The local government unit

While the team was establishing the youth centre, the CDA, and the school, the establishment of a localized government unit became a priority. Boghada belonged to a fairly large local government unit, responsible for the provision of electricity, water, roads, etc., and the unit included some 60 villages. Its funds and services were stretched too thin, so once again Saad, Mohsen, and the team of concerned citizens suggested that the local unit be split into two units, each overseeing approximately 30 villages.

From 2003 to 2005, Saad and Mohsen undertook the painstaking process of bringing this idea to fruition. They prevailed upon former senior government officials to assist with compiling the required paperwork. This was an extremely cumbersome task but these two young leaders and their advisors convinced the governor of Ismailia that he would enjoy a lot of credit if this local government unit were established while he was in office. The governor in turn met with the prime minister with the completed dossier presenting their case and the request was granted in 2005.

This meant that about LE500,000 in annual funds would be extended to the new local government unit. This would pay for overseeing 35 villages, instead of 60, as per the initial arrangement. Conflict arose over the location of the new local government unit because of a misconception that the village hosting it would receive certain privileges. Thanks to Saad and Mohsen's conflict mediation skills, which they describe as the ability to persuade, all of those concerned were invited for a meeting at the hall of the Boghada CDA. It was explained that a consensus had to be reached in order not to forego this opportunity. It had been the case in several villages that *kheir*, in the form of government funds, for youth centres, schools, etc., had been revoked because the community could not resolve its own issues. '[Conflict] automatically sends a signal to the government that the community is incapable of managing the funds,' explained a teacher from a nearby community (personal communication, 2007). Essential to resolving the conflict was the location, selection, and naming of the new unit. A central location was chosen for the local unit on the premise that all villages served would lie within a limited radius. A neutral name was chosen – *Shorouq* (meaning sunrise) – that did not represent any one village and was not associated with historical heritage. The naming of the local unit is strategic in that it signifies alliance with the government, and it invokes a sense of newness associated with 'striding forward' in populist rhetoric, and most importantly, does not favour any one village.

Saad was appointed head of the new *Shorouq* local unit in 2006, which is a testament to his leadership capabilities. It was explained that this appointment instilled a sense of pride in the community and that Boghada was capable of growing leadership from within. It also reaffirmed the value of collectivism and extended it into the realm of leadership. In a meeting organized to announce this appointment Saad explained, 'we are all leaders of the local government unit' (personal communication, 2007).

Yet this great achievement also took its toll. A larger responsibility for overseeing the multiple institutions established has now fallen on Mohsen, who is employed full-time at the district office of the Ministry of Education. Mohsen noted: 'Saad is now deeply immersed in fulfilling the local government unit's financial obligations, such as reporting to the government office in charge, handling budgets, etc. He cannot make any mistakes. Everything is calculated in monetary terms. Auditors do not understand the value of volunteering; they need to see everything accounted for in exact pounds and *piasters*' (personal communication, 2007).

The Boghada team was wary that Saad's appointment might place Boghada under scrutiny from surrounding villages. Members of these communities might have had the impression that his newly acquired influence would allow the funnelling of funds to Boghada at the expense of other villages. And so, in another strategic move, Saad and Mohsen held a meeting of village representatives at the youth centre and announced: 'Boghada is self-sufficient, and thus we decline any service from the local government unit unless there is a surplus at the end of the year' (personal communication, 2007). Since the establishment of the local unit in 2005, Boghada has only availed itself of one benefit, earned through its volunteer efforts. Local government unit funds are of two types. One is an 'infrastructural plan' in which funds are allocated

The Community Development Association is an eye-catcher for passers-by and a sign of Boghada's persistent efforts.

for projects relating to infrastructure and a contractor is hired to implement them. The second is the *Shorouq* plan in which services are contingent upon the non-monetary contributions of a community. Boghada benefited from the latter. For example, to acquire new PVC water pumps for irrigating the soccer field the community contributed manual labour for their installation.

A sceptical perspective

While these stories have been described here as successes in terms of being community-driven, a more nuanced discussion of who has the power and responsibility to act in these circumstances is required. In this section, this is addressed by first discussing whether such community-driven initiatives absolve the state of some of its responsibilities, and second, by looking at the extent to which the community-driven process is inclusive or consensual.

Onus on the community

One question that might be raised about these stories is whether, in fact, they showcase a power differential between the community and the state where failure of the state to provide social services has increased the burden on communities to provide for themselves. It may be outrageous to think

---

Box 1.2: Decentralization

Egypt is divided into 26 governorates under the Ministry of Interior Affairs, which is then divided into 126 administrative districts. According to the Egypt Human Development Report, whose theme for 2004 was decentralization: 'local government does not control the bulk of wage expenditure, it is just the agency responsible for disbursing it on behalf of line ministries' (UNDP, 2004: 55). The report alludes to a very limited level of decentralization on the part of the government and very limited autonomy in fiscal and non-fiscal matters at the level of local government. This lack of fiscal autonomy on the sub-national governmental level is also confirmed by the UNDP's Programme on Governance in the Arab Region (POGAR), which indicates that transfers of funds from the central government account for 90 per cent of local revenues. The UNDP report confirms that the absence of capital at the local level undermines the ability of these governments to initiate development projects.

Source: Civil Society Index Report for Egypt, 2005.

---

that children have to endure six years in a mud classroom, or that youth must work relentlessly for nine years before the government finally fulfils its duty of building a proper school or youth centre. By declaring these successes, does the state evade its responsibilities and place an increased burden on communities?

And so, to assess the success of the Boghada case implies passing judgement on what the respective roles are – or ought to be – of citizens relative to the state. When this issue was raised at a Cairo workshop in 2003, in which this case was discussed, community members responded that the answer is different depending on whether the context is urban or rural. In the rural situation, the government technically owns no land. A community member clarified: 'If we go to the state and request a service, the first question that will be asked is: where is the land?' (personal communication, 2007). The predominance of reciprocal relations among villagers in the rural context is contrasted with its absence in the urban. In fact, reciprocity is seen as the distinguishing characteristic (or the pretext) that makes it possible for citizens to take initial action and for the state to supplement those actions. As Mohsen, and other community members, explained:

> We exert the initial effort to demonstrate to the state that we are up to it. Then we bombard the state with letters and demand officials to come and see. We essentially say to the state: 'Put us in your plan.' After that the state never fails to fulfil its side of the agreement. (personal communication, 2007)

Citizens of Boghada never doubt that the state will eventually offer support. Perhaps the people are mystified by the attitude of government officials, but it seems more plausible that they are highly pragmatic. They have learned over the years that this is the way things are in Egypt, and that unless they take the initiative, nothing will be done for them. This is their way of challenging the status quo and exercising political activism. The people of Boghada have taken a situation that disadvantages them as rural citizens and transformed it into a situation that leverages state resources to maximum effect – resources that would not have been acquired had it not been for their initial efforts.

Power, conflict, and friction

'Development' in Boghada is about more than increasing income; it is also about a process of conflict mediation and conciliation inspired by an older generation of Boghada citizens who remain committed to resolving conflict through dialogue rather than external means. Conflict mediation does not take any prescribed form, except for an astute sense of reading the situation and responding through versatile communication skills. Saad and Mohsen have inherited what they refer to as 'the art of persuasion' from the older generation. Because of their leadership status, whenever there is a situation of tension, the two friends call for a meeting where issues are settled through dialogue. Each situation warrants a different strategy, with some disputes such as those over land or irrigation water being more divisive than everyday neighbourly disputes for example. But what is common in all incidents of conflict is that Saad and Mohsen always manage to craft a framework of collective responsibility. For instance, when disagreement arose over the use of the vacant land a certain rule of thumb was used: communal use would benefit a greater number of people than private use. Moreover, the two friends always found a common denominator around which all stakeholders could coalesce: the youth in the soccer field initiative, a neutral name and location for the local unit, *kheir* to be bestowed on the community in the case of the day-care project. The idea is to show that there exists some larger, higher-order interest that community members should strive towards, while concurrently demonstrating the adverse impacts of not resolving conflict. Within the village, Boghada is usually compared to other communities that lost the promise of *kheir* because people could not resolve their conflicts.

The highly collectivist and egalitarian philosophy demonstrated in Boghada may indeed overshadow the existence of conflict or power differentials. Yet there may be a deliberate relationship between the two. Collectivism is a structure that minimizes or alleviates conflict; it is an imperative that precedes rather than follows conflict situations. So the issue is not the apparent absence of conflict or power differentials but the application of collectivist values to avoid conflict, and to resolve it once it arises. Collectivism is more than a mere nicety; it is achieved by the community as an absolute necessity. Power relations are dealt with before they actually form.

The community's prizing of amicable relations and the urgent action taken to resolve conflict leads to an alternative interpretation of power, inviting a shift in emphasis from the conventional 'power over' to 'power to' and 'power with'. In the former, power is treated like a 'thing' of which there is a finite amount in a closed system; if one party gains power it would be at the expense of another – a zero sum game. While 'power over' certainly exists in Boghada and may manifest itself in unequal access to land, irrigation water, or other forms of wealth, it seems that the more relevant model of power here is the 'power to' or 'power with', which draw on a generative definition of power. Here power grows when people stimulate activity in each other to realize what capacities and knowledge can be developed in a collective way (Nelson and Wright, 1995). Indeed the Boghada community, through its collectivist mantra and conflict resolution practices, constantly tries to suppress the existence of 'power over' in order to grow the power 'to' make change 'with' each other.

This levelling of power relations has been a considerable challenge. 'Don't be misled into thinking that this was all easy. It took years and years of work. The CDA is the outcome of ten difficult years,' reminded Saad (personal communication, 2007). Moreover, there were times when the two leaders felt disheartened and burned out. Mohsen recounted that some people often questioned Saad and Mohsen's leadership, insinuating that they must have had ulterior motives. On one occasion in particular, Mohsen was fed up and told Saad that he would quit community work as soon as they had finished a scheduled meeting with a government official. At the meeting, Saad directed Mohsen's attention to a framed saying by the Prophet Muhammed that hung directly above the official's desk: 'God has assigned certain people to assist others, making them love *el-kheir* and bringing them closer to *el-kheir*. Those will evade hell's wrath' (personal communication, 2007). From then on, Mohsen and Saad developed the conviction that they had a mission – to assist people of lesser fortune. It would be *haram* (against God's will) if they were to abandon this role.

Assessing assets positively or negatively

Assets can be described in terms of what they can do for, or what they confer upon, in terms of identity and capacity, those who have them. Depending on one's perspective and circumstances, the same set of assets can be perceived positively or negatively. A negative perspective foregrounds the limitation of one's capacity to act and is reflected in statements such as: 'Those (assets) are all we have. We get by.' Assets in this sense are utilized out of a sense of coercion, stemming from the absence of alternatives and lack of choice. By contrast, in the case of Boghada, people chose to see themselves positively as having an abundance of assets, which led them think in terms of possibilities for action.

Everything they did was a matter of choice and not limitation. Relating this to Sen's argument, we could say that the people of Boghada defined their asset base (that others might see as meagre) positively, precisely because of the community's varied capabilities, which in turn enabled it to choose how to function in certain situations. These capabilities include various skills such as leadership, the community's ability to communicate its progress to others, and its adeptness in attracting government officials. The capabilities also include the philosophy that the community itself constructs to propel it forward, such as reciprocity, philanthropy, and collectivism.

Of course, Boghada exists within a larger power structure. 'Development' is often criticized for being shaped into an apolitical machine, offering technical solutions rather than political ones because political solutions would threaten the state by drawing attention to its failure to account for the poor (Fisher, 1997; Ferguson, 1990). The people of Boghada are aware of the power structure in which the community exists, but instead of confronting, challenging, or dismissing the state, they choose to engage and work with the system.

Applying an asset-based lens

This section will illuminate the most pivotal assets in the Boghada case and review, in more detail, how government funds have been leveraged.

Human versus natural assets

It is quite evident that a number of assets were utilized throughout all the years of Boghada's development. The community has an aptitude for recognizing even latent assets and putting them to good use, whether these assets initially belong to the community or not. In recounting how they obtained assets, people shamelessly used the verb *shahatna*, which literally means 'beg,' but in the Egyptian dialect this in fact means acquiring something for which its owner no longer has use.

Boghada used numerous assets to establish the four institutions discussed earlier in this chapter, including physical assets such as buildings and water pipes; natural assets, such as land; and human assets, such as solid leadership. When asked which of these was most important, a debate ensued with some claiming the land and others claiming human assets. There is no doubt that land is critical in Boghada. It could be argued that without the vacant land for the soccer field, or the other plots donated, no activity would have occurred in Boghada. Land is more than an asset in Boghada; it is embedded in the wider social pattern of the community.

On the other side of the debate was the view that even if land were abundant, it would remain idle if it weren't for the human and social assets that converted it into something useful. By 'human assets', the community referred to leadership, the youths' commitment and enthusiasm, and the various skills exhibited by members of the community, from knowledge of government structures and mechanisms, to skilfulness in planting and irrigating patches of desert land.

The role of empowering leadership

There is no doubt that Saad and Mohsen appear as the prominent leaders of this movement of active citizenship or public-spiritedness in Boghada. They are leaders because of three factors. First, they embrace their own leadership and justify it in terms of the religious argument discussed in 'The school', above. By voluntarily taking charge of various projects, they see themselves acting as good Muslims. They have also earned this tacit status by championing various activities, starting with the soccer field that was seized from them back in the 1980s. Finally, the community confers leadership on them, as Saad and Mohsen continually demonstrate their capabilities with each challenge.

As mentioned above in 'The local government unit', the community extends collectivism into the leadership realm. This collapses the traditional hierarchical relationship between leader and follower, and dispels the heroic model in which a powerful and charismatic leader directs others or bestows knowledge upon followers. One manifestation of this type of leadership is the way it recognizes and values the capabilities of others. For example, the water pump earlier donated by a villager was no longer required once PVC water pipes were installed. When the youth suggested removing the pump, Saad and Mohsen refused, explaining that it should be left to commemorate philanthropy and the good man who donated it. 'We never forget el-kheir', stated Mohsen (personal communication, 2007).

Another manifestation of this collective form of leadership is its empowerment of others – especially younger generations – to take on leadership roles. This occurs through the constant reinforcing of capabilities and subtle reminders of Boghadian values. For example, when the Ministry of Youth hired a contractor to build a wall around the soccer field and convert the field into one that met professional standards, the youth might have been relieved of arduous tasks. Yet, as Mohsen commented, they 'keep organizing clean-ups, and other day-long activities, lest we all forget the spirit of volunteerism' (personal communication). An elder had always advised Saad and Mohsen to create a 'second row' of community champions who will take charge of Boghada's development, and indeed, the two friends are keen on building the youths' capabilities through subtle, ongoing pedagogical approaches. The youth readily accept the responsibility and the challenge. Mahmoud Khalil, one of the younger citizens explained: 'our colleagues from other villages always tell [the Boghada youth] that we are too involved in this community. They think it consumes all our life. I say to them "that is because everything that we work on in Boghada is relevant to other life experiences." I will use this learning in whatever life throws at me' (personal communication, 2007).

Assets as means of exchange

There are many ways of talking about the value of assets. One is the sociological sense of what is ultimately good, proper, or desirable in life. In Boghada, this logic applies to natural assets, such as land, and human assets, in the form of volunteerism, and the value attributed to them. In another sense, assets could be defined economically, particularly by measuring how much people are willing to give up to obtain them. Physical assets in Boghada, such as the school or the youth centre, could be defined in this way because people gave up money (in the form of donations) and time (in the form of volunteerism) to construct them. Yet another theory of value in people's action is most relevant to this case. When people's capacity to act is 'transformed into concrete perceptible forms' (Munn in Graeber, 2001: 45), the assets exchanged serve as a medium, with the real value lying in the act of exchange. So when community members donated ducks to help build the school, the real asset was not so much the donation – in this case, live birds – but the *act* of exchange itself. In other words, the birds would have no value in this situation had it not been for the exchange relation. This *act* of exchange is an important capability in Boghada.

This case is an example of open-ended reciprocity, when people give and receive to widen the circle of exchange so that any individual can access the resources of the entire group. Such exchange relations signify two interrelated things: social capital and capabilities. Social capital is defined by Putnam as 'features of social organization, such as trust, norms [of reciprocity], and networks [of civic engagement], that can improve the efficiency of society by facilitating coordinated actions' (Hulme, 2000: 4). Exchanging donations (ducks) for buildings (a school) is an example of an act that solidifies reciprocal relations and builds social capital. Capabilities do not only refer to particular skills such as leadership or communication, but also to how the people of Boghada construct reciprocal relations that keep the community moving forward. Sen's definition of poverty as capabilities and functionings argues that: '...the constituent part of the standard of living is not the good, nor its characteristics, but the ability to do various things by using that good or those characteristics' (Sen, 1983: 9). In this light, physical, natural, financial and human assets act as media because they enable social capital to strengthen and accrue, enabling people to do various things by using them.

Leveraging government funds – the role of 'external' agency

Boghada's strategy for obtaining government funds has been simple, yet very effective: the community pools both monetary contributions and time to establish a makeshift institution, and then the government provides the funds necessary to shift from a temporary to a permanent structure. Boghada has not been successful, or perhaps not keen enough, to obtain funds from donor agencies, despite the fact that it is known to the donor community.

Boghada has solidified its relationship with the government on all levels, partly because of proximity and access to local government officials. Several citizens of Boghada have enjoyed prominent government posts and these people have been instrumental in guiding Saad and Mohsen. Boghada's relationship with government, especially at the local level, is premised on partnership and the understanding that the state cannot invest in an initiative without securing land first. As explained succinctly by a villager: 'the government also wants to do its job. It's a win-win relationship. We do the work and provide the land, and they fulfil their end of the bargain. In the end, we get what we want and the government can demonstrate progress' (personal communication, 2007).

An example of the capabilities discussed by Sen is Saad, Mohsen, and the Boghada team's intuitive communication skills. They know exactly what attracts government officials, and they are confident that once an official visits Boghada, he or she will provide access to resources. Over the past decade, Ismailia has had three governors, all of whom have known Boghada well. Mohsen explained, 'Any new government official is interested to know who are the active members, the change agents, the "makers and shakers", within his jurisdiction. They are drawn towards these people and wish to build alliances' (personal communication, 2007). Of course, prominent government officials would not seek out Boghada, a tiny village off a dirt road, so the community must invite them first. As Mohsen puts it:

> Some people establish relationships with governors and other influential people by inviting them to weddings. We have found that it is much more effective to invite them to any event that signifies progress in the community – like the inauguration of the local government unit. (personal communication, 2007)

Mohsen mentioned that the governor was planning to make a fleeting appearance on the day of the inauguration, but ended up staying two hours because he was so impressed.

Boghada's skills in leveraging government funds, in communicating with government officials, and exerting influence over the community's own development all challenge the 'idea of the state as a concrete, overarching, encompassing reality' (Ferguson and Gupta, 2002). This idea – that the state is above civil society and community with inherently top-down planning – ultimately benefits the state because belief in the idea entrenches its legitimacy, thereby granting it more rights to intervene and control local development processes.

The Boghada example illustrates that the lines between 'state' and 'community,' and between 'internal' and 'external,' are often blurred. With Saad's new position as head of the local government unit, it is difficult to draw a line between insider and outsider, or between state and civil society. Boghada's engagement with the system, rather than its confrontation, has a political result in that it alters power relations (or perhaps perceived power relations) between the state and civil society. The image of the top-down state dictating development agendas no longer holds in this case. Boghada remains the driving force of its own development, and even defines the very notion of development in its own terms.

Nevertheless, there is some danger then when assessing a community's capacity to drive its own development. The danger comes from depicting a community as a neatly delineated entity with distinguishable boundaries when 'endogenous' (or internally driven) is pitted against 'exogenous' (or externally driven). As clearly demonstrated in this case, community leadership was effective because it worked at these boundaries, linking internal capacity to external opportunity and blurring these notions of *endogenous* and *exogenous*.

Concluding remarks

Boghada provides a remarkable example of agency: community action in the context of a government structure that expects more from the rural poor than from the urban poor. As such, it contradicts commonly held assumptions about the capacities of the poor, found in popular characterizations such as 'a culture of dependency,' 'weak work ethic,' 'eroded values,' and 'apathetic attitudes'. Boghada also provides a counterpoint to theories that attribute poverty to the culture of a people where internalized self images of poverty are passed on to succeeding generations and become enduring cultural ways of seeing the world and acting within it (Howe, 1998).

In Egypt, it is common to find vestiges of these attitudes, even today. Privileged groups express their anguish over the dismal state of the country and blame the poor for their poverty, but it is less common to blame the wider socio-economic circumstances or the political structure.

Boghada has suffered the deprivations of war, scarce resources, weak economic conditions and a state development policy that favours urban over rural populations. Yet, instead of conforming to the stereotype by expressing a negative view of itself, the leadership of Boghada has managed to instil a belief in possibility derived from an appreciation of its capabilities. Community members have ingeniously realized that by fuelling diverse capabilities they can function and exercise a measure of choice, as they have demonstrated in their ability to turn state development policy to Boghada's advantage. In exercising this choice they have shown that assets only take on value through people's actions. These actions, ranging from forging reciprocal relations to attracting high-profile government officials, are the capabilities discussed by Sen that enable a community to exercise choice in its development endeavours.

Endnotes

1. From 1922 to 1952, the number of CSOs is said to have grown from 300 to more than 800, including Private Voluntary Organizations (PVOs), eight political parties, labour unions, professional associations, chambers of commerce, and one industrial union.
2. According to Egypt's administrative divisions Boghada qualifies as *ezba* ('estate'), which is an even smaller unit than a 'village'.
3. A *feddan* is the Egyptian measure for an area of land and is equivalent to roughly 21 metres by 200 metres.

References

El Daly, M. (2006) *Philanthropy in Egypt: A comprehensive study on local philanthropy in Egypt and potentials of directing giving and volunteering towards development*, Centre for Development Services, Cairo, Egypt.

El Karanshawy, S. (2005) *The relation between private property and capital in Egypt*, Centre for Development Services, Cairo, Egypt.

Ferguson, J. (1990) *The anti-politics machine: 'Development', depoliticization and bureaucratic power in Lesotho*, Cambridge University Press, Cambridge, UK.

Ferguson, J. and Gupta, A. (2002) 'Spatializing states: Toward an ethnography of neoliberal governmentality' *American Ethnologist*, 29: 981–1002.

Fisher, W.F. (1997) 'Doing good? The politics and antipolitics of NGO practices', *Annual Review of Anthropology*, 26: 439–464.

Graeber, D. (2001) *Toward an anthropological theory of value: The false coin of our own dreams*, Palgrave, New York.

Howe, L. (1998) 'Where is the culture in the "culture of poverty"?' *Cambridge Anthropology*, 20(2): 66–91.

Hulme, D (January 2000) *Protecting and strengthening social capital in order to produce desirable development outcomes*, Social Development Department, SD SCOPE Paper No. 4. Institute for Development Policy and Management, University of Manchester, Manchester, UK.

Infonex Corporation and Center for Development Services (2005) *An overview of civil society in Egypt, CIVICUS Civil Society Index Report for the Arab Republic of Egypt*, CIVICUS, Cairo, Egypt.

Nelson, N. and Wright, S. (1995) 'Introduction: Participation and Power' in Nelson, N. and Wright, S. (eds) *Power and participatory development: Theory and practice*, ITDG Publications, London.

Sen, A. (1983) 'Poor, relatively speaking', *Oxford Economic Papers, New Series*, 35 (2): 153–169.

Sen, A. (ed) (1987) *The standard of living*, Cambridge University Press, Cambridge, UK.

UNDP (United Nations Development Programme) (2004), *UNDP Human Development Report 2004: Cultural liberty in today's diverse world*, Oxford University Press, New York.

World Bank, The (2005) *World Development Report 2005: A better investment climate for everyone*, Oxford University Press, New York.

Author's note

Interviews for this case study were conducted in 2005 and subsequently in February 2007. I talked with the two recognized leaders in the community – Saad and Mohsen, various community members of different occupations, the active youth volunteer group, and staff of some of the community-led initiatives including the day-care centre, the youth centre, and the veterinary unit. Preliminary discussions revealed that Boghada citizens generally have an astute sense of what counts as resources ('resources' in Arabic resonated more than the literal translation of the word 'assets') and how to use those resources. By 2007, a relationship based on trust had been fostered with the community, and since appreciative inquiry seemed to obscure the more contentious, and conflict-laden topics, I chose to probe into some potentially negative terrain. Through that, stories about the initial conflict surrounding the soccer field, and some community gossip about the two leaders were revealed. It was through these stories that I could get a sense of how the community manoeuvres tough terrain, especially when it comes to mediation of conflict, which appeared to be an integral part of the daily life and cultural repertoire of Boghada.

The story of Boghada is a special one for me, because the community's progress seems to run parallel to my own personal development over the past three years. When I first visited the small village back in 2005 I was delighted to be part of a comparative case study research and found it particularly refreshing to be looking into positive examples, within a line of work dominated by depressing stories. I was impressed by their tenacity, wisdom, and sense of morality.

Three years and an anthropology degree later, I was still impressed with Boghada, all the more for different reasons. I could still see their tenacity, wisdom, and sense of morality, but what I found myself infatuated with was their sense of agency. Boghada embodies agency – an over-used and tired word in the development discourse. Despite all the odds stacked against the village, the community seizes every opportunity, makes use of every resource, and activates every relationship in order to achieve its objectives.

Equally fascinating to the story itself was the way in which the people welcomed me and *chose* to communicate their story. I often found myself reflecting on my own position in the research and how, what we might traditionally refer to as the researcher-researched relationship, offers insight into the Boghada way of doing things. The people I interviewed largely drove the research, using me as a means of communication to the 'outside' world and as a means of solidifying their current relationships. Unlike the frequently encountered attitude of suspicion, Boghada entered into the conversation from a stance of pride. I, to them, was living proof that word of their success had circulated outside the village, outside the boundaries of the governorate, and even outside the typical communicative spheres for such small villages. I was proof, and was used to 'show-off', for lack of a better word, how Boghada was now attracting researchers residing outside of Egypt. If there were people that needed honouring, my presence was an opportune time. People from neighbouring villages were invited to converse with me, not so much for data gathering, but to communicate to them that they were respected and that it was Boghada's privilege to have them represent Boghada to the researcher.

I was constantly aware of this dynamic. This was a manifestation of agency. And if people in Boghada used me as they did the train (referred to in this case study) to communicate their news, then that is all the more reason to recognize their astuteness and cleverness in this case study.

CHAPTER 2

God created the world and we created Conjunto Palmeira: four decades of forging community and building a local economy in Brazil

Rogerio Arns Neumann, Alison Mathie, assisted by Joanne Linzey

Abstract

Forced to resettle by the Brazilian military junta in the 1970s, the residents of Conjunto Palmeira began organizing and demonstrating in order to secure basic services and infrastructure. One struggle followed another – for water, electricity, a sewage system, a bus service, garbage disposal and the construction of a canal to drain the swamp where the neighbourhood was located. Once this was accomplished, the local Residents' Association organized to build the local economy through the creation of Banco Palmas. Offering loans to small entrepreneurs, it has also experimented with issuing a unique local currency to promote local consumption and boost the local economy. The Banco Palmas model has now been replicated in other parts of Ceará State.

Introduction

Conjunto Palmeira is an urban neighbourhood on the outskirts of the tourist city of Fortaleza in the north-east of Brazil. For the regular tourist, or the middle class residents of this modern city, Conjunto Palmeira has no particular attraction – on the contrary, its location would be more likely to be associated with poverty and crime. However, this neighbourhood has attracted considerable attention internationally because its residents have achieved social and economic successes that have eluded other low income neighbourhoods. Emblematic of this success is its Community Bank – Banco Palmas – with its loan scheme and its own local currency, used to promote the local economy.

This achievement is the latest demonstration of community solidarity and initiative that has taken place over a 40-year period, starting when its first residents were forcibly removed from coastal areas and relocated to desolate land 15 km from the city centre. Decade by decade, residents forged a sense of community by organizing themselves, calling upon each other's skills and resources, securing basic services from the local authorities, and then challenging themselves to produce and consume in ways that would boost the local economy and generate employment. It is a story of struggle and resilience; community organizing and strategic partnering with external agencies; openness to new ideas; and an astute use of the media to capture outside interest and attention.

The significance of this story is in how the character of community organizing has itself evolved and changed over the years. In a climate of political repression, people had to rely on each other for survival, and organized themselves accordingly. With the end of the dictatorship, organizing strategies could be channelled towards campaigning for services from local government and building project management capacity. And then, in its most recent form, community organizing has reached a new threshold as Conjunto Palmeira's producers and consumers try to build a local economy that offers hope and opportunity to a younger generation. These historical threads are picked up by each new generation of leadership, motivated to build on the reputation of their predecessors.

Brazil in the last forty years: the context for the achievements of Conjunto Palmeira

In 1973, when the first residents began to settle in the area of Conjunto Palmeira, Brazil was experiencing one of the most contradictory periods in its history. These were the so-called *Anos de Chumbo*, or the Years of Lead, a dark period during which the military dictatorship gave legal power to arbitrary rule and political repression. Assuming power during a military coup in November, 1964, the dictatorship enacted legislation that repressed citizens' rights for ten years, from 1968 to 1978. The National Congress was closed, individual rights were suspended, people were not allowed to gather in groups, and demonstrations were prohibited.

And yet, this period was also associated with strong economic growth, known as the Brazilian Miracle. Between 1968 and 1973, the Brazilian economy grew at an average rate of 11.5 per cent per year, helped by foreign loans and newly adopted neo-liberal reforms, and by 1980 it was one of the fastest growing economies in the world (Pinheiro et al., 2001). Pride in the 'Miracle' blinded the government to the social costs of the inequalities that economic growth was generating. An influential slogan created by the military government captured this cavalier attitude: 'Brazil, love it or leave it.'

This pride began to waver when the first oil crisis hit in 1974, and interest rates on foreign debt began to rise, threatening the viability of the Brazilian economy and leading to the external debt crisis in the early 1980s. For many poor Brazilians the end of the 1970s came without gains: their rights had not been respected, nor had they received a slice of the economic pie. It was in this climate of repression and exclusion that people began to organize in Conjunto Palmeira.

During the 1980s, the economy remained in crisis; as elsewhere in Latin America, its external debt burden resulted in a 'Lost Decade.' Successive economic plans attempted, but failed, to rein in inflation, which at times was running rampant at 20–30 per cent a month. But popular pressure was building for political change, and as a result steps began to be taken towards political openness and reconciliation. Exiled politicians were allowed to return to Brazil, and an amnesty was granted to members of the military junta accused of torture. Political parties began to form. In 1982, state government elections were held, the first elections since the military coup in 1964, followed by mayoral elections in the state capitals three years later. Mass demonstrations prompting these steps towards democracy finally resulted in the election of the first civilian President of the Republic in 1985. Thus, the period when Conjunto Palmeira campaigned successfully for the provision of basic services was also a time when the power of popular movements, new political parties, and trade unions was uniting the country around promises of democratization.

Closing the decade on a note of optimism, Brazil adopted a new Federal Constitution in 1988, with specific emphasis on citizen participation in decisions at the municipal level. Pioneering a new model of decentralized democracy, public services affecting the day-to-day lives of citizens were decentralized to local governments. Decision-making boards were created, especially in the area of social services – health, education and social assistance – with half of the board members representing civil society and the other half representing government. Each board had the power to propose public policies and set guidelines for the budget for each sector. To this day, despite challenges, few countries in the world offer their population so many avenues for participating effectively in public administration as does Brazil. The partnership of the residents of Conjunto Palmeira with government in the construction of infrastructure during the early 1990s illustrates early efforts to put these principles of citizen participation into practice.

The 21st century began with a new agenda for development. With inflation under control and the currency stabilized since 1994, the national debate has focused on economic growth and income redistribution. The paradox still confronting Brazil is that while it currently enjoys the position of having the eighth largest economy in the world and a respectable overall record in terms of life expectancy, income per capita, and education, these successes continue to coexist with extreme inequality and poverty. The vitality of the economy has allowed for some social mobility but income disparities remain stark: the wealthiest 10 per cent of the population earns nearly 50 per cent of national income, while the poorest 10 per cent earns only 0.7 per cent. According to 2003 data, about one-fifth of the population live on less than US$2 a day and 8 per cent live on less than US$1 a day (The World Bank, 2007), with north-east

Brazil experiencing lower standards of living than elsewhere. Urban violence has become a recurrent issue and is a sign of looming social upheaval that has been decades in the making. In this context, the residents of Conjunto Palmeira have attempted to claim their share of economic prosperity and social mobility, and create a 'solidarity economy.'

The story of Conjunto Palmeira

The story of Conjunto Palmeira is inscribed in collective memory as well as in several *litaratura da cordel* (literally meaning, 'literature hanging on the clothesline,' because the booklets had to be dried after printing). These clothesline stories were produced in the 1980s, when community leaders collected statements from residents on the history of the neighbourhood's struggles. In this section of the case study, these stories, enriched by interviews with current residents and supported by more recent publications produced by Banco Palmas and university researchers, are organized in the way leaders in the community organize their own stories, according to distinct phases in the community's growth, decade by decade.

The decade of migration: early efforts to organize in the 1970s

I am not going to Palmeira this way. I will stay in my shack until they knock it down. The breadwinner ... will be worse off with his family if they move [him] to Palmeira. He will miss his bus, sleep on the street and be late for work. Why can't they move us closer to the city? There are many empty plots of land. (Os moradores de favela do Conjunto Palmeira, n.d.: 8)

The words of Inácio, cited in *Memories of our Struggles,* expressed a common sentiment at the time: Conjunto Palmeira was an undesirable place to live. Situated in a swampy area, it not only lacked basic infrastructure, such as drinking water and electricity, but was also far from the city centre where many people worked or were looking for work.

The move to which Inácio refers was the result of a policy of slum removal and urban improvements along the city's waterfront begun by the city of Fortaleza in 1973 during the military dictatorship. Fishermen and other working families of this coastal region were forced to leave their homes and were transported by truck to an area outside the city limits that would become known as Conjunto Palmeira, named after the large number of palm trees in that area (*palmeira* means 'palm tree' in Portuguese). Following these fishing families, people from other neighbourhoods of Fortaleza and from the state of Ceará were also moved to Conjunto Palmeira. The experience of Carmo illustrates what happened:

In 1974 I was living in Lagamar when we had the great flood. I lived for a month in the sports arena and then the City brought us here to Palmeira. We came by truck. They gave us 500 roof tiles and six hay forks and we had to figure out the rest (Os moradores de favela do Conjunto Palmeira, n.d.: 7)

The city of Fortaleza assigned building lots and donated materials for the construction of a one room building per family. This had to be built within a month, otherwise the right to the land would be forfeited. Thereafter, people could purchase the land in instalments. However, the makeshift dwellings, combined with the lack of basic infrastructure and services, soon earned the area its reputation as a slum. Minimal services were provided, but only gradually. The first school was set up in 1974, in a barn. Only in 1976 did the community finally receive a regular bus service so that people could get to Fortaleza for work.

One of the earliest examples of community organizing was 'Community Emergency Assistance' (CEA), started in 1977. Medical facilities were only available outside Conjunto Palmeira, and people had to be taken there in donkey carts or hammocks. Through a donation of an old car, community leaders organized a means to transport emergency cases to hospital. Approximately 600 people joined this initiative, and contributed a monthly fee to maintain this service. Then, during a municipal election campaign, a candidate for election to the city council donated an ambulance that would provide the same services to the community for free. Three days after the election, however, the ambulance was taken in for repairs and never returned to the community. According to a community activist at the forefront of the CEA initiative, this breach of trust was a salutary lesson. People realized that they would be better off relying on each other rather than outsiders: 'People wanted to believe in something bigger [outsiders] and this is what happened' (Filho, personal communication, 2007).

By the end of the decade, government services in the community included a health centre, a public school, a community centre, and a police station. A Catholic church was established, and local priests were instrumental in supporting local organizing efforts, such as the cooperative day-care centre that still exists today. And connections were made through the priests to a now active NGO sector in Brazil. With NGO support, Delivery House, an initiative of residents to ensure accessible and safe birthing facilities, was established at this time.

These early organizing efforts were significant, but small in scale compared to the severity of their living conditions. The population of Conjunto Palmeira kept growing – reaching almost 20,000 at the end of the 1970s – and the lack of basic infrastructure such as water and sanitation, electricity, and garbage disposal pushed people's patience to its limits. By the end of the 1970s, the residents were ready to take action.

Box 2.1: Leadership in Conjunto Palmeira: Marinete's story

Marinete's story illustrates how she began to see herself as a leader and activist. She grew up in the interior of Ceará state, where she later married. But her husband died when she was expecting her first child, and with neither husband nor father to help her, she moved to Fortaleza to find work as a maid and later as a manicurist. She married again and had three children. However, since the land where she lived was going to be developed, the government relocated her, together with her family, to Conjunto Palmeira in 1975. At the time, it was an isolated community with nothing: no houses, no roads, no water, no sewage system, and no power. It was there that she and her husband owned their first house. It was very small and made out of boxes, but it was theirs.

Marinete recalls how, in the 1980s, throughout Brazil, people were starting to organize against the dictatorship. The residents of the community recognized that they too were going to have to organize in order to put pressure on the authorities to get basic services. She and her husband agreed to hold meetings in their house as there was no other place to gather. As she listened to the conversations, she gradually became more involved and eventually became a community activist in her own right. There were risks involved, since organizing locally was linked to larger scale political activism. She describes clandestine meetings with political activists operating in the area, and a growing determination to resist the dictatorship, despite the threats of violent reprisal.

She is particularly well known for her role in mobilizing volunteers and obtaining materials for the Residents' Association building. That success inspired other leaders to emerge. Today, more than 30 years later, Marinete is still deeply involved in the organizing of her community. While she makes her living by selling clothing at local markets, in her volunteer role she is the elected secretary of the Residents' Association, connecting people to programmes and services offered through the Association or through other organizations. As she points out, commenting on the changes she has seen: 'in the eighties no one wanted to live here. Now, there is more money in the town and people want to come and live here.... We are still in control of our development. There are no partners who can tell us what to do' (personal communication, 2007).

The decade of community participation: mobilizing, organizing and confronting the authorities in the 1980s

Of particular significance at this time was the formation, in 1981, of the Residents' Association of Conjunto Palmeira (ASMOCONP). It began as an informal gathering of concerned community members meeting in the home of Marinete (as described in 'Marinete's Story' below) and her husband. Once it was formed officially, it gave them the confidence to confront the authorities in a more organized way and paved the way for other community organizations to establish themselves soon after.

Yet the Residents' Association needed a physical presence in the community, and so proceeded to organize the construction of a building. Community leaders went from house to house in the neighbourhood asking for donations – building materials, money, tools, volunteer labour, or whatever people were willing to contribute. When the actual construction took place, community leaders like Marinete used a loudspeaker, calling for the bricks, roof tiles, and volunteers that had been promised. The overwhelming response was a strong indication of the support for the Association, and of the strength of the

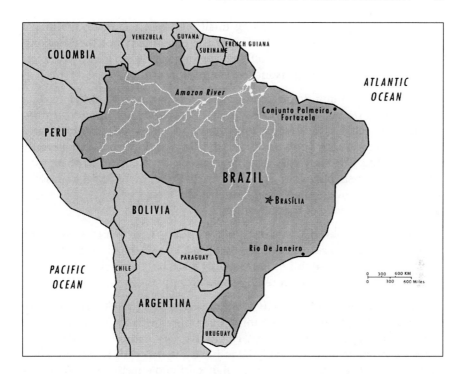

community. As Marinete said, this was not an activity that was carried out by a few community activists but by a groundswell of active community members: 'It wasn't just me, it was us' (personal communication, 2007).

Marinete was one of several leaders who paved the way for later campaigns. With each success, it was easier to organize community members. For example, after the Residents' Association was built, the next issue they rallied around was access to electricity. The story of how the community persuaded the power company to provide electricity services is now legendary. Jose Valdo remembers the strategy they used to make their point:

> So we decided to get organized. We were 2,000 residents who went to the electricity company. We made our case and insisted on bringing the engineer to Palmeira at nightfall. It was very dark. As he walked around the community he fell and tore his clothing. After that we got electricity for 14 blocks. (personal communication, 2007)

The fact that 2,000 people could be mobilized in this way is evidence of an extraordinary level of community solidarity and organizational capacity. Even though many of the community members didn't know exactly what they would be doing once they arrived at the power company, they were still willing to go. Moreover, as Jose Valdo explained, community leadership was able to leverage this success by astute use of the media:

When the houses [in one section] finally received electricity, the mayor and the press showed up. That's how the community got them to keep another promise, which was fulfilled later: to provide electricity to the rest of Conjunto Palmeira. (personal communication, 2007)

In 1983, the community mobilized again to draw attention to the need for public transportation. Conjunto Palmeira is located 18 km from downtown Fortaleza. It could take three to fours hours to get to the downtown area because there were few buses and those that did pass through the community were often full. The story goes that the municipality claimed that there were 12 buses, whereas only four actually passed through the neighbourhood. Angered by this discrepancy, Jose describes the tactics he and a few others used to force the hand of the authorities:

> … A few colleagues and I would stay at the bus stop from four in the morning until midnight to count the buses that came by and the number of people on them. We showed this to the Mayor's Office, but they doubted us. So we damaged some buses in protest. (personal communication, 2007)

This action resulted in the city's withdrawal of this route's bus service for several days. People in the community were furious with the local leadership, but they also appealed to the city. Finally the city authorities added some buses to the route and eventually established the first express bus service in Fortaleza, taking passengers from the neighbourhood directly to downtown. A three-hour journey could now be accomplished in 45 minutes.

By this time, Conjunto Palmeira was well-known to the local authorities and there was a certain level of respect for the community's tenacity. A fourth instance of effective community mobilizing illustrates people's attempts to collaborate with local authorities rather than use confrontational tactics, at least at first. The issue was garbage disposal. Frustrated by the lack of garbage collection, the Residents' Association began a campaign of Alternative Clean-up in 1987. Striking a partnership with the city authorities, residents were hired by the city to collect the garbage in mule-drawn carts. A year later, the partnership ended, on the grounds that the partnership was not permitted under local authority regulations. In protest, residents and cart drivers picked up garbage accumulated over several days and took it in a convoy of mule-drawn carts to the nearest municipal building, where the garbage was dumped. To draw even more attention to the situation, the Association invited the local press to publicize the event.

Emboldened by their successes, the Residents' Association then decided to take on the issue of the water supply, which had been raised as a serious public health concern. Ironically, the water supply for Fortaleza was piped through Conjunto Palmeira, but the residents did not have access to it. In 1988, the community organized itself again to put pressure on the government, giving the Water and Sewage Company of Ceará a 30-day deadline to provide the community with access to the piped water supply running through to the city. Under the slogan, 'if the water doesn't arrive, *olé olé olá*, Fortaleza will dry up,' the residents threatened to break the water pipe. Sensing this level of determination, the state government authorized construction to allow for the distribution of piped water to the community.

According to several of the leaders who emerged during the 1980s, the motivation to organize was prompted by their experience of well-intentioned, but often inappropriate, outside assistance. Food-for-work programmes organized by state and municipal authorities were widely considered to be 'make-work' programmes; their effect was demoralizing. Leadership emerged in reaction to the patronizing treatment residents experienced at the hands of social workers (or 'social insisters,' as they were dubbed) who administered these food-for-work programmes. One community leader remembers how people began to reject some of this assistance: 'We learned to stand on our own two feet. We realized that they were bringing in ready-made things that we should have been doing ourselves. We wanted someone to help us, not someone to tell us what to do' (Marinete, personal communication, 2007).

Not all interactions with outside organizations were negative. In fact, an initiative of a group of health-care professionals that led to the creation of the Nutrition Centre of Conjunto Palmeira in 1984 gave the community an experience of a positive relationship that could benefit and strengthen the community. This group of health-care professionals respected the way the community was already organized and recognized the skills and capacities that the community members were willing to contribute. In the face of chronic malnutrition and a high infant mortality rate, the health professionals trained community members to work as health monitors and provide basic health education to children's families in their own homes, while simultaneously providing medical services for critical cases of malnutrition at the nutrition centre. The Block Leaders (*Representantes de Quadras*) selected to be health-care monitors did not need to be literate; a sophisticated visual tool with simple pictures and symbols was designed so that health data could be recorded by all these volunteers, regardless of literacy levels. Programmes such as those offered by the Nutrition Centre helped people develop skills to monitor children's health and deliver basic care, while simultaneously raising awareness about the social, environmental and economic factors affecting children's health.

It was during the 1980s, therefore, that the community began to assert itself in the face of neglect by the authorities, earning respect for its tenacity and perseverance. This reputation would stand community members in good stead as they headed into the 'decade of construction' that followed.

The decade of construction in the 1990s

Looking at Conjunto Palmeira today and remembering the community the way it was, I am amazed at everything we built. When I say 'we,' I mean the associations, the church groups, and people in general. We [did not] have drainage or a basic sewage system, we didn't have anything... We were completely forgotten. After everything that we have achieved, Palmeira now has more life! (Conceição, personal communication, 2007)

During the 1990s, Conjunto Palmeira underwent another transformation. As Conceiçao looks back on this period, three observations stand out. First, the community finally acquired basic infrastructure – water, sanitation, a drainage canal. Second, the community itself was responsible for building and managing the construction. Third, it marked a time when the community was no longer being ignored by the authorities but was working in partnership with them.

By the early 1990s, there were 26 community organizations in Conjunto Palmeira and its population had grown to 25,000. It had established a reputation for itself as a well organized, active community, but with the majority employed in casual, minimum wage employment or in petty trading, and many living in very poor conditions.

Through the network of local and international NGOs operating in north-eastern Brazil at the time, staff members of the German organization, Deutsche Gesellschaft für Technische Zusammenarbeit (GTZ), heard about Conjunto Palmeira. Based on its reputation and the discussions between members of the Residents' Association and GTZ staff members, Conjunto Palmeira was identified for a programme that would build on the community's organizing and mobilizing capacity and revitalize the local economy. GTZ, City Hall, and the State Government worked with the community to organize a series of workshops for community leaders. The first of these, called 'Inhabiting the Uninhabitable,' took place in 1991. Emerging from these discussions was an agreement among community leaders to form a Union of Associations and Organized Groups in Conjunto Palmeira (UAGOCONP). The leaders took responsibility for developing a ten-year strategic plan to transform the neighbourhood into a place where people could live with dignity. Over this 10-year period, with support from GTZ, City Hall, and the State Government, community members managed to drain the rivers, install a sewage system and pave the streets, transforming what had been described as a slum into a desirable residential neighbourhood.

The construction of a drainage canal was the first priority. The flooding and landslides of 1986 had resulted in extensive damage to 600 houses: over 1,000 people had been left homeless. A permanent solution was necessary.

The construction of the canal required community organizing, planning, and managing at an unprecedented level. Using a participatory methodology, community members mapped out land use, drew up socio-economic profiles of the residents, made an inventory of the organizations in Conjunto Palmeira, and listed other information about resources that the community could mobilize. Each resident was committed to carrying out construction work in his or her neighbourhood. Community leaders held street meetings every time work began on a new part of the canal. People had to be kept informed and reassured that even if their houses had to be removed to make way for the canal, they would not be left homeless.

At the time, the usual practice was for government to manage the construction of infrastructure projects. But on GTZ's insistence, the community had to be in charge of construction, through the Residents' Association. 'The Canal', as it is known locally, became a landmark not only because it improved the living conditions in the community, but also because of the experience people gained in administering such a large project. It was also an experiment in innovative partnership. The financial investment was huge: one million *reais*, in total, of which GTZ contributed 50 per cent, the Municipal Government paid 25 per cent, and the State Government contributed the remaining 25 per cent. They set up a local board – consisting of representatives of 26 community organizations working alongside municipal staff members – which was responsible for decisions relating to the construction. The workers on the construction project were local residents, many of whom were specially trained to work on this project.

The project required a unique partnership with local government. The government architect and technical advisor were part of the management unit responsible for purchasing equipment and hiring community workers, and were accountable, not only to the city authorities but also to the community. According to the local government architect, having the construction supervised directly by community representatives resulted in cost savings, even if the weekly meetings slowed down the work itself at times (Garcia, personal communication, 2007). The priority was to build on the skills of community members, and allow them to acquire new skills and increase their income-earning potential. Matias, who at the time was the treasurer of the Residents' Association, had to do the books with the management unit every month. He remembers, with pride, how 'we could account for every penny' (personal communication, 2007). This experience stood him in good stead: it was during his term as President of the Association that Banco Palmas was created in 1997.

The ten-year plan, of which the canal construction was a major part, was completed in seven years. In 1997, at a follow-up workshop, discussion revolved around the consequences of the community's success. Proud though people were of their achievements, Conjunto Palmeira had, however, now become an expensive place to live, as the newly established infrastructure required formalized services, with the result that people had to pay municipal taxes for electricity, water, and sewage disposal. A study done by the Residents' Association revealed that 30 per cent of the residents had been living in the neighbourhood for less than two years, and that one out of every three residents who had fought for the improvements to the neighbourhood could no longer afford to live there. A spate of speculative purchasing of real estate had started, now that the newly upgraded neighbourhood had begun to attract new residents. If the now 'habitable' Conjunto Palmeira was to be affordable for all its residents, there would have to be more opportunities for people to earn a living.

At this time, it was estimated that 80 per cent of the residents relied on the informal economy for their livelihood and that 90 per cent of households lived on the equivalent of two minimum wages (Stichting Aktie Strohalm, 2003). And so, during the next community planning phase, the priority was to create opportunities for income generation. Small loans were needed to help people establish themselves in micro enterprises, but there was neither a bank, nor a small loan facility in Conjunto Palmeira. Turned down by the state government for a loan fund, community leaders eventually succeeded in convincing a local NGO (CEARAH Periferia) to approve a grant of R$2,000 (approximately US$1,180 at 3 March 2008) to start a credit scheme in 1997. News spread fast – too fast, even on the TV and radio. Community members clamoured to get access to the credit, not realizing that the supply of funds was so limited.

In the midst of this turmoil, the Residents' Association of Conjunto Palmeira established a community bank – Banco Palmas – in January 1997, to manage the new credit scheme. Strictly speaking, it remains a financial institution, rather than a bank, because it is not authorized to hold savings, although this may change in the near future. Offering loans and credit facilities, it was founded on a modest sum of money, but its vision was ambitious: to ensure that economic development in Conjunto Palmeira would be inclusive, with opportunities for people with more limited means to stay and contribute to the continued development of the community. Gradually, funds came from other NGO sources (Oxfam UK and GTZ), thanks to the connections through CEARAH *Periferia*, and the loan fund grew to R$20,000. However, it soon became clear that while money was coming into the local economy from various sources – wages, pensions, petty trading, and sometimes illegal activity – very little was being spent in the community. Not only was it going to be necessary to provide loans to local businesses to provide local services and products for people to buy, it would also be necessary to encourage consumers to buy locally if the local economy was to flourish.

The decade of economic development in the new millennium

The way we consume defines the kind of society we would like to build. Consumption is not only an economic attitude, but it is also a political attitude. When we consume products that have been produced in our community, we are generating jobs and income for local residents. When we consume products by companies that have no social responsibility, we are only enriching the business people who use the profits for their own benefit. (Joaquim Melo and Sandra Magalhães, 2003)

It was in this spirit of building a community – one that consumed, as well as produced, with a 'political attitude' – that Banco Palmas was established, building on past accomplishments of organizing and on the trust earned by broad-based leadership. The focus of the community began to shift. The residents had fought for, and had won, basic infrastructure, organizing themselves to make demands of outside institutions, particularly government. At the end of the 1990s, when a sustainable local economy became the priority, they began to make demands of themselves. People started to look within their own community for solutions.

To assess the potential for stimulating the local economy, the Residents' Association calculated that the community spent around R$15 million or R$428 per capita per year (based on a population of 35,000). Set against this potential spending power, there were very few retail stores and services offering competitive prices or opportunities to purchase on credit. Hence, money was draining out of the community that could, potentially, be 'captured' by local businesses. It took 45 meetings with local producers, merchants, members of the Residents' Association, and residents to come up with a plan to encourage people to buy locally rather than going elsewhere to shop. Innovative financial products and services were one part of the plan (a credit card, and various loan products, outlined in detail in Box 2.2) but still more creative ideas for a local currency were also proposed.

Experimenting with a 'solidarity economy': testing the idea of a local currency

Within a few years, community leaders had begun to establish links with a global network of activists, academics and development practitioners experimenting with strategies for a 'solidarity economy.' Those who attended the first Brazilian Meeting of Culture and Socio-economic Solidarity in Rio de Janeiro in June 2000, picked up on the idea of an Exchange Club, already common in Argentina. Back in Conjunto Palmeira, 30 to 40 local traders agreed to try this out by getting together every two weeks for a day to exchange clothing, crafts and food. Essentially a bartering system, the value of each product for sale was expressed in units of 'social currency.' This experiment lasted approximately two years, but because basic goods such as rice, beans, eggs and flour were not produced locally and were therefore not offered for exchange, the initiative ultimately lacked the overall utility necessary to succeed.

During the World Social Forum in Porto Alegre in 2002, the Strohalm Foundation looked for a partner to test a method of stimulating the local economy by introducing unique local currency into the local economy. Banco Palmas agreed to be the partner and the '*palma*' was introduced as a unit of currency. At first, the value of the *palma* was tied to the value of the *real*, but the exchange of *palmas* to *reais* was not permitted, in an effort to maximize the demonstration effect of buying locally with *palmas*. But it soon became clear that unless it was possible to exchange *palmas* for national currency (the *real*) those businesses or producers accepting *palmas* would be limited in what they could purchase, and wages in *palmas* would have limited spending power. For

---

Box 2.2: Promoting 'prosumers' in a solidarity economy

Promoting local consumption

The PALMAcard was the first innovative idea for encouraging people to buy locally. It is a credit card with a limit of R$20 that can only be used in local stores. Consumers repay the credit at Banco Palmas at the end of each month in either *palmas* or *reais*. Since the card operates on the same principle as a major credit card, businesses pay a 3 per cent fee when claiming their Brazilian *reais* from Banco Palmas. The fee represents acknowledgement that Banco Palmas, through the credit card, has steered local consumers to local businesses. The introduction of a local currency (*palmas*) further encouraged local consumption.

Promoting local business

Producer credit is designed to help small businesses start up and expand. The minimum loan size is R$50, making credit more accessible to low income borrowers than would be the case at commercial banks, where the minimum loan size is R$300. The maximum loan size is R$5,000, but, on average, the loan size for initial loans is between R$300 and R$400.

The interest rate charged on these loans is low compared to commercial banks, and it runs counter to mainstream lending practices: the smaller the loan, the lower the interest rate. (On loans up to R$300, the interest charged is 1 per cent; on loans up to R$600 the rate is 1.5 per cent; and 2 per cent for R$1,000). The reasoning behind this is to encourage people to come together as a group, with each individual paying 1 per cent on his or her share of the loan.

With its low rate of interest, there is a potential risk of individuals borrowing at the low rate and on-lending at a higher rate. However, Banco Palmas makes business loans everyone's business. Because the lending system relies heavily on social relationships and character references, leakages like this have not occurred, nor have there been defaults on loans to any significant degree (1.5 per cent). As yet, these transaction costs, in terms of staff time, are being borne by the project funds that support the bank. This clearly raises financial sustainability issues which the next phase of Banco Palmas will have to address. The formation of a credit union with a savings facility is under discussion and may be part of the solution.

Currently, there are 249 individual loans and group loans. Of the individual loans, 86 per cent are for women. For women who are at home, this loan scheme helps them to achieve some independence and financial security. Currently, while many men in Conjunto Palmeira have waged employment and are therefore registered and eligible for state pensions, women have fewer opportunities, given their family responsibilities, and are ineligible for state pensions.

---

example, the supermarket could only pay its staff in *palmas* if they were from the community and spent their money there, but they could not pay other staff members, let alone their suppliers in *palmas*.

So Banco Palmas and the Strohalm Foundation decided to take the experiment further. The decision was made to allow the *palma* to be exchanged 1:1 with the *real*. In this new phase 20,000 *palmas* were brought into circulation. Little by little, local merchants began to offer discounts of between 2 and 10 per cent for those paying in *palmas*, stimulating local consumption even more. Remarkably, in the early days, people began to bring their *reais* to exchange for *palmas* and the *palma* currency continues to be widely accepted in the local economy today.

The idea behind the local currency was to create more opportunity for local business development and employment. Soon it became clear that unless people were paid in *palmas*, the amount of money circulating locally would be limited. The Residents' Association then negotiated with the Strohalm Foundation to construct a building for PalmaTech, a Community School of Socio Economic Solidarity, in the grounds of the Residents' Association, and use the process of building it to further test the impact of the new currency on the local economy. A grant from ICCO (Interchurch Organization for Development Co-operation) for R\$55,000 would cover the costs of construction. The plan was to convert as much as possible of this grant to *palma*, then use this to purchase building supplies locally and to pay 80 per cent of people's wages. By doing so, *reais* were 'saved' and used for micro credit loans by Banco Palmas. It was explained to the workers that the *palmas* they earned could be spent locally, while the 20 per cent of their wages in *reais* could be used for the goods and services that were not available locally. Banco Palmas offered interest-free loans in *reais* to local merchants, and would accept repayment in *palmas*. As businesses began to see the advantages of this arrangement, and as people began to spend their wages in their own neighbourhood, *palmas* began to gain credibility.

The expectation was that all of the *palmas* paid out would return to Banco Palmas, balancing the amount of money loaned in *reais* with what was paid to the workers in *palmas*. In fact, the new currency began to circulate in the local economy, just like the official *real* currency. According to the Strohalm Foundation's evaluation report (Stichting Aktie Strohalm, 2003), during the construction phase, over 40 participating businesses agreed to accept *palmas*, offering 200 different products. Examples included local pharmacies, bakeries, groceries, fast food shops, and accessory stores. Over 300 consumers and 'prosumers' used the new currency in their transactions, generating a significantly higher multiplier effect (15 per cent higher) than would have been the case if *reais* rather than *palmas* had been injected into the economy.

A local currency: educational tool or threat to the national banking system?

In 2003, the Central Bank of Brazil began to get nervous about this new currency and threatened the Residents' Association with court action, on charges of forging money. Eager to demonstrate that the local currency was complementing the national currency, not trying to compete with it, the director of Banco Palmas made his case at a hearing. He argued that the currency was, in fact, no more than an educational tool, demonstrating the benefit of local consumption for local economic development, and providing incentives to change local expenditure patterns. The judge agreed: according to Joaquim Melo, the judge commented that the real crime was allowing such levels of poverty to exist, not the effort to give people in Conjunto Palmeira an opportunity to increase incomes through developing the local economy (personal communication, 2007).

Scaling out the Banco Palmas model

From this point on, Banco Palmas went from strength to strength. In 2005, Banco Popular do Brasil (a bank specializing in micro credit) agreed to provide it with R$250,000 in loan funds. Its latest partnership with Banco Popular do Brasil enlarges its loan fund to R$500,000. Its employees now act as advisors by scaling out this model of community banks elsewhere. To date, eight new community banks have been established in other parts of Ceará State, and five are established in other parts of Brazil. Banco Palmas is earning a fee for its advisory role in the start-up of these new banks. With these banks restricted to providing loans, the formation of a credit union with a savings facility is the next logical step.

Whether the *palma* currency will outlive its usefulness is another question. If patterns of expenditure continue to favour buying locally, then the *palma* currency may no longer be necessary. On the other hand, a local currency may help local merchants draw customers back to the community once they can provide the diversity of products that its consumers have been purchasing elsewhere. Members of the recently formed Business Association now take up these issues with Banco Palmas, strategizing how to continue to build the economy through loans for small business, financial services for 'prosumers,' training opportunities for youth, and the continued use of *palmas*. The story of Bezerra (Box 2.3) illustrates how local entrepreneurs have both contributed to, and gained from, this investment in the local economy.

Bezerra's account, as a relative newcomer who has seen the reputation of this urban neighbourhood rise in the eyes of outsiders, is a familiar one. Young people described how coming from Conjunto Palmeira used to count against them, but how employers now actively seek young employees from this neighbourhood.

A growing local economy

Through a series of initiatives, economic development in Conjunto Palmeira has continued to grow, not only in terms of quantity but also in terms of complexity. With the Residents' Association at the helm, partnerships with external funders have made it possible to share investment in a number of local economic initiatives. In total, between 1998 and 2007, five small-scale manufacturing businesses were directly created within the Residents' Association, and 130 small businesses started up in the community as a result of the loan scheme. This translates into direct employment for 1,000 and indirect employment for a further 400 people (Melo, personal communication, 2007).

Box 2.3: Bezerra's story: a local entrepreneur

Bezerra's parents thought he was crazy and his wife threatened to leave him when, ten years ago, Bezerra said he wanted to move to Conjunto Palmeira to open a grocery store. He eventually persuaded his wife to move, convincing her that there were good business opportunities in the community. He wanted to get involved in the community and has been an active volunteer from the beginning. For many years his main focus was his involvement with the development of Banco Palmas. He is now the president of the newly formed Business Association.

Today, Bezerra has a ten-year old grocery store. His was the first business to accept *palmas*. With a Banco Palmas loan he has now opened a computer training centre called Data Curso. To date, 500 students have registered for the course and 350 have already completed the eight-month programme.

Over the years he has noticed a change in how the community is portrayed in the press. In the past, the media focus was on violence and crime in Conjunto Palmeira, but now there is more attention paid to the social progress of the community. This positive media attention has helped attract donors for the community projects carried out through the Residents' Association.

Bezerra and his wife are sure that the move they made ten years ago was the right one. He remembers going to a mall outside the neighbourhood to buy something when they first moved to the community. When he gave his address the salesperson was shocked, given Conjunto Palmeira's reputation, embarrassing Bezerra and his wife. Recently, however, Bezerra went to a big store to buy a mobile phone. When he was filling out the form, the store manager looked at the address, and mentioned Banco Palmas and the local currency. And the manager offered an invitation to Bezerra: 'Would you mind spending time with my team explaining your initiatives to strengthen the local economy?'

In addition, to ensure sustained commitment to a solidarity economy, the Residents' Association runs the *Bairro Escola de Trabalho* (Neighbourhood School of Work), which trains young people to understand the cooperative economy of their neighbourhood and creates opportunities for internships in local businesses. As an expression of solidarity, income earning opportunities for the disadvantaged have also been established, such as *Incubadora Feminina*, founded in 2001 to assist at-risk women, with external NGO support (from the Coordenadoria Ecumenica de Servicos (CESE). Fifty women took part in professional training and were provided with an opportunity for work experience in local businesses. Since then, they have applied for producer credit from Banco Palmas for small business loans or received support in their job searches.

Forging a community: an analysis of internal agency

'God created the world and we built Conjunto Palmeira.'
(quoted on a poster illustrating the canal construction)

It was in this can-do spirit that the residents took responsibility for transforming an inhospitable area into a desirable place to live. In the process they forged a community. Through its associations, particularly the Residents' Association,

The palma is accepted in many stores as local currency.

the community has become internally and institutionally connected, continuously building on its reserves of local skills and assets. Embedded in these associations are the less tangible characteristics of this community that have contributed to its success. Some of these have to do with larger social, economic and political struggles and successes with which community members were directly or indirectly engaged and which influenced the type of assistance offered by outside agencies. Some, however, were specific to the community itself and we focus on six of these here.

First, the residents of Conjunto Palmeira have been opportunistic and enterprising. In a period of political repression, the only opportunity for people was to draw upon their own resilience and survival skills. Later, as the political climate in Brazil changed and social justice began to be heard in government rhetoric, community members seized opportunities to hold their elected officials to account, and resisted the kind of help that would weaken their resolve. They deliberately sought out partnerships with NGOs that recognized their capacities and invested in them. Today, a growing national economy, combined with international criticism of the widening social inequality this generates, allows Conjunto Palmeira to demonstrate that it has both the right and the capacity to seize a larger portion of the economic pie. In so doing, it sets an example for others to follow.

Second, the community has developed effective internal communications and has been able to make use of the media to communicate its aspirations and successes to the outside world. For example, community stories have been recorded and shared as a common reference point. People of different ages and diverse life experiences talk about the same struggles and initiatives. This local history, or micro-history, has been a powerful instrument in developing a local identity and a sense of community. Also, the community has used the media strategically to draw attention to its struggles and successes, sometimes embarrassing local authorities to fulfil obligations, and sometimes impressing potential investors.

Third, this sense of identity has relied on expanding the relationships of trust. This is a large community where many people are strangers to one another. Yet through its associations and activities (mobilizing neighbours to make demands of government, building a canal, or establishing *Banco Palmas*, issuing loans, and establishing a viable local currency) trust has enabled these initiatives to succeed and has been further strengthened as a result of that success. The associations have been the means by which the capacity to organize in a crisis (demonstrated in the 1970s and 1980s) has become institutionalized and sustained.

A fourth factor in the success of Conjunto Palmeira is the capacity of its leaders to change perspective, using the lessons from each struggle to organize better each time. The lessons from the experience of building the canal, for example, prompted community members to think about economic development in a different way. Before, the focus had been to bring people together to demand external intervention, primarily from government. The challenge with regard to the canal was for leaders to bring people together so they could introduce 'interventions' themselves, with external support. Sometimes, success can tie people and their organizations too rigidly to the attitudes that made them successful in the first place. Resisting this tendency, the Residents' Association has been able to redirect its focus. Building a community is like a game of chess, demanding patience, flexible strategies, and an awareness of risk. In Conjunto Palmeira, the leaders have demonstrated all of these skills and more.

Fifth, in telling their history, no one leader is identified. People never say 'I,' only 'we,' thus embracing all those who had earned legitimacy as leaders at different stages, at different times, and with different groups. The challenges of life in the community transformed many residents into leaders, and they continue to do so. It is another example of the capacity on the part of the leaders to be able to change their views, and to step back when others are ready to move forward.

Finally, while many of the original leaders remain active, forming new leadership among the younger generation is considered so important that the by-laws of the Residents' Association require it. Over the 40-year history of the Association, different residents helped establish it, led the large community campaigns, and then fostered local economic development through Banco Palmas. Now a new generation of young people are being identified and trained to lead the development of the community in the years to come.

Stepping back: relationships with external organizations

Over time, the Residents' Association negotiated for partnerships with external organizations that respected the aspirations of the community expressed through the Residents' Association and the Union of Associations and Organized Groups in Conjunto Palmeira. People were proud of their existing achievements, yet they were aware that they did not necessarily have all the skills required to manage large-scale projects. In the case of Conjunto Palmeira, the turning point for people was the experience of building the canal. While the Association could count on technical assistance from the city and GTZ, it retained control. The practical lessons in community governance were invaluable.

The attitude of external agencies is therefore very important. As Neumann and Neumann write:

> If, when looking at a community, one sees only poverty and poverty-related issues, one tends to throw a number of structures and projects its way to change what is there, ignoring or even shutting down development initiatives that have come from the residents themselves. But if one looks at a community and sees the human talent, community and organizational resources already available, one tends to strengthen what is already there. (Neumann and Neumann, 2004:19)

Viewed from this perspective, the quality of the relationships initiated by external organizations has been of fundamental importance. The priests who came in the 1970s, the health professionals who started the Nutrition Centre and volunteer health monitoring in the 1980s, GTZ in the 1990s, and Strohalm Foundation, ICCO, and the Banco Populaire do Brasil in this decade have all modelled their relationship on valuing the contribution and achievements of the residents of Conjunto Palmeira. They were responsive, not directive. Now this type of partnership is expected and well understood: organizations that support the community do not look at residents as less capable individuals who need to be 'fixed.'

Conclusion

Conjunto Palmeira has transformed itself from a collection of hastily constructed dwellings built in the 1970s to an urban neighbourhood of 30,000 with services and amenities and a growing local economy. An older generation of leaders is proud of the results of the struggle, but concerned now about how to ensure that opportunities exist for the younger generation. Deliberate efforts to prepare and position young people for leadership have been built into the work of the Residents' Association, opportunities for skills training are provided through PalmaTech, and loans for small business and a service to link young people to job opportunities exist alongside the regular banking services of Banco Palmas. These efforts, and the social life that revolves around

Bezerra's supermarket in Conjunto Palmeira, where Palmas – a local currency issued by Banco Palmas to stimulate the economy – are accepted.

these activities, reach into the larger community and, to some extent, protect it from threats – a drug culture that permeates poorer neighbourhoods of most Brazilian cities, for example, is no stranger to Conjunto Palmeira.

Nevertheless, one of the concerns raised by the leaders of the Residents' Association is how to continue to sustain the forward momentum. The character of the community has changed, as have the aspirations of its members and its motivations to organize. The newest association – the Business Association – is indicative of its new focus. From the point of view of community members, Conjunto Palmeira continues to undergo transformation, and this means meeting opportunity while at the same time contending with new struggles such as the social and economic challenges facing youth. As one long-time resident commented, in the early days the community organizers would talk long into the night strategizing. Now, because of increased crime, they are on their way home from community meetings by 9 p.m. Historically this community has been able to adapt, devise new strategies and find solutions; new partners that recognize this capacity are still needed to support their endeavours.

Conjunto Palmeira is best known for Banco Palmas, but as this case study illustrates, Banco Palmas rests on the shoulders of those who have spent decades organizing. Under a repressive regime, leaders in Conjunto Palmeira organized so that people could survive conditions of physical neglect. This initial organizing evolved into organizing to access the services that a new democratic regime was obliged to deliver. Finally, with the infrastructure in place, people organized to ensure that the country's economic growth did not pass them by.

In the last 20 years since the end of the dictatorship, three different presidencies have offered different brands of political and economic change, with Lula's current presidency elected on the promise to redistribute wealth more evenly. Yet the structural transformation required to change the course of Brazil's development has, so far, been slow to materialize. Although a popular saying states that 'God is Brazilian', God has not yet performed the miracle of building a socially equitable, economically solid and environmentally sustainable country. Conjunto Palmeira is a place where people have taken the situation into their own hands. They want to continue to build solidarity and create their own version of social and economic success.

References

Melo Neto, J. and Magalhães, S. (2003) *Bairros pobres, ricas soluções: Banco Palmas, ponto a ponto* [Poor neighbourhoods, rich solutions: Banco Palmas, step by step] Expressão Gráfica, Fortaleza, Ceará, Brazil.

Neumann, L. and Neumann, R. (2004*) Desenvolvimento comunitário baseado em talentos e recursos locais – ABCD* [Community development based on local talents and resources], Global Editora, São Paulo, Brazil.

Os moradores de favela do Conjunto Palmeira [The residents of the favela of Conjunto Palmeira] (n.d.) Memorias de Nossas Lutas : favela de Conjunto Palmeriras: Habitando o inabitavel. [Memories of our struggles: The settlement of Conjunto Palmeiras: habitable or uninhabitable]. Vol. 1. Unpublished document.

Pinheiro, A., Gill, I., Servén, L. and Thomas, M. (December 2001) *Brazilian economic growth, 1990–2000: Lessons and policy implications*, 2nd draft. Prepared for Global Development Network Conference, Rio de Janeiro, Brazil. Available from http://www.gdnet.org/pdf/draft_country_studies/ BrazilianEconomicGrowth1900-2000RioDraftI.pdf [Accessed 5 September 2007]

Stichting Aktie Strohalm (2003) *Project 'Formento Fortaleza': Final report*, Stichting Aktie Strohalm, Utrecht, The Netherlands.

World Bank, The (n.d.) *Brazil country brief*, available from: http://go.worldbank. org/UW8ODN2SV0 [Accessed 5 September 2007]

Authors' note

Research for this case study was carried out in January 2007 in Conjunto Palmeira and Fortaleza, north-eastern Brazil, by Rogerio Arns Neumann, Joanne Linzey, and Alison Mathie with assistance from Sarah Riedl (translation) and Nathalia Cardoso (interview transcription).

In 2006, the Coady Institute invited Rogerio Arns Neumann, currently working with the Odebrecht Foundation, to identify a community in Brazil that would illustrate citizen-driven development in an urban context. With many years experience working in community development in Brazil, he identified four possible communities. Conjunto Palmeira was our first choice because it was an urban setting in one of the poorest regions of Brazil, and because its history was already well documented by community members themselves as well as by academics and some NGOs. Rogerio contacted the Residents' Association who responded enthusiastically to the idea. Joanne Linzey offered to assist in the fieldwork because of her experience working in collaboration with Rogerio in Brazil in her capacity as the Chief Executive Officer of Metro United Way in Halifax, Canada. Alison Mathie's role was to coordinate the research effort and help in the writing once an initial draft had been translated from Portuguese into English.

In Conjunto Palmeira, we conducted group and individual interviews with staff and elected representatives of the Residents' Association in Conjunto Palmeira, staff of Banco Palmas, members of the Business Association, individual entrepreneurs and community members. Mostly these interviews took place in the Residents' Association with the various activities of Banco Palmas, Palma Limpe, and the Business Association going on all around, and with preparations for Carnival in full swing. We encouraged community members to analyze their own stories, and offered the Residents' Association some popular education and facilitation tools in the process.

Deepening our understanding of the history of the neighbourhood, we also conducted interviews with representatives of *Centro de Nutricao de Conjunto Palmeira*, and a teacher at the local school. Accounts of the construction of the canal were gathered from community members and the local government architect, Paulo Garcia. Details on the history and the impact of Banco Palmas were provided by Joaquim de Melo (Banco Palmas) and Dr Jeova Torres of the University of Cereá. Particular thanks go to Joaquim de Melo, the Director of Banco Palmas, for his assistance in facilitating interviews, for giving his own time so generously, and for reading an earlier draft of this case study. Altogether fourteen individual interviews and four group interviews were conducted. These interviews were recorded and transcribed, then analyzed along with existing documentation, cited in the text.

Efforts were made to get in touch with some of the organizations that had assisted Conjunto Palmeira in the early days, but key individuals in these organizations had moved on. Their role, although important at key intervals, remains in the background, with the community perspective more prominently placed in the foreground. One of the reasons community members were willing to participate, according to Joaquim de Melo, is that the story was not confined to a single project (Banco Palmas, for example) but highlighted the cumulative effect of community organizing, each new development standing on the shoulders of the efforts that preceded it. As outsiders, the researchers therefore promised to deliver an inside story, and on that basis the conversations began to flow.

CHAPTER 3

Building the Mercado Central: Asset Based Community Development and community entrepreneurship in the USA

Geralyn Sheehan

Abstract

In a relatively short period of time, new Latino immigrants in Minneapolis, USA, have been able to establish a cooperatively owned market place that incubates small businesses catering to Latino (and non Latino) consumers. In the process, a run-down area of downtown Minneapolis has been revitalized. This process of social and economic integration was set in motion by local church groups assisting new immigrants with a place where they could come together as a faith community and hold services in Spanish. This assistance then extended to opportunities for local training, which in turn led to a deliberate exercise in identifying the skills and resources of new immigrants and how these could be linked to opportunities for small business development. As such it illustrates the power of organizing based on a recognition of assets, motivated by aspirations for a strong community integrated into the larger local economy.

Introduction

The story of the Mercado Central is one of Latino immigrants who believed in their capacity to realize a collective vision of home and neighbourhood. The Mercado Central, a retail business cooperative and incubator in Minneapolis, is the result of creativity, tenacity, and collaboration with faith-based and other community organizations to build a traditional marketplace in an inner-city American neighbourhood.

Centrally situated in an area that is home to an estimated 8,000–9,000 Latinos, the Mercado Central offers an alternative vision for other inner-city neighbourhoods, where recent immigrants are often marginalized and faced with serious challenges to integration with the wider American population. As a result of this vision, the Latino population in Minneapolis has been able to gain much wider acceptance and appreciation for its cultural traditions. It has created a culturally relevant economic development vehicle that has enabled its members to integrate into the city's economic life.

Latino community members were determined to create a neighbourhood that felt like home and supported their efforts towards economic advancement. In doing so, they firmly believed that they had much to contribute to the city they had moved to. They were encouraged by leaders of a coalition of churches and local organizations who were committed to economic development in the community. A diverse group of actors developed a common vision which forged a path forward by recognizing the skills and talents of community members. Currently housing over 40 businesses, the Mercado Central is a reality because of the synergy that developed among these groups as they worked together to bring their community-based initiative to fruition.

This experience demonstrates the capacity of immigrant communities to revitalize a largely abandoned inner-city area, highlighting the opportunity for other positive developments and economically viable initiatives in similar neighbourhoods throughout North America. The Mercado Central offers a sense of possibility for underestimated and marginalized communities to make inner-city neighbourhoods home by revitalizing and reclaiming them from within.

Context

In recent decades, the make-up of many North American cities has been dramatically altered. Fuelled by shifts in global economic trends, government policies, and a withdrawal of industry from urban areas, the economic viability of many inner-cities began to collapse in the 1970s and 1980s. The 'urban decay' that ensued is characterized by city centres which are faced with high unemployment, a migration of wealthier residents to the 'suburbs,' property devaluation, increasing crime rates, and frequently bleak urban landscapes. In contrast to many European cities, where this phenomenon tends to affect the outskirts of urban areas, families, schools, and businesses have often withdrawn from inner cities, as people choose to build their homes and livelihoods on the periphery of their cities. Urban sprawl and suburban lifestyles have thrived alongside an increase in poverty, marginalization and crime in inner cities. This has been the case in inner-city Minneapolis.

The 'Twin Cities' of Minneapolis and St Paul constitute the largest urban area in the American state of Minnesota. The Mercado Central is located in the commercial area of Minneapolis' Lake Street which, historically, was the centre of commerce. In the 1960s, however, older, established businesses began to close down, homeowners fled the city, city taxes were reduced, and city services could no longer keep up with the need to upgrade the aging infrastructure. By 1970, Lake Street was known as a 'seedy' district with adult sex businesses, pawn shops, bars, and liquor stores.

Nonetheless, Lake Street was becoming a neighbourhood hub for a growing Latino community. While the majority of Minnesota's Latinos are American-born, during the 1990s alone the state of Minneapolis saw its number of foreign-born residents double, from 110,000 to 240,000. In the year 2000, 24 per cent of this population was of Latin American origin (The Minneapolis Foundation, 2004: 8). This is significant, considering that America's growing concentration of immigrants has created pressure on local institutions to address issues such as the need for access to employment, job training, affordable housing, and English as a second language. Latino immigrants are often monolingual, some arrive without legal documents or higher education, and many have a limited number of skills with which to compete for well-paying jobs. This can leave them vulnerable to poverty and social isolation.

Given steadily increasing rates of immigration in the United States, this has become a highly political issue. Between 1970 and 2003, America's foreign-born population rose from 5 per cent to 12 per cent (Hanson, 2004). According to the US Census, more than one in eight people, or nearly 40 million, in the United States were of Hispanic origin in 2002. Approximately 40 per cent of this population is foreign born, and two thirds are of Mexican origin, with others having roots in Central and South America, Cuba or Puerto Rico (US Census Bureau, 2003). Now surpassing the African American population in number, there is much speculation regarding the future impact of the Latino population as the largest minority group in the country.

As Robert Putnam has pointed out, increasing ethnic diversity and social heterogeneity is one of the greatest challenges currently facing the industrialized world. While immigration and diversity produce important cultural and economic benefits in the long term, in the short term, the impact tends to be a reduced sense of solidarity and social capital. According to Putnam 'New evidence from the US suggests that in ethnically diverse neighbourhoods, residents of all races tend to "hunker down". Trust (even of one's own race) is lower, altruism and community cooperation rarer, friends fewer' (Putnam, 2007: 137).

It is in this context that the Latino community of Minneapolis has crafted an inspiring and innovative strategy for challenging the status quo. Drawing upon deep religious beliefs and diverse leadership styles, the effort to establish the Mercado Central has allowed Latino community members to redefine their roles and identities in America. It also suggests that recent immigrants are able to integrate socially and economically much more quickly than others, such as Putnam, have suggested, and offers important lessons for community organizers operating in similar environments. By consciously and proactively organizing around shared interests, building upon existing community strengths and forging meaningful relationships with strategic external actors, the development of the Mercado Central offers important insight into community-building in traditionally marginalized communities.

Building community: laying the groundwork through organizing a congregation

The story of the Mercado Central begins in 1990, when five Salvadorean immigrants approached Juan Linares, a Catholic Charities social worker originally from Mexico City. This initiative was the catalyst which set a chain of critical events in motion.

The men requested Juan's support in making St Stephen's, the local Catholic church, available to the community throughout the week. As with most inner-city churches, it was locked during the day, thus depriving families in the neighbourhood of a space to pray together. They also voiced their concern that there were no Spanish masses available at any other local churches. Although accustomed to providing support in the form of food stamps, transportation tokens, and rent assistance, Juan was unclear about how to proceed. He reflected that the men 'challenged me to help meet their spiritual needs. Most of these people are from far away and feel they are in a strange land. They miss the strength that comes from belonging and working together' (personal communication, 2002). Until this point, he had been distracted by more immediate needs and requests for financial assistance, and had neglected the community's more intangible spiritual needs.

With the assistance of *Isaiah,* a multi-denominational, congregation-based community organizing coalition in Minneapolis, the first Spanish mass was conducted at St Stephen's in 1991, with 35 families attending. The deacon, Carl Valdez (who had been approached by Juan) arranged for 12 bilingual priests to commit to a weekly rotation. Meanwhile, he conducted over 200 meetings in the homes of local families to discuss their desire to build a spiritual community, their ideas, fears, interests, and willingness to help. Over time, more and more people came to the now regular Spanish masses, until in 1995, a church was established within St Stephen's Parish called *La Comunidad Catolica del Sagrado Corazon de Jesus* (the Catholic Community of the Sacred Heart of Jesus) – or simply *Sagrado Corazon.* What began with a simple request to open the church for five families by 1999 had resulted in over 750 Latino families regularly attending the new Spanish-led church, reflecting the desire for community among the city's new residents. The church would eventually become the centre from which Latino residents would mobilize to build their local economy and address other community concerns such as the treatment of Latino residents by the Immigration and Naturalization Service (INS).

To mobilize large-scale action, a 'sponsoring team' of community members was formed to develop an action plan around unfair immigration practices. Termed the 'Campaign to Preserve Immigrant Families,' the strategy was to demand that the INS transform its interactions with Latino residents in ways that respected language barriers and other concerns. Although the Mercado organizing activities were distinct from the immigration organizing that took place during the same period, many community members were involved in both sets of activities and considered them two components of the larger community transformation that they were trying to achieve. These activities built a base of intra-group trust among diverse Latinos, as well as inter-group trust among non-Latino churches committed to addressing the immigration issues of Latino families. The majority of the membership within the *Isaiah* project was from non-Latino churches, and for many Latino immigrants, it was the first exposure to 'outside' assistance and support. Ultimately, the partnership enabled the Latino community to build the skills, leadership, self-confidence, and group trust that allowed them to take on the large and complex Mercado Central project, while remaining in charge of their own development.

As the story of the development of Mercado Central unfolded, the active community members forming the coordinating committee would find that different styles of community organizing sometimes led to conflict, not about their end goal, but about the means to achieve it. Many *Isaiah* leaders adhered to and promoted a traditional, more confrontational community mobilization approach to 'win' ground, while others believed in focusing on areas of mutual benefit and negotiating through the identification of common goals as a way to achieve the desired end goal.

Community Talent Inventory

The Mercado organizing activities began when Juan Linares and Salvador Miranda, one of *Isaiah's* community organizers, began working with congregation members to create a 'Community Talent Inventory' (CTI) aimed at identifying entrepreneurial skills within the community and building relationships among community members. Based on the first 75 completed inventories, three themes emerged: confirmation of wide-ranging business expertise and entrepreneurial talent; a desire for targeted entrepreneurial training; and an interest in addressing immigration issues collectively as a community. This demand for entrepreneurial training came to the attention of two local organizations, the Whittier Community Development Corporation ('Whittier'), providing specialized business development training for local entrepreneurs and the Western Initiative for Neighbourhood Development (WIND), which operates the Neighbourhood Development Centre (NDC), a non-profit organization that responds to local needs for entrepreneurial training, loans, and technical assistance to micro-entrepreneurs and small business.

The entrepreneurial training course: a community-building opportunity

Since an entrepreneurial training programme in Spanish was already offered in the neighbouring city of St Paul, NDC agreed to offer the training in Spanish in Minneapolis as well. Instrumental in its decision to do so was the evidence generated through the CTI of residents' interest in starting small businesses. The economic development specialist from Whittier participated directly, facilitating the business planning session with the budding entrepreneurs. The courses were offered at *Sagrado Corazon* as a way of confirming to community members that their efforts in building the church were paying off, and that their collective aspirations were inspiring positive action and immediate local change. The church served as concrete reality that they could achieve common

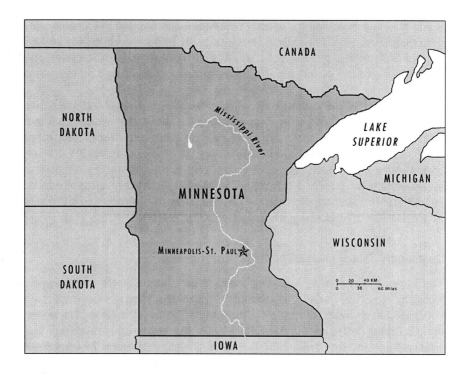

goals through their own planning and actions. Early 'wins' on immigration and church-building inspired leaders to believe that they could reach their next goal – the development of their own businesses.

The 16-week-long entrepreneurial training provided was a vehicle for continued community organizing as well as learning. At the individual level, the curriculum provided entrepreneurs with the technical information required to develop viable business and marketing plans. At the community-building level, the group talked about how to effect broader change in the community and play a role in revitalizing the local economy.

Juan Linares attended each session in order to continue to build relationships with and among the entrepreneurs. The participants in the training programme represented some of the most motivated and creative people in the Latino community. During the training, the entrepreneurs began to think and talk about themselves as leaders and to assume roles that reflected that leadership.

As the entrepreneurs progressed through the training programme, they were challenged to think about how they could develop individual businesses that would be competitive in the larger marketplace without competing with one another. They had worked hard to achieve a level of trust and cohesion as a group, and each of them recognized the benefits. This challenge led the entrepreneurs to consider the idea of a cooperative, a vehicle that would enable each business owner to achieve financial success while simultaneously working together and supporting others' efforts. For the entrepreneurs in the class, part of the challenge was to create a successful network of businesses surrounded by friends, family, and community support.

The Mercado Central idea is born

Reflecting on their own traditions, Latino immigrants realized that they shared the experience of a central market place where people gather to shop, socialize, share news, celebrate and grieve as a community. Traditional *mercados* in Latin American cities are in the centre of town and are designed to be an informal place for families to eat and socialize. Much more than simply the centre of commerce, it is the heart from which one can sense the pulse of a community. As discussions continued along with a growing confidence and business acumen, an idea emerged that directly related to the entrepreneurs' cultural experience as Latinos: they would build their own central marketplace for the people of the neighbourhood and citizens of Minneapolis as a whole. As a diverse group of individuals primarily comprising Mexicans, Ecuadorians, Nicaraguans, and Salvadoreans (including those living in America both legally and illegally, and others who were American-born), their affiliations, language abilities, and life experiences varied widely. One common element which supported the development of a cohesive unit, however, was their faith, and belief in the importance of a faith-based community. The idea of creating a central marketplace was therefore conceived as an economically viable option for the Latino entrepreneurs as well as a 'gift' to the city and to the wider American population, who the Latino community members perceived to be lacking a central site to enjoy as the 'heart' of community life – an element of city living that all Latinos, regardless of their country of origin, appreciated as the core of a healthy community.

The idea soon became known as the Mercado Central (central market). During the first entrepreneurial training course, the idea became the basis of how the emerging merchants saw their ongoing work together as community businessmen and women. And as a community, they began to identify with the notion that: *'El pueblo vive como sujeto de su propia historia, no vive ya como objectos de un historia que otros han escrito'* (People live as the subjects of their own history and no longer objects of a history defined by others for them).

Investing in the development of both leaders and businesses

Through their connections with *Isaiah*, and inspired by the organizing of the *Sagrado Corazon* congregation, some of the entrepreneurs from the training course had participated in a leadership training based on the Alinsky model (Alinsky, 1972), offered through the Gamaliel Foundation. At the same time, the entrepreneurs established a Mercado Central coordinating committee to make necessary decisions until a legal entity could be formed. The members of the coordinating committee were all graduates of the first entrepreneurial training class who had already launched their businesses. They agreed to meet between two and four times each week to develop the legal and operating policies for the Mercado Central.

The committee's time commitment over the next decade and determination to maintain local control over the project (versus allowing well-intentioned external professionals to take on key roles) must be emphasized at this stage of the Mercado's development. Conflicts sometimes arose about how best to work – whether to organize a public confrontation or media event, effectively used by traditional community organizers; or to focus on mobilizing their own groups' assets and resources (skills, abilities, expertise, networks), and to then identify other like-minded groups with which to later leverage additional resources. As each committee meeting began in prayer, the value all members placed on their faith served to diminish potential conflicts among individual agendas and promoted internal cohesion. This environment was another essential component of the process.

Getting over the initial hurdles in creating the legal vehicle for the Mercado Central was not easy. Seeking advice from the economic development specialist of Whittier, the Mercado Central entrepreneurs on the coordinating committee spent long hours of deliberation and planning to establish a legal cooperative. While the notion of a cooperative appealed to most, some local non-profit developers believed that the development of a cooperative would greatly complicate the project.

After substantial discussion, the group decided to form a cooperative to serve as the vehicle for property ownership. A co-op structure would place management responsibilities in the hands of a Mercado Central Board of Directors and also serve as a leadership training structure. Members were officially elected to the Mercado Central Board by the new cooperative membership at its first meeting, and the project was under way. In laying the groundwork, the organizers identified resources for planning, training, and expert advice for community members as they moved the project forward. By leaving the central roles to community members while providing them with supportive resources, local control of the decision-making process was maintained, as was validation of the ability of local people to re-shape their own community. A few months later, the coordinating committee decided on a vendor-owned cooperative. The cooperative model represented a creative and intentional deviation from the standard business incubator model, which usually creates an entity operated by a non-profit business developer. Because the coordinating committee wanted to ensure that the Latino merchants would have total ownership of the cooperative, they decided to sell shares to each merchant.

For the Mercado Central board and members, the entire process reflected the principles of building community from the inside out. The critical first step of identifying internal assets allowed for building bridges to external assets, and finally leveraging additional assets both internally and externally.

A multi-pronged community economic development project

The plan that emerged from the work of the coordinating committee and the new board of directors reflected a complex undertaking. To achieve the vision of a community gathering place, the Mercado Central needed land and a building that would eventually be owned and controlled by the cooperative members. The cooperative was also seen as a vehicle for business development that could provide business training, support, and access to financing – a retail business incubator for emerging Latino retailers. Part of the idea was that as individual businesses successfully grew, they would leave the Mercado Central and move into available storefronts in the surrounding area, eventually creating a Latino shopping district with the Mercado Central as the anchor.

This expansive vision required that several distinct strands of activity be undertaken to develop each component. Ultimately, this meant that a multi-pronged community economic development project would have to be launched, in three distinct phases. First, it would be a real estate development project, with a building to house the Mercado Central. Second, it would be a business development project, with support for 30 business start-ups, plus several expanding businesses occupying vendor space in the Mercado Central. Third, it would be a member-owned cooperative development project, with the establishment of a board of directors, an operating structure and the formulation of the *Mercado Central Cooperativa* as a legal entity.

Any one of these activities would have required an enormous commitment from local people and institutions. But for the Mercado Central vision to be successful in its entirety, all three components needed to be developed simultaneously. The economic development specialist from Whittier acknowledged his lack of experience in an economic development endeavour of this scale, but pledged his support in helping to move all three project areas forward. Most Mercado Central members aligned themselves with at least one of the three development areas, and because it was impossible for every individual to be part of every aspect of the work, members learned to trust one another to fairly represent their interests on occasions when they were unable to be present.

The total financing for all three projects was almost US$3 million, derived from about 25 sources, including banks, foundations, the City of Minneapolis, non-profit development organizations, local corporations, and the Catholic Campaign for Human Development. The real estate project financing totalled about US$2 million alone. Most of the renovation costs were covered by grants to substantially reduce the debt on the property, allowing rents that could be managed by the vendors. Financing for individual businesses totalled over US$500,000.

Real estate development

With an architect's plans as a guide, the organizing committee began to look for real estate in the commercial stretch of Lake Street, which had been targeted for significant reinvestment and revitalization work by the City of Minneapolis. At the same time, a non-profit community developed organization known as Project for Pride in Living (PPL) was working with a small business association on a local development effort. As the coordinating committee launched inquiries about property in the neighbourhood, they were approached by PPL with an invitation to consider a property on the corner of Lake Street and Bloomington Avenue.

As talks progressed, PPL offered to handle the financing for the purchase and renovation of the existing property and to remodel as much as was feasible. With these guarantees, the committee agreed that the Mercado Central would be the anchor tenant for the project. Although working with an overall purchase and renovation budget of US$2.4 million dollars, there were significant challenges involved in upgrading the building. Nonetheless, by the summer of 1999, the Mercado Central was able to begin leasing space with an option to purchase the entire building if, at any point during the following 10 years, it could afford to do so.

The Mercado Central began to lease the first floor to strategically selected start-up vendors and assumed responsibility for marketing, maintenance, cleaning, and security for the first floor. This floor originally hosted 27 vendor stalls and six restaurants, with a shared kitchen space for food vendors. Most vendors on the first floor sell a variety of Latino-oriented products and services; two-thirds of these merchants are start-up businesses. The first floor also provides a larger open space for cultural events, music, and dining, central to the idea of building a community environment, as well as a marketing tool for the Mercado Central.

Project for Pride in Living leases out the second floor and is responsible for its maintenance, cleaning, and security, as well as overall maintenance and security of the exterior and the parking lot. This floor is occupied by more established Latino businesses, including the city's Latino newspaper, a travel agent, accountant and tax service provider, jewellery store, leather goods, music store, Spanish language school, and offices for the Mercado Central and WIND Neighbourhood Development Centre. These businesses pay slightly under market rent for their space.

Business development

The Mercado Central Cooperative vision was designed to allow small businesses to take advantage of the larger customer base that would be drawn to a Mercado Central as a destination because of the variety of small businesses. Priority recruitment was done among entrepreneurs whose businesses offered the key products and services that reflected a desired retail mix. According to Becky George, the original Board had a 'wish list' of businesses (personal communication, 2007). Their primary list of anchor businesses included a tortilla shop, café, butcher, bakery, supermarket, and various restaurants. Their secondary list included merchants offering flower services, Mexican sweets and piñatas, clothing shops, jewellery, music, among others. The Mercado Central recruiters looked for a mix of established and start-up businesses. Keeping in mind the vision of a family atmosphere, they also took into account the types of vendors that they didn't want, including tattoo parlours, fortune tellers, and illegal 'pyramid' businesses in which participants earn profits through recruiting new members (George, personal communication, 2007).

There are a number of requirements for a business to be part of the cooperative. The business owner must first be a graduate of the Neighbourhood Development Centre's entrepreneurial training course or other Mercado Central-approved training programme, and must offer goods or services that meet the needs of the Latino community in the Minneapolis metropolitan area. Finally, the vendor must agree to purchase US$1,000 in stock in the cooperative.

Today, 44 businesses and services are thriving in the Mercado Central, including six restaurant stalls; a variety of clothing vendors; and entrepreneurs specializing in videos, flowers, music, sporting goods, Christian books and gifts, Latin American traditional crafts and clothing, and natural products. In addition, a number of vendors offer services in tax and bookkeeping, clothing design and alterations, real estate, travel, insurance, Spanish language and translation, beauty services, and custom embroidery.

Neighbourhood development centre training

The required NDC training programme creates a 'feeder' system of entrepreneurs, through a popular 16-week entrepreneurial training course. The close connection between NDC and the Mercado Central assures members that they will not have a problem filling stalls that are vacated in the future due to businesses that either move to a larger location or close. This system recognized a gap in the community and provided the opportunity for skill development and the nurturing of local and sustainable leadership capacity.

The Mercado's customer base stems largely from the neighbourhood and city of Minneapolis. Eighty-five per cent are Latino, with 70 per cent of this population coming from surrounding neighbourhoods and the wider Minneapolis area. The typical Latino shopper lives in the neighbourhood and may stop in at the Mercado Central to send a package to relatives in Mexico through one vendor, buy fresh tortillas from another, a dozen tamales from a third, and a bag of dried peppers from another. This shopper will pass several booths selling Latino clothes and shoes, a booth selling typical Latino party novelties and cards, and will make a note to come back the following week since there are important birthdays coming up. As this shopper turns to leave, he or she will see a leather soccer ball imported from Mexico that

Shopping at the Mercado Central.

represents the perfect gift for a child in the family. Most conversations will be in Spanish with people the shopper knows, and most shoppers will also make new acquaintances through the Mercado Central shopping experience.

A second kind of customer is someone from the Latino community in the broader metropolitan area. This type of customer returns to the Mercado Central once or twice during the week, thus circulating money he or she has earned elsewhere to other members of the Latino community. The sense that the Mercado Central is a Latino institution will motivate them to become loyal shoppers. This type of shopper appreciates having contributed to the development of a Latino institution that builds Latino businesses and employs Latinos. These shoppers will be drawn by the availability of Latino clothing and will stock up on food products or other speciality items not available from more mainstream retailers. Their purchase totals will be higher but will occur less frequently.

A third type of customer is the non-Latino who seeks a unique international experience. This shopper may be looking to enjoy an evening of Latin music or food; he or she may be drawn to the available arts and crafts that are a reminder of past Latin American vacations. This customer will target the craft artisans, will visit the Mercado Central infrequently, but could generate high individual sales on every visit.

Cooperative development

The Mercado Central Cooperative provides opportunities for ownership at two levels. First, each vendor is an owner in the cooperative itself. Second, owners of mature businesses who have readied themselves to move out of the Mercado Central are in a strong position to buy a larger storefront space on Lake Street. With the maturity that results after five to ten years of business experience in the more protected cooperative setting, Mercado Central business owners have a much better chance of success when they launch out on their own as independents.

Over the course of the development, the relationship between PPL and the cooperative has experienced typical landlord-tenant tensions and conflict. As Becky George explains, some challenges existed due to the diverging priorities of the PPL and the Mercado Central management (personal communication, 2007). With its expertise in residential housing, the PPL was new to working in commercial property management. Likewise, the Mercado Central, as a new venture, experienced a number of growing pains. Over time, the differences were resolved through a commitment from both parties to developing a smoother relationship, and support from NDC. During a period of financial difficulty, NDC was able to provide contracted management services, realizing that such services needed to be culturally appropriate. PPL accepted the proposal and management of the second floor was eventually transferred to the Cooperative (George, personal communication, 2007).

During the real estate development stages of the project, PPL and the board met weekly or bi-monthly until the development was completed. The purpose of these meetings was to enhance the balance of power and decision-making between the board and PPL. Board members raised important issues and discussed concerns, vendor needs and ideas, and changes to the original plans. After the physical development of the facility, the meetings began to occur monthly, and currently take place annually in order to evaluate the performance of the Mercado Central and establish an operating budget for the coming year.

Overall impact

The many results of the Mercado Central effort reflect the goals of the various partners in the development effort. As Leonard Inskip (1999) points out, the Mercado Central is important not only as a model of cooperation, but also a model of reciprocity: '[It is] a model of cooperation between immigrant churchgoers, the broad faith community, non-profit urban institutions, city neighbourhoods, federal and local government, leaders and philanthropic donors'. Likewise, as Becky George, current Manager of the Mercado Central, original cooperative member, and former board president, notes: 'I feel that I have been fortunate to witness the Mercado's growth in many areas ... I have been so blessed to be a part of the [personal and commercial growth] of the members' (personal communication, 2007).

While the financial results of the projects have been impressive, the more general community and leadership benefits that have resulted from the project also represent important outcomes. The Mercado Central was created through the commitment of local Latino community members combining their skills, abilities, and visions for the future to create an economic opportunity that none of them could create on their own. Because it was built from within the community, the community was able to leverage outside resources to support its unified vision and goals. As John Flory, an economic development specialist, commented, investors recognized the value in this approach and vision: 'This project was unique from the start. I have been doing economic development work for 14 years, and never have I had banks call me to say, "We want to invest in this project." It happened here' (personal communication, 2002). The unique approach of the project was immediately obvious and attracted unusual attention.

The leaders of the Mercado Central project were focused on their two-pronged strategy to bring the project to fruition. They needed to create a mechanism to continuously draw potential entrepreneurs into the project while also attracting outside resources (including the city, funders, government, and other business owners). Marketing the unique assets of the Latino community became the mechanism to bring both elements together.

The Mercado Central provides a mechanism for entrepreneurs to access capital financing, technical assistance and ongoing support as they venture into business ownership. Over half of the businesses in the Mercado Central are first-time, start-up micro businesses. The Neighbourhood Development Centre works with merchants to clarify the technical assistance needed, as well as to provide individualized advice and problem-solving to merchants. Because the merchants are all graduates of the entrepreneurial training course and are located under the same roof, the cost of delivering services is minimized. General services offered include: legal assistance; sales and marketing support (e.g. combining marketing dollars allows merchants to advertise their businesses to a broader market than otherwise possible); bookkeeping; one-on-one business planning; and personal technical assistance available with an on-site business advisor (available 20 hours per week).

The Mercado Central follows a Latin American tradition whereby *mercados* are an informal community-gathering place. It is a venue for public forums of particular interest to Latino families. Forums in the first year included topics on immigration, the 2000 Census, and county resources. It has hosted Catholic Church services on special occasions and holidays. The Mercado Central has also been a mechanism for distributing information to the community, as well as a social hub hosting dances, concerts, poetry and other cultural events. As J. Trout Lowen (1999), a local newspaper columnist, commented: 'The Mercado Central becomes the province of families, mostly Latino, who find it a comfortable place in which to socialize'.

The Latino immigrant community has often been stereotyped as low-wage farm workers with few transferable skills. The Mercado Central challenges those conceptions. It demonstrates in a visible way the success of Latino business people and that Latinos are savvy entrepreneurs and community leaders. The Mercado Central creates a bridge between Latino community members and non-Latino community. Schools have used the Mercado Central as an educational destination for field trips. It is a safe environment in which individuals or groups can explore another culture. Food, products, people, and environment all share the telling of the story, and provide a link between new and more established community members. As envisioned at its conception, the Mercado Central has emerged as the Latino community's 'gift' to the city of Minneapolis.

A revitalized economy

Across America and beyond, inner cities are experiencing the impact of economic and social change, and most have experienced some degree of disinvestment. 'Turn-around' strategies have included identifying key properties for development on a commercial corridor. Good solid 'pioneering businesses' are expected to draw additional development to fill in the gaps. Recognizing the Mercado Central is just such a pioneer, Inskip (1999) commended it as 'a model of community cooperation'.

Over time, a commercial corridor can be transformed, providing a key deterrent to crime. Business owners along the corridor naturally establish a stake in the community, which encourages their collective voice demanding reinvestment by the public sector. A 'virtual circle' is thus established that will lead to reinvestment in the community. The Latino neighbourhood in Minneapolis is a prime example of how proactive economic planning can yield impressive results.

Initial financial benefits to the Lake Street area included: US$2.4 million dollars invested in the purchase and renovation of three dilapidated buildings on Lake Street; over US$277,000 in small business loans made to new Latino businesses; 44 businesses established and/or expanded; over US$2 million in first year sales; 70 people employed by Mercado Central businesses, and over US$80,000 in sales tax paid by Mercado Central merchants in their first year of operation alone.

More recently, the building has been valued at US$1.7 million, and property taxes paid in 2006 totalled US$54,000. Although overall sales figures are difficult to confirm, estimates suggest that US$6,900,000 in annual sales tax was paid by Mercado merchants in 2006. The Mercado Central now directly employs between 125 and 150 people, and taking into account the expansion of businesses outside of the cooperative, approximately 70 more jobs have been created by Mercado business owners.

Because of the project's unique design, many of the financial benefits remain in the neighbourhood. Creating an economic engine like the Mercado

Central has allowed neighbourhood income to remain in the local economy where it can be spent again and again. This recycling of income produces ever-increasing neighbourhood income (e.g. through salaries and through the profits earned by local owners). This virtuous cycle multiplies the economic benefit of the Mercado Central, as well as establishing it as a new economic asset for the entrepreneurs, the Latino community, and the entire neighbourhood.

For instance, the Latino Economic Development Centre, which offers its services to the cooperative membership, has recently transformed a neighbouring, abandoned building – the Plaza Verde – into a viable business and community gathering space in partnership with a number of other organizations. Plaza Verde is now able to accommodate the growth of original Mercado Central vendors who have expanded their operations.

Now a thriving, multi-cultural marketplace, the Lake Street area is now home to a number of Mexican, Ecuadorian, Ethiopian, and Chinese restaurants; four Mexican bakeries; three East African halal shops; and a variety of speciality shops. Over the past three years, the neighbourhood has experienced reconstruction efforts featuring wider sidewalks with improved lighting, benches, signage, cameras along Bloomington Avenue to deter crime, and community murals in place of graffiti.

A sustainable local economy is created as local people start businesses, spend more of their money locally, and more fully engage in the commercial life of the community. As more people in the local committee have money to spend, and when they spend more of it locally, the neighbourhood economy grows and the initial investments are multiplied.

Community assets

The financial benefit figures capture only a snapshot of the Mercado Central's economic value to the community. The figures do not include the long-term impact of the Mercado Central on the overall Lake Street revitalization effort. While some of the benefits are immediately obvious, the hidden value of an alternative retail incubator that can nurture and support emerging businesses will only be apparent after many years.

By early 2003, several vendors were considering embarking on independent commercial ventures outside the Mercado Central. In addition, the presence of the Mercado Central has encouraged other Latino businesses to locate nearby. A Latino grocery store has opened across the street, and a number of Latino professionals, such as attorneys and accountants, have located their offices within a block or two of the Mercado Central. The results have attracted the attention of the larger Minneapolis community as well, and enthusiastic support for the success on Lake Street continues to grow.

In terms of organizational assets, the Mercado Central effort resulted in the creation of two new Latino community groups: *Sagrado Corazon* and the Mercado Central Cooperative. Both of these entities emerged where no organized voice existed previously; both created organized structures through which members have accomplished their specific community-building goals. These new community associations represent a new mechanism through which the Latino community can mobilize for the continuing support of the Mercado Central vision, and nurture community members' visions for the future. Perhaps one of the most important outcomes of the Mercado Central work is the creation of these sustainable community groups dedicated to building on the assets of their members.

The most important, yet not easily quantifiable, impact of the Mercado Central has been in the hearts and minds of the community's residents and families. One aspect of this change is the degree to which local people have assumed leadership positions in the activities related to the Mercado Central, the cooperative, local associations, and the broader Minneapolis community. Individual business owners have improved their skills and their confidence levels to contribute to local and more extensive community discussions. They had the positive experience of seeing their personal efforts contribute to their own improved financial well-being and the commercial heath of the community, and gained the kind of self-assurance that comes from their success.

Also of critical importance is the role that members of the Mercado Central's board of directors have played in maintaining a consistent, dedicated commitment to the longer term vision. Key leadership figures (both male and female) such as Becky George and Ramon Leon have been involved from the inception of the Mercado Central and continue to provide essential contributions to the cooperative's growth and development.

Many other members of the board are recognized as community leaders among members of the Latino community, local business associations, and the larger Minneapolis area. Ramon, for instance, has co-founded the Latino Economic Development Centre of Minnesota. One leadership figure has since been asked to join the Governor's taskforce on a small business development, while another has been invited to take part in an advisory committee to the Archbishop of Minneapolis and St Paul. Yet another has served on the Latino Advisory Board to the Mayor of Minneapolis. Without their experience and leadership roles within the Mercado Central effort, these individuals' capacities might not have been recognized by these mainstream institutions.

Mercado Central leaders continue to use their extensive experience in small business development and training and work with immigrant groups throughout the Twin Cities area.

Lessons: learning through doing

Looking back, the key actors in the development of the Mercado Central recognize a number of important lessons in effective community organizing. They identified the opportunity to harness local energy and mobilize local assets to build relationships that allow individuals to express their own talents and aspirations for the future. Those involved with *Isaiah* realized that its efforts with the Community Talent Inventory would have been wasted had they not also invested time in building connections between assets identified through the inventory process. Without care, mapping local assets and recording local capacities could have become just another exercise in data collection. Members of *Isaiah* learned that it is the quality of the information gathered, not the quantity, that matters and that 'less is often more.' Because *Isaiah* allowed the inventories to guide the action of its members, and because they moved rapidly to mobilize the assets identified, momentum was maintained, and the Mercado Central was born.

Knowing how information will ultimately be used is critical to a successful capacity inventory effort. Before getting started, *Isaiah* was clear about what information it wanted to gather and what would be done with it following the collection process. People understood that asking questions out of curiosity is only an exercise, but that directed questions whose responses serve a purpose are more effective. With clearly identified goals, they further capitalized on the energy that began to surface by developing an association of citizens, in this case the new church, and utilized this as a vehicle for ongoing support and development of community leadership, ideas, and actions.

It is important to consider how leadership roles can be shared among people in such a way that skills and abilities are complementary. Salvador and Juan were both leaders who respected each other's skills and perspectives. When asked about leadership abilities of these two individuals, community members responded that they were a combination of Salvador's strong and strategic 'head,' and Juan's relationship-oriented 'heart.' Both were vital to the success in organizing leaders to build the *Sagrado Corazon* church and create the Mercado Central. Neither could have led this endeavour alone; each would have lacked the specific leadership capacities of the other. It was critical to have a multi-dimensional leadership dedicated both to developing authentic relationships while focusing on the deployment of multiple strategies.

In the Mercado Central project, the original cooperative board members became the sustainable community voice and local guides for the Mercado Central. There was consistent commitment on the part of the Latino community businesses to work collectively toward the creation of a mutually owned cooperative. During the development process, it was critical that Juan Linares and John Flory were paid by their organizations to provide consistent and ongoing technical support in their various areas of expertise. The timelines stretched beyond the initial timeline set by all parties, yet staff members were allowed to remain on the project without interruption. Similarly, the project maintained flexibility in order to accommodate the reality of (much lengthier) cycles of community-led organizing, rather than attempting to adapt to timelines imposed by external agents and organizations.

Those involved in the Mercado Central project understood that there is value added to investing in collective action rather than simply pursuing individual action. When a group of people engage in developing a vision, strategize how to achieve it, and then invest in making it happen, their relationships are solidified and they have built a sense of community. Early experiences of community members working together accumulated over time, so they developed a great sense of assurance and faith in collective action. Spending time developing a cooperative legal structure was complex work that could not have been achieved without the earlier group success in building the church.

Leadership figures in the Mercado Central effort were able to win over the media as a powerful community-building tool. By cultivating strategic relationships with columnists and local reporters, Salvador was able to make effective use of the media to help change unfavourable perceptions of the Latino community in the Twin Cities. Although the media often reinforce ethnic, racial and class stereotypes, Salvador was able to feed newsworthy stories to his media contacts. He was able to effectively position information according to the interests of the wider community, which ultimately served an educational role.

Over time, community leaders began to develop greater skills in time management. They learned that, when involving community members, increased effort is needed to be inclusive and assure ongoing ownership and authority among community members. They developed creative structures and ways of communicating to develop a broader and deeper network of people involved. When involving multiple partner organizations, the group adopted a general rule of multiplying the anticipated timeline by the number of diverse partners involved. In order to more effectively organize, a single person would oversee the general coordination and communication process.

The group learned to expect different agendas and conflict among members in an alliance of supporting organizations. Attempts were made to clearly identify the roles that each organization would assume in the project, identify the goals and objectives of each, and clarify how the project would benefit from their work. A process for negotiating conflicts was also developed. In 2002, an extensive list of operating procedures was formalized, and it was determined that members would be fined for failing to adhere to regulations (George, personal communication, 2007).

Community members in the Mercado Central project were often torn between a desire to focus solely on starting their business and to urge *Isaiah* to provide leadership in community-organizing activities. These differences in goals among partners created tensions and conflicts that had to be taken seriously and resolved. Clarifying expectations from the beginning helped to reduce the need for conflict resolution later on.

In order to prioritize long-term sustainability, it is essential to maintain consistent involvement of community members. Often a project begins with high levels of involvement, but after a few months, only a handful of people remain to do the majority of the work. When this happens, the project has lost the energy of the community. Those involved in Mercado Central considered a number of strategies to avoid this type of situation. First, they made certain that short-term 'wins' occurred (small, intermediate goals that could be accomplished easily), so that community members could see results that kept them active and involved. People's work on church issues provided many such positive results along the way to the larger goal, and kept them involved during the long development process of the Mercado Central. Next, they expected turnover in participation as people's lives and commitments changed. In anticipation of this inevitable situation, the Mercado Central needed a strategy for developing leaders in an ongoing way. The entrepreneurship classes served such a purpose for the project and became a source of new leadership. Finally, they created ongoing mechanisms for individuals to connect with one another and act jointly. The creation of a church and legal cooperative entity were critical community mechanisms that allowed for sustained local action. The Mercado Central Cooperative provides continuity in development and operational support for Latino businesses.

The complexity of the Mercado Central project required ongoing support well beyond the official grand opening. Although Whittier has not played an active role in the Mercado since 2003, the project is still heavily dependent on PPL and NDC, which have worked consistently with the board of directors to address endless changes, adaptations, and modifications to assure growth and success for individual vendors and the cooperative itself. This consistency in leadership and partner support has been critical to the success of the project.

Conclusion

Today, the Mercado Central includes over 44 established businesses. It is a thriving commercial space, the hub of a community, a place for families to gather, and a place of pride and culture. It is a testament to what the power of community can do. Although many successes are already apparent, much of the longer term impact remains to be seen. As an organizing vehicle for the Latino community, it has been a clear success. As a demonstration of the positive contribution that low-income immigrants can provide to an inner-city community, the Mercado Central has been a triumph. It has also been successful as a public relations project. The larger-scale economic development impact, however, will take several more years before it can effectively be measured.

Nonetheless, there are a number of important stories to explore within the Mercado Central. There is the story of *Isaiah,* a coalition committed to developing leaders and building organizing skills among community members. *Isaiah's* leadership training and organizing techniques successfully assisted leaders in building the first Twin Cities church based on the vision and faith of diverse Latin American immigrants. *Isaiah* also linked Latino community members to church allies, connected them with non-profit organizations that offered needed expertise, and, through media connections, brought them together with the Twin Cities community-at-large. As a church, *Sagrado Corazon* has established a powerful faith-based association from which Latinos can be unified in achieving their goals.

Then there is the story of the Mercado Central Cooperative itself, made up of Latino small business entrepreneurs. Individuals with little financial security risked US$1,000 each and placed their money in a cooperative where success depends on unity of purpose and community effort. This new association of Latino businesses, with the support and guidance of partner organizations, then built the Mercado Central, drawing almost US$3 million of investment into an inner-city neighbourhood that others had abandoned. Members of this community have rallied together, fostered by a dedicated group of leadership figures from the Latino community in order to bring a long term goal to fruition.

The building of *Sagrado Corazon* and the Mercado Central stories are rooted in the use of the gifts, talents, and personal potential of individuals. In each story, the actors are community members who have realized the vast breadth of experience within the Latino community and leveraged this to achieve a commonly shared and developed vision. They are both the beneficiaries as well as the change agents who are writing their story. As the Spanish saying clearly points out, communities thrive when: 'the people live as the subject of their own history rather than as objects of a history written by someone else.' The creation of the Mercado Central has allowed the Latino community in Minneapolis to be 'the subject of its own history.'

References

Alinsky, S. D. (1972) *Rules for radicals*, Vintage Books, New York.

Inskip, L. 'Mercado' on Lake Street is a model of community cooperation. Star Tribune. July 6, 1999.

Kretzmann, J. and McKnight, J. (1993) *Building communities from the inside out: A path toward finding and mobilizing a community's assets*, Institute for Policy Research, Northwestern University, Evanston, IL.

Lowen, J.T. Mercado Central: Marketing dreams. Siren. October 19-November 1, 1999 issue.

Putnam, R. (2007) 'E pluribus unum: Diversity and community in the twenty-first century. The 2006 Johan Dkytte Prize Lecture', *Scandinavian Political Studies*, 30(2): 137–174.

Minneapolis Foundation (2004) *Immigration in Minnesota: Discovering common ground*, The Minneapolis Foundation, Minneapolis, MN.

US Census Bureau (June 2003) *The Hispanic population in the United States: March 2002*. Available from http://www.census.gov/prod/2003pubs/p20–545.pdf [Accessed 14 August 2007].

Author's note

This is a story of community members believing in their ability to realize their dreams, and the leadership required to achieve a common goal.

My exposure to this story begins in the 1980s, when I was working with Cuban and Haitian families in the Twin Cities as a refugee settlement officer for Catholic Charities. Through my work with Latino refugees and political asylees, I had the honour of working and learning from community members who, years later would become the key leaders in the development of the Mercado Central. I left the Twin Cities during the 1990s and upon my return, many old friends agreed that the Mercado Central story was ready to be told.

My thanks and admiration go to the members of the Mercado Central Cooperative for their openness in sharing their story, especially Manuela Barraza, Ramon Leon, Becky George, and the many merchants at the Mercado. Their courage from the initial immigration fights, to the church building of *Sagrado Corazon*, to the successful development of their individual businesses, and ultimately to their leadership in the Mercado Central is an inspiring story to those committed to build community and support community-driven economic development.

This is also a story of committed community partners working together and being open to the dreams of the community. I am grateful to Salvador Miranda and Juan Linares for introducing me to community members, providing background materials, and helping with translation when needed. Thanks to Father Larry Hubbard and Carl Valdez for their insight and perspective on the community impact of this project; Rachel Dolan and Mike Temali from the Neighbourhood Development Centre; John Flory of Whittier Community Development Corporation; and staff from Project for Pride in Living for sharing their work, photographs and perspective on how this opportunity was made a reality. Everyone's work has been an inspiration to us all.

CHAPTER 4

The Jambi Kiwa story: mobilizing assets for community development in Ecuador

Gordon Cunningham

Abstract

The Jambi Kiwa cooperative in Ecuador has evolved from a small group of indigenous women sharing herbal remedies in local markets to a community-wide cooperative enterprise now selling medicinal and aromatic plants in global markets. This case documents how these women, and then communities in the region as a whole, recognized the potential of local natural assets and how they organized to ensure maximum returns to producers. It also highlights how initial success at organizing production by cooperative members was used as leverage to attract investment by a wide range of external donors, NGOs, and private business interests without compromising control by cooperative members. As such it demonstrates the possibilities for 'marginal' areas to link to the globalized world.

A seed is planted

The story of the Jambi Kiwa cooperative is about the struggle to create a new enterprise that holds the possibility of improving the livelihoods of hundreds of families in dozens of small rural villages throughout the mountainous region of Chimborazo. It is also a story about building on natural assets, reclaiming and valuing traditional culture, knowledge, and practices, and in the process, redefining what it means to be an indigenous people in Ecuador today. Throughout its brief history, Jambi Kiwa has demonstrated that it is possible for a community-driven initiative to develop partnerships with dozens of external stakeholders without ceding control of the decision-making process. Beginning as an informal enterprise of a few women harvesting medicinal plants in the wild, Jambi Kiwa is now processing and exporting plants in the global marketplace. As the business has grown, so too has a tension within the organization to find a business model that blends a larger social vision and the cultural norms of shared decision-making with the imperative of running a nimble, efficient and profitable enterprise.

Jambi Kiwa's history is intertwined with the nationwide movement for indigenous rights in Ecuador. A semi-feudal *hacienda* ['estate' or large plantation]

Box 4.1 Rosa's story

My name is Rosa Guamán and I have 5 children. I live in the town of Licto – I was born here. I lived here with my family until I turned 11 years old but, because of family problems, I had to leave home. With school finished, I went to the coast to find work. For the next eight years I did domestic labour to earn an income. It was during this time that I began the search for my identity and commitment – I wanted to change my life.

At 19, I returned to Licto and immediately noticed differences in the way domestic help was treated in Licto as compared to the treatment I received on the coast. In Licto the treatment of domestic help workers – and women in general – was awful.

Most native women in Licto were illiterate. At school there were no native girls and very few women among us had finished primary school. We had very low self-esteem, we felt very little self-worth. A woman's words were almost never valued within the home and it was even worse in the general community; we would often hear comments like 'What does she know? She is just an Indian.' On the public buses from Licto to Riobamba women could only sit in the back. And worse, if *mestizos* [people of mixed European and indigenous non-European ancestry] entered, women had to ride standing. As women we didn't count.

In our traditional culture, women had great knowledge, but after the conquest of our people, this has changed. Instead of using their knowledge and natural resources to provide for their families, women now relied on donations of milk, semolina, oil and flour from NGOs. It was humiliating to live in a country with many resources and not be able to provide for ourselves.

I was so frustrated with this situation that I began to seek out other women who were determined to fight such injustices. Many women were interested, but we all needed to make sure that our children were fed and so we didn't take drastic action. In 1974, however, Fr Estuardo Gallegos came to Licto to be our parish priest, and he motivated us... to get jobs and start making changes in our lives. Through his liberation theology work, he said that it was important to examine and encourage positive changes among the marginalized and exploited. His teachings seemed radical to us because the Church had not always been a place that we, as native people, felt welcome. In those days discrimination and racism were present everywhere. The Church was one of the worst discriminators, often using religion to put down the peasants and Indians. We were considered a lesser social class; we were not allowed to sit on the benches in Church and we always had to kneel on the floor. Fr Gallegos began to win our trust by painting the church benches the same colour, arranging them in one row and allowing everyone to sit as equals.

So we began to organize. We offered literacy classes for women and then offered classes in cutting, sewing and knitting. We started doing traditional craftwork together. As we talked about our work, word spread, and more and more women organized themselves. We were not only learning trades, we were becoming the protagonists of our own development.

The women's organization grew to become the Christian Network of Rural Women at the provincial level. Then, in 1999, we started the Association of Producers of Medicinal Plants – Jambi Kiwa. In starting this work, our struggle and commitment has also been to work for equality. While the idea of gender equality had taken root in many projects, social equality had been somewhat overlooked. It was too big for NGOs to want to take on so we had to do it ourselves. As a woman, it was difficult for me to confront such large social issues but I managed to do it. I was elected to the parish council, the main governing body of our small town. People supported me because they saw that we were trying to change things with our organization and valued our accomplishments.

We all have our personal journeys in life... my personal journey has [involved] a lot of hard times but the challenge is not to be bitter. I gradually began to realize that the *mestizos* had been born into a system where they exploited the indigenous: this had been going on for centuries. I also realized that the way forward is for us all to come together.

system had continued for more than 150 years after Ecuador's independence from Spain, perpetuating the exploitative service tenure structure in which the indigenous peasantry were employed. The first serious challenge to this system came during the 1940s and 1950s when the communist-inspired Federation of Ecuadorian Indians (FEI) organized unions of *hacienda* workers around securing wage labour. Although unsuccessful, this uprising helped to create the foundations of an organized indigenous peasants' struggle throughout Ecuador which set in motion land-redistribution policies and an end to service tenure. However, by 1970, only 3 per cent of land in Chimborazo had been transferred to indigenous peasantry (less than a fifth of which was cultivable land).

A significant force in the indigenous peoples' struggle for land was the Catholic Church. Being the largest land owner in Chimborazo, the Church was in a unique position to enact land reform. Monsignor Leonidas Proaño, Bishop of Riobamba and a liberation theologian, was instrumental in turning over large portions of Church land to peasant communities and ensuring that the poor had access to low-interest credit to buy *hacienda* land. He became a vocal advocate for the rights of indigenous peoples at the national level.

By the 1980s, national efforts were shifting towards a land reform model whereby peasants could purchase plots of land. Forceful land appropriations by indigenous groups also became more frequent, as did violent confrontations. As indigenous movements throughout Ecuador strengthened, many of them became part of a national movement known as the Confederation of Indigenous Nationalities of Ecuador (CONAIE). In 1990, it organized a national uprising to demonstrate its frustration with the government's failure to act on indigenous issues. With the participation of roughly 70 per cent of the rural population, the CONAIE brought the country to a virtual standstill.

Following this uprising, dialogue between the national government and the CONAIE increased significantly but the CONAIE continue to have difficulty getting their issues on the government's agenda. Indigenous people also struggled to break up the dominance of the *mestizo*-controlled national and regional markets.

While large sections of the best agricultural land in Chimborazo are still controlled by *hacienda* owners, many indigenous communities have been successful in maintaining or obtaining rights to communal and individual land. Today, however, new land issues are emerging. These include the increasing division of family property into smaller and smaller plots and the related issue of desertification, due largely to overgrazing, hillside farming and deforestation. These factors have led many small land-holders to either sell their land (often to the large landowners) and migrate or continue farming with financial support from family members who have already migrated to the cities or abroad.

One of the ways in which the Bishop of Riobamba supported the development of indigenous leaders in rural villages throughout the province was by training pastoral workers to work closely at the community level, keeping people informed and supporting their efforts to improve their livelihood.

These efforts laid the groundwork for the emergence of community-driven initiatives like Jambi Kiwa.

One of those former pastoral workers, Rosa Guamán, plays an essential role in this story Her work began with organizing indigenous women and their communities, and continues today in her role as one of the founding members and inspirational leaders of Jambi Kiwa.

In 1997, she was invited to attend a meeting of a group of women in Guayllabamba. This group had been working with an agronomist with the Canadian Centre for International Studies and Cooperation (CECI) on a number of small income-generating projects such as rearing cattle, growing fruit trees and vegetables and raising cuys (Andean guinea pigs).

At the meeting Rosa discovered that the Guayllabamba group had recently attempted to grow and sell traditional medicinal plants but were about to give up on this idea because it seemed time-consuming and unprofitable. Rosa and her friends not only recognized a potential income-generating activity, they also saw an opportunity to improve the health of their communities. However, given the difficulty persuading local women to put time and effort into preparing land and planting a new crop, Rosa suggested they start by gathering medicinal plants growing in the wild. They could immediately take these plants and display them in the local market as a way of reintroducing women to the medicinal qualities of local plants.

As they had promised, the very next week Rosa and her colleagues attended the local market in Licto to display several plants. As they were explaining their idea to a crowd of women who had gathered around, the leader of the diocese's pastoral programme happened to overhear the conversation. He later offered small stipends to Rosa's two colleagues to continue promoting medicinal plants. He also provided the use of an attic in an old church building to dry and store the plants.

With minimal support, Rosa and her colleagues organized many groups of women over the next year to collect medicinal plants and bring them to the church. With a small grant provided by UNDP, Rosa's colleague Josée was able to purchase plants from the groups. Purchases were made each Saturday, since cash on delivery was an incentive for the plant gatherers. Josée also found a reliable buyer in a tea company in the city of Ambato. As a result, the plant gatherers who began by harvesting 5 to 10 kg of plants each week now started bringing up to 100 kg of fresh plants to the church each weekend.

As the attic filled up with drying plants, Rosa and Josée saw the potential for these women to process the plants into a variety of medicinal products. As Josée recalls, it was significant that the women had begun to rediscover the traditional medicines of their ancestors:

> What I saw was women gaining confidence. They started coming to the courses we offered... We would pay older people to come in and show the women how to make traditional medicines or shampoo and soaps. I can remember some of them remarking: 'Oh my grandmother used to

do this.' Then they would take this rediscovered knowledge back to their communities. It was an exciting time. (personal communication, 2004)

By mid-1999, Josée's placement ended and CECI agreed to hire another cooperant. CECI also commissioned a market study to explore the potential for commercialization within Ecuador. Before she left, Josée also convinced her supervisor that CECI should hire Rosa. This was the first time CECI-Ecuador had hired an Ecuadorian as a project staff member.

The shift to commercialization

By the spring of 1999, Rosa and her colleagues in the women's medicinal plant producer groups were starting to attract the attention of other external agencies. One of these organizations was the *Centre de Solidarité Internationale* (CSI) in Quebec, Canada. Rosa asked CSI if they would partner with CECI to support a Jambi Kiwa proposal to the Canadian International Development Agency (CIDA) for money to purchase a used mill and dryers. The diocese responded by providing an old warehouse to house this equipment.

While its application to be an official association under Ecuadorian law was under consideration, Jambi Kiwa began small-scale production of shampoos, expectorants, diuretics, slimming formulas, etc. By the spring of 2001, a makeshift factory was ready to be inaugurated, coinciding with the time when the association was granted legal status.

The transition from an informal group to a legal association of medicinal plant producers marked a turning point in the evolution of Jambi Kiwa. For the group to be registered as an association, a formal, federated structure had to be created. Prior to this, each village-level producer group elected a representative, but as the number of producer groups grew, a new system was introduced. The result was the creation of three zones, each with an organization representing several producer groups (see Figure 4.1).

In April, 2001, Jambi Kiwa landed its first large scale contract to supply dried and milled herbal plants to CETCA, a national tea company in Quito. Executives of the tea company, recognizing the growing national and international markets for herbal tea, had begun to look for local herb suppliers. Jambi Kiwa responded to their advertisement in the local newspaper. The general manager, Jaime Macias Flores, agreed to the proposal put forward by these small producers, namely that intensive harvesting on small land plots had the potential to produce high yields of good quality plants.

Taking a personal interest in Jambi Kiwa, Flores showed them how to handle the herbs, provided the plans for the design of a new dryer, and helped them with the designs of the new factory. He was clear, however, that if Jambi Kiwa was going to be a supplier, it would have to follow certain procedures, such as artificial drying, to guarantee quality. Over the next few years, the relationship between CETCA and Jambi Kiwa evolved into a partnership through which medicinal herbal teas were sold in Panama, Costa Rica, and Colombia under the joint label Jambi Kiwa/Sangay.

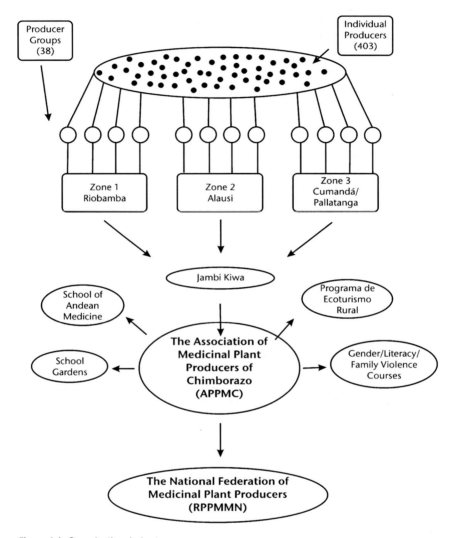

Figure 4.1: Organizational chart

In May 2001, when CECI sent two more cooperants, Jambi Kiwa was still in its 'honeymoon phase'. CECI continued to administer the project, provide funds to the producers and locate markets for their products. As a result, as one of the cooperants observed:

> There were no demands on the producers... There were no annual dues, no expectation that the producers should contribute their labour to the emerging organization and there was no certification process. Producers would show up at meetings and only be concerned with when the truck was coming to pick up the plants. (Walsh, personal communication, 2004)

Jambi Kiwa members were shaken out of this complacency by a national economic crisis that gripped Ecuador starting in early 2000 (see Box 4.2). In response to growing debt and rapid inflation, the government took the drastic measure of adopting the US dollar as the national currency. Dollarization increased Jambi Kiwa's costs, particularly for fresh plants and labour. In late 2001, association members were asked to pay dues and contribute labour at the factory in order to keep the business viable. As a result, some members left the organization, but the committed ones remained. Rosa describes the struggle to maintain a clear vision among members:

> I can recall a situation when a group of producers came and wanted to become members of Jambi Kiwa. They wanted to know what the profitability was going to be each month. I said, 'Our benefits are not just economic and financial – they are about learning, training, improving the biodiversity of the community and having a better diet.' That is the challenge – finding people [who] are willing to be part of this vision. (personal communication, 2004)

Despite financial constraints, committed members continued to emerge and Jambi Kiwa was able to grow. With growth, however, came a need to restructure the production process. A factory manager and two factory staff were hired. At the same time, a young industrial engineer was hired to offer support to the new factory manager, a bookkeeper assumed much of the day-to-day accounting required by CIDA for the CSI/CECI project and a marketing director was trained. To increase potential markets, producers also needed training that would earn them 'green seal' status (certification) from Bio Control Systems. To increase the volume of production needed to successfully commercialize the business, a permanent facility with new equipment became a priority.

Outside organizations respond

Over the next two years, Jambi Kiwa was able to progress in terms of both commercialization and its larger social vision of reclaiming and valuing traditional knowledge and culture by forming relationships with a series of external organizations. Some of these organizations sought out Jambi Kiwa, attracted by its early success. Others were approached by Jambi Kiwa members to support a specific aspect of its work.

Several relationships resulted from the reputation that Jambi Kiwa had developed within the donor community. Small grants allowed Jambi Kiwa members to make use of a second building for a temporary factory, purchase a new mill, replace an electric dryer with a gas model, and create a root drying facility. A staff member was sent to take training courses on marketing natural products at the Inter-American Cooperative Institute (ICI) in Panama. Rosa was able to put together a consortium of Canadian donors (CIDA, Scarboro Missions and the Comart Foundation) to secure funding for a permanent

---

Box 4.2: A recent history of Ecuador's economy

In the 1980s, two economic trends had enormous impact on indigenous communities: economic liberalization and falling oil prices. In response to Ecuador's growing national debt, international financial institutions pressured the state to implement neoliberal reforms. Trade liberalization led to the flooding of local markets with cheap imports while government austerity measures led to cuts in public sector jobs, tightening the labour market and lowering wages throughout the country. In 1997, the price of Ecuadorian oil (the country's leading source of foreign exchange at that time) fell to US$7 per barrel.

Perhaps sensing disaster, wealthy individuals began moving their money out of the country. In a two-week period in 1999 more than US$1.5 billion was withdrawn from the financial system. Several banks collapsed, hundreds of thousands of Ecuadorians lost their savings and inflation soared. In an effort to combat this crisis, Ecuador adopted the US dollar as its currency. Dollarization stabilized the currency but had many negative impacts on Ecuador's domestic economy and the lives of its people. The cost of labour in Ecuador rose relative to Peru and Columbia and, as a result, many of Ecuador's manufacturers moved their operations outside the country or went bankrupt.

These factors led to a mass out-migration of Ecuadorians, which began during the economic crisis, and has continued to be a major issue. Particularly hard hit are the rural areas, where some towns have seen most of their men migrate to one of the major cities in Ecuador, Spain, Italy or the United States. Between 1999 and 2004, nearly one quarter of the population left the country. While migration has depleted labour force in rural areas, it has also proved to be a major source of income for rural families. In 2003, remittances (money sent home from family members working in cities or abroad) from Spain alone totalled US$849 million dollars, US$103 million more than the previous year. It has become Ecuador's single largest source of foreign exchange, even greater than oil. One of the effects of these remittances is that they have allowed families to continue living in rural areas even when they don't make a profit on their farming activities.

---

factory building, solar energy technology, a truck and management training for several women leaders. Jambi Kiwa also became an attractive placement for a wide range of volunteers from Canada, the US and Ecuador.

Jambi Kiwa 's social vision was attracting attention by this time. The new partnership included funds to expand the School of Andean Medicine. Now it could provide further training to traditional healers and midwives and implement medicinal garden projects in a number of indigenous schools.

> [In addition to medicinal plant production], our goal is to increase people's self worth to such a level that our healers can talk as equals with doctors... In Jambi Kiwa we prioritize the participation of indigenous *campesinos* [farmers] and women. We try to generate employment for these groups. (Guamán, personal communication, 2004).

In keeping with this goal of increasing the self-worth of members, gender equality programmes were implemented, with particular emphasis on women's literacy and addressing family violence. The impetus for this came from the personal experiences of many of the women of Jambi Kiwa (see Rosa's Story in Box 4.1).

The Association further strengthened its literacy efforts by convincing the Ministry of Education in Chimborazo to give stipends to eight Jambi Kiwa

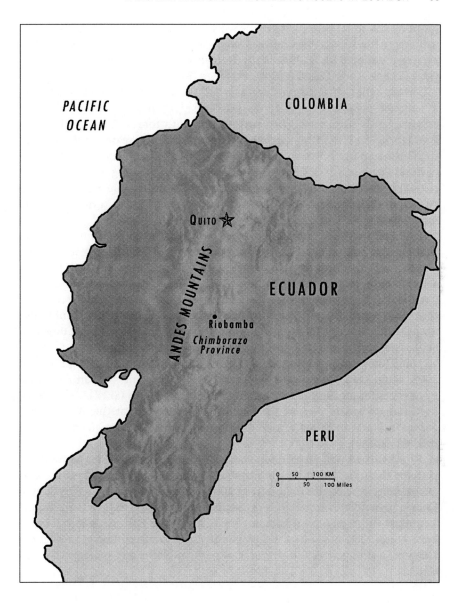

members to carry out literacy training with women's groups. This programme was advantageous for Jambi Kiwa as it financially supported the women trainers who were, in turn, providing training to women's groups in the cultivation and use of medicinal plants.

Buoyed by the interest that external organizations were showing, Jambi Kiwa began to look for new partnership opportunities. In May 2002, Jambi Kiwa members participated in a workshop in Guayaquil with a national parastatal organization formed to promote the development of export markets for non-traditional exports. After the workshop, Jambi Kiwa emerged as a lead member of the *Red de Productores de Plantas Medicinales Mashi Numi* (RPPMMN), a nascent national association of these organizations. At its first meeting, Rosa Guamán was elected head of this new federation.

Through the *Corporación de Promoción de Exportaciones e Inversiones* (CORPEI), a national organization that was established to promote non-traditional exports, Jambi Kiwa established partnerships with three other organizations: EcoCiencia (an NGO that specializes in conservation research and training), the Organization of American States (OAS) and the Latin American Network of Rural Producers (FOMRENA). Jambi Kiwa began working with EcoCiencia to train its producer members in environmentally sustainable methods for the collection of wild plants and the cultivation of plants that, until then, had only grown wild.

Jambi Kiwa also successfully approached OAS for funding for additional training and equipment over a three-year period. FOMRENA (created by the German aid organization GTZ) provided partial financing for a dryer through a local credit cooperative and then asked Jambi Kiwa to make installment payments as if it were repaying a loan. These repayments were actually returned to an account that Jambi Kiwa was able to use for other activities. Jambi Kiwa adapted this strategy for a revolving fund to assist members in creating seed banks and purchasing tools and equipment to improve their farms.

Jambi Kiwa was beginning to gain national and international recognition. In 2002, Jambi Kiwa was awarded 'Best Rural Women's Business in Latin America' by Services for an Alternative Development in the South (SENDAS). In 2004, Rosa was invited to present the Jambi Kiwa experience at the World Social Forum in Brazil and then at a GTZ-sponsored event in Nicaragua celebrating rural enterprises.

While this kind of recognition was positive reinforcement for Jambi Kiwa, perhaps the most important international recognition came when the first export sales were finalized. In June of 2004, Jambi Kiwa was invited by Salinas Cooperative in Bolivar province (a member of RPPMMN) to help them supply a contract they had recently obtained with a buyer in Italy. Only four months later, Jambi Kiwa made its first independent international sale to Le Clef des Champs, a producer and distributor of organic plants and extracts based in Canada.

Understanding the Jambi Kiwa story: an Asset-Based and Community-driven Development perspective

Jambi Kiwa's success was created through the mobilization of a wide range of community assets that were, in turn, used to lever considerable outside resources. Jambi Kiwa's members combined their indigenous knowledge of medicinal plants with traditional skills in cultivation, their access to individual and communal land, their history of communal labour, a cadre of strong indigenous women leaders and their savings to start the enterprise.

Jambi Kiwa members' plants being weighed at the roadside en route to the factory at Riobamba.

The commitment they demonstrated impressed a number of external agencies that agreed to become stakeholders; from government agencies that had a shared interest in promoting exports or preventing the depletion of wild plants, to non-governmental organizations that shared their social, economic or environmental vision, and to private businesses that welcomed a new supplier of medicinal plants.

In this section we examine the various assets built or enhanced at the household, community and societal levels during the enterprise development process. Secondly, we explore the different and complementary roles played by internal and external agency in this process.

Household level

By eliminating intermediaries, Jambi Kiwa has been able to raise the price paid to producers for fresh plants (from 8 cents per kg in 2001 to 20 cents per kg in 2003). Several producers reported sending between 200 kg and 300 kg of fresh plants to the factory each month, representing an increase of approximately US$40–50 monthly in income. As a Trigaloma member pointed out, 'Every extra cent is a cent more I can spend on my children' (personal communication, 2004).

Medicinal plants have enabled producers to diversify. Soldador Toltora, for example, had been experiencing losses because of low prices for his crops of broad beans and potatoes. His solution has been diversification:

> Now I grow medicinal plants... [and] each month we harvest about 200 kg of artichoke leaves. As well, each month we harvest between 180–200 kg of chamomile. This represents an additional US$30–35 each month and helps us to cover our family costs...I would like to increase production. (personal communication, 2004)

Box 4.3: Cuatro Esquinas: in the face of adversity, value what you have

Cuatro Esquinas is a small rural community of 60 households on the side of Mount Chimborazo. Survivors of conquests by the Incas and the Spanish, these former warrior people are described as 'always having fire in their eyes.' and a history of fierce independence. Until the 1960s, they were famous for running a contraband trade in distilled sugarcane from the coast. They are also known as the ice-men of Chimborazo; to this day they carve ice from the glaciers to be sold in the markets of Riobamba.

The people of Cuatro Esquinas have always directed their own development. In 2003, they took their children out of the Spanish school in the area and created a bilingual school to ensure the survival of their language. They have a reputation for being entrepreneurial and independent, while successful at leveraging outside resources. Luis Guamán (no relation to Rosa), a villager from Cuatro Esquinas, explains that even though they don't have funds, they have started such projects as a small tourist lodge and an interpretive centre. Now they take tourists with them when they cut ice. As he explains: 'We have lots of things we think we can do together...We have a new school with more than one building and a garden. We have all invested in training ourselves, as carpenters, welders and weavers and we want to revive the *randeem* [traditional barter system] which is part of our culture' (personal communication, 2004).

The first woman to start collecting medicinal plants in Cuatro Esquinas was Maria Francesca Ochoa. She had heard about Rosa Guamán and the effort to buy medicinal plants at a meeting in a nearby town. Together with a friend she began collecting plants and taking them to Riobamba. She recalls, 'We walked all over these hills collecting plants. It was profitable, [an] important source of cash for us. Then Jambi Kiwa started to interest us in cultivating...[and] we didn't have to leave home. That's when our group started to grow.'

Now the 14 women in the group are all certified organic producers. Two members of the group have assumed leadership positions with Jambi Kiwa. Ochoa is a member of the Association's supervisory committee while another group member is the president of the zone committee. Although Jambi Kiwa requires producers to have a minimum of 400 m² for cultivation, most members in Cuatro Esquinas have nearly doubled that.

Ochoa's garden is a model of diversity. It is surrounded by malva trees which provide a windbreak and leaves with medicinal properties. In addition to medicinal plants, the garden contains plots for seed potatoes and carrots that are sold as cash crops. Even though experts determined that bees would not survive at this altitude (over 3,000 metres above sea level), Ochoa has several beehives that provide honey and increase pollination of plants. She also raises sheep, llamas and donkeys and she has developed a large compost area which utilizes vermiculture. When asked why people like Maria Francesco Ochoa and the community of Cuatro Esquinas have been determined to succeed, Luis Guamán responded, 'There is an incentive to value what is ours. Because we are poor, we can't risk losing our land' (personal communication, 2004).

The additional household income gained for producers and their families is not merely a seasonal phenomenon. Medicinal plants are grown and harvested all year round. Thus, the income received for plants is spread throughout the year, reducing household vulnerability to periodic or seasonal shocks. As a producer from Trigaloma explains, 'This area [can be] hit particularly hard by frost and when we lose other crops to frost, we have this to fall back on' (personal communication, 2004).

Other producers report the importance of Jambi Kiwa in helping them develop skills for identifying, collecting, growing and harvesting medicinal and aromatic plants. One Jambi Kiwa member points out, 'The plants which we have here were unknown to us. Thanks to Jambi Kiwa we can now identify them. And we know what they are used for. That is why we are cultivating them' (personal communication, 2004).

In other instances, Jambi Kiwa has worked with groups such as the local affiliate of Germany's Bio Control Systems to certify its members as organic growers. To date, more than 420 producers in 38 communities have been certified and steps are being taken to train an additional 175 members in techniques for soil and water retention and in the preparation of organic fertilizers and biocides.

During the last two years the Andean School of Medicine has held monthly workshops facilitated by traditional healers skilled in ancient remedies and therapies. Today more than 35 Jambi Kiwa healers and midwives have been trained in the practice of natural medicine. The health and income benefits are significant. Maria Francesca Ochoa comments, 'We are going to the doctor less; we have our own medicine here and we've been trained. We know [which] plants can be used for what' (personal communication, 2004). There is pride in the rediscovery of an asset previously taken for granted: 'a hospital and pharmacy in our own front yards' (personal communication, 2004). These household 'pharmacies' are now complemented at the community level by a health centre covering 3 indigenous rural communities. Healthcare workers trained in the use of medicinal plants are supervised by a Jambi Kiwa health worker based at the health centre.

Community level

At the community level, livelihood prospects have been enhanced, not only because Jambi Kiwa offers a new source of income, but also because production and processing have created new social ties and strengthened others. With this new source of livelihood, many members have continued living in, or have returned to, their communities, and there is greater optimism that Jambi Kiwa can play a role in stemming the tide of migration that is draining Ecuadorian communities of its best and brightest.

However, the ability of Jambi Kiwa to continue providing new economic opportunities for its members will depend on whether the Riobamba factory can become a centre of innovation. If it can develop value-added products (currently the larger profits from processing the plants into finished products are mainly being earned elsewhere) and thereby retain income earning opportunities, it will realize one of Jambi Kiwa's most important goals. For example, profit can be increased from US$3–4 per kg to US$50 per kg if Jambi Kiwa can move from loose-leaved to pre-packaged tea bags. To this end, members have worked hard to secure a new factory and invest in drying, milling, storage and tea-bagging equipment. Producers are also encouraged to add value to their plants before they are sold to Jambi Kiwa by cleaning and preparing them, thereby reducing the processing required at the factory.

Many of Jambi Kiwa's producers recognize that they will have to maintain consistent quality and quantity if they want to compete in a discriminating marketplace, and maintaining these standards is considered not only the responsibility of individual producers, but a joint responsibility. Working collaboratively, producers have shared techniques and supported each other in both production and processing. For example, in one community each producer has an individual garden, but 22 women are also working together on a model garden: '[We grow] cilantro, lemon verbena and oregano. We sell the [plants] for 16-20 cents per kilogram. Right now we are happy because yesterday we sold the plants from the garden. And each one of us received US$6' (Jambi Kiwa and El Centro de Communicacion Indigena, 2003).

Despite such positive developments, the leaders of Jambi Kiwa face a challenge in reversing the natural asset depletion that has occurred in the sierra. Edison Suarez, the Jambi Kiwa agronomist, observes that because of global warming, a serious water shortage is looming. Rainfall will not be enough to provide water for farmers. Erosion and chemical contamination have also compromised the soil. Those who are trying to restore it remain in the minority: 'In short, we are facing a serious ecological problem' (personal communication, 2004).

Jambi Kiwa has introduced sustainable agricultural practices to its members, but change can be slow. However, the over-harvesting of wild plants has been significantly reduced and some leaders in the Ecuadorian development community believe that the move to organic production will gather momentum as farmers see the benefits. The Coordinator of Swiss Aid in Ecuador, Pancho Gangotano, is an organic farmer himself. He explains:

> When your land was yellow and now it is black you don't need to go to labs to know what is happening. And when you see a tiny little wasp controlling the aphids and if you see your cilantro or fennel attracting certain insects, and you see that the nitrogen, phosphorus and potassium can be obtained from certain plants...this is a very powerful thing. You can say that development has started. (personal communication, 2004)

Societal level

Less tangible are the assets Jambi Kiwa is striving to build at the societal level. Some producers express the hope that membership of Jambi Kiwa will improve the balance of power in the local markets. Middlemen have an advantage over small, independent farmers because they are better organized. And since they have vehicles and capital, they have access to larger markets in Quito, Guayaquil and Cuenca. Jambi Kiwa's solutions to this have been twofold. First, collaboration among producer groups in villages and zones has given them more influence in the marketplace. Second, a new supply chain has been created for medicinal and aromatic plants. Indigenous producers now sell directly to the factory, bypassing *mestizo* intermediaries.

Raising the profile and bargaining power of indigenous farmers has been extended to enhancing the status of indigenous women. A transformation in the capacity of indigenous women has been one of Jambi Kiwa's most notable achievements: 'The women I met at the beginning were not the same as [they are now]. They are more open... and sure of themselves. This is a big success. Even if Jambi Kiwa ends today it will have changed these women' (Tremblay, personal communication, 2004).

Perhaps the most significant societal level impact that Jambi Kiwa may achieve is the creation of a new economic model for indigenous and *campesino* communities in rural Ecuador. Integrated into the larger economy, these communities have experienced dramatic changes in lifestyles and aspirations over the past 30 years. Indigenous and *campesino* communities are simultaneously looking for ways to maintain autonomous cultural space, build their economic assets and make claims on the state on the basis of their citizenship (Bebbington, 1999). If Jambi Kiwa can compete in a globalized economy while also fulfilling its cultural, environmental and asset building ambitions, it may help to redefine what it means to be indigenous in Ecuador today.

The roles of internal and external agency

Internal agency

A community-driven initiative is characterized by a high degree of internal agency, that is, the ability of the community to determine and maintain control over the development agenda. This requires local leadership that is able to generate a strong 'motivation to act' among community members. External agency refers to the actions or power exerted by individuals and organizations outside the community, such as governments or NGOs. A community-driven initiative is also characterized by external agency that is responsive to the efforts of internal agency.

There is evidence to suggest that governments and NGOs are, in fact, attracted to strong internal agency (Kretzmann and McKnight, 1993). Many of these organizations have had experience with projects initiated and implemented from the outside that have collapsed as soon as external support is withdrawn.

A growing number of external agents realize that community development initiatives are more likely to be sustainable when local communities or groups are driving the process.

Leadership

The leaders of Jambi Kiwa have developed strong internal agency by motivating members and staff in three distinct ways. First, they have clearly articulated a vision to address the issues facing the indigenous *campesinos* of Chimborazo. They have been able to convince people that cultural assimilation, the environmental degradation of their lands, the exploitation by middlemen and the loss of their young people to the cities of Ecuador, North America and Europe will only be overcome if they organize themselves. Second, they have drawn on indigenous cultural belief systems of the area – the Andean cosmo-vision of being at one with the earth and sharing responsibility for the welfare of future generations – and the region's long history of community mobilization and action. Third, they have identified concrete opportunities for members to contribute to the growth of a 'social enterprise' that tries like any other business to make a profit but which also aims to restore the land and preserve indigenous knowledge, culture, traditions and values.

Rosa and her colleagues have prioritized building the capacity of a cadre of grassroots women leaders. The Association provides training to its members in basic literacy, the uses of traditional medicine (through the Andean School of Medicine), and the organic cultivation of medicinal and aromatic plants. The existing leadership has also created space for the development of new leaders both in the Association and the business. The main vehicle of this is the Association's policy of electing new leaders to the board every two years. During her tenure Rosa has managed to create an organizational culture where leadership is recognized as action, rather than position. This has been crucial for building the Association and the business to this point. A key question in moving forward is whether the existing leadership has anticipated the kinds of leaders and skills that will be needed to balance the growth of the business and the larger social vision of the organization.

Ownership of the process

Jambi Kiwa members see themselves as part of both a social movement and a social enterprise. As Rosa points out, Jambi Kiwa is an organization with roots, because its members feel a moral responsibility to make it work. She emphasizes that it is 'not merely a good idea with financial backing' (personal communication, 2004). Producers and staff alike seem highly motivated by the possibility that Jambi Kiwa can provide a new enterprise model for ensuring the survival of rural indigenous communities. The staff at the factory in Riobamba also seemed motivated by the ways in which they were encouraged to actively participate in some element of the business.

The main difference between Jambi Kiwa and many indigenous NGOs in Chimborazo is that Jambi Kiwa is member-owned and member-run; even the staff are members. Edison Suarez describes Jambi Kiwa as an 'inside-out' organization as compared to the 'outside-in' NGOs he has worked for.

With other projects, the outside NGO works on the basis of goals, tasks, results and deliverables. But from outside you don't zero in on what really needs to be done to make the initiative effective. When you are working from within an organization you look at where the bottlenecks are occurring. Here we have monthly meetings and determine what has to be adjusted. This feels more like I'm working for a company than a project. (personal communication, 2004)

These differences are also reflected in the way in which the Jambi Kiwa staff relates to members at the community level. Suarez explains:

We do what we call 'accompaniment'[1] [sic: Wilson and Whitmore, 2000] where we don't pretend we can replace the *campesino*'s knowledge. Rather, together we investigate the situation and try to come up with a solution together. The producers learn by setting up demonstration plots where they can test out solutions...We also work with the local schools to set up demonstration gardens so the children can learn [how to grow] traditional medicinal plants. (personal communication, 2004)

As a member from Trigaloma puts it, 'There have been times when the leadership has had to push us a bit but now we feel that this project is ours' (personal communication, 2004).

Nina Pacari, the first indigenous woman in the Ecuadorian parliament, describes the history of indigenous community-driven development by noting that such groups are developing small local economies that have moved beyond subsistence. They are also not reliant on government funding. This reveals a movement that is modern in its outlook, yet traditional at the same time:

In the matter of agriculture, natural resources and in the relationship of 'person-nature-society', [these initiatives] come to constitute themselves... in the case of native peoples, as a matter of recovering aspects which have been part of the philosophy and life of these peoples. (Jambi Kiwa and El Centro de Communicación Indigena, 2003)

People in Caliata lent support to this claim. One villager stated, 'We have a history of working together. We did that with a communal house [which is used as a school]. We pooled the money for a piece of property and then built the house on it' (personal communication, 2004). In Cuatro Esquinas, a local citizen declared that everything in the community, from the school to the roads, had been built through the *mingas* (traditional work-sharing groups). These self-help associations pool labour to undertake community initiatives (they are known as *yanapacu* in Bolivia and *ayni* in Peru). In the *paramo* (high sierra), there is also a long history of communal land ownership. In other words, group ownership is part of the very spirit of indigenous communities in Chimborazo.

External agency

Breaking from tradition

A community-driven initiative that has developed external relationships on its own terms is the exception rather than the rule in Ecuador. Community development is often seen by government and non-government organizations as an exogenous rather than endogenous process. According to Pancho Gangotano, relationships between NGOs and community-based organizations in Ecuador are typically structured along the lines of patron and client. He observes that when community members analyze their problems, they often look to external organizations to provide technical assistance. Since the answers come from outside, he says, 'people no longer trust their *vivencia*, [or] their life experience' (personal communication, 2004). The unfortunate consequence is that communities develop an inferiority complex. He has concluded that, in general, NGOs tend to reinforce this sense of inferiority, rather than alleviating it:

> We promote it; we have big programmes...to solve problems. We get technicians and money. Everything is external. If an outside technician is present, communities will defer [to that individual]. But if a technician is not there, the community will go and see how their neighbours did it. They will...carry out the initiative, and when they finish, the community will have ownership and pride. (personal communication, 2004)

Rosa adds her impression of traditional relationships between NGOs and communities in Chimborazo:

> There are two dynamics going on: one, a long history of the NGO as protagonist where almost all the work is palliative...and two, people have become complacent, almost like beggars. Whatever NGOs have [they] will take. (personal communication, 2004)

Jambi Kiwa has never operated this way. In addition to motivating members at the community level, its leadership has been able to reach out to external networks and support. The sheer number of external relationships is impressive (see Figure 4.2). According to Bebbington and Perreault, this is a sign of strong local leadership: 'Simply put, good leaders tend to mean wider networks, greater external support, and thus a more active organization; weak leaders lead to little external support and moribund organization' (1999, p.16). Jambi Kiwa's decision to reach out to external organizations did not come easily. Members had to be convinced to seek out partnerships, since it meant breaking with the indigenous tradition of remaining independent.

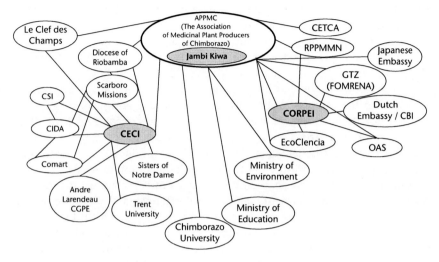

Figure 4.2: External relationships

In spite of their lack of experience, Jambi Kiwa's leaders have managed to forge external partnerships that support its development agenda. Rosa points out that she and her colleagues had to learn how to deal with government and non-government organizations: 'Even though we did not have experience in negotiating we are now able to sit at the table, listen and observe what is happening and come back, discuss and make a decision' (personal communication, 2004). Jambi Kiwa's leaders learned valuable lessons from their early external relationships that helped them in later negotiations. 'Those in government live in a completely different world from us. But I believe that when you sit chair to chair with them you learn something' (Guamán, personal communication, 2004).

Responding rather than driving

The relationships between Jambi Kiwa and external organizations can be broadly characterized as partnerships, though each is unique. One of Jambi Kiwa's longest running partnerships is with the Diocese of Riobamba. From its early support of women's groups to its provision of the church attic and subsequent loan of the first warehouse, the diocese continues to help Jambi Kiwa flourish without controlling the initiative or creating dependency.

Since 1998, the most important NGO partnership for Jambi Kiwa has been CECI, through which Jambi Kiwa has made linkages with UNDP, the Sisters of Notre Dame, CSI, CIDA and Comart. CECI has also placed five full-time cooperants with Jambi Kiwa over eight years. In addition to providing technical assistance, experienced cooperants helped Jambi Kiwa develop relationships with customers, donors and technical support organizations. Members have since taken charge of developing new external relationships now that there are no longer any CECI cooperants.

Another very important partnership for Jambi Kiwa has been CORPEI, which has not only directly connected Jambi Kiwa to a variety of training opportunities but has also indirectly, given Jambi Kiwa credibility with a wide array of organizations including government ministries. Jambi Kiwa now works closely with the Ministry of Education in developing and delivering literacy training for its members. As well, the Ministry now recognizes agricultural extension training carried out by Jambi Kiwa's agronomist and the trainers for EcoCiencia. Certificates are given to Jambi Kiwa's producers in recognition of this training, a formal tribute to the value of indigenous knowledge.

Similarly, Jambi Kiwa has cultivated a positive relationship with the Ministry of the Environment. Jambi Kiwa anticipated the requirement of environmental licences for the export of all natural products. It has kept the Ministry in Chimborazo informed about plant domestication and cultivation, as well as steps to counter over-exploitation of wild plants. They share an interest in reducing harvesting in high elevations, which are environmentally sensitive. They also work together to improve agricultural practices, such as terracing and setting up windbreaks, as well as establishing crop rotation and intercropping throughout the sierra. According to the regional director of the ministry, Patricio Hermida: 'Once people start to realize the economic value of their plants, they will be more encouraged to preserve and develop a system which is beneficial to the environment' (personal communication, 2004).

Jambi Kiwa's many external partnerships have prevented the organization from becoming dependent on a single donor or technical assistance provider. Managing the large number of relationships does, however, pose a challenge to Jambi Kiwa's staff and leaders. As the business evolves, it is possible that Jambi Kiwa's portfolio of partnerships will change in composition. It is likely that there will be fewer relationships with donor organizations and NGOs and more business partnerships with other producer organizations and domestic or foreign trade organizations or companies.

The challenges ahead

Production and marketing

Jambi Kiwa is poised to take advantage of the overall growth in international markets for medicinal and organic produce. The new factory, which opened in January 2005, provides Jambi Kiwa with the capacity to quadruple its output. In preparation for this, Jambi Kiwa has simultaneously tried to increase its producer membership while improving productivity through training. Producers are also encouraged to make use of the revolving fund for such farm enhancements as seed banks, fencing to keep out animals, and tubing for irrigation.

For Jambi Kiwa members, the transition from small-scale domestic operations to large-scale production and export may prove demanding. The relationship between producers and managers can become strained. For example, in an attempt to boost production of medicinal plants, Jambi Kiwa raised the minimum cultivation area required of producers from 100 to 400 m^2 and at times they also encouraged producers to grow a certain plant only to have the market disappear by harvest time. For its part, Jambi Kiwa sometimes has to contend with brokers offering its producers higher prices for plants. When the immediate need for income has been great, some producers have overlooked the potential benefits of being long-term owners of a successful company.

Jambi Kiwa has struggled to achieve a viable economy of scale for its operations and get its costs in line with its competitors.[2] Members have been asked to make certain sacrifices. For instance, a minimum number of plants is now required on pick-up day to make transport worthwhile. Yet sometimes members have to wait to be paid because funds from Jambi Kiwa's buyers have been delayed. While these factors have cost Jambi Kiwa some members, most have stayed. As one member from Trigaloma put it 'There has been strong motivation to persist' (personal communication, 2004). Her group felt proud and hopeful in the knowledge that plants that they have grown are now being sold internationally.

Jambi Kiwa is in the process of deciding on a strategic direction for production for the next few years. While it could continue to increase sales of dried or powdered ingredients to international manufacturers and continue joint labelling in Ecuador, this approach may not be profitable for many years. Most Jambi Kiwa export items have little value-added. As a result, profit margins are quite small. Certain value-added products are sold domestically through a joint labelling agreement but, to date, these products have failed to generate profits for Jambi Kiwa (see Table 4.1). For instance, while the partnership with the tea company CETCA has allowed Jambi Kiwa to get its teas nicely packaged and placed on the shelves of major Andean supermarkets, CETCA's calculation of the revenues and expenses for these product lines have not shown any net income to be shared with Jambi Kiwa. CETCA has also developed designs for the Sangay herbal tea line that greatly resembled Jambi Kiwa's own labels. When Jambi Kiwa objected to this practice, CETCA made only modest design changes.

Despite challenges, Jambi Kiwa continues to work on a three-pronged marketing strategy. The first prong is to pursue large buyers of low value-added (dried and milled) plants in Europe and North America. Large international customers of medicinal plants are becoming interested in supply chain management and looking to find long-term reliable suppliers of natural ingredients. The second prong is to try to break into the international fair trade networks. Jambi Kiwa's application to the Fair Trade Labelling Organization (FLO) in Belgium has been accepted and in 2006 two containers of plants were shipped to France with two more containers on order for 2007. Jambi Kiwa is currently negotiating sales to businesses in Belgium and Canada. The third

Table 4.1: Jambi Kiwa at a glance

	2001	2002	2003	2004	2005	2006	2007*
Number of active members	603	475	403	403	503	350	400
Number of members with organic certification			228	403	503	350	400
Number of producers in transition			175	100	50	0	0
Number of communities	60	60	46	38	45	45	45
Average price paid to producer per kilogram of fresh plants	.08	.12	.18	.21	.22	.22	.22
Number of wild species (collected)	15	17	20	20	20	23	23
Number of cultivated species	25	27	28	28	28	30	30
Fresh plants purchased (tons)	80	84	96	100	118	140	96
Total sales in USD (1,000s)	21	32	42	53.4	63	54	111.5
Ecuador	21	32	42	42	48	48	38.5
International				11.4	15	6	**73
Semi-processed	20	30	39	48	50	45.6	56.9
Products with added value	1	2	3	5.4	10	8.6	54.6
Profits (losses)	(6)	(9)	(15)	(24)	(20)	(24)	(12)

*   Sales figures for 2007 are only up until September of that year.
**   Not included in this figure is a contract to supply four containers of herbal teas to France later in 2007 at US$47,000 per container.
***   All financial figures appear in USD.

prong is to continue to pursue the domestic and regional market. Jambi Kiwa plans to continue joint labelling of high value-added products such as herbal teas and medicinal formulas in the Andean region.

The products which hold the most promise commercially are herbal teas. A consultant, Jean-Guy Godbout, with Canadian Executive Services Overseas (CESO), has recommended that Jambi Kiwa be incorporated as a separate business owned by the Association and to seek out a joint agreement with a North American company and focus almost exclusively on the herbal tea market. From his perspective, such a business partner could provide capital and technical assistance to the factory and place Jambi Kiwa's products, possibly under a different label, in North American supermarkets.

Jambi Kiwa's leadership has major concerns about the direction the consultant has proposed. They are worried that an exclusive focus on herbal teas will be at the expense of the development of other medicinal formulas. They are also fearful of gradually losing ownership of Jambi Kiwa to a larger, more powerful company.

Organizational model

As Jambi Kiwa moves into the export market, one of its biggest challenges is whether or not to follow a conventional business model. As a social enterprise, there is a clear tension in the organization between the need to be responsive to the demands of the market and aspects of their shared vision such as the desire to follow the Andean traditions of communal ownership, consensus building, and rotating leadership. Rotating leadership is essential to a good democratic organization and is also an Andean tradition (Martínez, personal communication, 2004). Respecting this tradition, the Association holds an election for its board and President every two years, often resulting in a complete turnover of board members. Presidents are only allowed to serve one two-year term, according to the current system, though other representatives are eligible for re-election. This prevents incumbent leaders from becoming entrenched, allows member interests to be represented, and develops a cadre of people with valuable leadership knowledge and experience.

Yet it also means that each time new leaders take their positions, there are delays in important decisions: 'It can take Jambi Kiwa months to make a decision...The competition can be making four or five of those decisions a day' (Walsh, personal communication, 2004). While members have a sense of ownership of the decisions because of the time taken to make them, the consequences can be bad for business, at least in the short term.

Internal debate has delayed the final approval of Jambi Kiwa's new strategic plan. On the surface, this debate is about whether Jambi Kiwa should focus on relationships with existing clients or concentrate production on more value-added products (like herbal teas) where they do not yet have solid commitments from buyers. At its core, this debate is about which management model Jambi Kiwa will adopt: the current model with a manager handling day-to-day factory operations and the board making most management decisions; or a more conventional business model consisting of a management team with a board focusing on policy, making strategic decisions and overseeing operations. In all likelihood, Jambi Kiwa will face enormous pressure from customers and donors to move to a more conventional business model.

Jambi Kiwa will also face market pressure to establish a consistent business culture within its membership. There has been some resistance within both the leadership and membership toward adopting such a culture. The fear is that such a move will jeopardize the social vision that led to the creation of Jambi Kiwa in the first place. Some leaders and members feel that if they continue to submit to the demands of the market, Jambi Kiwa will be abandoning its indigenous peasant roots. Others contend that if Jambi Kiwa does not become more competitive and fully adapt to the market, it will never make a profit. The best way to promote community development, the latter argue, is to maintain a profitable business which will improve producers' incomes and generate money for the Association's community development projects.

Conclusion

Jambi Kiwa is both a community-driven development initiative and a business. This duality is what has energized its membership and attracted support from technical assistance partners, donors and some customers. Rosa and her colleagues did not begin their work by submitting a proposal to an NGO or donor organization. They began by rediscovering indigenous knowledge and motivating other women to collect and sell medicinal plants. In other words, they mobilized their own assets before seeking assistance.

Most of the organizations that support Jambi Kiwa have an investment rather than a charity orientation. These organizations tend to see themselves as stakeholders in Jambi Kiwa. This makes them aware of, and sympathetic to, the challenges Jambi Kiwa faces in integrating its business and community development roles. Although Jambi Kiwa has yet to turn a profit on any single product, annual revenues have increased each year, Jambi Kiwa members and external organizations alike expect this trend to continue if the organization can resolve its internal debate on how best to develop a commercially viable business while maintaining its strong social vision (see Table 4.1).

A great deal of human capital has already been built by Jambi Kiwa members, staff and leaders. Indigenous knowledge has been reclaimed. Members have acquired new skills in collecting, growing and processing medicinal plants. Health and literacy programmes have been introduced. Within Jambi Kiwa there is room to build more human capacity especially in the area of business and finance. As the strategic planning exercise has highlighted, decisions on such issues as investment, production and marketing are going to be difficult to navigate without these skills. Fortunately, Jambi Kiwa has developed strong linkages with a wide variety of individuals and organizations that may be willing to help build the capacity of its leaders.

One external asset Jambi Kiwa has not exploited is the potential market provided by members of the Andean diaspora. There is evidence that these populations are a potential market for specialized value-added products. In early 2005, Jambi Kiwa sold 10,000 bags of *horchata* (a traditional package of herbs popular in the Andes) to an Ecuadorian man living in the US. Jambi Kiwa's capacity to target such niche markets will improve when it can streamline production and develop stronger marketing strategies.

At the core of Jambi Kiwa's success has been the ability of its leaders to motivate members, mobilize existing assets, and lever outside resources. Even with financial contributions and hands-on assistance from numerous external agencies, Jambi Kiwa has managed to retain control over its strategic direction. External agencies have responded to an agenda set by Jambi Kiwa, providing grants, loans, technical and economic advisors, and volunteers.

Jambi Kiwa as a social enterprise has much to contribute to larger indigenous political and cultural movement in the Andean region and perhaps elsewhere. Jambi Kiwa provides a 'leadership laboratory' that nurtures and develops indigenous women leaders. In some ways this represents a break from tradition in the indigenous community where men are still very much at the centre of decision-making in most organizations. Where many indigenous leaders are focused on confrontation, the leaders of Jambi Kiwa have put their energy into building both the enterprise and the national and international relationships with other organizations necessary to further their agenda. These emerging women leaders may well inject the Ecuadorian indigenous movement with new energy and a fresh outlook in the years ahead.

When asked what she would like to see in 10 years, Rosa said she wanted to see better incomes for member families and more opportunities for young people to stop the migration to the cities. She added:

> I want to see that the Andean culture will be strengthened, that these efforts we are making to revalue and extend the ancestral knowledge of medicinal plants, this training, will have paid off and that mothers and fathers [can] pass [it] on to their children. I want to see the Andean vision become part of the overall [vision for]...Ecuador. And I want to see Jambi Kiwa as a model for others...one that contributes to the new society. (personal communication, 2004)

Rosa put this in perspective by concluding that 25 years ago she would have been happy to have children and see her family working on the land. Now she and her colleagues have a much wider vision.

Endnotes

1. This describes the concept of accompanying and supporting someone else's process, and allowing local people to lead the process of social change.
2. *Le Clef des Champs* reports that shipping costs from Ecuador (CAD400 per cubic metre, (approximately US$406 at 3 March 2008) are four times higher than China and five times higher than Europe. In China, a ship is leaving every day for 'Canada; in Ecuador a ship might leave every three weeks. In addition, Jambi Kiwa has to pay all it producers and factory workers in US dollars, putting it at a cost disadvantage with its Andean neighbours: Colombia, Bolivia and Peru.'

References

Bebbington, A. (1999) 'Capitals and capabilities: A framework for analysing peasant viability, rural livelihoods and poverty', *World Development,* 27(12): 2021–2044.

Bebbington, A. and Perreault, T. (1999) 'Social capital, development and access to resources in highland Ecuador', *Economic Geography,* 75(4): 395–418.

Jambi Kiwa and El Centro de Communicacion Indigena (2003) *Las plantas magicas de Jambi Kiwa* [Motion Picture] (Available from Associación de Productores de Plantas Medicinales del Chimborazo, Apdo. Post. 06-01-403,Riobamba, Ecuador).

Kretzmann, J. and McKnight, J. (1993) *Building communities from the inside out: A path toward finding and mobilizing a community's assets,* Institute for Policy Research, Northwestern University, Evanston, IL.

Wilson, M. and Whitmore, E. (2000) *Seeds of fire: Social development in the era of globalism.* Fernwood Publishing, Halifax, Nova Scotia, Canada.

Author's note

Jambi Kiwa was brought to our attention by members of the Comart Family Foundation when they visited the Coady International Institute in the fall of 2003. Comart had supported Jambi Kiwa in the early commercialization phase of their development and family members who had visited Ecuador had been struck by the degree to which the initiative was driven by Rosa and her colleagues. Comart expressed an interest in funding the Coady Institute to write a case study about Jambi Kiwa. This experience eventually led to Comart funding the production of 10 other case studies in this book.

Primary research was carried out in Chimborazo province in October 2004 by a research team consisting of myself, Martha Caranqui (a staff member of Jambi Kiwa since its inception and a Board member of the Association of Medicinal Plant Producers of Chimborazo), Thomas Walsh (a former cooperant with Jambi Kiwa under the auspices of the Canadian Centre for International Studies and Cooperation), and Aaron Steeghs (a graduate student at Dalhousie University).

One of the biggest challenges in producing this case was ensuring that people's voices were reflected accurately. Interviews in Quechua had to be translated first into Spanish (Martha) and then into English (Tom). After publication in English the document was translated into Spanish and then into Quechua. As a way of minimising the chances of inaccuracy, Aaron and I transcribed the English versions of the interviews each night and checked them for accuracy with Martha and Tom while the interviews were fresh in their minds.

I am grateful to the following people and organizations who generously gave their time to be interviewed as part of this research: Rosa Guamán, Estela Espinoza, Luis Sisa, Maria Guzmán, Marlene Espinoza, Edison Suárez, Medardo Bastidas, Melchor Vacacela, Ernesto Paguay, Wiliber Ibarra, Maria Francesca Ochoa, Cuatro Esquinas, Felipa Lema, San Jose de Gaushi, Anna Bukai, Pungol, Aurora Borja, Santa Rosa, Mama Sebastián, Gallo Rumi, various producers/farmers from Trigaloma, Maria Arguello, Maria Jose Borja, Sandra Edwards, Jaime Macias Flores, Anne Marie Flynn, Pancho Gangotano, Charlie Gervais, Jean-Guy Godbout, Patricio Hermida, Josée Lagarde, Inti Macias, Luciano Martinez, Nelson Martinez, Carmina Matton, Martha Rice, Julie Rice, Victor Hugo Torres, Louis Michel Trembley and Günter Viteri. I am especially grateful to Dona Aurora who successfully treated my eczema with a traditional remedy made from local plants while I was in Ecuador.

CHAPTER 5

When bamboo is old, the sprouts appear: rekindling local economies through traditional skills in Hanoi, Vietnam

Jim Delaney and Nguyen Duc Vinh

Abstract

A bamboo cooperative in a community on the outskirts of Hanoi, Vietnam reclaims its traditional mastery of bamboo, years after local bamboo forests had disappeared, despite a context in which community-led initiatives have, until recently, received little support from a highly centralized and 'top-down' government. This case explains how and why this cooperative evolved in Vietnam's transition from central planning, combining the social imperative of providing local employment to young people with the economic opportunities explored through linkages with an international NGO and government agencies. The challenges posed by the promises and contradictions in present day Vietnam are played out in a highly localized context where a small group of villagers fashion a cooperative that builds on cultural traditions while participating in a market economy that is national in scope.

Introduction

In early 2001, Mr Le Phan Nghi returned to a village on the outskirts of the Vietnamese capital of Hanoi that he had often visited during his youth. The village had not yet seen the rapid urbanization that had marked much of urban Vietnam in the previous decade. At the end of his visit, he wrote a story for *Nhan Dan* (The People), the Communist Party of Vietnam's newspaper, published on 2 February 2001, 'Mot lang nghe dang bi lang quen' [A craft village is forgotten], in which he lamented the sad fact that, in the wake of urbanization and economic change, Thu Thuy village's traditional trades in bamboo construction had all but died. Thu Thuy, otherwise known as Thu Hong by earlier generations, had been well known throughout the region for its bamboo products. Artisans from the village travelled the whole of Northern Vietnam to build houses and village gates; they built chairs and beds, and wove mats that were popular in the city. But during Mr Nghi's visit, he saw none of the activity that he remembered from his youth. The village, and the trades that supported it for generations, were forgotten.

This story tells of how the bamboo construction trade contributed to new economic activities and community pride in Thu Thuy village. The title of this case study draws from a Vietnamese proverb *Tre Gia, Mang Moc,* or 'when the bamboo is old, the sprouts appear.' The saying speaks to the regenerative powers of nature and the renewal that comes with generational change. It hints at the often latent possibilities for individuals, communities and enterprises to draw upon traditional and aging assets to support new forms of endogenous development.

In a time of economic boom, it is easy to focus on the large enterprises, industrial zones, and the agricultural revolution that have provided much of the steam for Vietnam's economic locomotive. It is at this scale – that of the nation, the region or the city – at which most analysis of development success remains. On the other hand, in terms of community initiatives, there is also a tendency to highlight programmes that have attained critical levels of success. The expansion of once small organizations and groups to 'scale up,' and in so doing reach and mobilize an ever greater number of participants and beneficiaries, is a common goal of most local development programmes.

This case study takes a decidedly different approach, instead telling the story of one small bamboo construction cooperative located on the outskirts of Hanoi. Thu Hong Traditional Bamboo Production Cooperative is a small cooperative that has, with perseverance and ingenuity, carved out a role for itself in a fast-paced economy where small enterprises are increasingly left behind. Its role is that of a social enterprise that is committed simultaneously to individual profit and overall community development (Borzaga and Defourny, 2001). The Thu Hong story offers insights into the important roles that individual agency and social networks play in developing and maintaining any successful social enterprise, and sheds light on how intangible community assets embodied in traditional skills and knowledge can be mobilized so that communities may benefit from economic change. Finally, it offers a counterpoint to the all-too sharp contrast that is often made between endogenous and exogenous development. Indeed, one of the key lessons of Thu Hong is that networks of relationships between those on the 'outside' and 'inside' of the community have been pivotal for its ongoing success.

Doi moi and rural development in Vietnam

What follows is a short overview of the political and economic changes that have characterized Vietnam's highly successful period of *Doi moi,* or renovation. In 1996, the Sixth Party Congress of the Communist Party of Vietnam officially recognized the economic stagnation that followed the reunification of the country in 1975 and the difficulties of implementing socialist collectivization and industrialization. To respond to these concerns, the *Doi moi* policies moved away from a subsidy-based central planning model towards a mixed economy through wide-ranging price reforms and other macroeconomic initiatives. Government investment was reoriented by giving priority to agriculture, consumer goods production and the expansion of trade and foreign relations. Collectives were broken up and householders were offered long-term leases on their plots of land and the freedom to farm them as they wished.

Western and Vietnamese scholars alike have argued that the process of political and economic reform in Vietnam, though sporadic and at times halting, was largely bottom-up in nature, as higher level politicians and bureaucrats reacted to shifts that had already taken place on the ground (Kerkvliet, 2005). On the whole, farmers and industrial workers refused to put up with the arbitrary controls of socialist collectivization and the subsidy economy (*bao cap*), and through their everyday forms of resistance and mundane entrepreneurial behaviour, managed to push the Communist Party of Vietnam to bring about major changes in economic policy. This interpretation of the foundation of Vietnam's programme of economic renewal is important, for it offers a more empowering vision of the role of peasants, petty officials and otherwise hidden groups in initiating political and economic change, and provides an antidote to the – at times – dominant assumption that communities and villagers simply have things done for them, or to them, by all powerful governments.

The primary achievement of the *Doi moi* policies was to reconfigure economic life to ensure that incentives were available for individual households and businesses to enter into private enterprise. In other words, *Doi moi* shifted the management of the economy to allow villagers to allocate and build their own assets, without the constant and heavy intervention of the socialist state. Economic growth has averaged more than 8 per cent annually from 1990 through to 2006. This has helped to raise GDP per capita from US$114 in 1990 to US$414 in 1996 to more than US$600 in 2001 (World Bank, 2003; 2004).

It would be difficult to argue that *Doi moi* has been anything other than a major achievement. The World Bank has listed Vietnam time and time again as one of development's major success stories (World Bank, 2000). Yet despite these achievements, there remains a concern that meeting the challenges of continued improvement in the lives of the poor will be difficult. The demands posed by remote, mountainous areas with large and diverse ethnic minority populations and deteriorating natural environments are becoming more acute (Rambo and Jamieson, 1993). The large-scale and unavoidable migration of peasants to the booming urban areas of Vietnam also provides major challenges for the provision of social services and for planning urban communities so that unserviced slums do not become the norm. Furthermore, and of direct relevance to this case study, is the stark fact that Vietnam's urban boom, even as it has been unquestionably beneficial for many, has also led to dislocation and disempowerment for many others. Even as incomes in urban Vietnam have increased, many have seen increased vulnerability, particularly those who are forced to migrate for work or live in environmentally degraded surroundings.

Thu Hong village

Thu Thuy village, historically known as Thu Hong village, is located in Xuan Thu Commune in the suburban Hanoi District of Soc Son. Soc Son makes up almost a third of Hanoi's total land, and therefore is home to an extremely varied economy, including Hanoi's Noi Bai International Airport, one large, export-oriented industrial zone, with another zone currently under construction to serve local Small and Medium-sized Enterprises (SMEs). According to reports from the District People's Committee, industrial production in the district increased by 12 per cent in the year 2006 alone, and is set to increase by much more in the coming decade with the expansion of the two industrial parks. The People's Committee has further plans to develop the region's tourism potential through the building of a number of golf courses, a horse racing track, and a nature-tourism resort to the district's north. The landscape of the district varies widely from lakes and hills, to rice-fields, and from urban streetscapes and industrial parks to rural villages. This very diversity holds within it a wide-ranging array of development patterns and social groups.

For understandable reasons, much of the district's leadership is in thrall to industrial development and modernization. Interviews with government officials, including representatives of the economic management office, indicated that there was little interest in traditional trades and micro-enterprises. District officials define a small enterprise as one that has 200 to 400 employees, and it is at this end of the small enterprise scale that they are concentrating their efforts. 'In 20 years,' an official from the People's Committee stated, 'this area will look like Kuala Lumpur. Do you know Kuala Lumpur? It will be like that; very modern and beautiful' (personal communication, 2007). The vision of industrial progress that drives the official imagination in Soc Son largely excludes small and marginal enterprises such as the Thu Hong cooperative.

Thu Thuy village, home to some 2,400 people, is among the poorest areas of Soc Son District. Its average income of 280,000 Vietnamese Dong (VND – approximately US$17 at 3 March 2008) per month, much less than US$1 dollar per day, is just barely above Hanoi's poverty line. Thu Thuy lies in close proximity to the Ca Lo River, a tributary of the famous Red River that winds past Hanoi to the ocean. The farmland surrounding the village is at a lower elevation than the river, and therefore suffers from seasonal flooding and crop loss. Historically, because of this poor land, the people of Thu Thuy have had to look elsewhere to secure their livelihoods. The village's tradition of creating bamboo goods is said to date back to the time of the Ly dynasty (1010-1225 AD). Village elders tell a story of two generals from the previous regime committing suicide because they did not want to submit to the Ly kings. Residents of the area, then known as Thu Hong, built a temple for the two fallen warriors. It was here, in the creation of the village, that the bamboo arts began to seed, for without the resources to build a wooden temple, they constructed an edifice out of bamboo with a straw roof. Village elders claim that this was the first time that people in the village built such a structure from bamboo, and because of the popularity of the temple, the village quickly began to gain recognition for the craft. Its trade in building bamboo houses continued from this period. On 12 September of every lunar calendar, the village has a festival during which people worship the two generals, thanking them for the founding of their village and for the craft that gave them their livelihoods.

For hundreds of years, there has been a thriving local market for bamboo construction: housing in the area was built primarily from bamboo, as were the fences and gates that sealed off villages from the outside world. In colonial times, when the economy was oriented toward serving the French, the bamboo trade offered the one market that villagers could access. One elder explained that, 'under the French, if we did not have this trade, we would have died of hunger' (personal communication, 2007). Another village elder, and a well-known craft master, told the story of how he built a school in the North for children who were fleeing Hanoi during the American war in 1966. Villagers also supported the war effort by travelling to Hanoi and to other provinces in order to build houses and barracks for the army. It is because of this long history that Thu Thuy village built its reputation over time, one that is closely tied to the village's traditional name of Thu Hong. Even as the bamboo sector in Thu Thuy managed to survive through periods of colonialism and economic shocks, providing an important safety net to villagers, it stagnated during the 1970s and 1980s, coming perilously close to disappearing entirely. The reasons for its decline are many, and can be explained both by the changing nature of demand for bamboo products and the specific nature of economic organization in the area. Villagers noted in interviews that, due to the extreme poverty under the time of socialism, few households were interested in household decoration or the purchase of anything but basic commodities and products. Bamboo products, along with other handicrafts, were a luxury (albeit a relatively inexpensive luxury), that few could afford. Poverty and the lack of demand for primary products serve as one important explanation for the decline of the bamboo trade under collectivization.

But another, perhaps more plausible, explanation can be found in the role of the state in overlooking villagers' assets and the potential of the bamboo sector. This intangible asset held by the whole community was hardly recognized by government planners and poorly mobilized under the subsidy economy. With the development of collective farming in the 1960s and 1970s, households were organized into collective farms, with a primary focus on rice production, leaving trading in bamboo products as a side industry, with trade remaining highly localized within the commune. 'During that time,' explained one villager, 'we only sold to our friends and relatives who lived nearby' (personal communication, 2007). Any trade outside of the commune was outside of the state collective system, and therefore labelled as capitalist and 'illegal'. This stands in contrast to the numerous bamboo production cooperatives that were developed during the same period in Ha Tay province. Unlike Thu Thuy, these collectives were actively supported by state trading companies and offered export markets, primarily to Eastern Europe. In a world of state control, Thu Thuy's relative isolation – as one of only two handicraft villages in Son Son District – led to limited state support. And given this lack of support from state planners, the top-down, output-oriented planning of the area did not bode well for the development of the industry.

But even while bamboo production stagnated, it did not disappear. Even during hard times, up to 90 per cent of men in the village knew basic techniques of bamboo construction. Villagers continued to build certain items, such as beds, for local consumption. This provided some black market supplement to their incomes, and helped them to survive during some very difficult times. The bamboo trade, explained many locals, could not disappear: 'you cannot forget this...it is our village trade' (personal communication, 2007). That the bamboo trade did not disappear is a testament to the deep roots that it has in the area and to the strong sense of history within the village. But we must also look to the individuals and institutions that played a key role in its revival.

Everything old is new

Doi moi was a mixed blessing for Thu Thuy village. The opening of the economy in the 1990s meant that jobs were increasingly available, and farmers could sell their own produce and labour as they wished. But the village was still stuck in the trap of having poor agricultural land, which limited the ability of most residents to benefit from Vietnam's first agriculture-led boom. Moreover, despite the growth of industry in Soc Son District, very few local youth have been able to find employment in the industrial estates that have sprouted up nearby. The educational requirements for these modern jobs were simply too high. Farmers told stories of friends and relatives who, having agreed to sell their land to the new industrial parks on the condition that their children could apply for work in the new facilities, learned that their sons and daughters could not pass the rigorous entrance exams. As a result, many villagers found themselves travelling 50 to 200 km from their homes to work as day labourers. Many of these workers spent their time in the bamboo sector, often travelling to other craft villages in Ha Tay province to take on contract work building houses or working in the other province's burgeoning handicraft enterprises. While in many cases people were content with the wages of up to US$70 per month, they were less than pleased with the long stretches of time they often had to spend away from their families. During interviews, many complained that they were often hired as day labourers because of their knowledge of working with bamboo, particularly traditional techniques that are increasingly valued for handicrafts. But once employers learned enough from them to train other local workers, their contracts were cancelled, forcing them to look for more work elsewhere.

The lack of local work has led local people to experiment with a wide range of income-generating activities. Most important among these has been the growing recycling trade. Over the past seven years, villagers have begun to gather materials for recycling, including plastic, paper and metal from Hanoi and neighbouring provinces to resell for a profit. Village leaders have estimated that up to 90 per cent of households were involved in recycling in one way or another, and that up to half of a household's income could come from recycling. Recycling offers money, much more than could be earned through farming, the making of bamboo products, or even woodworking. It is for potential profits that villagers are willing to travel far from their village for extended periods to gather materials and endure the gruelling labour and low status that comes with the trade. Elders complained that the wholesale uptake of recycling was a matter of short-term thinking: in an economy and society increasingly preoccupied with economic growth and consumption, people were willing to do anything in order to make some money. 'Our children...recycle now because the money is good,' claimed one elder, 'but once the money is not so good, they'll come back to the village trade' (personal communication, 2007). Recycling, he and his colleagues claimed, was a simple economic activity, one that the young were engaged in to make some quick money. But it did not have roots in the village, and did not have meaning to its members. It was 'only' money making. Bamboo, on the other hand, was something quite different, since it offered a sense of identity and pride of place that other trades could not.

The Thu Hong Cooperative

While the story of the Thu Hong Cooperative is one of how internal assets are mobilized, we do not claim that the villagers built the Thu Hong cooperative within a bubble; quite the opposite, since, in many ways, it was outsiders from the Hanoi government who provided the impetus for Thu Hong's establishment. The newspaper story in *The People*, mentioned at the outset, generated a good deal of interest within the Hanoi leadership about the state of the Thu Thuy craft village. In particular, the article attracted the attention of the Vice President of the Hanoi People's Committee, who was concerned about the state of the village, and about how a traditional trade could flounder in a time of economic growth throughout the city. A delegation was soon dispatched to visit the village, led by representatives of the People's Committee and the Hanoi Cooperative Alliance. The goal of the delegation was to look into the reasons for the decline of bamboo in Thu Hong and to assess what could be done for the village. The group arranged for a meeting of village elders and craft masters, who were likewise concerned about the decline of the bamboo trade and interested in what could be done to revive the business.

One man who took a particularly keen interest in the trade was Mr Phan Van Khai, a local elder who had recently returned home to Thu Thuy after retiring from a position as a government engineer in Thai Nguyen province.

Mr Khai himself had memories of working with bamboo as a child, something that he had been involved in less and less during his years of working for the state company. His father, a local government official, was a well-known house builder, and his brother was, and continues to be, known as one of the finest craftsmen in the area. At the very first meeting of craft masters concerning the establishment of a new bamboo enterprise, all were excited about the opportunity to take bamboo production beyond the household level in the area. And though they were too old to participate in the new venture, they agreed that they would ask their children and grandchildren to join the cooperative, but only if Mr Khai agreed to be the leader. Mr Khai, they understood, had the expertise of a skilled craftsperson, combined with the management skills and technical knowledge of an engineer. He combined the respect of a well-known village elder with the energy and enthusiasm of an entrepreneur. Indeed, his skills of working with people and developing networks, as we will show later, have been key factors in the success of Thu Hong cooperative. In the end, 30 people were asked to join the cooperative, and 15 agreed. This group subsequently formed the core of the new enterprise.

The cooperative was registered under the 1998 Law on Cooperatives as an Industrial Cooperative. The goal of the group, written at the time of their incorporation, was:

> To develop a centre for restoration and development of traditional trades, to contribute to the creation of jobs for local workers, and to participate in local economic development, poverty reduction and to contribute to the furthering of the local identity of Xuan Thu Commune. (Khai, personal communication, 2007)

The ambitions of its members were clear in the goal statement. Thu Hong cooperative was not founded as a 'mere' business; instead, its primary goal was to create jobs within the local area and to provide a catalyst for the redevelopment of traditional trades in the area. The name Thu Hong was chosen to reflect the traditional name of the village, both in order to draw upon the great prestige and recognition that went with it, and also, in the words of Mr Khai, 'to thank the ancestors for the traditional trades that they had passed down to us' (personal communication, 2007). In this way, the members were able to forge a link with their past, and tap into an important source of village pride.

The Thu Hong Traditional Bamboo Cooperative is primarily a construction enterprise. The majority of its projects consist of the construction of small bamboo buildings, houses, and gazebos, primarily for restaurants and cafés in and around Hanoi. The group sends small teams, supervised by one of the more experienced builders, to complete a finished project on-site. Most members claim that the ability to mobilize groups in this way is one of the prime benefits of the cooperative; previously, families had worked on their own, and had difficulty taking on large commercial projects. The cooperative also builds a number of products – primarily furniture – in its own workshop.

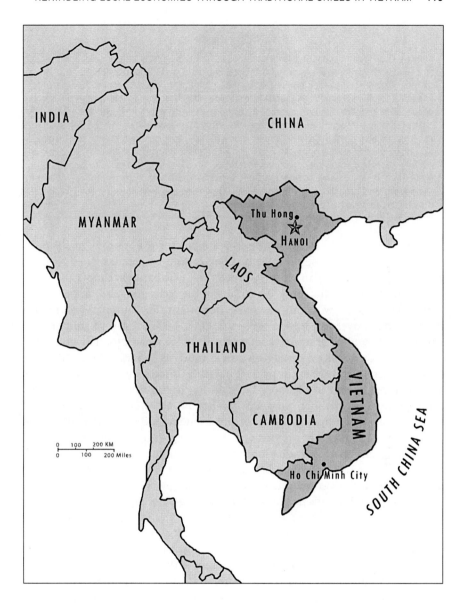

These include tables, chairs, and beds, as well as other small items that are becoming increasingly popular in the city. All items are made to order, and usually created in small quantities.

In 2003, the group was able to acquire the rights to use a small piece of land near one end of the village. This land is now the site for a central operations base for the cooperative and contains an office building, a gazebo for production, a wood-working shop, and an area for treating bamboo. The property also houses a warehouse to store bamboo, which is critical in that

> **Box 5.1: Sourcing bamboo**
>
> Though Thu Thuy village – and the vicinity – was once the site of large stocks of bamboo, one is now more likely to see a motorcycle plant nearby. For this reason, the Thu Hong members are forced to look elsewhere for their bamboo. In the early days, before having enough capital in advance to purchase materials, Mr Khai was forced to use his social connections to borrow unused bamboo poles from other local families, with the promise to either replace or repay them at another time. With the establishment of the cooperative, Mr Khai is able to purchase materials from traders who obtain bamboo from remote provinces such as Ha Giang in the north and Thanh Hoa on the central coast. As recently as three years ago, Thu Hong members were forced to travel long distances to buy bamboo, particularly if they wanted to find speciality kinds for particular products. Today, following the rebirth and growth of the trade in Thu Thuy, bamboo traders bring their products directly to the village.

it allows the cooperative to stockpile materials for the months of February and March. During these months, bamboo cannot be purchased, as access to bamboo is restricted in an effort to protect the new bamboo shoots.

When founding Thu Hong, Mr Khai and his colleagues also tapped into a trend that was, and will continue to be, important. The current world market for bamboo is over five billion dollars (INBAR, 2006). A recent study of the potential of bamboo as a sustainable substitute for wood products notes that Vietnam's industry alone could be worth as much as US$1.2 billion within the next ten years (Oxfam Hong Kong, 2006). While China currently dominates the international market in bamboo, Vietnam has begun to play an increasingly strong role. Most bamboo products in Vietnam are produced in specialized craft villages with differing degrees of development and access to markets and technologies. In Hay Tay province, an increasing degree of industrialization has led households to specialize in production of unfinished bamboo products and to access markets through linkages with SMEs (Tacoli, Hoang, and Dang, 2005). Indeed, it is important to note that, along with important support from well-placed friends in government agencies, the members of Thu Hong Cooperative benefited from a rapidly changing external environment, with a booming market for bamboo products both nationally and internationally. Without this emerging market – driven in part by changing senses of style and the appreciation for tradition that comes with higher incomes – the new enterprise might have lacked buyers for its wares. Therefore, Thu Hong's success is due, in large part, to a successful reaction to broader changes taking place outside of the village of Thu Thuy.

A cooperative or a social enterprise?

When asked why he chose to create a cooperative rather than a private company, Mr Khai replied that he simply 'knew nothing about business' (personal communication, 2007). Having worked the whole of his career in a state enterprise, founding a cooperative simply seemed to be the most natural course of action. Creating a private enterprise, on the other hand, would have required him to have a level of formality and management expertise that went beyond his knowledge and financial means. At the same time, he was well aware of the limitations of establishing a simple household enterprise: the lack of formality would make for thorny relationships with banks, trade organizations and local government. The cooperative provided a useful middle-ground of formality.

The form of the cooperative is worth reflecting upon here. The dismantling of the system of collectives through *Doi moi* in the early 1990s did not mean an end to the cooperative system. Indeed, the 'new style' cooperatives, such as Thu Hong, were an important platform of *Doi moi* policy: in 1996, Decree 68 committed both the party and the state to support the new cooperatives, and develop a coordinated movement to set them up throughout rural Vietnam. The fundamental difference between the new and old forms of cooperative can be seen in the voluntary nature of the new ones. The eminent Vietnamese social scientist, Pham Xuan Nam, has argued that the old pre-*Doi moi* collectives 'violated the principle of free will, democratic management and mutual benefit which characterize the civilized system of cooperatives' (Pham and Hainsworth, 1999: 94). These new cooperatives are based on cooperation (*hop tac hoa*) rather than collectivization (*tap the hoa*), and therefore do not denote a loss of control, as did earlier collectives, but instead allow for new forms of local control and participation.

For Thu Hong members, the ability to make profits and maintain them within the cooperative has been paramount. The management board and members decide on the distribution of the surplus during an annual meeting, following rules laid out by the Law of Cooperatives and subsequent decrees. The Thu Hong cooperative also departs from many other contemporary cooperative models in that it has a mix of cooperative members (*xa vien*) and workers (*lao dong thue*). Today, the cooperative has eight members and approximately twenty workers, whose numbers vary with the number of contracts. Cooperative members, all of whom were founding members of the organization, participate in management decisions and allocate surplus capital in an annual meeting each year. Most decisions are taken by a management committee, including the president and two vice-presidents, one of whom is responsible for overseeing workers and the other of whom is responsible for management and finance. Workers do not participate in decision-making, and instead receive a monthly wage for their labour, including no dividends from increased sales. During interviews, few of the workers indicated knowledge of, or indeed much interest in, the management of the cooperative.

This mixed nature of the cooperative, which is part cooperative unit, part joint stock enterprise, is worth highlighting, as it is an important aspect of the enterprise's success. Mr Khai expressed no interest in increasing the membership of the cooperative, and instead plans to keep the overall membership steady at eight. The small number of members allows for easier control and management of the cooperative, and surpluses he noted were much too small to divide too many times. Mr Khai clarified that the role of the Thu Hong cooperative was to create employment for local people. Understood as such, the cooperative is like many other social enterprises in that it combines a modest private gain for a small number of owners with the social mission of providing jobs for a wider range of people. The fact that it has been incorporated as a cooperative has eased the red tape associated with creating an enterprise. It has also been useful in helping to tailor marketing strategies to certain forms of organizations and buyers. Indeed, some foreign exporters and Vietnamese state organizations have shown considerable interest in Thu Hong because it is a cooperative. Its cooperative status has also helped the members and workers alike to get training and other assistance from the Hanoi Cooperative Association, and its training centre, the Hanoi Assistance Centre for Developing Business.

Although Thu Hong attempts to operate like a business, it does not operate like just any business. As a social enterprise, it relies on good communication with its employees. Given that the goal of the enterprise is to create jobs, it would simply not do to exploit them and treat workers as simple inputs to the cooperative. All of the management board members are expected to provide manual labour and work just as the other labourers. Likewise, the cooperative puts great effort into ensuring that management's expectations of employees are clear, that employees have steady work, and that they are properly compensated for their efforts. The cooperative's accountant explained that 'sometimes the workers do not understand their wage, and get angry when I pay them. But then I explain to them what the profits were [for] that quarter, how much the members have made, and how much they make. So they are then much happier' (personal communication, 2007). Indeed, one worker had recently quit as a member of another cooperative to work for Thu Hong because

Table 5.1: Annual income of Thu Hong Cooperative (1 US$ = 16,000 VND)

Year	Income (VND)
2002	206,708,505
2003	417,895,000
2004	297,527,500
2005	394,974,200
2006	299,143,000

Source: Khai, 2006.

Table 5.2: Monthly wages for workers (1 US$ = 16,000 VND)

Year	Monthly wage (VND)
2002	319,000
2003	415,000
2004	459,000
2005	670,000
2006	750,000

Source: Khai, 2006.

The artisans of Thu Hong Cooperative craft chairs by hand rather than with machinery. This leads to a much finer, though at times more expensive, product than that produced by larger enterprises.

of the steadier work offered. Another spent one year working at another local bamboo cooperative, but moved to the Thu Hong Cooperative because he felt that the other was working too much like a 'private business' (personal communication, 2007). Though the pay was higher, the other cooperative did not have a time sheet and did not manage itself in a transparent manner. And though his salary was higher at his original place of employment, he never knew whether he was going to work or not.

In many ways, Thu Hong's transparency and commitment to its workers can be considered to be an important asset. It has allowed the cooperative to continue to draw quality employees and to develop its reputation with local workers, buyers, and with government. Indeed, an examination of the cooperative's financial statements (See Tables 5.1 and 5.2) show that the salaries of its workers have raised much faster than the cooperative's overall profits. And while this 'asset' may be one that can be taken for granted, it need not be. Managing a business in a socially responsible manner is, unfortunately, far from the norm for many small enterprises. The decisions that the Thu Hong founders made at the outset, to concentrate on improving the local economy and providing quality jobs, have been important to its development. The constant focus on these factors distinguishes Thu Hong from other local enterprises, contributing not only to good relations with workers, but also to improved relationships with outsiders, who appreciate the way it is run, as well as the coherence of its mission (Hanoi Cooperative Alliance, personal communication, 2007).

From its inception, Thu Hong was founded with a two-pronged social mission: to create employment for those who had fallen through the cracks in the modern economy and to contribute to the development of the village. Mr Khai is explicit in this regard when discussing his business. He said that modern businesses supported by the district are very good for promoting business and economic development, 'but they know nothing about community development' (personal communication, 2007). In addition to the jobs created within the workshop – which are of a better quality than those offered in other bamboo workshops – the cooperative hosts training sessions for young people in such skills as weaving and construction. Indeed, the district has recently offered to move Thu Hong to a new industrial park, and to subsidize its land rents, electricity, and other infrastructure needs. But to move to the park would mean moving outside the village, a possibility that Mr Khai and the cooperative members are not willing to entertain. Business is important for the members, as are profits and growth; but not at the expense of providing jobs for local community members. For this reason, the cooperative's growth plans call, not just for an expansion of the bamboo trade, but also a diversification into other areas, such as tailoring and woodwork. The rationale for this expansion is that the members would like to provide jobs for different kinds of people and workers; women, for example, make up only a small part of the cooperative's workforce. Expanding into other areas such as weaving and textiles can provide work for these other groups who may not be interested in, or be able to play a central role in, bamboo construction. In short, while the goal of Thu Hong's leaders is to grow, they do not want to grow their business at any cost. They argue that they would like to remain true to their mission of providing jobs in Thu Thuy and contributing to the village's revival.

The exclusion of most workers from participating in decisions and benefiting directly from the distribution of surpluses calls into question whether calling Thu Hong a 'cooperative' is at all useful. At the same time, as we have tried to show earlier in this section, it cannot be assumed that workers in Thu Hong are *substantively* excluded from decisions and do not benefit from the enterprise's success, even if they are *formally* excluded by lack of full membership in the cooperative. One question that remains concerns the degree to which Thu Hong will continue to be responsive to its workers following inevitable changes in leadership that will take place in the future. Without institutionalized means of including workers, such as through full membership in the cooperative, Thu Hong's overall social responsiveness seems to be tied to the whims of its leadership. By all accounts, this has worked well to date, but the sustainability of the social nature of this social enterprise remains in question.

Mobilizing assets: pooling money and resources

We have already discussed the key assets that cooperative members wanted to mobilize to develop their village: traditional knowledge of the bamboo trades would be used to create new jobs on a greater level, and expand the trade beyond simple household production. While the cooperative members had high ambitions (such as eradicating poverty in the village) and joint commitment to a cause, they lacked two resources – land and money – that would be necessary for the development of a truly viable cooperative. In short, they were rich in many assets, including knowledge and social relations, but quite poor in the financial assets that they needed to mobilize these other strengths.

At the outset, the cooperative worked with little or no capital. Following the guidelines of the Law on Cooperatives, members were asked, initially, to purchase shares in order to provide for initial start-up capital for the venture, but most were too poor to offer anything other than their labour. Because few had the resources to purchase a share, waivers were offered to many members, who were obliged to pay at a later date following receipt of some of the profits of the cooperative. This has been common practice with many of the 'new' cooperatives in both northern and southern Vietnam (Fforde and Huan, 2001). But this move, while necessary, given the poverty of the new cooperative's members, left the group with no start-up capital with which to purchase tools and rent land. Seeking a loan to purchase tools, land, and other basic supplies, the founding members approached the Bank for Agriculture, the Hanoi Cooperative Federation, and a number of other agencies. However, due to their own lack of collateral, loans were not forthcoming. In those early days, members were forced to improvise. During their first jobs, some brought tools from home, while others borrowed basic tools from other friends and relatives. One member, in exchange for a waiver of his share purchase, offered the use of his home as an office and workshop.

Without access to any formal financing, members of the cooperative were forced to look to informal arrangements. Money was borrowed from friends both locally and far afield, from private companies, from the Hanoi Assistance Centre for Developing Business, and from a small Hanoi-based NGO. Most of these loans were completely interest-free, and offered long term flexible repayment rates. The various scraps of money were mobilized through the personal and professional connections of various cooperative members, but Mr Khai was central to the initiative's success. Indeed, while Mr Khai had very little collateral to use to secure a loan, he used his own pension book as collateral to borrow the equivalent of US$350 from a private moneylender. In total, the young cooperative had about US$700 in cash for start-up capital. Much of this money was used up during the early stages of registering the cooperative (in order to pay for the registration itself), on hosting visits by local officials, and on other administrative fees. In fact, Mr Khai explained that most of the working capital of the cooperative was exhausted before supplies could be purchased or work could be started on any building projects.

This ability to access informal finance was largely due to Mr Khai's strong networks of relationships within and outside of the community. Having worked away from the village for an extended period in a state-owned factory, Mr Khai had good connections, education, and a solid reputation within the village. A longstanding member of the Communist Party of Vietnam, and son of a teacher who taught Chinese for many people in the commune, Mr Khai held the respect and trust needed to mobilize this informal support.

Mobilizing assets: networking and external support

While the main goal of this chapter is to examine the endogenous changes that spurred the growth and development of the Thu Hong cooperative, it remains important not to overlook the role of exogenous influence, in the form of general market trends, institutional changes, and the role of institutions and individuals that provided support to Thu Hong in its formative years. Indeed, as we have reviewed earlier in this chapter, it was 'outsiders' in the form of representatives from the Hanoi People's Committee, who provided the impetus for Thu Hong's establishment. In this section, we would like to review the role of outsiders, and in doing so question the sharp distinction that is often made between the outsider and insider in community-driven development.

One of the major external resources that Thu Hong has been able to tap is that of membership in the Vietnam Federation of Craft Villages (VFCV), a membership-based organization established under the auspices of the Vietnam Fatherland Front, a mass organization with close links with the Communist Party of Vietnam. The Association works on behalf of member craft villages and individual craftspeople through its support of training, exchange of information and marketing of products by way of producing and distributing catalogues and hosting trade fairs. The federation's representatives were not in a position to offer Thu Hong the financial resources that it needed to grow; but they were able to plug Thu Hong into the burgeoning, nationwide network of craft villages and buyers. The cooperative's first big break came when Mr Dan, the Deputy Chair of the Federation, arranged to invite Mr Khai to display some wares at a major exhibition – the Spring Fair for promoting Vietnamese Culture – at Hanoi's renowned temple of literature. Not only did VFCV waive the fees for Thu Hong's display, but the cooperative was also contracted to build three temporary houses on site for the exhibition organizers. The exhibition represented the first time that Thu Hong Cooperative, and indeed any of its members, were able to market their wares on a large scale, and it provided the foundation for a series of social and business connections that would pay off over time. The contract for the houses, added to a small number of other contracts, allowed the Thu Hong cooperative to save enough funds to purchase some tools.

Another important institution that offered external support was Maryknoll, a Catholic missionary order with a strong social development mission. In 2002, Maryknoll entered the second phase of its work with Soc Son on a district-wide poverty elimination programme. In its Soc Son programme, the NGO worked closely with the local vocational skills centre to finance and offer technical assistance for people to obtain training in tailoring, carpentry, electricity and plumbing. The focus of the training was to assist unemployed youth to enter the growing job market in local industrial areas, the District Centre, and Hanoi. Maryknoll's interest in vocational skills training was supported by a second pillar of activities, consisting of work with traditional craft villages in the vicinity of Hanoi.

Maryknoll's first attempt to support traditional trades in Soc Son District came in the form of a partnership with a small basket weaving village in Xuan Lai. A short-lived project with a village-based agricultural cooperative had not been successful because of heavy and obtrusive management at the local level, high salaries claimed by management board members, and a general lack of interest in local ownership. Rather than continue to help maintain an unsustainable project, the organization drew it to a close after three months and asked its district partner to locate another village more willing to drive its own development process. Soon after, Maryknoll's project officer visited Thu Hong village and happened to see the newly erected sign for the cooperative at the side of the road. He was told by his partners that it had been recently established by a retired man, and so he arranged a meeting with the manager. It was not long before Maryknoll signed an agreement with Thu Hong cooperative to support its development. The 'inputs' provided by the Maryknoll project were modest. They included offering small financial grants to develop sample products to take to craft fairs, supporting the printing of brochures and name cards, and accompanying Thu Hong's leaders to exhibitions and trade shows, first in Hanoi and later further afield in Ho Chi Minh City in southern Vietnam. Maryknoll's staff members also helped to connect Thu Hong's management board with some export companies in Hanoi, and with some foreign importers as well, including a group of Belgians, who visited the cooperative following an exhibition.

What is useful to highlight in the case of Maryknoll's involvement is not that the order assisted in the development of the cooperative but rather how it supported the cooperative in its early days. Following the initial meetings between Mr Khai and the Maryknoll programme manager, the cooperative leaders asked the organization to offer them a grant or loan for working capital. The Maryknoll officer was forced to explain that funds could not be donated. However, he could provide technical support, and the project centred around this support. Two important factors should be underscored with regard to the role of Maryknoll and other external agencies in supporting the cooperative. The first was that of upgrading the members' technical skills, including working with bamboo and 'soft skills' of marketing and management. The second, and more important, were the many networking opportunities that work with outsiders provided.

It would certainly seem counterintuitive to claim that, while the key asset used by these villagers was their traditional knowledge of bamboo construction, one of the most important roles of outsiders was to improve upon this knowledge. Mr Hoi, a 90 year-old craft master who had been working with bamboo since his youth, told us that each household used slightly different techniques. Because the techniques were not standardized, the quality of products produced by the village could vary significantly. The range in quality often made it very difficult to sell goods on any large scale. Some new skills, such as techniques to stain and preserve bamboo with chemicals rather than water, also improved the quality of villagers' lives, since the harsh smell given off by wet bamboo was eliminated. Other techniques, developed through the partnership, focused on skills that the cooperative members could use to finish their final products for the market. For example, they hired a fine arts teacher from the Hay Tay Fine Arts School to train the members in painting and general design techniques for furniture. The relationships between 'local' knowledge and external expertise – perhaps best seen as the relationships between 'insiders' and 'outsiders,' are useful to highlight here.

On top of offering 'hard' skills to help cooperative members work with bamboo and design products, Maryknoll provided assistance in 'soft' skills such as marketing and advertising. When they are asked about marketing, most cooperative members exude bewilderment. Most claimed to want to know more, but thought of marketing as such a complex field that they could never grasp it with their level of education. Yet the simple assistance offered by Maryknoll has led to great dividends. The cooperative has taken on projects in the south of the country, and has built restaurants and other buildings in Hanoi that would have been impossible had the cooperative not moved beyond word-of-mouth advertising. Today, Mr Khai conducts most of the cooperative's marketing on his own, including advertising in both Vietnamese and English in a number of newspapers and trade magazines, and he ensures continued attendance at local trade fairs. Mr Dan, the head of the Hanoi Cooperative Federation, has said that all of this effort in marketing and networking is paying off: 'many more people know about the cooperative, and when you mention bamboo furniture, they know about that cooperative' (personal communication, 2007).

The second field of support from Maryknoll, closely connected with marketing, was that of helping the cooperative develop networks. The networking opportunities provided by the partnership perhaps eclipsed anything else that was provided by Maryknoll. Visits by cooperative leaders to fairs in Hanoi led to increased work there, and a visit to a fair in Ho Chi Minh City, in southern Vietnam, resulted in a number of contracts to build houses for restaurants and offices in Ho Chi Minh and Long An provinces. These opportunities have been important to both the leadership of the cooperative and its general members. One junior member of the cooperative stated in an interview that 'though my salary was higher before I joined the cooperative, I have had many opportunities to learn and travel. [Before the cooperative] I would never have been able to develop the relationships with new people that I now have' (personal communication, 2007).

Networking was not only an activity of the project, but also a way of acting throughout the project. Indeed, as an input, it was small: the whole budget for the Thu Hong project was less than US$10,000. Various informal types of networking and learning, with which the Maryknoll project officers assisted Thu Hong, however, had greater impact than more official project interventions. For example, Maryknoll's project officer travelled on numerous occasions to the cooperative to offer free translation for foreign visitors interested in its bamboo products. In a business such as Thu Hong's, which relies on direct orders and relationships with customers, it is the initial forging of the relationships that has been most important. Not unlike Mr Khai's ability to command respect because of his government experience and Party membership, Maryknoll has garnered respect for the way it uses its own networks to provide Thu Hong with new customers and outlets for its wares. Most of this support has been highly informal, and took the form of looking for, and exploiting, opportunities, rather than following a rigid plan.

Once these connections were made, however, it was up to the cooperative to build relationships. One customer of the cooperative, who hired members to build a restaurant near the Noi Bai airport, said that it was a combination of an advertisement and Thu Hong's reputation that spurred him to hire them: 'I saw [it] advertised on the internet...but I also knew that Thu Hong was very famous as a craft village. They have been doing this for hundreds of years...they do very good work, and are the best village for building bamboo houses' (personal communication, 2007). Certainly, it was the combination of Thu Thuy's traditional reputation as a craft village and the profile offered by Maryknoll's marketing assistance that allowed the contract to be secured. Each on its own would likely not have been enough to compete with other companies. Furthermore, the cooperative's high-quality work with the same customer has led to further work of building a beer stall for the customer's niece; he is also considering hiring Thu Hong to build more restaurant buildings at the end of 2008.

Networking alone is quite obviously not enough. Through the work and initiative of Mr Khai, Thu Hong cooperative has been able to employ what Robert Putnam (2000) has called 'bridging' and 'bonding' social capital. On one hand, the cooperative leaders have played a strong role in bonding together with workers within the cooperative and with other members of the village. The ongoing mobilization of workers did not simply happen. Rather, the fact that cooperative leaders treated their workers with respect, offering them steady work even during downturns, and managing relationships with village elders and other local officials, has been central to Thu Hong's very survival. Ongoing support from local craft masters and other village residents has also been actively cultivated by the cooperative. All bamboo tradespeople with whom we spoke mentioned the fact that Mr Khai was highly skilled in involving them in different projects when needed. But the cooperative, through its leadership, has also provided a bridge to other institutions and communities. This initial bridge to key individuals has opened new relationships with other organizations, for example, just as the partnership with Maryknoll has led to connections with trade associations in the south of the country.

Mobilizing assets: knowledge as an asset

If there is any one asset that can be considered critical to Thu Hong's success it is the knowledge of working with bamboo. But this asset is much more than mere 'human capital' created by educational institutions and expressed in measurable skills and knowledge. Instead, the knowledge of bamboo is an excellent example of 'tacit knowledge' (Polanyi, 1962), an intangible asset that is difficult to transfer and codify, but which is of critical importance to the success of the initiative. Workers both inside and outside the cooperative described a similar process of informal apprenticeship, when they were in their early teens, following fathers or uncles by working on small building projects. Even those no longer working in the bamboo trade described early experiences of learning the basis of the craft within the family. It is also a skill that is difficult to learn in the formal classroom. The local Vocational Skills Training Centre in Soc Son does not provide any training in bamboo or rattan, for the simple reason that there is no demand for bamboo skills. The trade is passed down within the family: 'People here learn quickly...it is not hard...anybody can do it' (personal communication, 2007). Even while the artisans of Thu Hong claimed that working with bamboo was easy (though it is not!), it is certainly not a skill that is easily learned through training or rote learning. As one elder asserted:

> Everybody in Thu Hong knows how to do it already. And it is difficult for people outside of Thu Hong to learn the trade when they are older. I think it is the kind of skill that you learn when you are young. (personal communication, 2007)

Knowledge of working with bamboo is not simply limited to rote knowledge. Craft masters like to speak of the intricacies of their craft, and how the work of Thu Thuy is often quite distinct from that of other villages. For example, in home building – their staple enterprise – the new cooperative uses a traditional method of making joints for beams by carefully weaving the large bamboo poles together and around each other. To many outsiders, it is difficult to tell the difference between this and the metal pegs that are used by others. But for the connoisseur, the traditional techniques are important. They are perhaps most important to the members of the cooperative itself, who proudly display the joints to all visitors. The same pride is taken in smaller products, such as chairs, which are assembled by hand using traditional techniques. For this reason, Thu Hong's prices are significantly higher than those charged by larger enterprises that use industrial techniques and equipment. But Mr Khai does not see this as a problem for the time being: while it can be difficult to find new customers, once people see the quality of Thu Hong's wares, they come back and recommend them to other buyers.

However, the tacit knowledge involved in the basic building and construction skills that had been imparted from father to son in the commune was not enough to survive in the modern bamboo sector. Mr Khai's experience as an engineer has translated well into bamboo, and has served the cooperative well. The support in design and 'soft skills' development in marketing has also helped the Thu Hong members to better mobilize their traditional assets into a livelihood over which they have more control. The use of new designs is important, for while there is certainly a renewed taste for traditional products throughout Vietnam, this is combined with some more modern sensibilities. With the help of Maryknoll, the cooperative has found new designs from Chinese and Indonesian internet sites with the hope of accessing export markets. Mr Khai has also put his own design skill to good use by creating new products to serve the Vietnamese market. For example, the cooperative has recently designed a new folding bamboo bed built to suit Vietnamese students.

Mr Khai's vision for the cooperative is one in which traditional skills and modern production techniques can be brought together. He believes that the traditions of the village can only survive if they are strengthened by some appropriate industrial techniques and better management. Ms Dung, the cooperative's young accountant and secretary, spoke about her hope for the future, which also balances strengths with future growth:

> I want a model of a cooperative that is developed, [on] a bigger scale, that sells more to international areas. I want to see more long term customers... I hope that we can improve the quality of wares and make the highest quality models. (personal communication, 2007)

Assets, skills and safety nets

The Thu Hong story points to the strong role that traditional skills can play in providing a safety net for those who have been unable to find employment in the modern economy. Unlike some of the communities considered in this book, Thu Hong is located in an area characterized by breakneck industrial growth and economic expansion. Large numbers of the village's young find employment in Hanoi for salaries that far exceed the wages provided by the bamboo cooperative. But Thu Hong Cooperative, and the local trades in general, provide something that the modern economy cannot. On one level, it provides an opportunity for those who prefer to stay home in their village, close to family. All of the workers and cooperative members with whom we spoke highlighted the fact that working in the bamboo trade allowed them to earn an income without leaving their village. Naturally, this option is not

preferred by all. Indeed, out-migration is preferred by many of the villages'
young. But working in traditional trades provides a choice, one that would be
all but absent without enterprises like Thu Hong.

Similarly, most people interviewed for this study – including both members
and non-members – spoke of the fact that they were happy that the traditional
trades survived for those who were not capable of moving into the modern
economy. They gained a sense of pride from having a trade, and being able to
use that trade to make a living. Indeed, the very skills now used by villagers as
a primary means of making a living were once undervalued and underused; a
small supplement for those participating in the collective farms. People have
been working in bamboo crafts for centuries, and this is itself a source of pride.
In providing a link with the past, bamboo production confers an identity on
individual workers, Thu Hong Cooperative, and indeed to Thu Hong villagers
as a whole. Many people told stories of following their fathers to construct
bamboo houses, and learning skills from their uncles and their grandfathers.
Village elders with years of experience in the trade are called craft masters (an
approximate translation) locally, and are often approached for advice both
on traditional techniques and on ways to modernize the sector. The village
has also become better known within Hanoi, with articles about Thu Hong
appearing in major newspapers such as *Ha Noi Moi* (New Hanoi) and *Nhan
Dan* (The People). At the same time, we should be careful not to overstate
the feelings of pride that come with working in the village's traditional trade.
While all villagers and cooperative members interviewed told proud stories
of the past, and often hoped for a bright future for bamboo in their area, few
felt a burning need to see the village's future in bamboo production. When
asked if they would like their children to work with bamboo, most villagers
were clear to affirm that, while they would be happy if their children followed
their trade, they would not try to force it. What was important was that their
children had a trade and that they could use this to make a living.

Conclusion

By many traditional measures of success, it would be difficult to call Thu Hong
a major achievement. To date, there are only eight members, and at peak
times a maximum of 20 workers are employed. While income has increased
over time, it has been inconsistent, with peaks and lows over the years.
But Thu Hong's lasting impact on the village and on the workers goes far
beyond direct employment. Spurred in large part by Thu Hong, the village has
seen a renaissance in the bamboo trades, with the establishment of another
cooperative and the establishment and expansion of 300 household enterprises.
Just as important, success can also be seen in the pride that individuals feel
in 'having a trade' and using that trade to better their own livelihoods and
advance the quality of life in their village. The sense of pride in Thu Hong
also points to the possibility that much of its success and impact goes beyond
the improvements in the lives of individuals. Indeed, one of the key successes

of Thu Hong, as a social enterprise, can be seen in its role maintaining and furthering the development of a sense of place and forging strong community ties in Thu Thuy village. For the employees of Thu Hong and others working in the bamboo trade, the economy is intertwined with the history and culture of their village – to work with bamboo is very much part of what it means to be from the 'craft village' of Thu Thuy. The Thu Hong Cooperative in this way is as much a defence of place in a time of rapid economic change as it is the promotion of individual jobs and livelihoods (Escobar, 2001).

At the same time, we should be careful not to overemphasize the role of local factors in enabling Thu Hong. While this case study has not tried to conclusively answer the question of 'why' Thu Hong has succeeded, it is evident that many of the underlying factors lie far outside of the village gates. First, without the changes introduced by and under *Doi moi*, Thu Hong Cooperative, quite simply, could not exist. In large part, it was this new enabling environment that allowed people to mobilize their own knowledge and assets, both through the provision of economic incentives and through the reduction of central planning in managing the local economy. Second, the changing nature of the bamboo sector, with increased demand for bamboo products both within Hanoi, and internationally, has created a demand for a service to which members of the Thu Hong Cooperative were well placed to respond.

Furthermore, Thu Hong has benefited considerably from connections with many who would be considered to be 'outside' of the local community. Strong interest from the government in Hanoi and from other agencies, such as Maryknoll and the Association of Craft Villages, not only provided the impetus for Thu Hong's establishment, but have been important to its growth. At the same time, Thu Hong has remained an enterprise that is controlled and managed locally. Much of this local control, in fact, comes down to incredible individual agency on the part of Mr Khai. In all interviews, Mr Khai downplays his role as the driving force behind the cooperative, but conversations with him and others point to the profound role that he continues to play in helping the organization to achieve its mission.

The Thu Hong story offers an antidote to the all too frequent separation of exogenous or 'externally' driven development from that which is endogenous. As with most other case studies in this volume, local leadership has played a strong role in mobilizing local resources and spurring change. On the other hand, in this case, local leadership would likely not have grown were it not for the interest and intervention of a small number of concerned individuals from the Hanoi People's Committee. Likewise, there would be no demand for Thu Hong's products, nor ability for its workers to mobilize, were it not for the political and economic shifts of *Doi moi*. What we are left with is a complex network of individuals and agencies that make it increasingly difficult to state, unequivocally, what is outside and what is inside. Yet, because this network mobilized around the historic and present strengths of Thu Thuy commune, it is illustrative of a highly successful community-driven initiative. We would therefore emphasize, and, indeed, celebrate, the contingency and uncertainty that characterizes Thu Hong as an economic intervention. The fact that people are learning to live with this contingency, while continuing to work through networks and mobilize local assets, are the key lessons of Thu Hong.

References

Borzaga, C., and Defourny, J. (2001) *The emergence of social enterprise*, Routledge, New York.
Escobar, A. (2001) 'Culture sits in places: Reflections on globalism and subaltern strategies of localization', *Political Geography*, 20, 139–174.
Fforde, A. and Huan, N. D. (2001) *Vietnamese rural society and its institutions: Results of a study of cooperative groups and cooperatives in three provinces*, Aduki Pty Ltd, Hanoi, Vietnam.
INBAR (2006) *Strategy to the year 2015*, International Network for Bamboo and Rattan, Beijing, China.
Kerkvliet, B. J. (2005) *The power of everyday politics: How Vietnamese peasants transformed national policy*, Cornell University Press, Ithaca, NY.
Khai, P.V. (2006) *History of Thu Hong cooperative*. Unpublished manuscript.
Oxfam Hong Kong (2006) *Mekong bamboo sector feasibility study*, IFC, MPDF and Oxfam Hong Kong, Hanoi, Vietnam.
Pham X. N. and Hainsworth, G. (1999) *Rural development in Vietnam*, Social Science Publishing House, Hanoi, Vietnam.
Polanyi, M. (1962) *Personal knowledge*, University of Chicago Press, Chicago, IL.
Putnam, R. (2000) *Bowling alone: The collapse and revival of American community*, Simon and Schuster, New York.
Rambo, T. and Jamieson, N. (1993) *Upland areas, ethnic minorities, and development*, Rowman and Littlefield, New York.
Tacoli, C., Hoang, X. T., and Dang, N. A. (2005) *Livelihood diversification and rural-urban linkages in Vietnam's Red River Delta*, International Food Policy Research Institute and the International Institute for Environment and Development, Washington, DC.
World Bank, The (2000) *World development report 2000/2001: Attacking poverty*, World Bank, Washington, DC.
World Bank, The (2003) *Poverty: Vietnam development report 2004*, Joint Donor Report to the Vietnam Consultative Group Meeting, Hanoi, December 2003.
World Bank, The (2004) *Governance: Vietnam development report 2005*, Joint Donor Report to the Vietnam Consultative Group Meeting, Hanoi, 1–2 December 2004.

Authors' note

This case is based on research conducted between May and June of 2007 in Hanoi. In total, 26 workers, villagers and officials were interviewed for the study. While the study was crafted during this period, the process of research and learning stretches back to the earliest days of Thu Hong, when Nguyen Duc Vinh entered into a partnership with the cooperative through his then employer, Maryknoll Missions. Returning to Thu Hong and witnessing its growth and dynamism first hand was an opportunity to reaffirm the value of such ventures and to rekindle and deepen friendships. Throughout the text, Vinh is often a silent partner in the Thu Hong enterprise, at once supporting its members through training, networking and documenting their successes and challenges. This case study is an important step along this road of learning and discovery, but by no means a final one.

The process of crafting this study has been collaborative in the best of ways. The two authors, one Vietnamese and one Canadian, approached many of the questions from differing worldviews, and challenged each other on each assumption that was made. At the same time, seeing the potential of this community was nothing short of inspiring, and only reinforced our collective belief that the most profound examples of community development are small and often invisible to most beholders.

While the conventions of authorship force us to stamp our own names on this document, we should note that the voices and aspirations of Thu Hong's membership loom large throughout this case. Mr Phan Van Khai has left a particularly strong mark throughout, not only as an 'informant' but as someone who has shaped this case's narrative and argument from beginning to end.

The authors would like to thank the People's Committees of Soc Son District for facilitating the research, and the leadership and staff of the National Institute of Agricultural Policy and Projection for facilitating much of the administrative side of the research. Comments offered by all participants in the Thailand workshop helped to sharpen our arguments. Alison Mathie and Gordon Cunningham offered detailed commentary and advice.

CHAPTER 6

By their own hands: two hundred years of building community in St Andrews, Nova Scotia, Canada

Gordon Cunningham and Kate Fiander

Abstract

Building on the legacy of pioneering Scottish and, later, Dutch immigrants, a rural agricultural community in Canada has been able to muster active and enthusiastic volunteers for a series of ambitious community initiatives – the building of a community centre, a curling rink and a senior's housing complex – and has sustained a thriving community into the 21st century. This case explores some of the reasons why this has been possible. At its base is a set of values that puts a premium on self sufficiency, community spirit, and care for others. By pooling resources, ideas, and talents, it has been able to build tangible community services. Success has not only motivated community members to continue with new projects, but has inspired confidence in local partners and investors, both in government and the private sector.

Introduction

This is the story of St Andrews, a small rural community of 1,100 people in north-east Nova Scotia that has been driving its own development for more than 200 years. What makes St Andrews unusual is that it continues to swim against the tide of government-led community development in the region. Since its early days as a French – and subsequently a British – colony, Nova Scotia has been shaped by waves of immigration layered on top of an existing indigenous culture. For the past 120 years the province's population and economy have failed to grow at the rate of some of Canada's bigger and richer provinces. In the 1970s the federal government began transferring annual equalization funds to so called 'have not' provinces, including Nova Scotia. While these funds have been important in building and maintaining the province's public sector programmes and infrastructure they have also created a dependency on the federal government. One of the consequences of this dependency is that many Nova Scotian communities now look to governments to initiate and fund activities that they once would have undertaken on their own. St Andrews, though, represents one of the exceptions. This chapter will look closely at three specific projects undertaken by the people of St Andrews in the last two decades in order to better understand how and why this community has been able to create and sustain the capacity of citizens to act for their own development.

The community of St Andrews: early history

As local historians recount, in 1801, a ship set sail from Fort William in Scotland carrying 500 economic and political migrants bound for Pictou, Nova Scotia. Among the passengers were many Catholic 'Highlanders,' descendants of the Scottish clans that had been engaged in an armed rebellion against the English in the mid-1700s. The rebellion was squashed and laws were subsequently enacted to prevent the expression of Highland culture, such as the gathering of the clans or the teaching of the Gaelic language. Even before this period of repression, few Scots had legal rights to land, relying instead on the clan leader's protection. The result was a migration of Highland Scots to various parts of the world in search of a better life and land they could own. The ship's passengers dispersed in all directions looking for land, and eight Highlanders, five of them brothers, found what they were looking for in what would later become known as the community of St Andrews.

The early settlers of St Andrews had to work extremely hard just to survive. Upon arriving, their most pressing need was to provide shelter for their families, which at first consisted of no more than a lean-to of poles and brush until more permanent lodging could be constructed. (MacDonald, 2000). The first settlers created a beachhead in the new world that, within a decade, had attracted dozens of families to relocate from the Scottish Highlands to rural Nova Scotia. These new families set about clearing the land and building barns, houses, roads, and bridges. They also built a chapel, and later a large church, and as many as nine schools, one for each district of the community. The largest of these schools, the St Andrews Grammar School, built in 1838, is considered by many to be the foundation for what is now St Francis Xavier University in Antigonish (MacDonald J., personal communication, 2007).

All of these accomplishments were achieved in St Andrews without any local government support. Municipal government was not established in Nova Scotia until 1879, three quarters of a century after the first Scots arrived in St Andrews. The British refused to allow any form of local 'town hall' democracy because they 'attributed some of the unrest in the American colonies to their unfortunate habit of meeting together and airing their grievances' (Service Nova Scotia, n.d.). Instead, the church became the focal point of community life and in addition to satisfying the spiritual aspects of peoples' lives, it was also the place where consensus was reached and people mobilized to undertake community initiatives.

The period between 1801 and Confederation in 1867 was a boom time for the local economy of St Andrews. The population was steadily increasing due to migration from Europe, and local demand for agriculture and forest products was high. The rapidly expanding market of the north-eastern United States absorbed any surplus production. In St Andrews, the water of the South River was used to power sawmills (lumber), grist mills (flour), and carding mills (wool). A cheese factory, tannery, and a shingle mill were established and several shops supplied general merchandise as well as blacksmithing and shoemaking services (MacDonald and Dunn, personal communication, 2007).

The second half of the 19th century witnessed a reversal of fortune for rural Nova Scotia communities including St Andrews. The 'long depression' between 1873 and 1896, the end of free trade with the US, in 1866, at the time of Confederation, and a new national railway that brought with it freight policies that favoured central Canada at the expense of the Maritime provinces all led to the decline in demand for Nova Scotia's main export products. This had an immediate effect on those in the primary industries of farming, forestry, fishing, and mining, and a long-term effect on the province's manufacturing base. In St Andrews, the practical effect was that one son or daughter would stay at home to look after the farm and his or her parents, while other grown children left to find work in the north-east United States or western Canada (J. MacDonald, J. and Dunn, personal communication, 2007).

In the first half of the 20th century, those who remained in St Andrews found innovative ways to continue building their community in spite of a depressed economy. Led by Dr Hugh MacPherson, who was born in the St Andrews area, the community established a wool cooperative in 1914, and the first cooperative store in eastern Canada in 1917. The co-op store was a centre of innovation, allowing cash, credit and barter (one of the oldest community members, Mary 'Tommy' Chisholm, remembers seeing people trading butter for kerosene there). The store also developed a hospitalization scheme for members.[1] Later, it initiated a mobile co-op store, in the form of a truck that was driven from one farm to another. MacPherson, the first recognized soil scientist east of Ontario, helped introduce the use of marl from local deposits to lower the natural acidity in the soil, and he encouraged the use of both organic and chemical fertilizers (which were new to Nova Scotia farmers). Under his leadership, St Andrews established a creamery and organized a grading and marketing system for lambs. When the electric power grid reached Antigonish in 1931, the people of St Andrews provided volunteer labour and local poles to run a 20-mile extension line to their community. Like many other rural communities in Canada, St Andrews set up a mutual telephone system whereby each household wanting a phone contributed money and volunteered labour to help string wires. The community built a house for a switchboard operator in lieu of having to charge each caller for this service. As well, a decade later, they dug, by hand, a mile-long trench and laid a wooden pipeline to bring drinking water from the South River to the heart of the community. In 1933, the people of St Andrews established their own credit union. The first loans of the St Andrews Credit Union rarely exceeded CAD100 (or Canadian dollars, equivalent to approximately US$102 at 3 March 2008), but these loans were crucial for the purchasing of farm equipment and livestock, and the building of barns and houses.[2] This early experience with cooperative activity in St Andrews formed a 'laboratory' for a group of professor priests at nearby St Francis Xavier University, who, under the banner of the 'Antigonish Movement,' helped spread the development of producer, consumer and savings and credit cooperatives throughout north-east Nova Scotia in the 1930s and 1940s (Boyd, 1949).

Recent history

One hundred and fifty years after the arrival of the first Highland Scots, St Andrews began to attract another group of industrious immigrants in search of land they could own and a better future for their children. In the aftermath of the Second World War, Holland was trying to rebuild its infrastructure and economy. Famous for their system of dykes holding back the North Sea to allow the reclamation of land, and well-known also for the social organization created to build and maintain them, the Dutch lost more than 16 per cent of reclaimed land to the North Sea during the war years. Thousands of Dutch farming families were looking for opportunities to farm in other countries, and Canada was an attractive destination. Canadian churches were encouraged by the federal government to find sponsors for immigrants and search for suitable properties in their areas. Between 1950 and 1956, 110 Dutch families came to the Antigonish Diocese, and through loans from the Catholic Church and the government's Land Resettlement Program, roughly one quarter of these families purchased vacant farms in the area of St Andrews.

For the first generation of Dutch immigrants, life wasn't much easier than it was for the early Scots. The Dutch were able to use their intensive farming techniques to make long abandoned land productive again, but it took years and many Dutch families had to rely on money borrowed from the parish priest and a helping hand from their Scottish-Canadian neighbours. While they were not universally accepted, the Dutch were embraced by the majority of the St Andrews community, their shared Catholicism making this easier. It was not uncommon in the 1950s and 1960s for long-time residents of St Andrews to volunteer days of labour to help a Dutch family build a barn or replace a roof (MacDonald, J., 2000).

Within a generation, the Dutch had contributed to reshaping the dairy industry in the region. Until the 1950s, dairy production in north-eastern Nova Scotia had been on a very small scale with most households owning their own cow. The Dutch experience in dairy farming helped develop the dairy industry into one of the main engines of the St Andrews economy.

Today, the economy of St Andrews is relatively strong, at least when compared with neighbouring rural communities. While the number of family

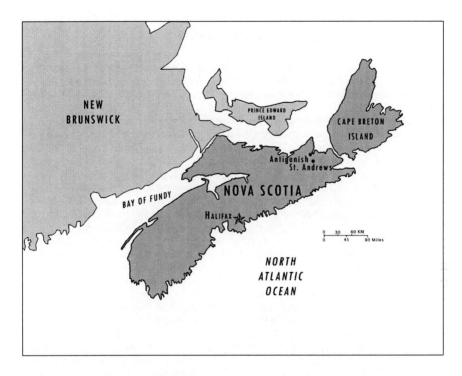

dairy farms has decreased over the last 30 years, those that remain are highly capitalized and somewhat protected by a sophisticated supply-management system. The dairy sector is complemented by the presence of several small construction firms, a reforestation company, a poultry and egg business, and a hardwood flooring mill. In addition, a new subdivision in the community now holds approximately 30 families who work outside the community, many in professional employment fields. This diversity of livelihood activities has produced a wider range of skills and a higher average income than in most rural communities in the region.

In the modern era, the people of St Andrews have continued to build their community from a solid base of cooperation and volunteerism. During the last 30 years they have set up their own baseball field on land donated by a community member, upgraded their church and school (including a computer lab), and built their own volunteer fire hall (see Box 6.2). Not restricting themselves to local projects, they have also raised money to dig several wells for villages in India (see Box 6.1). In the last decade and a half, the community also built their own curling rink and community centre. In 2006, St Andrews opened the first phase of a community-owned and community-managed housing project for seniors. Although each of these initiatives are worthy of more in-depth description and analysis, this case study will focus on the three latter initiatives.

Box 6.1: Wishing Wells

In the mid-1970s, St Andrews resident Mary van den Heuvel and her family hosted a Catholic priest from India who had come to Canada as a participant in the Coady Institute's five-month community development diploma programme. During his short stay, Father Boniface Mendes, fondly known as 'Bonnie,' became a loved and trusted friend to many in St Andrews.

Following his return to India, Fr Bonnie and the van den Heuvel family remained in close contact through the exchange of many letters. Several years later, Mary received an unexpected letter from a brother of the Missionaries of St Francis de Sales (MSFS) informing her of Fr Bonnie's sudden death. When Mary offered to support a development project in memory of his colleague, a well for a rural parish in Karivde, Maharashtra, was proposed. Mary was intrigued by the idea, but upon learning that the project would require CAD3,400 to complete, she was hesitant to accept. It was ultimately Mary's husband who urged her to take on the challenge, telling her, simply: 'If you want to, you can do it!'

In 2000, several community members decided to organize a 'Wishing Wells' concert in the St Andrew's Catholic Church. Although donations were never solicited, news of the event began to spread, and Mary began to receive spontaneous offers of support from across the country. As an unexpected bonus, several well-known artists and musicians, such as Men of the Deeps (a choir of coal miners from Cape Breton) and Mary Jane Lamond (a well-known Nova Scotian singer in the Gaelic tradition), offered to participate in the concert. Their participation was significant, given that they are highly regarded in the region for their efforts to revitalize and promote respect for traditional ways of life, culture, and language through music.

Nearly 300 people, including young children and international students from the Coady Institute, attended the first concert. Many were 'filled with emotion,' Mary recalls, and 'everyone was so cooperative... almost like they were just waiting to take part' (personal communication, 2007). The concert raised over CAD4,000, prompting a community commitment to support a second well in India and another concert the following year. Seven years later, a total of seven wells have been completed in two districts of India.

'Wishing Wells' is now a registered society, which enables it to operate as an independent body under a local board of directors. Its aim is to provide financial assistance where needed for sustainable water systems to improve the quality of life for rural communities.

The people of St Andrews have developed a deep connection to the project and take pride in supporting rural community development in India.

The St Andrews district community centre

In 1989, the citizens of St Andrews decided it was time for a new community centre. The old parish hall, built by the community in 1912, was considered too small and too structurally deficient to be worth repairing. The volunteer church members, who made up the parish council – which oversaw the operation of the building – began to discuss whether the new structure should be a 'parish' or 'community' centre. After some debate, a vote was held and it was agreed that a hall built and managed by, and for, the broader community, was preferable. The parish priest at the time supported the decision as he felt the running of the old hall was taking parishioners' time away from more church-related activities. A committee was created that included representatives from every geographic area of the community and several important local associations.

The first two priorities of the committee were to determine the possible uses and location of the new building. A former committee member, Patricia MacDonald, pointed out that 'from day one, the priority was not the funding, but the land and the structure: we felt that if we had these two items settled the funding would follow' (personal communication, 2007). The Diocese of Antigonish agreed to donate 5.6 acres of land next to the fire hall. To come up with an appropriate structure, the committee members polled the various associations in the community (i.e., the Seniors' Association, the 4-H Club (rural youth association), the St Andrews Parish Council, the Volunteer Fire Department, etc.). Committee members also travelled to see other community centres in the province asking questions about the advantages and disadvantages of each structure.

Once the land and building design issues were settled, the committee set about raising money. In order to also raise the profile of the new community centre campaign, the committee began with the organization of public dances and concerts. The first big event was an open-air concert in a local farmer's field featuring the Rankin Family (a very popular musical act in north-eastern Nova Scotia at the time). Local carpenters and electricians donated their time in setting up the stage, other community members donated materials and several 'baby barns' (small storage sheds) to be used as places to sell food and goods at the concert. A car dealership in a nearby town was approached and the owners agreed to donate the use of a travel trailer for the band. A second open-air concert was held one month later, during 'St Andrews Come Home Days' (an occasional celebration that draws former residents back to the community) and the proceeds were split between three local associations, including the community centre. One of the more unique fundraising ideas was to produce and sell a calendar featuring the historical buildings of St Andrews. Community members searched their collections for old photographs that were turned into pen and ink sketches by a local artist who donated her time. So many local and area businesses were willing to advertise in the calendar that there wasn't enough space to accommodate them all.

The two most successful fundraising schemes were a lottery and a pledge campaign. The lottery involved selling tickets for cash prizes that would be awarded each week. Over a one-year period, 930 tickets were sold for CAD100 each, which amounted to a profit of CAD60,000 for the building project. Representatives from each part of the community sold tickets to their neighbours and former community members were solicited through the mail. Even though some community members did not want to support what they saw as a form of gambling, most found a way to give cash donations instead of purchasing lottery tickets. The lottery was followed up with a very successful pledge campaign that raised CAD55,000 from the 300 families targeted. If families could not afford a cash pledge, they offered their labour or food for volunteers during the building phase. In total, the committee raised CAD260,000 in cash through all of its fundraising activities.

When the old parish hall was closed for safety reasons, the committee decided to start construction of the new building in the spring of 1993, even though their fundraising targets had not yet been reached. One of the committee members was hired to supervise the construction effort. Thirty-five volunteers, mostly local firemen, cleared the land. Other community members used borrowed equipment – a bulldozer and an excavator – to level the ground and dig the base for the foundation. More than 15 local truckers hauled donated gravel from three private pits, accepting no payment except money for fuel. A local contractor donated the use of a boom truck to help the men installing and welding steel beams for the floor. The underground plumbing was carried out by a local union plumber and two helpers charging nothing for their time. Several local volunteers installed the floor joists and more than 20 community members helped assemble the walls and put in the roof trusses. The roof was shingled in one day, and at one point, volunteers counted 54 people working on the roof at one time. Each day a group of community members cooked food donated by local businesses and households for those working on the building. Whenever speciality work needed to be contracted from outside, volunteers offered their time in order to lower the cost.

By November 1993, approximately two-thirds of the way through the construction phase, the committee began to run out of funds. A decision was made to take a loan from the local credit union for CAD100,000 in order to finish the building. The continued use of community volunteers and local materials kept down costs enough to ensure that the building could be completed with the additional loan. The electrical work was carried out by local volunteers over a one-month period. Community members cut ash trees on their land and delivered them to a local sawmill owner, who cut, planed and dried the wood for the interior lower walls. The firemen volunteered to do all the drywall work and offered, as well, to build new tables for the centre. The head of the local plumbers and pipefitters' union designed the hot water heating system and 22 union members donated their time to install it, even though only two of the union members were actually from St Andrews. Several union bricklayers also donated their time to complete the masonry work. The hardwood floors were laid by 26 community members over a two-day period. Most of the landscaping work was done by 4-H leaders and youth members who donated hundreds of hours to the task. To get an idea of the value of all the volunteer labour and donated materials, an insurance estimate after construction placed the building's value at over CAD800,000. The cash cost to the community was only one third of this amount.

After community members had spent five years designing, fundraising, and constructing, the St Andrews District Community Centre opened its doors in September 1994. The new 7,800 ft^2 centre was a multi-purpose building with something to offer most groups in the community. It included a large room with a kitchen, bar and stage that was used for weddings, funeral teas, dances, concerts and both meetings and fundraising events for a variety of community associations. A second kitchen and meeting room were reserved for senior citizens. Seniors and the 4-H Club were not charged for their use of the building. Funeral teas as well as first communion and confirmation receptions were also held in the building without any charge. The parish was allowed to use the building five times a year at no cost. Five years after the building opened, a mortgage-burning party was held to celebrate the fact that the St Andrews District Community Centre was now debt-free.

The people of St Andrews are justifiably proud of their community centre and how it was built. Patricia MacDonald, one of the original committee members and the first part-time administrator of the community centre, boasted 'this centre was financed by the people and built by the people' (personal communication, 2007). Community members are also proud that they have provided inspiration to other communities. Shortly after the centre was completed, a delegation from Judique – a community situated 100 km to the north-east – came to St Andrews to learn how to plan and build a new community centre. In 1995, the St Andrews District Community Centre won a provincial achievement award.[3]

Just as impressive as the funding and construction of the building is the way in which the community manages and maintains the structure. A volunteer runs the bar and makes arrangements to pick up the bar supplies for dances each Friday. Other volunteers, who help at the dances and events, often do not get home until the early hours of the morning, after everything is put away and that evening's revenues and expenses are balanced. It is not uncommon to see the part-time administrator and a few volunteers decorating the hall late at night for a wedding the following day. Commenting on the learning experience of running a busy centre, one key volunteer, John B. MacIsaac observed, 'it's one thing to build it; it is another thing to run it' (MacDonald, P., personal communication, 2007). Yet the ongoing commitment of volunteers to operate and maintain the community centre has not flagged, demonstrating that the spirit of cooperation that was drawn on so heavily in the building of the community centre has been replenished through the collective pride and sense of accomplishment the community centre has generated.

The Highlander Curling Club

In the early 1990s, when volunteers were busy planning, designing and raising money for the community centre, another community-driven project was conceived, funded and built.

The idea for a curling club[4] in St Andrews came about as the result of a confluence of several factors. The only curling rink in the area, in nearby Antigonish, had burned down several years earlier, and people in that community had not been able to build a replacement. At the same time a group of more than 20 people from St Andrews had organized a social outing to a curling rink in a neighbouring county. The success of this trip inspired several more such trips – often initiated by the fire department – to other curling rinks in the region and the resulting bus rides generated some discussion about what it would be like for St Andrews to have its own curling rink. After one of these trips, a local community member started calling those in charge of curling rinks across the province asking them how they built their rinks and how much these had cost.

Some time later, at a Big Top Dance during 'St. Andrews Come Home Days' at the old parish hall, two community members, John Juurlink and Leroy MacEachern, began talking in earnest about the idea, and together they agreed to call a meeting and invite a few other people whom they thought might be interested. In September 1990, a group of five people met at the fire hall and at the end of the meeting they all agreed to recruit one community member each and start meeting each Sunday night to develop a business plan. By early January, group members began going door-to-door to talk about the idea with their neighbours. At the end of the month, they called a community meeting during which they unveiled their plan.

A series of meetings were held in the neighbouring community of Antigonish, to see if there would be support from curlers there for a rink in St Andrews. The planning group met quietly with members of a number of service clubs and associations before calling a big meeting at the Antigonish high school auditorium. Most people in Antigonish were impressed with the business plan but one man stood up and suggested the rink should be built in Antigonish. A member of the St Andrews delegation replied that this business plan was for a building in St Andrews, but that if for any reason the rink in St Andrews did not get built, his group would be happy to give all their research and the business plan to the people of Antigonish. From that point on, curlers in Antigonish began to see the rink in St Andrews as a viable possibility.

The part of the business plan that impressed everyone was an innovative scheme to raise the capital needed to build the rink. Leroy had seen a prospectus from a golf course in another part of the province for which shares were sold to members to raise funds to build the course. Since the development of a legal prospectus would cost tens of thousands of dollars, and involve specialized legal help, the group in St Andrews designed its own system of preferred and common shares. For every CAD500 unit of investment, an investor member would receive a CAD400 preferred share and a CAD100 common share. The preferred shares would be treated as loans from the investor members to the curling club. If and when the curling rink became a financial success, the preferred shares would be paid back to the bearer at the curling club's discretion with no tax implications, since the investor would be reimbursed with his or her own money.

The scheme was a huge success. Within four months the curling club had raised CAD232,000 in pledges to purchase shares. The planning group simply asked for a percentage of each pledge as the money was needed during the construction of the rink. By the time the rink was built the group had raised CAD302,000. To date, the curling club has paid back two thirds of the preferred shares to members and has still been able to finance improvements to the building. And as one member proudly stated, 'we have done this without grants or loans from the government or financial institutions – all our money was borrowed from our members' (MacEachern, personal communication, 2007).

There was one point, however, at which the share scheme seemed in jeopardy. In the mid-1990s, the very public collapse of a mining scheme in Nova Scotia, through which shares had been sold to the public, triggered a review of all share schemes by the provincial Securities and Exchange Commission. When the Commission discovered that the group in St Andrews had not developed a legal prospectus they summoned the Board of Directors to a meeting in Halifax. Upon realizing that the project was not a business venture but a community-owned curling rink, they agreed to allow the group's original business plan to be treated as a prospectus. They allowed this provided that every investor member was informed, in writing, of the error and was offered his or her money back. Not one member asked to have his or her share redeemed.

The share scheme was not the only risk taken by members of the planning group during the creation of the curling rink. Leroy MacEachern and John Juurlink each invested substantial sums of their own money to purchase used equipment, resulting in huge savings for the curling club. Before construction of the building began, Leroy wrote a personal cheque for CAD5,500 to buy used kitchen equipment from a seafood restaurant that had gone out of business. Around the same time, John Juurlink discovered a used ice plant (machinery that freezes the ice on the floor of the rink) for sale at a hockey arena in another part of the province. On the spot, he paid CAD3,500 for the equipment that arrived in St Andrews on two large trucks the next day. As he recalls, 'from that point on we all knew it was really going to happen – it was...real' (personal communication, 2007).

As with the community centre, the curling rink was largely built by volunteers. The land was cleared and levelled by volunteers with borrowed equipment. The framing, wiring, plumbing, and roofing of the building were carried out by volunteers under the direction of two paid carpenters. Other than the work of these two carpenters, the only other contracted tasks were those of pouring the concrete floor and hooking up the ice plant to the pipes, which had been laid by volunteers. Leroy was amazed at the range of skills of people in St Andrews: 'You can be living next door to someone and have no idea what skills they have' (personal communication, 2007).

The construction phase went so smoothly that the building was completed before the deed for the land had been registered. A well-known local resident, Judge Hugh MacPherson, had donated the land for the curling rink. It had only taken 10 months from the sale of the first shares to the first game of curling in the new building. And it had happened at the same time that many in the community were preoccupied with the planning and fundraising stage of the community centre. As a measure of the success of the project, Pugwash, another village in the region, was inspired by the experience of St Andrews and has since replicated both the design and process of building the curling rink.

The level of cooperation between those involved in the building of the community centre and the curling rink was exceptional. Several community members credit both committees for meeting before any shares in the curling rink were sold and agreeing to support each project. Along with the fire hall, the curling rink and community centre now created the physical 'heart' of the community. Once the curling rink had been built, most of the volunteers who had helped during the construction phase also helped build the community centre. Some community members had developed skills while working on the curling rink which they could apply to their work on the community centre, particularly the coordination, supervision, and feeding of large numbers of volunteers. Because the curling rink went so well, it raised the confidence of the community centre committee members. They realized that the centre could be completed largely by volunteers. Once the curling rink was complete, the new Highlander Curling Club donated 100 chairs and a propane stove to the community centre. In the words of St Andrews resident Ron MacIsaac, referring to the two, almost simultaneous, projects, 'we say around here that one built the other' (personal communication, 2007).

The seniors' apartments

The idea for affordable housing for elderly people in St Andrews first emerged in parish level discussions in the mid-1970s. There was concern that there was nowhere in St Andrews for elderly people to live independently once they could no longer look after themselves in their own homes. A number of efforts were made to convince the various levels of government to build some apartments for seniors in St Andrews, but it never happened. In the early 1990s, the federal and provincial government had budgeted for 10 units in St Andrews but this money ended up being combined with money set aside for 15 units in Antigonish instead, where an enriched, converted seniors' complex of apartments would be attached to an existing nursing home allowing tenants to acquire housekeeping and meals on a fee-for-service basis.

In 2000, the idea of housing for seniors was revived, but this time people in St Andrews began thinking about how they could do it without depending entirely on the government. Joe van de Wiel recalls a conversation he had with John Juurlink at the curling rink one night. John had looked around at the bustling curling rink and said to Joe, 'What do you think – is it time to take on another community project?' Joe thought of the apartments for senior citizens that had been discussed for some time. Ron MacIsaac, one of the committee members for the community centre, remembers Joe approaching him around that time and saying, 'I think we've been going about this the wrong way. If we're going to build seniors' apartments we're going to have to do it like we did the community centre' (personal communication, 2007). When Joe took this idea back to the parish council he was asked if he would head up a seniors' housing committee, which would later become the St Andrews Seniors' Housing Association (SASHA).

The first thing Joe did was to engage leaders from the curling rink and community centre projects. He recalls looking for people who 'weren't afraid to handle something' (personal communication, 2007). Then he made a list of people he felt wouldn't give up easily if things didn't work out initially. The easiest way to find these types of volunteers, he felt, was to look for the busiest people in the community: 'I've learned that if you want to get something done around here you ask a busy person' (personal communication, 2007). One of the people Joe recruited was Leroy MacEachern.

The committee members felt it was critical for the seniors' apartments to be self-financing once they were built. Committee members thought it was unrealistic to expect people to permanently subsidize something that only benefited a relatively small number of citizens. Leroy had a finance background, and after costing out the building of the apartments, he convinced the committee that they would need the government as a partner. Even with donated land, discounted building materials, and volunteer labour, there was no way to reduce the unit cost, and thus the necessary monthly rent, to an affordable amount for a senior citizen. However, Leroy had seen an article in a provincial newspaper about a new government affordable housing programme and he offered to investigate it.

Tom Moore, Regional Director for Housing Services for the Nova Scotia Department of Community Services, recalls that his initial, major concern was the capacity of a small non-profit group to build, manage and sustain a multi-unit housing project. 'And then,' he recalls, 'we got the tour...we saw the curling rink [that had been] funded by selling of shares, [and] the community centre. We were amazed at how well maintained everything was' (personal communication, 2007). Martha Dunnett, Tom's colleague in Halifax, also recalls the trip to St Andrews being the tipping point in the decision to provide a CAD25,000 per unit subsidy for an eight-unit building: 'We gave them conditional approval based on all the other things they had done...You need to know you are dealing with folks who know how to manage and maintain infrastructure. These people had a great history' (personal communication, 2007).

The committee was also successful in leveraging money from the municipal government. Leroy MacEachern remembers local government officials also being concerned with the capacity of the community to manage the apartments on an ongoing basis: 'We [SASHA] told them, OK, we will build the building ourselves and then turn the keys over to you, but on the condition that you run it up to our standards' (personal communication, 2007). Shortly thereafter, the Municipality of Antigonish[5] granted CAD50,000 to the housing project.

Several local businesses also assisted the project. The St Andrews Credit Union agreed to donate land next to its building and provide a line of credit so that construction could begin. A local engineering firm agreed to do the initial drawings that were needed for the application to government, without charge. A cement company came back to the committee with a price that was one-half that of their main competitor. When asked how they could supply the cement so cheaply the company representative replied that an anonymous citizen of St Andrews had given the cement company CAD6,000 to lower the price.

Two local building supply companies agreed to supply materials at very favourable prices. Both companies further agreed to approach their suppliers for special pricing on such items as flooring, windows and trusses. The owner of one of those companies, Steve Smith, gave three reasons for why his firm agreed to support the project 'We did it because many of our customers live in St Andrews and this is a way of giving something back to them; some of our employees also live in St Andrews; and what these people are doing is very important for the survival of rural communities and we want to be involved in that' (personal communication, 2007).

As with both the community centre and curling rink, the construction of the seniors' building depended heavily on volunteers. Nothing was put up for tender. The preparation of the ground, along with the work on the foundations, was done by two local contractors for their cost. Following the example of the curling rink, two skilled carpenters were hired to provide the expertise and to direct the work of volunteers. Seven farmers agreed to give a day of their labour to put in the roof trusses, but they stayed an entire week to finish the roof. At one point, Joe recalls being struck by the sight of a 15-year-old girl and an 83-year-old man working together.

The parish youth group, which had previously been engaged in social activities, was looking for something more community-oriented and asked if its members could help in the project. Even after the success of the curling rink and the community centre, Ron and June MacIsaac were taken aback at the spirit of volunteerism in their community: 'Some of us thought that getting volunteers to work on housing for seniors would be difficult as it is sort of a business in that it pays for itself. But it wasn't that way at all. In fact, people would say to us, "thank you for asking me – if you need more help just call"' (personal communication, 2007).

The seniors' complex was full of tenants one month after construction and the committee is already planning to build another eight units. The provincial government officials involved in the project clearly see it as a success story. Tom Moore has called the St Andrews seniors' building the 'poster child' of such projects in Atlantic Canada. Martha Dunnett said that what most impressed her was the strength of the entire committee rather than just one or two strong members. 'Another thing that struck me,' she said, 'was that they made sure that nobody spent more time than they needed to on site. They didn't burn anybody out. They had the experience from the other projects. If you start to burn out you don't feel ownership any more, and it becomes a job.' (Dunnett, personal communication, 2007)

Community members spanning generations work on the construction of the St Andrews Seniors' Housing Association.

Community-led development in St Andrews

It is clear that the people of St Andrews have a long history of being the 'agents' of their own development. What is less clear are the reasons why this community has been able to create and sustain such a strong level of internal agency. The following section will explore possible explanations in the history, culture, associational life, and leadership of St Andrews.

The St Andrews of today is a product of 200 years of community evolution. The latest generation of community projects have been built on the skills, traditions of cooperativism and motivating memories of previous initiatives. It also seems likely that the resilient, independent and self-reliant nature of the community comes from a history of both risk-taking and cooperation. The community is still largely made up of the descendents of Scottish (and later Dutch) settlers who carved homes and enterprises out of the bush. They risked everything by coming to Nova Scotia, but they also had to cooperate to survive, even though many were in economic competition with each other. The cooperative spirit that the Scots had developed in the New World was reinforced by the influx of Dutch who had spent generations helping each other build communal dykes to hold back the sea.

Both the Scots and the Dutch were able to respond to negative economic shocks with innovation. In the late 1800s and early 1900s the Scots were able to change the way they practised agriculture – the Dutch helped revolutionize the dairy industry several generations later. In the early part of the 20th century, the community's primary producers helped survive the Great Depression through the development of producer, consumer, and financial cooperatives. Today the people of St Andrews continue to innovate in creating new ways to structure and finance non-profit organizations.

Many St Andrews' residents acknowledge the importance of resilience, industriousness, and the value placed on education in the Scottish and Dutch cultures. Even when times were hard, people retained a strong sense of integrity. Long-time resident Mary McCarron recounts an old family saying, 'you can be poor, but you don't have to be dirty,' meaning you should never lose your pride despite your material circumstances (personal communication, 2007).

Mary McCarron and many others also credit their Catholicism, and time spent together at church, for creating a strong feeling of unity in the community. Some feel that this shared faith allowed the Dutch immigrants to integrate so well with the Scots. Loyola MacDonald thinks faith was at least partly behind the principles passed on to her generation by parents: 'We were taught to share with others, to place other people ahead of ourselves. There is a willingness here to "pay it forward" [to repay kindness shown to you by helping others]' (personal communication, 2007).

The pride people show in the accomplishments of their ancestors seems to drive present day community members to succeed. This sense of pride is evident in both the number of amateur historians in the community and the number of immaculately maintained cemeteries. There is an obvious respect for elders in St Andrews, and this may have something to do with the choice of seniors' housing as a community priority. Leroy MacEachern speaks with pride about his late grandfather's role as one of the first members of the board of directors at the St Andrews Credit Union. He also recalls his feelings when he, too, was asked to join the board: '"You don't want to let your ancestors down." I remember saying to myself, "there is no way this place will close while I am on the board"' (personal communication, 2007). One community resident suggested there was a particular feeling of pride that St Andrews could build a curling rink when the much bigger community of Antigonish couldn't seem to get people organized to do it. The pride shown by local residents in the creation of the first cooperative in Atlantic Canada a century ago, or illustrated by the successful fight to keep the school in operation a generation ago, is the same as that demonstrated by current residents in the development of a new share model for financing their curling club or the establishment of the only rural community-owned seniors' apartments in the region.

Associational life

As in many other communities in rural Nova Scotia, there are dozens of vibrant voluntary associations in St Andrews. Associational life in St Andrews, however, is particularly well-coordinated. The homogeneity of religion has allowed the parish council to act as an unofficial umbrella association to reach community consensus and give legitimacy to new initiatives. Both the community centre and seniors' housing initiatives emerged from discussions at the parish council. The other associations in the community tend to have some of the same key members, which led to a tremendous level of cooperation between associations. For example, the parish council helped the volunteer fire department convince the Diocese of Antigonish to donate land for both the fire hall and the community centre.

Box 6.2: St Andrews fire hall

When a local home in St Andrews was destroyed by fire in the 1970s, community members began an intensive lobbying effort to build a local fire hall. When a meeting was called to determine community interest and feasibility, over 60 community members attended and immediately created investigative and finance committees in order to explore the next steps of moving the idea into reality. At the time, the fire hall in the nearby town of Antigonish was responsible for serving a wide geographical area which, due to limited resources and large distances, was cause for concern among residents.

In the 'can do' spirit of St Andrews, the fire hall was incorporated just 13 months later. Unlike other fire departments in the province, it was decided that a volunteer board of directors would be formed. According to long-time fire fighters in St Andrews, this system is a good model in terms of accountability due to a tradition of careful monitoring and fiscal responsibility. Given that board members are *not* fire fighters, volunteers report that the model of decision-making further serves to 'take the heat off the chief' (personal communication, 2007).

Well before acquiring a building permit and beginning construction, members of the investigative committee purchased a used tanker truck for CAD1,960 from a regional oil company, and collectively installed a pumping system. A functional fire fighting system was in place shortly thereafter, despite the fact that there was no permanent 'home' for it. Thirty community members initially volunteered to become fire fighters and training sessions were held every second Wednesday by Alan Young, who had previous experience and a willingness to support the initiative. Volunteers were sent for more intensive training at a fire fighting school in another region of the province as time and finances allowed.

At a time before '911,' the fire hall created an emergency number for community members to dial in case of fire. When this number was dialled, five separate homes in St Andrews received the call and a rotating calling system would continue until a fire crew was assembled.

The issue of access to land for the building was solved when the local parish and Department of Highways collectively agreed to donate land. The question of access to a water supply was resolved when the nearby community centre donated an area of land which was dammed and converted from a swamp into a pond.

With these solutions in place, start-up funds and pledges began to flow in from the community. All initial funds were raised by the community and, using borrowed equipment from a fire department in another small community, activities such as bingo, dances, auctions, raffles and bottle collections were organized as fundraisers by dozens of dedicated volunteers. When enough start-up funds were finally in place, construction of the building that stands today was under way.

Three decades later, St Andrews has developed an innovative means of securing sustainable resources for the fire hall. While its system still relies on volunteer fire fighters and board members, the community now funds the provision of fire fighting services through a property taxation system. A small municipal grant of CAD5,000 per year (compared with a structure now valued at an estimated CAD750,000) remains the only source of external funding for this community-driven and managed service.

Later, the fire department was also given access to a pond by the community centre, for filling the tanker truck. As has been noted, the firemen played key roles in the construction of both the curling rink and the community centre.

The fire department also provides an example of the way in which local associations have been organized to minimize conflicts of interest and maximize efficiency. When the fire department was established, volunteers were selected for two separate functions. A board of directors was selected and charged with raising money for construction of the fire hall, and the purchase of equipment, and providing oversight on the department's finances. The firemen who were recruited were free to focus their time and attention on training, maintaining equipment, and fire fighting.

The cooperation between the parish council and the fire department illustrates the bridging that takes place informally between one association and another. The fact that one association can overlap another, with members working towards mutual goals, is part of what gives this small community its strength of purpose.

Leadership

St Andrews has a legacy of progressive community leaders. Until the middle of the 20th century, most of these people were priests. Today, the community has a cadre of informal leaders from many different backgrounds: some are farmers, others have businesses in the community, while still others are professionals working outside the community. Kevin Bekkers, the local representative of the Nova Scotia Department of Agriculture, declared, 'the thing about St Andrews is the number of leaders they have. They have people who not only talk about things; they do them' (personal communication, 2007). Steve Smith agrees: 'they have some real movers and shakers, and real community-minded people' (personal communication, 2007).

One of those leaders, Leroy MacEachern, described four important characteristics of leaders in the recent community-driven projects in St Andrews. First, he says, 'leaders are more involved than anyone else. This means they are there earlier than everyone else and they are there at the end of the day after everyone leaves.' And, he adds, 'they put in their own money before anyone else.' Second, leaders in St Andrews have learned how to generate a feeling of ownership among the volunteers involved in the various projects:

> You find whatever ways you can to get other people involved in decision-making. I remember saying, 'Why don't you take a look at those samples and figure out what colour of siding we need?'...When they drive up to that rink ten years later, they will tell people, 'I picked out that siding' – that's what I mean by ownership. (personal communication, 2007)

Third, Leroy suggests that local leaders are inclusive, since 'they are good at identifying people's skills and are able to find a place for everyone who wants to help. They recognize that everyone wants to make a positive contribution to the community. Some people may not think they can do something, but it is up to the person organizing the work to make sure that they can...to train them' (personal communication, 2007). Finally, he says that local leaders have been good at knowing when to mobilize the community, and points out that timing is everything. As well, he observes that a plan is needed before leaders go out to the community to enlist support.

His strong, yet self-effacing, commitment to his community illustrates a salient point. Good leadership demonstrates that a leader can offer direction while simultaneously standing back to invite direction from others, without ever losing sight of the communal goal. In this way, leaders like Leroy MacEachern or Joe van de Wiel can inspire people so that initiative can come from the community as a whole.

The ability to sustain internal agency

What is so impressive about internal agency in St Andrews is that the community has been able to sustain such a high level of it for such a long period of time. Several community members volunteered their thoughts on why this was possible. A newcomer to the community, Paul MacLean, suggested that the various community associations are not insular but reach out to, and draw in, new members. He also lauds the way in which each association holds 'volunteer appreciation' events to recognize the dedication and work of their members. Other residents felt that the community had developed mechanisms to pass on the 'community spirit' from one generation to the next. The most important of these mechanisms was seen to be the role-modelling of parents. Some people also saw community sporting events as instrumental. Many farming families pointed to the local 4-H Association as an important vehicle for developing the next generation of community leaders. In addition, it was pointed out by many that St Andrews is also able to draw on its former residents, particularly for raising funds. A community newsletter called *The Causerie*, and reunions such as 'Come Home Days,' were thought to contribute to the connections between former residents and the community of St Andrews.

Another reason for the scale and scope of initiatives undertaken by this community is that many of the livelihood activities developed by the residents of St Andrews have generated the skills and equipment necessary for building and maintaining community infrastructure. A former St Andrews Consolidated School principal exclaimed that whenever any community improvements needed to be made 'it seemed like everyone in that community owns a bulldozer' (personal communication, 2007).

Yet the overriding reason that internal agency has been sustained over time is that community members are determined to preserve their ability to drive their own development. According to Joe van de Wiel, 'What really drives people around here is a common faith in doing good for others' (personal communication, 2007). This non-traditional concept of faith has been attributed as a source of unity and sense of pride. Joe recounts his reaction to a priest who once referred to St Andrews as a highly self-interested community: 'That really hurt me ... and I tried to do something about it' (personal communication, 2007).

People in St Andrews see a correlation between the level of internal agency and their quality of life, and thus make it a priority to engage in reciprocal and volunteer activities that build both social capital and community spirit. As Joe MacDonald declared in *St Andrews Then and Now*, 'One of the greatest assets of the community of St Andrews is an apparently unlimited supply of volunteers, for whatever worthy cause' (MacDonald, J., 2000, p. 109).

As Leroy MacEachern puts it, 'We are really lucky in St Andrews that when people decide to take on a project other people are ready to support them' (personal communication, 2007). Part of the reason for this is that St Andrews is not factionalized. Owen McCarron, who represents St Andrews on the municipal county council, points out 'People here don't try to tear down someone who is successful. They just do not get jealous of success. And, if anyone needs assistance, people will drop whatever they are doing to help' (personal communication, 2007). John Juurlink, one of the informal leaders behind the curling rink, suggests that part of the spirit of community in St Andrews is the 'spirit of compromise.' This may explain why the decision to replace the parish hall with a 'community' centre did not divide St Andrews the way it might have done other communities in northern Nova Scotia.

Striking the right balance between internal and external agency

Running through the story of St Andrews are the undercurrents of both community and government in the community development process. What is different from the early days in the development of St Andrews is that today there are certain entitlements that all residents in north-east Nova Scotia can expect from the state by virtue of their citizenship and in exchange for their taxes, such as health care, public education for their children, and the maintenance of roads. In many communities, the evolution of governments into service providers has led to the atrophying of individual or associational initiative for even simple improvements in community life. Leroy MacEachern points to the 1970s as the time when 'society's expectations were that the government should be doing everything in communities' (personal communication, 2007). There were even small grants given to pay people to undertake activities that had, until that time, always been done by volunteers.

The citizens of St Andrews have found a way to maintain their role as initiators of community development activities. Part of the challenge in claiming this space is being able to differentiate between when support from the state is helpful and when it undermines or overwhelms community initiative. For example, the people of St Andrews did not see a role for government in building either their community centre or the curling rink. They did, however, see a role and a responsibility for government in reducing the cost of building the seniors' apartments, so elderly people on fixed pensions could afford the monthly rent. The people of St Andrews do not see this government funding as a subsidy; rather, they see it as a public investment, a way for a small amount of public funds to make possible a larger community and societal impact. Similarly, the fire hall was, initially, built and equipped with community money. But rather than have to keep fundraising for a service that most residents now see as an entitlement, community members agreed to a levy on property taxes to fund the fire department on an ongoing basis. In this case, the community agreed to finance a community association as though it were a public institution. The people of St Andrews have become pioneers once again, but this time, instead of creating homesteads and farms, they are experimenting with new types of relationships between the community and the state.

Conclusion

Despite a successful history, the citizens of St Andrews face several important challenges as they move forward. The majority of the community's young people now migrate to the province's largest city and to other parts of Canada for employment after they graduate from secondary school, much as they did in the late 19th and early 20th centuries. Those who remain have begun to place as much importance on virtual communities as the one in which they live; they could become less committed to their real community in the future. Many members of St Andrews' voluntary associations are 'greying,' and a number of the current generation of community leaders are at, or near, retirement age. Due to a number of factors, several farmers may not encourage their children to continue in the business.[6] As well, St Andrews is becoming a 'bedroom community,' meaning that people live there, but work elsewhere.

While these challenges are formidable, St Andrews is in an enviable position compared to most rural communities in the region. All of the challenges mentioned above are also being faced by other communities. But unlike most rural communities in Nova Scotia, St Andrews is now attracting new residents. These newcomers report they are drawn by the quality of life in the community and its close proximity to Antigonish, which has schools, shopping facilities, a University, a hospital and a golf course. In addition, many of the community's sons and daughters who have moved away to find work indicate that they would like to return and raise their families in St Andrews. And technology is starting to make it possible for people to be based in a small, rural community and 'telecommute' to work in urban areas thousands of miles and several time zones away. Optimistic about the future, local resident Owen McCarron sums it up: 'As one type of community identity fades, another flourishes. The cornerstones of the community that we have built over the years will help us weather any changes' (personal communication, 2007). While McCarron is referring mainly to the physical infrastructure built by the community, one can't help thinking that it is the social infrastructure that is the real foundation upon which this community has been built and will continue to thrive. Perhaps that is why the actual cornerstone embedded in the wall of the community centre does not bear the name of a local, provincial or federal politician, but instead bears the simple, yet profound, motto: 'Community Spirit.'

Endnotes

1. Decades before universal Medicare was introduced in Canada, the St Andrew's Co-op was one of a number of organizations (several mining organizations in Cape Breton and Pictou county were others) to pioneer an early medical insurance scheme, whereby members would make regular contributions to a fund that could be drawn upon in medical emergencies
2. In 1960, a school credit union was established to introduce the credit union concept to young people. In 1987, the St Andrews Credit Union amalgamated with the Bergengren Credit Union in Antigonish, leading to the building of a new full-service branch in St Andrews in 1992.
3. Bluenose Achievement Award from the Recreation Association of Nova Scotia.
4. Highly popular in St Andrews, as in many parts of Canada, curling is played by two teams of four players on an indoor sheet of carefully maintained ice. Curling teams take turns sliding heavy, polished granite stones along the ice towards a target known as the *house*. The complex nature of stone placement and shot selection has led some to refer to curling as 'chess on ice'.
5. St Andrews is part of the Municipality (or County) of Antigonish, one of 77 local governments in the province. The municipal government is headed by a Warden (similar to a Mayor) and nine councillors. St Andrews is represented on the council by the councillor for District 6, who also represents the adjacent community of Lower South River. The Municipality of Antigonish provides a range of local government services such as planning, water and sewage, solid waste disposal and maintenance of some roads. Monies to pay for these services are raised through the assessment of property taxes
6. High real estate values of land and high value of milk quota, combined with the potential challenges to the supply management system through trade agreements, make selling their farms and quota a more attractive option than staying in business.

References

Boyd, A. (1949) *The history of the co-operative movement in St Andrews, N.S.* Unpublished master's thesis, St Francis Xavier University, Antigonish, Nova Scotia, Canada.

MacDonald, J. (2000) *St Andrews: Then and now*, Casket Printing and Publishing, Antigonish, Nova Scotia, Canada.

Service Nova Scotia (n.d.) *Municipal facts, figures, and history – The history of municipal government in Nova Scotia*. Available from: http://www.gov.ns.ca/snsmr/muns/info/history/originHIST1.asp [Accessed 30 August 2007]

Authors' note

I first heard about the community of St Andrews on an early morning regional radio broadcast in which a regular contributor from our area spoke of this amazing local community that had built their community centre and curling rink without any government help. Several months later my wife and I had a chance to try curling at a 'learn to curl' evening organized by her employer. At that event I met Leroy MacEachern who filled me in on the history of the curling rink. A few months, and several visits to St Andrews later, Alison Mathie, Kate Fiander and I were convinced that we had found a story of community-driven development not more than 10 km from the Coady International Institute.

In June 2007 Kate Fiander sent copies of the draft case to twenty five citizens of St Andrews who had been interviewed the previous month as part of the research for the case. Most of the feedback we received was very positive but one comment stood out for us. Several people commented that the case played up the role of only a couple of key leaders, in spite of the fact that in St Andrews there were many leaders working behind the scenes. However, when we tried to interview a person who several people put forward as a behind-the-scenes leader, she told us she didn't want to be interviewed (in keeping, obviously, with her *modus operandi*).

Kate and I would like to thank the people of St Andrews, former residents and others who have supported or worked with the community on its various projects, including officials with the provincial government, for giving so generously of their time. This included finding and providing archive material, being interviewed and agreeing to read the draft case to check for accuracy. In particular we would like to thank (in alphabetical order): Kevin Bekkers, Fr Vern Boutlier, Archie Boyd, Mary (Tommy) Chisholm, Benny Ten Brinke, Fraser Dunn, Martha Dunnett, Marie Feltmate, Marianne Forbes, John Juurlink, Joe MacDonald, Loyola MacDonald, Patricia MacDonald, Alistair MacDonald, Leroy MacEachern, June MacIsaac, Ron MacIsaac, Paul MacLean, Mary McCarron, Owen McCarron, Tom Moore, Cathy Sears, Steve Smith, Mary van den Heuvel, and Joe van de Wiel. We hope that this case does justice to the efforts of more than eight generations of St Andrews residents who have built their community from the ground up.

Gordon Cunningham

CHAPTER 7

The hardware and software of community development: migrant infrastructure projects in rural Morocco

Natasha Iskander and Nadia Bentaleb-Maes

Abstract

This case study highlights villages in the Moroccan Souss, long neglected by government, and how people there collaborated with émigrés returning from France to help improve livelihoods in their villages of origin. The need for basic infrastructure to power irrigation prompted innovation in both the technical aspects of electricity generation and distribution (the hardware) as well as in the way communities could organize to maintain and distribute services (the software), adapting traditional forms of organizing. The case extends the idea of community beyond the boundaries of residence to include émigrés still identifying with their place of origin.

Introduction

The Moroccan Souss, a narrow valley pinched between two chains of Morocco's Atlas Mountains, had suffered neglect in a policy framework dating back to France's control over Morocco before World War II that favoured urban Morocco over the subsistence agriculture in the kingdom's heartlands. While the state had encouraged large-scale horticulture enterprise in the valley for the export of vegetables to Europe, investment in these operations stood in stark contrast to the lack of attention to the surrounding mountainous areas of the Souss. Compounded by geographical isolation and the slow strangulation of a drought that was becoming endemic from the mid-1970s, the Souss' predicament produced some of the worst human development indicators in the Arab world. In response to the dismal economic prospects of the area, out-migration became the structural feature of the local economy. Soussis, as the locals are called, emigrated to Morocco's burgeoning cities as well as to Europe's industrial areas in large numbers, turning villages throughout the valley into crumbling adobe shells.

In recent years, the same emigration that was once viewed as proof of the region's economic distress began to reverse the Souss' decline. Migrants from the region, and international migrants in particular, began to quietly but profoundly transform the region's political and economic landscape. In concert with their communities of origin, they elaborated a vision of economic development in the Souss that began with the provision of basic infrastructure, and experimented with organizational and technological models to make that vision a reality. More significantly, they brought the state in as a full partner, not just into the process of equipping villages in the region with infrastructure, but also into the process of imagining the possibilities for economic change that new services allow. Soussi migrants and their communities did more than compel the state to abandon its habit of chronic neglect and commit long overdue resources to the valley. They drew the state into community-generated processes of innovation.

The results of the ongoing exchange that Soussi communities established with the state have been dramatic, for the Souss region and beyond. The Moroccan government has connected villages to basic infrastructure and services at rates that would have been inconceivable even as recently as the mid-1990s. Tens of thousands of households that until a few years ago depended on candles and firewood now enjoy reliable access to electricity, and the hum of electric-powered irrigation pumps can be heard in the early mornings as orchards and fields – some of them on land newly reclaimed from drought – are irrigated. Schools for boys and girls have been established at unprecedented rates, and weekly markets have sprung up at the intersections of roads that were just dirt pathways until 1998, when hundreds of kilometres of fresh pavement were rolled out to link isolated villages to regional centres.

The catalyst behind the transformation of the mountainous areas of the Souss was a non-governmental organization called Migrations et Développement. Established in the mid-1980s by Soussis who had emigrated to France, the organization began by providing independent rural electricity networks to hamlets dotted throughout the upland valley slopes. This case study follows their lead and shows how their community-generated solutions to electricity provision ultimately led to major reforms in the Moroccan government's strategy for rural electricity supply. The process on which the organization relied to devise new approaches to rural electricity provision, and to inform government infrastructure policy, was repeated over and over again in other areas of infrastructure provision, from roads to schools. This process hinged on two key features. First, Migrations et Développement created an institutional structure for ongoing and participatory discussions that included emigrants, their communities, a handful of European infrastructure experts, and eventually, the Moroccan state. It blended the ideas of all of these actors to create an innovative solution for infrastructure, reshaping the way that communities and the state provided services like water, roads, and schools. Second, Migrations et Développement used the provision of infrastructure 'hardware' – the physical structures and buildings that make up infrastructure – to cultivate the 'software' of economic development, enhancing 'soft' assets such as social deliberation, planning skills, and management capabilities.

On a conceptual level, the participatory process Migrations et Développement fostered in the Soussi villages calls into question definitions of 'community' that rest on representations of communities as self-contained entities with more or less exclusive membership. The ongoing discussions the migrant organization launched between Soussi emigrants, villagers in their communities of origin, French allies, and eventually the state, criss-crossed the boundary that defined what was 'inside' the community and what was 'outside' with such frequency that the boundary was ultimately erased. The deliberations between Soussi emigrants and their communities of origin blurred the distinction between them, and reinforced migrants' sense of belonging in their communities even as they anchored them more firmly in networks far beyond the Souss valley. Similarly, the repeated exchanges that would occur between the state and rural communities were so dense that they bridged the chasm that had been hewn by decades of policy neglect and mutual suspicion. As the conversations between the various actors began to dissolve the distinctions between them, the importance of the deliberative process in generating innovative solutions to development challenges became clear. It revealed that who contributed an idea was less important than how it was contributed. What mattered was the participatory process through which that idea was appropriated, amended, and reinvented as a creative intervention for infrastructure provision and, ultimately, for economic transformation.

Organizing for infrastructure

Migrations et Développement grew out of a struggle over lay-offs and severance packages in a valley much further north, in a small town in the shadow of the French Alps called Argentière-la-Bessée. One of France's largest aluminium processing companies, Péchiney, had a plant in the town, and the Soussi emigrants who founded the association had been labourers there. Like most of French heavy industry, Péchiney had been suffering a slow but inexorable decline since the oil shocks of 1974. To cope with its economic crisis, the company resorted to repeated waves of downsizing in the early 1980s. Péchiney's workforce, immigrants and non-immigrants alike, fought the lay-offs tooth and nail with the help of the CFDT (*Confédération Française Démocratique du Travail*), the labour union that had been representing them. Shedding workers proved an insufficient measure to salvage Péchiney, however and, in 1984, 16 of the company's plants were slated for closure, with the Argentière plant topping the list. To cushion the massive lay-offs this entailed, and to rescue Argentière from economic disaster, Péchiney extended start-up funds to former employees so that they could establish small firms in the region (Daoud, 1997).

Fifty-four North African immigrants, with several dozen Soussis among them, decided to return to their countries of origin rather than try to rebuild their lives in Argentière. When the immigrants approached Péchiney for the funds to start small businesses in their communities of origin, the company refused, insisting that the funds were tagged for the development of the Argentière valley. Countering that they had equal rights to the aid since the award was, in fact, a form of severance pay, the immigrants, supported by the CFDT, took the company to court, and after a protracted legal battle, Péchiney was forced to disburse the same funds to the immigrant plaintiffs as it had to the rest of its workforce. The Soussi immigrants began planning for their return (Daoud, 1997).

The plans the migrants had were modest: they wanted to make marginal agricultural improvements to family land holdings, open grocery stores and gas stations, and set up agro-processing firms that produced for local markets. Although small in scale, the migrants' projects were impossible. Most of the migrants would be returning to hamlets without electricity, running water, passable roads, or telephone lines. The infrastructure necessary to support their plans simply did not exist in their villages.

In order to address these infrastructure gaps, in 1986, the returning Soussi migrants, already organized because of their legal battle with Péchiney, formed an association under French law called *Retour et Développement* – Return and Development – which they would later rename, in 1998, Migrations et Développement. The migrants decided to pool a portion of the start-up funds they received from Péchiney to fund small-scale infrastructure projects. The members of the group then began to lobby their communities of origin to join them in their efforts. Lahoussain Jamal, the group's founder, remembers his soapbox speeches to his family and neighbours: 'You have to get involved; the state won't do anything for you. Let's take the initiative ourselves. With your participation and ours, we can breathe life back into our village' (Daoud, 1997: 20).

Imgoun, a small village hugging the slope where the Souss Valley rises to meet the Atlas Mountains, and Lahoussain Jamal's birthplace, was chosen as the group's first project site. In early 1985, Migrations et Développement conducted an informal assessment of village needs. Members of the organization asked villagers about the problems they faced and found that they were many, each one compounding the last: overgrazing and deforestation leading to desertification, retaining walls for cultivated terraces in such serious disrepair that the steppes were being washed away in the rains, wells briny and dry from overuse and neglect. The migrants' questions also revealed that the villagers' top priority was getting electricity.

Electric power would enable them to run motorized water pumps that could draw up water for their parched agricultural plots from far deeper in the ground than a standard well would allow. Motorized water pumps had also come to represent the divide between the rich and the poor in the village: only the wealthiest residents, with those households receiving remittances from emigrants newly counted among them, could afford the cost of gasoline to run them. The fuel was made expensive by the long haul up to the village on dirt roads only passable during some seasons of the year. Emigrants concurred with residents on the choice of electricity as the first infrastructure priority. Without it, none of their modest business plans would be feasible.

Imgoun's lack of electricity was typical of the vast majority of villages in Morocco's countryside. In the 1980s, over 60 per cent of Morocco's population was rural, and no more than a fraction of villages had access to electric power. While data for the 1980s are sketchy at best, rural electrification rates were estimated at anywhere between 4 and 18 per cent. The data in the 1990s are slightly more reliable, but they still show that Morocco's rural electrification rates, hovering at between 21 and 25 per cent, lagged far behind those for similar income countries in the region (ONE, 1999; World Bank; 1990). By 1990, Algeria had achieved 70 per cent rural electricity coverage and Tunisia was close behind with 60 per cent (World Bank, 1990). The Moroccan government explained away its poor performance in this area by claiming insufficient revenue and bureaucratic obstacles. In the early 1980s, the Moroccan central government, pressured mainly by the World Bank, embarked on a rural electrification programme, but by all accounts, it was a half-hearted effort with little impact: between 1982 and 1996, the state hooked up a mere 70 villages to electricity per year on average (ONE, 1999). At that rate, it would have taken Morocco over 300 years to provide electricity to its 34,000 villages. As the former director of the National Office of Electricity, Dress Benhima admitted: 'between 1960 and 1990, [rural electrification] was not a priority' (Daoud, 1997: 40). If the residents of Imgoun and the emigrants from the village wanted electricity, they would have to get it on their own.

Connecting electricity and water

For help with their electricity project, the migrants of Migrations et Développement contacted the *Agence Française pour la Maitrise de l'Energie* (AFME)[1] in 1986 about the possibility of setting up a solar-powered electricity network. The migrants were able to get access to the French government for energy management because the leadership had ties to the CFDT, the union that had supported the migrants in their struggle against Péchiney. The man who had been president of the union during the migrants' legal conflict with the aluminium company, Michel Roland, had since been named president of the AFME.

The migrants' project piqued the interest of the AFME because the agency had already been commissioned by the Moroccan National Office of Electricity to study the provision of decentralized solar power to rural areas. For the AFME, Imgoun represented a potential site for a pilot project, and in the agency Migrations et Développement found an experienced partner to help it set up an independent electricity network.

To investigate the feasibility of a solar project in Imgoun, Migrations et Développement conducted an extensive needs assessment of energy usage in the village that year, in consultation with local authorities. In the intimate setting of the village of slightly over a thousand inhabitants, the survey, though thorough, was carried out in a very informal manner. The people conducting the survey were mostly emigrants from the village, and they went house to house, chatting with their friends and kinfolk about how they used energy. The needs assessment evolved into a series of open-ended discussions with people about what they viewed as their priorities for energy usage, about what family resources they devoted to securing the energy they needed, and about how they would imagine themselves using energy if it were readily and cheaply available. Through these conversations, villagers articulated their patterns of energy usage, many of them implicit in practice, and identified the ways that energy consumption was tied to other household and agricultural practices.

The study yielded two unexpected findings. First, motorized water pumps did not represent the village's primary energy consumption by any stretch. Instead, to the migrants' and residents' surprise, the study found that the village's largest energy consumption was at the household level, in the form of butane gas, candles, and batteries for lighting and audiovisual use, and of wood used for cooking. In fact, wood provided an average of 80 per cent of the energy used in households, with about a quarter of the wood used scavenged from the already denuded slopes surrounding the village. Moreover, the poorest 20 per cent of the village population relied much more heavily on found wood, scavenging more than half of the wood they used. The second unanticipated finding was that households were spending an average of 30 per cent of their income on energy, an amount well above the villagers' own estimates (Missaoui, 1996).

These two findings made it clear that energy could shape villagers' access to water, but not through water pumps that dredged it up through rapidly falling underground sources, as the villagers had thought. Rather, a reliable supply of energy could stop the over-harvesting of wood that was leading to desertification in the region. However, in order for this virtuous relationship between electricity and the protection of water supplies to hold firm, all villagers had to have access to electricity, regardless of the ability to pay. If excluded from the network, the poor would continue to scavenge wood, and even as the rich enjoyed a cheaper source of power to feed the pumps, they would still need to reach subterranean water pools, the level of which would continue to fall. The challenge, then, for Migrations et Développement, was two-fold: to create a network that was affordable, reliable, and safe; and to ensure that all villagers could tap into it, irrespective of income.

Getting power

In order to construct an electricity network that met these two requirements, the organization would have to link technological expertise about electricity networks together with local knowledge in an on-going way. The rich discussions and participatory processes that emerged during the needs assessment that Migrations et Développement conducted in collaboration with the AFME, seemed, to the organization's members, essential to achieve that. Migrations et Développement began creating a structure to support the on-going exchange of ideas at the village level and, in 1988, established a village association called the Anour Association to house community deliberation about the proposed electricity network.

The village association was modelled on the *jema'a*[2] (a traditional council of elders) that had for centuries governed the management of natural resources in the villages of the Souss. Often celebrated as an indigenous form of proto-democracy, the *jema'a* elected its leader each year and most decisions were made by consensus (Mernissi, 1997; Haas, 2003). The *jema'a*'s functions were varied, including determining each household's contribution, in resources or in labour, to the maintenance of community infrastructure, like terraces and irrigation canals, settling family disputes between families, and negotiating with central government authorities on behalf of the village. While participatory in its process, the *jema'a* was exclusive in its membership. With seats on the *jema'a* restricted to male members of land or water-owning clans, the council was dominated by the wealthier families in the village. Families that were newly wealthy, thanks to emigrant members abroad or in Morocco's coastal cities, were generally excluded from the *jema'a*. They began to chafe at the authority of the traditional council, claiming that it favoured traditional notables over the rest of the village. These tensions, combined with changes in agricultural and husbandry practices, including the spread of water pumps had, by the 1980s, undercut the authority of the *jema'at* in the region so significantly that, in many villages, the once vibrant deliberative institutions had become cultural relics.

The migrants of Migrations et Développement revived Imgoun's *jema'a* by reinventing it. Their village association reproduced the *jema'a*'s participatory decision-making processes and its practice of reaching decisions by consensus. But in a radical departure from tradition, membership in the village association was extended to all villagers, regardless of wealth, land ownership, social status, age, or (to a lesser extent) gender. Migrants and locals were invited to participate in meetings, and in decision-making, and the association set its meeting schedule around migrants' yearly return so that their participation would be more than symbolic. As Migrations et Développement would later explain in one of its programme documents: 'the association enables everyone to get involved in the development of the village, and reduces their hierarchical inequalities between rich and poor, between young and old' (Migrations et Développement, 1996). Precisely because the village association was inclusive and open to all villagers and migrants, the village elders who had sat on the traditional council vehemently resisted the new community organization at first. They felt that it undercut their authority in the village, and was less a reinvention of the *jema'a* than a political manoeuvre on the part of migrant upstarts to marginalize the village notables and the wealthy families that they represented. Over time, the elders were swayed by the migrants' persistent and solicitous invitations to join the association, and more importantly, by

the migrants' ability to secure technical assistance from French electrical engineers.

In the case of women, although they were explicitly encouraged to take part in the village association meetings, gender norms in the village made them reluctant to participate until the village association was established as a vital and inclusive institution in the village. While women were rarely seen at the association's early meetings, their presence became progressively more important over time.

With the organizational groundwork in place in the form of the village association, Imgoun and Migrations et Développement still had to overcome the technological hurdles involved in setting up a durable, self-standing network. Migrations et Développement turned once again to French electricity providers. Through the AFME, Migrations et Développement forged a relationship with *Electricité de France* (EDF) with a non-profit spin-off set up by the French power company's employees, called Codev (later renamed *Electriciens Sans Frontières*). Intrigued by challenging topography and the technological puzzle it created, Codev sent 37 volunteers, armed with blueprints and a clear set of principles for electricity provision, to help Imgoun set up its electricity network (Daoud, 1997).

Once the Codev electricians committed to the project, they joined the conversations about electricity use that had been initiated with the needs assessment and sustained in the village association meetings. Consultation between the Codev, Migrations et Développement and the Anour Association convinced the village to abandon its plans for a solar-powered network, and opt instead for a generator-supplied network that could provide an electrical current better suited to the household uses that represented – and would continue to represent – the lion's share of electricity consumption in Imgoun. The deliberation over the best technological solution for the village continued even as the network was being constructed. Villagers and migrants worked side by side with the volunteer EDF electricians to build the electricity system, and when they ran into obstacles erecting the network, they problem-solved together. Finding it impossible, for example, to haul the ten-metre high concrete columns, mandated by French and Moroccan safety standards, up to the isolated village on rough dirt roads, the villagers and electricians decided instead to make the poles for their network out of stripped eucalyptus trunks, which were available locally and were easier to transport. This sort of ongoing and collaborative improvisation ultimately produced a network that differed significantly both from the blueprints that the electricians had brought with them and from the standards set by Moroccan government, but that was, as a result, well-suited to the local needs and local environment. Local materials, including recycled hardware, were used; the network capacity was scaled down to local usage requirements; and maintenance needs were simplified so that the villagers could manage the network on their own.

In addition to the exchange between the French electricians and the Imgouni villagers and migrants, the construction of the network rested on the huge organizational effort that the village association undertook to fund and manage the new electricity system. The village association collected financial contributions for the project on an income-based sliding scale firmly rooted in the principle that all should contribute what they could, but that no one would be excluded if he or she did not have the wherewithal to contribute. Wealthy villagers and emigrants living in France were asked to contribute 10,000 Moroccan Dirhams (MAD), or about US$1,330 (approximate equivalent at 3 March 2008), undocumented emigrants were asked to give 5,000 MAD (approximately 665 USD), and villagers only 1,000 MAD, with the poorest households exempt from contribution. The association also organized a rotation system for the accommodation of the French electricians in the village, with some households lodging the guests and other households taking turns feeding them. Once the network was up and running, the association took charge of maintaining the network and collecting fees based on the income-sensitive payment schedule it had designed. The association charged a slight premium over and above the cost of electricity production and distribution: the additional 'tax' was earmarked for future development projects that the community would decide upon through deliberations in the association. In carrying out these organizational functions, the association enacted the traditional fiscal and managerial functions of the *jema'a* in the community, but through an approach that was more inclusive and equitable than the mandates of the elders' council.

The discussions in the village association about what projects to take on next were equally inclusive. The wide-ranging deliberations at meetings and the multiple perspectives that were thrown into the conversations led to new insights about the economic possibilities that electricity could offer the village, and ultimately to a more creative take on the relationship between infrastructure and development. Villagers began to brainstorm about the possibility of using electricity for new water-saving irrigation techniques in 1989, which in turn allowed for the prospect of larger scale cultivation of high-value crops like saffron. The expanded cultivation of high-end crops gave rise to discussions in the early 1990s about the creation of a co-op for the export of saffron and other products to Europe, which in turn began deliberations about the need to provide the women who would be harvesting and packaging the crops with basic literacy, and led to plans in 1996 for an adult education centre for women. As further elaborated in Box 7.1, the electricity network in Imgoun, a piece of infrastructure 'hardware,' had become a catalyst for the social deliberation, the management skills, and the ambitious creativity that constitute the necessary 'software' for development.

The electricity network and the development dynamic that it set in motion quickly spread beyond Imgoun. An elder from a village not far from Imgoun recalled how this happened: 'Imgoun is across the way, just there. We saw that they had electricity. At night, it was all lit up. We went to Migrations et Développement and told them to come and bring us electricity too' (personal communication, 2004). By 1996, seven short years after the first electricity network was functional, Migrations et Développement had worked with over 70 villages to set up electricity networks and had a waiting list twice that number. Cognizant of just how critical the participatory processes of deliberation and innovation had been to the success of their first electricity project, Migrations et Développement stipulated that any village it assisted with electricity – and later helped with other infrastructure projects – create a village association as a structure to support creative discussions, and that it offer access to the service installed to all villagers, regardless of ability to pay. Additionally, Migrations et Développement asked that village associations join a federation that the migrant organization had spearheaded. By the mid-1990s, there were close to 200 federated village associations in the Souss region, many of them self-taxing, and all of them carrying out development projects ranging from electricity provision to the building of potable water networks to the creation of informal schools.

Bringing the state by the hand

The demands on Migrations et Développement from Soussi villages requesting help with infrastructure projects quickly outstripped the organization's capacity. By the early 1990s, Migrations et Développement had shifted its

Returning migrants discuss rural development options with Imgoun village elders.

perspective on community-sponsored infrastructure projects from a stand that advocated village self-help – and self-funded – infrastructure initiatives to one that considered that the state had an irreplaceable role to play in infrastructure provision. Lahoussain Jamal, director of the organization at the time, explained the revised position of Migrations et Développement: 'we want to take the state by the hand and bring it here. We don't have the resources the state does; we can never accomplish what the state can. What we want is for the state to do the work of the state *here*' (personal communication, 2004).

A few short years after Migrations et Développement had begun its work, it was able to achieve that objective by drawing the state into the participatory processes of deliberation and innovation that it had launched in communities throughout the Souss. The rudimentary electricity networks the organization erected would soon transform the Moroccan government's approach to rural electricity provision and enable the state to raise its rural electricity coverage rates dramatically.

Migrations et Développement made the government aware of rural electricity initiatives from the very beginning by formally registering their village associations with the state as non-governmental organizations, but soon Migrations et Développement went further and began to share insights about the best way to set up a network with government agencies. This exchange initially occurred through AFME employees who acted as intermediaries: the same French agency that was first to help Migrations et Développement with Imgoun's electricity network had been retained by the Moroccan government since the early 1980s. Several of its consultants volunteered with Migrations et Développement even as they assisted the Moroccan government in designing a pilot programme in rural electricity provision that it would launch in 1987. The consultants brought the knowledge they had gleaned from Imgoun about electricity usage patterns and network design to the government's pilot programme, but they also brought Moroccan state bureaucrats to the village

---

Box 7.1: The Anour Association, Imgoun: Mobilizing Assets and Driving Development

The Anour Association has shown the way forward for other villages in the area as a mechanism for mobilizing village-based assets for community-wide benefit; establishing linkages with external institutions to ensure sustainability; and maintaining control over development initiatives. Including migrants in its membership, it recognizes that loyalty to family and place endures the separation in time and space that occurs when people emigrate.

Mobilizing and redistributing assets

The Anour Association has built the capacity to mobilize and redistribute resources within Imgoun. The management of electricity services is a case in point. To pay for the service, households are metered. Rates are calculated on a sliding scale according to income level. An additional charge is added to each bill to cover the costs of providing electricity to public buildings – the mosque, the health centre, and the school. Finally, additional fees are charged to ensure sufficient revenue is raised to fund other projects in Imgoun. An example is the health centre, built in 1992, which was 50 per cent financed by revenues from electricity.

Over the years, its management capacity (building on generations of experience of the *jema'a*) has been put to the test on several occasions. In the 1990s, responding to the drought crisis, the association was the mechanism through which technical expertise (a French national with experience in drought-prone California), youth volunteers from France, migrants, and technical equipment from the local authorities were all organized alongside local villagers to stop ground erosion in the small valleys and build three hillside dams upstream from the village's sources.

Subsequently, a new association, Azourar, was formed to manage a large-scale irrigation project to reclaim large tracts of land left uncultivable by years of chronic drought. Managed on similar lines to the Anour Association, and building on its reputation, the new Azourar Association was able to access grants directly from the Moroccan government for the reclamation work and then sustain the service through user fees.

Establishing linkages

As members of the association, the migrants are both assets in themselves and effective as those who mobilize external assets and resources. Through Migrations et Développement, links to organizations in France providing volunteer support and financial assistance have been significant, especially with regard to the technical expertise required for infrastructure development. But the linkages have been still more extensive. For example, in 1990, youth groups from France (including both children of migrants as well as other French youth) came to help renovate classrooms, originally built by the *jema'a* in 1957. Later, a different group of youth came to assist with the construction of irrigation canals. Over a period of six years in total, the villagers accommodated and worked alongside these young French volunteers to get the work done. Now, with the children of migrants coming of age, another generation of people identifying with the Moroccan Souss is emerging to provide continued support.

As well, as deeper and wider links are strengthened with migrants in France, the association has solidified relationships with government to ensure that service delivery is sustained. It has also embarked on relationships with international organizations that have set an example for continued government investment. For example, an ILO programme in education and skills training for children and youth illustrates a clustering of interests: Imgoun wants to educate and train its youth in anticipation of greater employment opportunities in the future, international organizations want to discourage child labour, and the state has a responsibility to invest in education.

(continued)

(continued from previous page)

It is important to note that the Anour Association is linked to a federation of village associations that, individually and collectively, work in collaboration with Migrations et Développement and the government in a relationship that is unique in the region. The road construction project, requiring collaboration between several associations and the government, mediated through Migrations et Développement, is a case in point.

Driving its own development

Investment from outside organizations has had to be carefully handled to prevent it threatening the independence and autonomy of the Anour Association. In fact, Migrations et Développement had played such an important linking role in the early years that donors expected Migrations et Développement to act as the intermediary between the donor and the association. Over time, this stipulation threatened the positive dynamic that had developed between migrants and the association, independently of Migrations et Développement. The migrants wanted to deal directly with the village association. Thus, in 2003, as part of a road construction project stretching 47.5 km, the Anour Association took responsibility for collecting the 10 per cent funding required to leverage government funds for the 2.5 km stretch of road to link the village to the main highway. Migrants donated directly to this fund as well as to the funds necessary for the highway itself.

Reversing emigration: retaining and building local assets

Through these initiatives over the last 20 years, the neglect of the Moroccan Souss and the large-scale emigration from villages like Imgoun has found solutions in the combined resources of migrants and the local population, with Migrations et Développement playing the role of boosting people's confidence in their skills and their country, and aiming at increasing 'the attractiveness of the territory' in the eyes of the people: the youth in particular.

The establishment of basic infrastructure has now permitted attention to be focused on the next priority: economic opportunity. Villagers' experience in 'hard' technical skills, learned through infrastructure development, and in the 'soft' skills, organizing and managing, are now being applied to cooperative enterprises in saffron and olive oil.

itself to observe community management of the electricity network. The connection that the AFME consultants forged led to an on-going exchange between the Moroccan government and Migrations et Développement, one that lasted for the ten-year duration of the pilot programme. Government electricians transplanted practices observed in Migrations et Développement villages to a large number of their 200 pilot sites, and they tried out electricity technologies, new to rural Morocco, on the Migrations et Développement villages, considered by that time to have relatively mature electricity networks. Migrations et Développement appropriated and modified some of the practices introduced, like the use of fluorescent lights and certain generator maintenance techniques, which were then copied once again by government electricians in pilot villages throughout Morocco.

After five years of this exchange between Migrations et Développement and the Moroccan state, government electricians began to articulate the main lessons the experience offered for rural electrifications. They listed four main findings. First, in order to build a network that addressed village-specific energy usages patterns, a thorough needs assessment needed to be conducted in each community. Second, the electricity networks could be built using materials that were adapted to the topography of rural Morocco, that were locally sourced and less expensive, without compromising service or safety. Third, because communities already spent a significant portion of their income on energy, they were often able and willing to contribute funds for the construction of networks. Fourth, and most importantly, supporting electricity networks with some sort of social organization, akin to village associations, was the key factor for those networks to function properly and cost-effectively. Moreover, the associations would enable the new electricity grids to serve as an 'institutional motor to drive other developmental actions' (Berdai and Butin, 1993: 13). In other words, the impact of infrastructure 'hardware' depended on the 'software' of social processes that surrounded it.

In 1996, a crisis in the Moroccan energy sector created an opening for those lessons to permeate the kingdom's rural electricity strategy. After repeatedly failing to meet national demand, the National Office of Electricity was forced to privatize its energy production facilities and, to avoid closing the sizeable bureaucracy, the Moroccan government began to focus on electricity distribution instead. Overnight, rural electrification became an important government priority, and the National Office of Electricity launched a massive rural electricity programme, with the goal of linking 90 per cent of rural households to the national electricity grid by 2010. After a string of programme failures in the 1980s and 1990s, the National Office of Electricity abandoned its previous rural electrification strategy, which approached villages as if they were tiny, isolated cities that were extremely expensive to electrify. Instead, a programme was built from the ground up, using the lessons learned from the government's pilot programme, and more specifically, through interaction with Migrations et Développement-sponsored electricity initiatives. The new rural electrification programme mandated a needs assessment in each village; it revised national electricity standards to allow for equipment and materials that were less expensive and more readily available in local markets; it required some financial contribution from local villagers, but subsidized set-up costs by means of a tax levied on wealthier urban customers; and finally, the programme allowed for some degree of community management, though mostly in the very limited form of fee collection from households.

The results of the new electrification programme were dramatic. Rural electricity provision shot up from an average of 70 villages a year to 2,000 villages a year. By 2005, less than a decade after the programme was launched, the estimated rural electricity coverage in the kingdom rose from 21 to 81 per cent (ONE, 2005).

Lessons for rural development: the 'hardware' and 'software' of deliberative processes

The success of the rural electrification programme was a watershed in the Moroccan government's approach to rural Morocco: it made clear that community-based initiatives could yield insights pivotal enough to transform large-scale government programmes from embarrassing failures into policy triumphs. The Moroccan government began to look to other Migrations et Développement infrastructure initiatives for ideas about how to revamp other areas of rural infrastructure provision. The government turned to the discussions on water management that emerged in Migrations et Développement villages once electricity networks had been built and found, in the village-based deliberation, a host of innovative solutions for combining traditional water-harvesting methods with modern irrigation and potable water distribution. The resulting national programme for the provision of water in rural areas that the government launched in 1998 raised rural water access from 13 to 50 per cent in a little over five years, by 2005. Similarly, the government's collaboration with Migrations et Développement and its federation of village associations on road construction in the Souss region, beginning in 1997, prompted the government to revise the criteria it used to select the location of roads in 2005, causing it to shift its emphasis from number of kilometres paved to the number of people that a given road would serve. According to the Moroccan Ministry of Infrastructure, the roads planned according to the new measures have been more effective in alleviating poverty and isolation than roads planned under the previous scheme. Further collaborations between the government, Migrations et Développement, and village associations are currently under way in the area of adult schooling and health clinics.

Two important factors enabled a handful of small-scale community-based initiatives to grow into major reforms in national rural infrastructure provision. The first was the creation of an institutional structure to support a participatory process of innovation that included community groups, technical experts, and the state. Had Migrations et Développement not created a village association to protect those exchanges, those processes may not have been visible enough to attract government attention or robust enough to withstand the Moroccan government's sometimes overbearing involvement. The state's active participation in the exchange was most important: this is what enabled it to understand the rudimentary infrastructure set-ups in Soussi villages and to appreciate the conceptual principles that underlay them, which in turn allowed it to translate those principles into programmes that were national in scale.

The second factor that allowed for the spread of infrastructure innovation beyond a cluster of villages in the Souss region was the connection made between infrastructure 'hardware' and the 'software' of social deliberation. In all of the villages that Migrations et Développement worked with, infrastructure 'hardware' provided the focal point around which deliberative processes could grow, endowing those on-going and sometimes messy exchanges with a concrete purpose and a sense of urgency that kept them from dissipating into the mix of everyday conversations. Meanwhile, the 'software' of those deliberations generated the conceptual connections (between water and electricity, for example) and the creative ideas necessary for innovations in the infrastructure 'hardware.' Development 'hardware' and 'software' existed in symbiosis. Over time, the distinction between 'hardware' and 'software' became blurred as the projects that Migrations et Développement undertook in villages came to depend less on physical infrastructure and more on social organization. For initiatives like the saffron cooperatives and adult education programmes that the association launched in villages throughout the region, the buildings in which the activities took place mattered less than the coordination of community efforts, deliberation about strategy and curriculum, and the collection of funds to launch the programmes. However, the high-functioning community 'software' on which these initiatives depended could have been developed without the initial focus on 'hardware' with which Migrations et Développement began its intervention. The lessons Migrations et Développement drew from this experience are further elaborated in Box 7.2.

With donor agencies increasingly interested in supporting deliberative processes, and with infrastructure provision topping the priority list of a growing number of developing countries, the emergence of infrastructure innovations in the Souss valley offers an important reminder about the connections between participatory practices and the infrastructure services that lay the groundwork for economic development. Participatory practices are delicate and do need to be supported, particularly through the establishment of an institutional space to protect and nurture them, but social deliberation on its own is not sufficient to promote economic development. Likewise, basic infrastructure is an indispensable precondition for economic growth, but unless it draws on community-based processes of deliberation and innovation, the infrastructure provided may fail to meet the actual needs of the community. Furthermore, infrastructure initiatives that bypass community deliberation may forfeit the opportunity to be more than 'hardware' on the ground, and miss the chance to be the kind of catalyst for change that transformed the Souss from a parched, abandoned stretch of countryside into a hotbed of economic development.

Box 7.2: Lessons for providers of external assistance: the perspective of Migrations et Développement

1. The sooner local associations can take control of the projects the better. Taking control and assuming accountability ensures a sense of responsibility, signals victory over submission to poverty, and restores confidence in the options that are available to local people.
2. Solutions to problems can be found through combining 'insider' experience with 'outsider,' in a process that deliberately generates innovative ideas and 'out of the box' thinking, as was the case in building infrastructure and is now the case with finding markets for local produce.
3. Demand-driven, rather than supply-driven, development reverses donor logic. It means that development is shaped by local communities, not outsiders. In other words, development does not proceed by 'invitations to tender,' according to agendas elaborated in the North, but by responding to proposals put forward by local populations and migrants.
4. Building infrastructure first is important for two reasons. Not only is infrastructure essential for subsequent economic activity, but the collaboration on something with a concrete, visible outcome ('a tap in each house,' for example) provides the basis for shared learning and innovation between migrants and local populations. To support economic activities, more sophisticated know-how, fewer tangible assets, and more complex procedures are required. Without the villagers' experience of building infrastructure together with the migrants, this would have been difficult to accomplish.
5. Different donors are interested in different aspects of an initiative. Migrants, local populations, and Moroccan institutions are more likely to finance the 'hard' technology (construction of buildings or equipment). The niche for Northern donors is to finance the 'soft' technology (social mediation, coordination of participants, training for management, marketing of products, or technical studies).
6. Migrants provide an important link between governments in the North and local development activities in the South. Migrants' associations in the North that have credibility in development projects in their region of origin can be an important source of expertise and local knowledge.

Endnotes

1. This agency has now been renamed *Agence de l'Environnement et de la Maitrise de l'Energie* (ADEME).
2. The plural of *jema'a* is *jema'at*.

References

Berdai, M. and Butin, V. (1993) *Mettre en oeuvre l'électrification décentralisée dans une demarche participative: un nouveau service et une stratégie d'équipment rural: Le cas de programme pilote d'electrification rurale Décentralisée (PPER) au Maroc* [Implementing decentralized electrification by participatory means: a new service and rural equipment strategy: The case of the Global Decentralized Rural Electrification Pilot Project in Morocco], Ministère de l'Interieur, Royaume du Maroc, Rabat, Morocco.

Daoud, Z. (1997) *Marocains des deux rives* [Moroccans on both shores], Editions Ouvrières, Paris.

Haas, H. (2003) *Migration and Development in southern Morocco,* Ceres, Amsterdam.

Mernissi, F. (1997) *ONG rurales de Haut-Atlas: les ait débrouille* [Rural NGOs in Haut-Atlas: resourceful communities]. Editions Le Fennec, Marrakesh, Morocco.

Migrations et Développement and Migrations et Développement Local (1996) *Programme d'electrification decentralisée sur initiative locale.* [Decentralized electrification programme for local initiative], Migrations et Développement, Marseille, France and Rabat, Morocco.

Missaoui, R. (1996) *Le secteur informel de l'énergie dans les pays en développement: Cas du Maghreb* [The informal energy sector in development: The case of Maghreb], Ecole Centrale Paris, Paris. Unpublished Dissertation.

Office Nationale de L'Electricité (ONE) (1999) *PERG: programme d'electrification rurale globale* [Global Rural Electrification Programme], Office National de L'Electricité, Casablanca, Morocco.

Office National de L'Electricité (2005) *Le programme d'electrification rurale globale: L'electricité pour tous* [Global Rural Electrification Programme: Electricity for all], Office National de L'Electricité, Casablanca, Morocco.

World Bank, The (1990) *Staff appraisal report: Morocco, second rural electrification project (*8426-MOR), World Bank, Washington, DC.

Authors' note

Research is the process of creating a narrative, and although the researcher may be the person who ultimately articulates it, multiple hands collaborate in weaving together the story. This case study was no exception: as a researcher, I participated in the processes through which actors in this story made sense of what had happened and of its significance.

As part of the research for my dissertation on migration and development policy, I travelled to Morocco in the summer of 2001 and began to seek out initiatives that link emigration with local economic development. I heard about Migrations et Développement, rented a battered hatchback, and after a perilous drive that involved my car breaking down on one of the dizzying hairpin turns in the road that hugs the Atlas Mountains, made it to Talioune, where the organization had its local headquarters. From that very first encounter, the staff at Migrations et Développement were extremely welcoming and generous with their time and their information. The conversations that began that dusty afternoon would continue for the next five years, and would stretch to include multiple rural and urban cites in at least three countries. Migrations et Développement staff, the villagers served by their programmes, and migrants in Europe and in Morocco not only took the time to speak with me, but also hosted me in their homes, feeding me and often offering me a place to lay my head at night. I also interviewed current and former government officials in Rabat and Casablanca, and spoke at length with electrical engineers that had been involved in the Migrations et Développement electricity projects as well as in the national government's rural electricity programmes. I pored over reams of government documents, some published, some not, but saved in musty closets by people who perceived the significance of the experiment they had been a part of. I also spoke with observers of Migrations et Développement: people who, like me, were trying to make sense of the dramatic changes that Migrations et Développement's initiatives had set in motion in the Souss region.

Nadia Bentaleb was undoubtedly the most central of those observers. Before becoming director of Migrations et Développement she had, like me, gone to the Souss to do research on Migrations et Développement's electricity initiatives for her own dissertation. The conversations I had with her captured most vividly the dynamic that allowed the narrative presented in the case to emerge. Through back and forth exchanges, we built on each other's understanding of what had happened, and of how a small scale electricity experiment ultimately shaped Morocco's national rural electrification programme. (That exploration even broadened to include a consideration of the relationship of migration to development more generally, and in 2003, Nadia came to MIT to give a presentation at a conference on that topic that I had organized). The process of collaborative interpretation that characterized my interaction with Nadia occurred in almost all of my conversations over the course of my research. In a very real sense, it was the same process that allowed for Migrations et Développement initiatives to have such a profound impact on development, locally and nationally, as illustrated in the case. It was through those exchanges that a story was woven, and although Nadia and I are the authors of the case in this volume, we could not have presented the tapestry of the narrative without the threads many people provided.

In the same way that I was engaged in making sense of Migrations et Développement 's initiatives and their impact, the people I spoke with for this research interpreted the significance of my interest. Multiple views emerged as to what my doing research in the Souss meant, but one of those was featured in a book written by Zayka Daoud on Migrations et Développement. In her monograph, published in 2004, she presents my research as evidence that the quality of Migrations et Développement interventions as well as the organization's longstanding commitment to the communities it serves was being recognized internationally, and with those words, it was no longer I who was interpreting what I observed, but I who was being interpreted.

CHAPTER 8

A spreading banyan tree: the Self Employed Women's Association, India

Martha Chen

Abstract

The 30-year history of the Self Employed Women's Association offers insights into how women in India's informal economy have been able to mobilize and build their assets and to work proactively as an organized force for legal and policy changes in the sector. Women identify with the community of SEWA membership as a whole, as well as their particular trade group. They also play a valued role as SEWA members in their respective communities of place.

Introduction

Seeing itself as a spreading banyan tree, the Self Employed Women's Association (SEWA) of India supports its members through its many and various branches, drawing on the resources and capacities of its members. Thirty-seven years since the first seeds were sown in 1972, and now with a membership 500,000-strong in Gujarat State and 1 million across India, SEWA has grown into a movement of solidarity among self-employed women workers around the world and has steadily transformed the conditions of work and livelihoods of its members who work in an otherwise unprotected, yet substantial, sector of the Indian economy. It has allowed women to slowly and steadily accumulate productive assets, and insure themselves against the risks that constitute the norm, not the exception, in their work and lives. As such the tree nourishes and protects, spreading its influence through development services, collective bargaining, and policy advocacy for regulative and legislative change. As a member-based organization, it consolidates the 'agency' of each individual member as she contributes to household livelihood and community life, such that SEWA's collective power has influence locally, nationally and internationally – a fact aptly described in the title of the recent book by SEWA's founder Ela Bhatt: 'We are Poor But So Many' (Bhatt, 2006). This case study traces its history, how it developed a collective identity as a social movement, inspired by Gandhian principles, and how it interacted at the local, national, and international levels from a position of strength. Finally, recent challenges to that strength (by the Government of Gujarat) and SEWA's response to those challenges are discussed in terms of their implications for SEWA's future

SEWA's story begins

In 1920, inspired by Mahatma Gandhi, Ansooya-ben Sarabhai (the daughter of a textile mill owner) started a union of textile workers called the Textile Labour Association in Ahmedabad City, Western India. For the next 60 years, the textile industry – including the Textile Labour Association (TLA) and its institutional counterpart, the Ahmedabad Mill Owners Association (AMA) – dominated the economic and political landscape of Ahmedabad City. In 1955, a young woman lawyer named Ela Bhatt joined the TLA. In 1968, after working for more than a decade on labour issues, she was asked to head the Women's Wing of the TLA. The mandate of the Women's Wing was to provide training and welfare services to the wives of textile mill workers.

But in 1971, a small group of migrant women cart-pullers in the wholesale cloth market of Ahmedabad approached the Women's Wing to ask whether the TLA might be able to help them find housing. Ela Bhatt accompanied the women to the wholesale cloth market where she met another group of women who were working as head loaders, carrying loads of cloth to and from the wholesale market. The head loaders described their work, including their low and erratic wages. The head loaders were paid on a per trip basis by the merchants – not according to the distance travelled or weight carried. Because no records were maintained of how many trips they made, they were often not paid the full amount they were owed.

Under the auspices of the Women's Wing of the TLA, Ela Bhatt decided to organize a public meeting for the head loaders in the cloth market to discuss their problems. During the meeting, she told the women that they should organize if they wished to address their problems – the women agreed to organize themselves into a group and each paid 25 *paisa* (quarter of a rupee – US$1 is approximately 40 Indian Rupees, or Rs, at 3 March 2008) as a membership fee. Following the meeting, Ela Bhatt wrote an article for a local newspaper detailing the problems of the head loaders. The cloth merchants countered with their own news article in which they denied the allegations and claimed that they treated the head loaders fairly. The TLA Women's Wing responded by reprinting the merchant's claims of fair treatment on cards which they distributed to the head loaders to use to hold the merchants accountable: thus turning the merchant's rebuttal to the head loaders' advantage (Sebstad, 1982).

Word of the head loaders' moral victory spread quickly. Soon, a group of used clothing dealers approached the TLA Women's Wing with their complaints. Again, Ela Bhatt called a public meeting to which over 100 used-garment dealers and other women came. During that meeting, a woman from the crowd suggested they form an association of their own. Thus, on an appeal from the women and at the initiative of Ela Bhatt and the TLA Women's Wing, the Self-Employed Women's Association was born on 3 December 1971. The rest, as the saying goes, is SEWA's history.[1]

SEWA's name is significant because it has highlighted two underappreciated dimensions of India's economy. First of all, it has drawn attention to the fact that in India over 90 per cent of the labour force is informally employed: what SEWA prefers to call self-employed. Therefore, from Ela Bhatt's point of view 'Unless they are brought into the mainstream of the labour movement, it is no movement worth its name.' Secondly, the name has drawn attention to the fact that a major proportion of Indian women are poor and illiterate but economically very active:

> Work is their priority. If we bring these women into the movement on the basis of work, it is strategically the most effective way of organizing large numbers of women according to issues which are relevant to them. (Ela Bhatt, personal communication, in Rose, 1992: 36)

In effect, heralding a surge of interest in the value of the informal economy and the value of women's work that took off in the 1980s, SEWA stood as a challenge to the commonly held perceptions of those who don't have formal wage jobs as 'unorganized, unprotected, unregistered, marginal, informal,' or even constituting 'the black economy.' As Ela Bhatt commented in 1995, 'it is contradictory to describe such a vast, active workforce in terms that relegates it to a peripheral position, while in reality it is central to the economy' (personal communication).

Ela Bhatt soon began organizing two other overlooked and largely female segments of the textile industry – home-based garment-makers and quilt-makers (who made patchwork quilts from textile waste called *chindi*) – as well as street vendors. By 1975, membership in the SEWA Union had grown to 2,750 women from 15 trade groups of which the largest was street vendors (400 members) followed by head loaders, garment makers, used-clothing dealers, and bidi rollers (300 members each). In 1975, SEWA also began organizing agricultural labourers in several villages in Ahmedabad District. But it was only in 1989 that SEWA began to significantly expand its rural operations. By the end of 2006, there were nearly 500,000 SEWA members in Gujarat state from over 80 occupational groups.

Gandhian principles put into practice

As its overarching goal, SEWA is committed to the pursuit of what Mahatma Gandhi called India's Second Freedom: that is, economic freedom or freedom from poverty and hunger. After the First Freedom – political freedom – was attained in 1947, the founding fathers of modern India disregarded Gandhi's notion that the Second Freedom, 'Doosari Azadi,' should be based on agriculture and small-scale cottage industry. But, 25 years later, Ela Bhatt adopted Gandhi's notion of economic self-reliance as a basis for SEWA's work.

In SEWA's interpretation of Gandhi, the two key components of economic freedom are Full Employment and Self-Reliance. 'When there is an increase in her income, security of work and assets in her name, she starts feeling economically strong, independent, autonomous. Her self-reliance is not only on an individual basis, but also organizationally as a group' (personal communication). Unlike mainstream economists who use the term 'full employment' to refer to the level of employment in a country as a whole, SEWA uses the term to refer to the level of employment at the household or individual level and further defines it as employment that assures security of income, food, and social security (defined, by them, to include health care, childcare, and shelter). SEWA also uses the term 'self-reliance' in a holistic sense to refer to economic or financial self-sufficiency as well as control and autonomy as workers. Moreover, SEWA believes that collective self-reliance is as important as, if not more important than, individual self-reliance for its members. 'With collective strength the woman is able to combat the outside exploitative and corrupt forces like traders and moneylenders. Also her respect in the family and community follows soon' (Ela Bhatt, 1992).

In articulating its philosophy, SEWA evokes two overlapping sets of Gandhian principles. The first is a set of goals, namely: economic self-reliance as well as truth, non-violence, and unity or integration. The second is a set of guiding principles, namely: being truthful, being non-violent, being honest, retaining minimum possessions, controlling one's desires, using one's own labour, rejecting caste divisions, being free from fear, promoting local livelihoods (*swadeshi*), adopting a simple lifestyle (including diet), practising equality of all faiths (*sarvadharam*). These 11 Gandhian principles serve as SEWA's 'moral compass' which all SEWA organizers and members are encouraged to follow (SEWA, 2002).

SEWA draws its inspiration from sources other than Gandhi as well. It shares a commitment to promoting democratic representative membership-based organizations of workers with the international labour movement; a commitment to women-centred development and women's empowerment with the international women's movement; and a commitment to building the financial and physical assets of the poor with the international microfinance movement.

SEWA has translated these various influences into what it calls Struggle and Development: that is, union-style collective bargaining and campaigns to raise awareness, air grievances, and demand change; and development interventions to promote alternative economic opportunities and build assets. To promote this joint strategy, SEWA engages in 'organization, capacity building, asset building, and empowerment,' all in pursuit of the twin goals of Full Employment and Self Reliance.

Organizing, SEWA's central strategy, takes several forms. In addition to organizing its members by trade into its Union, SEWA helps its members to form cooperatives, producer collectives, and other local associations and marketing organizations. All members of SEWA belong to a relevant trade group and are voting members of the SEWA union; many also belong to one or more other membership-based organizations – cooperatives, producer groups, and (in rural areas) savings-and-credit groups. All members of these primary organizations are represented through elected leaders in the governance structure of the SEWA Union. Two types of these primary organizations – cooperatives and rural groups/associations – are also federated into separate state-wide organizations.

Complementing its organizing strategy are development services provided to its members. These include financial services (savings, loans, insurance), social services (health care, childcare, adult literacy), infrastructure (housing, sanitation, electricity, transportation), capacity-building (technical skills, leadership), and enterprise development and marketing services. While most of these services are offered on an on-going basis to as many members of SEWA as possible, some services are targeted to specific groups through special (often time-bound) schemes. For instance, SEWA joined a public-private partnership scheme to provide slum infrastructure services to some of its urban members in designated project slums; and SEWA has collaborated with government schemes to provide water resources to its rural members in designated project sites and to organize rural producers into local producer groups under a specific government scheme.

Over the years, to provide these various services SEWA has built a sisterhood of institutions, which comprises SEWA as a Union, SEWA Bank, SEWA Cooperative Federation, SEWA District Associations, SEWA Marketing, SEWA Vimo, SEWA Housing, and SEWA Academy. The first four – the Union, Bank, Cooperative Federation, and District Associations – are membership-based organizations, governed by elected representatives of SEWA members (see Table 8.1). The others are service units. But, reflecting SEWA's commitment to building sustainable local institutions, some of the services provided by these units are delivered, managed, or owned by membership-based organizations: Gram Haat and the Trade Facilitation Centre are owned and managed by SEWA producers; cooperatives of SEWA members provide health and childcare services; the insurance scheme developed by SEWA Security has been structured to become an insurance cooperative; and SEWA Academy provides communication services through a cooperative of SEWA members trained in video technology.

SEWA assesses the progress of its members towards Full Employment and Self Reliance against specific benchmarks – what SEWA calls its 'Eleven Points' – indicated as follows. A woman has to have *employment* to generate sufficient *income* to live with dignity, which in turn requires *ownership of productive assets, nutrition* and the fulfilment of basic needs such as *health care, housing and childcare*. She should have experience of *organizing in groups*, experience in *leadership, self reliance* as a group, and *education*.

Two final notes on SEWA's philosophy and practice are in order. First, SEWA is clearly centred on the working conditions of its members: all low-income working women from a myriad of trades and occupations. Second, although guided by the principles outlined above, SEWA is quite pragmatic in its approach. It does not take strong ideological positions. It is not, for instance, against globalization, liberalization, or modernity *per se*. Rather, it seeks to minimize the negative impacts and maximize the positive opportunities associated with these forces for its members. Reflecting this pragmatism, SEWA is willing to work with government, international donors, the World Bank, and private corporations, so long as they listen to its perspective and that of its members. Similarly, in working with various international movements – labour, women, and microfinance – SEWA seeks to reform from within: influencing the labour movement to organize informal workers (not just formal workers), the women's movement to focus on women as workers and on market relations (not just on gender relations), and the microfinance movement to focus on housing and consumption loans, savings, and insurance (not just investment loans).

Table 8.1: SEWA membership-based organizations and their membership: Gujarat State

SEWA membership-based organizations	Membership	Numbers
SEWA Union	All SEWA members	483,012 members*
SEWA Bank	All depositors are shareholders	49,909 depositor-shareholders
Gujarat Mahila Cooperative Federation	Members are SEWA cooperatives: producer, marketing, and service (childcare providers, health care providers, office cleaners)	100 SEWA cooperatives (63,477 members)
Banaskantha DWCRA Mahila SEWA Association	Members are producer groups organized by SEWA under a government scheme**	179 DWCRA producer groups (3,043 members)
Other rural membership-based organizations	Savings and credit groups, and cooperatives or producer groups	3,800 savings and credit groups (63,930 members) 4,321 other producer groups (64, 815 members)
SEWA marketing associations	Shareholders are SEWA individuals and/or SEWA producer groups and cooperatives	Gram Mahila Haat: 9 district federations, 5,060 groups (91,500 members) Kutch Craft Association: (20,002 members) SEWA Trade Facilitation Centre (3,300 members)

*   All SEWA members belong to the SEWA Union. Assuming individual members of the SEWA Union belong to only one other member-based organization – including the SEWA Bank – three-quarters (75 per cent) of SEWA Union members in Gujarat state belong to one of the other SEWA member-based organizations.

** In Banaskantha District, working in collaboration with a national government programme called Development for Women and Children in Rural Areas (DWCRA), SEWA has organized a large number of local producer groups – called DWCRA Groups – which are federated into the Banaskantha DWCRA Mahila SEWA Association.

Source: Author's elaboration, based on a variety of SEWA annual reports and discussions with SEWA staff.

SEWA members and leaders

How do individual women experience SEWA? What does it mean in their lives and work?

What follows are brief vignettes of two SEWA members-turned-leaders whose stories illustrate the transformative role that SEWA plays in the lives and work of its members.[2] They provide specific instances of the organizing, capacity-building, asset building and empowerment strategies as SEWA enables women to move towards Full Employment and Self Reliance. They also show how women build a strong sense of sisterhood or community with fellow SEWA members, as well as earn respect for their role in the communities where they live

Kamla-ben: a tobacco worker's story

Kamla-ben is from Napad-Wanta village in Kheda district of Gujarat. Born in 1956, she describes her life as full of *dukh* (pain). As she notes, '*Dukh* has been my constant companion. But my *dukh* has given me strength (*hemat*) as well as good qualities (*gun*) – or so people say. In recent years, since I joined SEWA, my life has been filled with *sukh* (happiness) as well' (personal communication).

Kamla-ben was the last of 13 children. Her parents were landless labourers from a Harijan community, the Vankars.[3] As was the custom in her caste, she was married when she was only two years old. When she was 12, she moved to her husband's home. His parents – also landless labourers – taught her how to work in the tobacco fields and factories. Since then, Kamla-ben has worked in the tobacco fields for half the year and in the tobacco factories for the other half. For the last 10 years, Kamla-ben has always worked with the same gang of seven co-workers – all members of the local SEWA savings-and-credit group. They get along well and try to lighten the load of work by singing, telling stories, teasing each other, and making jokes.

Kamla-ben and her fellow workers pluck tobacco in the fields during the winter months, working two shifts a day: one in the early morning, the other in the late afternoon. From March until the monsoon rains come, they work in the tobacco factories. The field work is back-breaking, as it involves bending over row after row under the hot sun – to pluck off the new unwanted shoots (called *peela*). They have to wear protective clothing as the tobacco resin on the leaves sticks to their hands, feet, and clothing and even their hair

The factory work is bad for their health – as the factories are filled with the soot and dust of the tobacco leaves. Employers are supposed to provide protective clothing and milk for the workers to drink to wash down the dust but this often does not happen. Although the work is arduous, Kamla-ben and her friends need the work. They worry about their future because many of the factories are mechanizing.

On the brighter side, since joining SEWA, Kamla-ben has found some peace and happiness. Because of her kind and caring personality she soon emerged

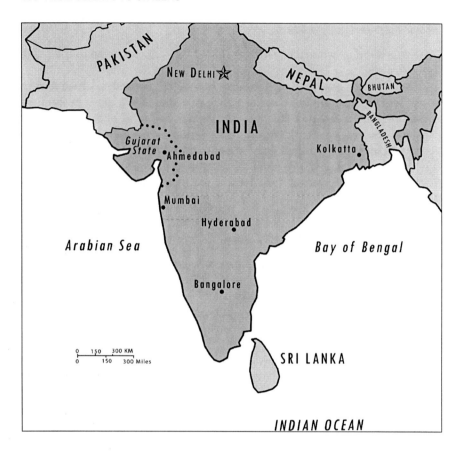

as the leader of her local SEWA savings association and then was asked to be a local area leader (*agewan*) for SEWA. In this role Kamla-ben has had the opportunity to travel to other villages and to other states of India. With loans from SEWA, she bought the bricks and cement needed to build two huts for her sons on a plot of land that she and her husband were allotted years ago under a government scheme for Harijans. With another loan from SEWA, she bought a mobile phone which helps in the organizing work she does for SEWA.

Kamla-ben and fellow members of the local SEWA savings association recently formed a *bhajan* (devotional song) association. They wanted to be able to sing and pray together – they meet 3–4 times a month. They collected donations from their employers to buy cymbals and drums. They plan to apply to the government, which has a long-standing fund for *bhajan mandalis* such as theirs, in order to buy some larger instruments as well. When this author spent several days with Kamla-ben, she attended one of these *bajan* sessions: as Kamla danced and sang, her worries and exhaustion (from a hard day of work in the fields) seemed, literally, to melt away.

SEWA's work organizing tobacco workers had a logical connection to its urban-based activities. Having unionized the bidi rollers in Ahmedabad City since the early 1970s (bidis are hand-rolled local cigarettes), SEWA became interested in organizing the rural women engaged in producing the tobacco that was used in the bidis. One of SEWA's organizers in Ahmedabad City was from Kheda district, where most of the tobacco in Gujarat state is grown. In 1986, she began organizing workers' education classes for tobacco workers in and around her home village. By 1987, SEWA had organized some 2,000 tobacco workers in Kheda District. At the end of 2004, there were 20,395 tobacco workers among SEWA's members (down from a peak of over 32,000 in 2002), representing 4 per cent of SEWA's total membership, 6 per cent of its rural membership, and 7 per cent of the SEWA members who sell their labour or services. By unionizing the tobacco workers, and despite opposition from the factory owners and farmers, SEWA has been able to ensure better wages and improved working conditions for the tobacco workers. In addition, they have provided childcare and financial services through local SEWA childcare cooperatives and savings-and-credit groups.

Madhu-ben: a construction worker's story

Madhu-ben grew up in a village in Ahmedabad District. Her parents were agricultural labourers, who would migrate for several months each year to neighbouring Junagadh District to harvest peanuts. When Madhu-ben turned 10, she began working alongside her parents. At 13, she was engaged to Magan-bhai, a man from her own caste who lived with his family in Ahmedabad City. A year later they were married and lived in the home of his parents. For the first two years of their marriage, Madhu-ben was not allowed to work outside the home but was kept busy doing most of the household chores. After some time, she began working as a construction worker. She would wake at 5 a.m. each day to make lunch for the extended family (nine persons at the time) before going for construction work, making flat breads (*rotis*) from five kilos of millet (*bajra*) each morning.

At construction sites, most women are involved in lifting and carrying cement, bricks, sand, and other materials. At larger construction sites, particularly for high-rise buildings, women have to walk up rickety bamboo scaffolding balancing heavy loads of bricks on their heads. The work is often hazardous leading to chronic aches and pains, injuries of varying severity, and even death. Accidents are quite common.

When Madhu-ben first began working in construction, she did not know how to pick up and lift the tin basins (*tagara*) of materials without spilling them. She suffered skin abrasions when cement spilled on her. While she can earn Rs60–70 a day (relatively high compared to other trades) she may only get 4–5 days work a month. Finding work is a daily struggle. In the early morning hours, construction workers gather at designated street corners – called *kadiya nakas* – across the city to wait to be signed up by the building contractors. On some days workers milling around with little prospect of getting work that day could spill over onto the street, jostling with vehicles for space on the road. The sharp rise in the price of cement and bricks since the earthquake of 2001; stricter government regulations; mechanization (notably cement mixing, digging, and lifting); and competition from migrant workers have all contributed to a recent slump in the demand for construction workers.

About 16 years ago, a neighbour of Madhu-ben's – named Jasu-ben – told her about SEWA. Jasu-ben had come to know about SEWA through a SEWA leader (*agewan*), named Kanku-ben, who lived down the lane. With encouragement from Jasu-ben and Kanku-ben, Madhu-ben opened a savings account at the SEWA Bank. For six months, she didn't tell her husband about the account. When he came to know that she had an account at the SEWA Bank, he asked 'What is SEWA?' After she described SEWA to him, he seemed satisfied and, indeed, has encouraged her participation in SEWA. Meanwhile, Kanku-ben had invited her to SEWA meetings.

After four years of being an active SEWA member, and having participated in two or three SEWA training courses (on SEWA as a movement, on the legal rights of workers), Madhu-ben was chosen to become a SEWA leader (*agewan*). As a local leader, her primary responsibility is to recruit other women to become members of SEWA. Magan-bhai helps her carry out this responsibility by taking her around to various neighbourhoods on his bicycle. Madhu-ben claims that she is able to recruit as many as 100 members per month. As a leader, Madhu-ben has had opportunities for travel and exposure. She travelled to a city in a neighbouring state to see a slum upgrading project; and she went to Delhi with a delegation of construction workers to hold a rally and submit a Memorandum to the Government of India demanding that the Government of Gujarat be forced to implement the national policy on construction workers.

SEWA first started organizing construction workers in 1998 and soon found that construction is a difficult industry to organize in, for several reasons. To begin with, it is an industry in which both men and women work. Since they began their organizing efforts at the recruitment corners where both men and women assemble, SEWA initially tried organizing both men and women construction workers. But the men soon began to dominate the meetings. Secondly, it is a capital-intensive industry in which, to leverage the amount of capital required and to secure lucrative bids, the building contractors often collude with city and state politicians, thereby further undermining the bargaining power of the workers. So SEWA stopped its organizing efforts for two months and, when they resumed, began organizing only women workers and only in their neighbourhoods, rather than the recruitment corners. When they get work, construction workers tend to work especially long hours, so that meetings have to be held at night.

Despite these constraints, SEWA has been able to organize 20,000 women construction workers since 1998 and to introduce some significant interventions – and policy changes – in support of construction workers. Most notably, SEWA has played a lead role in successfully lobbying for a state policy in Gujarat modelled on a national policy negotiated by other trade unions. The state policy includes a pension scheme for construction workers above 60 years of age, and a welfare scheme for construction workers and their families (financed by a 1 per cent *cess*, or tax, on building schemes with an annual net worth of Rs1 million or more). In addition, SEWA has introduced a scheme whereby construction workers are given 'diaries' to record their days and hours of work: the diaries, held by the workers not their employers, represent the only means the workers have to prove that they are eligible to be considered as construction workers (the legal criterion is 190 days of work per year). Like other SEWA members, many construction workers have subscribed to the SEWA insurance scheme, which helps cover the costs of treatment if they are injured at their work. Finally, SEWA has helped some women construction workers upgrade their skills by teaching them masonry and tile-work. Trained women construction workers are able to earn as much as Rs100 per day (compared to Rs60–80 earned by less skilled workers).

Unpaid local leaders, paid organizers, elected leaders

The organizing of construction and tobacco workers, and other trades in the SEWA membership, involves several layers of leaders and organizers. Kamla-ben and Madhu-ben are unpaid local leaders. In addition to several thousand unpaid leaders like Kamla-ben and Madhu-ben, there are some 30 full-time paid facilitators or organizers in SEWA Union.

Each of the individual leaders gives strength to the organization and derives strength from it. There is a palpable feeling of sisterhood among the organizers, leaders, and the members. When Kamla-ben and Madhu-ben described the kind of support that they received from SEWA organizers, both professional and personal, it was clear that the individual and collective strength nurtured through these personal connections reinforce each other.

The case of Jyoti-ben illustrates how women have been able to move into ever increasing roles of responsibility in SEWA. Jyoti-ben grew up in the same part of Gujarat state where Kamla-ben lives. From a family of tobacco workers, her mother was one of the first tobacco workers organized by SEWA. When she was very young, Jyoti-ben attended a childcare centre for the children of tobacco workers organized by SEWA. Despite their economic hardships, Jyoti-ben's mother insisted that she have the opportunity to go to school. After graduating from college, with a degree in commerce, Joyti-ben joined SEWA. Her first job in SEWA was to provide microfinance and other services to tobacco workers in her home area. She has worked for SEWA for over 20 years. At the last general elections of SEWA, which take place every three years, Jyoti-ben was elected General Secretary of SEWA: the first General Secretary who is the daughter of a SEWA member. When asked 'What is SEWA?' Jyoti-ben replies: *'I am SEWA'* (Macwan, personal communication, 2007). SEWA's membership – more than a million working poor women – *is* SEWA. And

SEWA gives its members an identity as workers, as members of specific trade or occupational groups, as members of a union and a sisterhood, and – for thousands of Kamla-bens and Madhu-bens – as leaders.

SEWA members: identity, agency, and assets

> When women organize on the basis of work, a woman's self-esteem grows - in the self-recognition that she is a 'worker,' a 'producer,' an active contributor to the national income, and not only somebody's wife, mother, or daughter. While participating in the organization and management of her cooperative or union, her self confidence and competence grow, a sense of responsibility grows, leadership within her grows. (Ela Bhatt, 1993, Keynote Address at the 1st Meeting of the South Asian Association for Women's Studies, Katmandu, Nepal)

Any self-employed woman in India who is 15 years or older is eligible to become a member of SEWA. In SEWA's use of the term, 'self-employed' refers to all economically-active persons who are not in formal salaried jobs.[4] Eligible women are recruited variously by SEWA members (who encourage a relative, neighbour, or co-worker to join SEWA), by local SEWA leaders (who canvas for new members in their neighbourhoods or hold local meetings for interested members), by SEWA organizers (in the course of their routine work or through special recruitment drives), or simply by word-of-mouth. Most commonly, the recruitment channel is through a given trade group or occupation, with a SEWA member or leader speaking to other women in her particular trade.

Identity through work

Drawn from different religious communities, castes and tribes – not only from different occupations – SEWA members face discrimination at work and in their daily lives by reason of their gender, caste, religion, and/or social class. SEWA seeks to build the identity and solidarity of its members (all women) as workers – as members of the working class and of particular trades or occupations – not as members of a particular sex, caste, religion, or social group. The primary channel through which SEWA members are recruited and the primary identity around which they are organized is their occupation or trade (a community of interest). But, as Kamla-ben and Madhu-ben's stories illustrate, SEWA members are often first recruited by neighbours in their own locality (a community of place).

SEWA members are engaged in a wide variety of occupations or trades which SEWA classifies into four broad groups: hawkers and vendors, home-based producers, manual labourers and service providers, and rural producers. Both Kamla-ben and Madhu-ben belong to the third group: those who sell their labour.

The members of SEWA are generally very poor. Available evidence suggests that half of SEWA's urban members live in households where income per capita is below the US dollar–a–day poverty line (Chen and Snodgrass, 2001). The wider environment – economic, regulatory, and social – makes it difficult for SEWA members and their families to improve their living standard.

Agency through organization

Organizing and capacity-building provide the essential foundation – organized local groups and trained local leaders – for all that SEWA does. As its central on-going strategy, SEWA recruits new members, organizes them into local groups, and convenes regular local group meetings to identify needs as well as the strategies to address needs. In the process, local grassroots leaders emerge, just as Kamla-ben and Madhu-ben emerged. Some leaders are trained and deployed as members of spearhead teams or as para-professionals to help carry out SEWA activities; while others are elected to serve as representatives of the general membership on the governing bodies of the Union, Bank, Cooperative Federation, District Associations and other member-based organizations of SEWA.

There are, therefore, three pathways through which SEWA's members gain agency or capacity in the organization. First, through its governance structure: as a member-based institution, all members gain voice through their elected leaders. Second, through its management structure, active leaders and members are specifically recruited and trained for responsibility in the delivery of its services. Third, through its collective bargaining and policy advocacy, active leaders and members become negotiators and advocates representing the collective strength of SEWA's membership.

Governance of SEWA Union

SEWA Union is the mother institution, so to speak, of the sisterhood of SEWA institutions. Union members pay an annual membership fee of Rs5 (roughly 12 US cents at the current exchange rate) and are organized into various trade groups who elect members to a Trade Committee. An additional fee is levied on trade groups which have benefited from struggles supported by SEWA. Since 1981, the President of the SEWA Union has been elected from the trade group with the largest membership. At the last election in 2006, an agricultural labourer, Bhanuben Danabhai Solanki, was elected President.

The trade committees meet once a month to discuss the problems faced by women in their respective trades and to plan strategies to deal with these problems. They serve as the 'nerve centre' of SEWA sending out signals as to what is happening locally and what the organization needs to do. The union hires paid organizers for each trade group who serve as member–secretaries of their respective trade committees.

Tobacco workers – members of the Self Employed Women's Association

Management of SEWA

In addition to or instead of serving as elected representatives in the governance structure of SEWA, local leaders are also recruited and specially trained to help SEWA implement its various activities. Every activity or programme of SEWA is managed by a local spearhead team comprising four local leaders and one SEWA organizer. Local leaders who have worked with SEWA for some time are trained to become spearhead team leaders. The goal is to have local leaders and members of SEWA assume the management and responsibility for all activities over time.

Advocacy of SEWA

Informed by its members and through the organized strength of its membership, SEWA pushes for structural changes in the wider environment. Some of these structural changes relate to the informal economy as a whole, such as legal recognition of the informal economy; legal recognition of SEWA as a trade union; and representation of informal workers in mainstream institutions at the local, state, national, and international institutions. Other structural changes relate to specific trade groups, such as increased wages or piece rates; worker benefits and social protection measures; licences to buy and sell goods;

access to new and improved markets. Some of these relate to specific issues of concern to SEWA members such as housing; infrastructure services (water, electricity, transport); land and other natural resources.

In shaping the wider policy environment, SEWA also seeks to change public understanding and appreciation of working poor women and their work and, thereby, to change the values, norms, and practices of society. This change may and should take place at different levels: husbands, families, and communities learn to value the contributions and understand the views of their wives, mothers, sisters, and neighbours; employers learn to value the contributions and understand the needs of their wage workers or their sub-contracted workers; and society learns to value the contributions and understand the needs of working poor women.

Of particular concern to SEWA is the fact that the working poor, especially women, do not have voice in most of the institutions that set the rules that affect their lives and work. This lack of voice – this exclusion from decision-making – has translated into lack of visibility in mainstream policies. Some of the relevant fora from which SEWA's members, other working poor women, have been excluded include: local councils; municipal, state, and national planning bodies; tripartite boards; minimum wage and other advisory boards; economic sector-specific business associations; local, state, and national labour federations. Thus, SEWA's strategy to impact policy includes gaining representation in key relevant institutions and, thereby, giving voice to the policy needs of its members and other working poor.

Assets through services

As noted earlier, SEWA provides an integrated set of services to its members, all designed to increase the assets of its members, including financial, enterprise development, marketing, housing, infrastructure, childcare, and health services. These services are designed and intended to increase various kinds of assets of its members, from financial and physical assets to human assets to social and political assets.

While seeking to build the assets of its members, SEWA also seeks to decrease their risks and liabilities. Consider the case of health. For most SEWA members, their labour power is their primary or only asset. For them, then, good health is their primary asset. Yet ill health is their most frequent source of economic stress. Illnesses and injuries can also be very costly in terms not only of medical expenses but also of foregone income. Illnesses or injuries that require hospitalization often prove financially catastrophic (Chen and Snodgrass, 2001; Ranson et al., 2003). Through its health cooperatives, SEWA provides health education and basic preventive health services; and, through its insurance scheme, it provides health insurance.

Consider also the case of housing. For many SEWA members, their home is not just their residence but also their workplace – or provides a storage place for what they sell and produce. For them, good housing is a basic physical asset: improving poor housing is an important goal of their savings and investment, and damage to or loss of housing is a significant financial liability. Through the SEWA Bank, SEWA provides housing loans; and, through the SEWA Housing Trust, SEWA provides a variety of housing services, including basic infrastructure services of water, electricity, and sanitation. And when disaster strikes, as in the case of the 2001 earthquake or the 2002 riots, SEWA helps its members rebuild or replace their homes.

It is also important to note that SEWA and its members see solidarity and bargaining power as key assets. Such political assets are different from social assets or social capital. Although they often build on social assets, they are not limited to bonding within communities or bridging between groups. They involve the ability to bargain with – to exert power or influence over – more dominant external players, including government officials, employers, and others with power or wealth. Thus, as noted earlier, SEWA is committed not only to building the organizational strength of its members but also to securing their representative voice in key policy-making and rule-setting institutions and processes. In other words, political assets require organization and representation, not simply services.

Finally, it is important to underscore that not all SEWA members take part in or take advantage of all of the strategies, services, or institutions described earlier in this section. Individual members of SEWA can be seen as belonging to one or another of four broad concentric circles of membership (see Figure 8.1).

It is not clear what share of SEWA's membership falls into each of these four categories.[5] There is roughly one local leader for every 100 members of SEWA, and one elected representative for every 200 members of SEWA. Assuming most (if not all) representatives are elected from the pool of local leaders, about 1 per cent of SEWA's membership is in leadership positions. Assuming all of those who joined SEWA in different years are alive and active, another 44 per cent are active members having been with SEWA for more than three years; and around 55 per cent of SEWA's members are general members having joined SEWA during the past three years. In sum, as one moves outwards from the inner circle of elected representatives towards the outer circle of general membership, the share of SEWA's membership in each of the concentric circles increases while the impact of SEWA is likely to decrease.

A spreading banyan tree

> SEWA is like a banyan tree. It grows, its canopy spreads, it bends in the direction of force, at the same time its roots deepen and give rise to new branches (new organizations). (Nanavaty, personal communication, 1995)

When asked to describe its organizational structure, SEWA does not draw a standard organizational chart. Rather, it depicts the organization as a banyan tree. The unique feature of the banyan tree is that it develops shoots from its branches, which eventually reach the ground, take root, and form new trunks.

In SEWA's vision of itself as a banyan tree, the Trunk – the SEWA Union – is seen to provide and channel strength to the tree as a whole; the Branches – the sister institutions and integrated activities of SEWA – give rise to the leaves, canopy, and roots. The Leaves – the Members – provide a canopy – the Membership. The various membership-based organizations put down Shoots that gain strength and sustenance once they reach the ground and begin growing new institutional Roots. The Banyan Tree – SEWA as a whole – is seen as a living organism generating new branches, spreading its canopy, putting down shoots, and taking root again and again.

From a local to a national union

During the 1970s and 1980s, SEWA's membership grew slowly but steadily from just under 4,000 in 1975 to nearly 20,000 members in 1988. During the 1990s, SEWA's urban membership grew nearly five-fold while its rural membership grew more than 14-fold. The dramatic increase in membership between 2000 and 2002 was due to a membership drive and to SEWA's relief and rehabilitation efforts in areas badly hit by the 2000 drought and the 2001 earthquake – many of the new members came from affected households in those areas. By late 2006, SEWA's membership in Gujarat state had stabilized at just under 500,000.

In the early 1980s, SEWA began expanding the scope of its operations to other states in India. Established in 1982, SEWA Bharat (literally, SEWA India) is the registered federation of SEWA organizations nationwide. With support and guidance from SEWA Bharat, eight SEWA organizations in six other states have been established over the last 20 years. By late 2006, membership in these eight SEWA organizations had reached nearly 500,000.

Given the numerical size and geographical spread of its membership, SEWA is now an officially-recognized national trade union which represents self-employed women all over India.

From a union to an international movement

Over the past two decades, an international movement has emerged in support of the working poor, especially women, in the informal economy. Much of the impetus and inspiration for this growing movement has come from SEWA. The success of a campaign to have the International Labour Organization (ILO) pass a convention on home working, and the requirement this generated for statistics on home work and the informal economy led to the creation in 1997 of the global research policy network called Women in Informal Employment: Globalizing and Organizing (WIEGO).

SEWA has also co-founded or inspired national and regional branches of home workers and their allies (called HomeNets) in South-East and South Asia; national alliances of street vendors in India and Kenya; an international alliance of street vendor organizations (called StreetNet International), and a

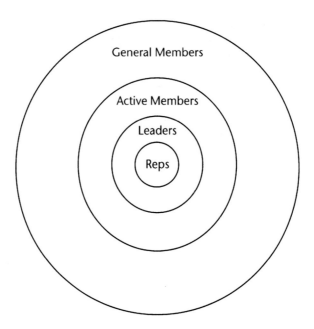

General Members: Members who have participated in only on SEWA service (notably, financial services) because they are either relatively new or passive members.

Active Members: Members who have participated actively in SEWA for three years or more by taking advantage of different services, becoming members in one or more membership-based organizations of SEWA (in addition to the SEWA Union), and participating in various events or field visits organized by SEWA.

Leaders: Leaders of the various groups and activities organized by SEWA who, in addition to general services offered by SEWA, receive special training as well as opportunities to travel, meet with government officials, and speak at public meetings. They are typically long-term members of SEWA.

Representatives: Elected representatives from the various trades groups in the SEWA membership who form the Trade Council in SEWA's governance structure and, like the leaders, receive training and exposure.

Note: These concentric circles are not water-tight categories – leaders are active, often long-term, members, and representatives are typically elected from the pool of leaders.

Figure 8.1: Concentric circles of SEWA membership

Grassroots Trading Network (GTN). Together, these organizations have helped foster a global movement of workers in the informal economy that continues to inform and influence policy debates nationally and internationally.

The strength of a banyan tree: responding to crises

> For poor women, one crisis is having a child. Having a female child is a risk. Having a good midwife and having clean water – these are all risks for the mother. Soon after birth, life is at risk. A woman's development is not at the forefront of anyone's thinking. Her education is neglected. She is married too early. Employment is always on piecework, and unemployment is always a risk. Old age is another risk. She becomes weaker. Widowhood is an even greater risk. She becomes dependent and if she has no savings she becomes vulnerable. (Ela Bhatt, Founder of SEWA, Opening Speech at SEWA Annual General Meeting, 2002)

SEWA's role has been to try to design programmes to address the risks that poor women face throughout the life cycle, with floods and drought, sudden factory closures, communal riots, an accidental fire.

SEWA has been able to help the majority of its members increase their employment and income; build and secure their asset base, including housing; and improve their nutritional and health status. In the process, many of its members have gained awareness, self-confidence, and bargaining power (both individual and collective), while membership-based organizations have been built and local women leaders have been mobilized and trained. But both SEWA's members and the organization itself are frequently buffeted by crises: predictable crises across a woman's life cycle that place financial stress on poor households; unpredictable widespread crises that often affect rich as well as poor households; and major underlying economic, social, and political changes.

As Ela Bhatt explained in her speech at the 2002 SEWA Annual General Meeting, SEWA has always been committed to helping its members deal with the predictable crises or financial stress events across their life cycles. The working poor, such as SEWA members, tend to have a relatively high exposure to many of the core common risks faced by all individuals and families, including illness, disability, property loss, and (premature) death; yet they have access to fewer resources to deal with these risks. Like better-off individuals and families, they also need funds to educate their children, celebrate religious festivals, arrange weddings for their children, and pay for death ceremonies. However, for the working poor, these common life-cycles events often turn into financial crises – as they earn too little to be able to save for them, they receive little (if any) help, and they live and work in vulnerable conditions.

In addition, the working poor face a wide-ranging set of work-related risks that persons engaged in more permanent and secure work do not. The 'hidden costs' of working informally include: high cost of doing business, including indirect taxes; great insecurity of work and incomes; few (if any) worker rights and benefits, such as paid sick leave, overtime compensation or severance notice and pay; little (if any) employment-based social protection; and uncertain legal status.

What is the role of SEWA in helping its members cope with these common and work-related risks? To begin with, SEWA Bank offers loans at a lower interest rate than loans taken from informal sources. In addition to lower interest rates, there are other (less tangible) benefits associated with borrowing from SEWA. SEWA members report that they prefer the anonymity of taking loans from SEWA Bank, compared to the shame associated with borrowing from family, friends, and neighbourhood moneylenders, and the disciplined regularity of repayments to SEWA Bank, compared to the whims of their informal creditors. Secondly, SEWA Bank offers loans for housing and for social expenditure (such as marriages). Thirdly, SEWA Bank offers a safe place to save money. SEWA members report several benefits of keeping their savings at the SEWA Bank: protection from theft or fire; unwanted claims by their husbands, children, or other relatives; and unnecessary withdrawals by themselves for their own or their families' spending needs. Fourthly, SEWA Vimo provides an integrated package of insurance coverage, including: illness, maternity, property loss, and death. Fifthly, SEWA Union negotiates with – and on behalf of – its members to minimize some of the risks posed by the wider social, economic, and political environment. Sixthly, SEWA Union, the Gujarat Mahila Cooperative Federation, and the district associations provide SEWA members with a fall-back position in the form of organized strength and mutual solidarity in the event of crisis. Finally, and of critical importance, SEWA Union, the Gujarat Mahila Cooperative Federation, and the district associations offer members avenues for alternative employment and livelihoods.

In addition to the chronic insecurities detailed earlier in this section, the members of SEWA – and other working poor – are affected by other more widespread and unpredictable crises. Over the past three decades, since SEWA's founding in 1972, a series of crises have affected Ahmedabad City and Gujarat state, including major changes in the economic, social, and political environment as well as so-called natural disasters of various kinds. During the 1970s, the textile industry of Ahmedabad – for which it was once famously called the 'Manchester of India' – began to decline. During the 1980s and 1990s, over 100,000 textile mill workers – many of them husbands, brothers, or sons of SEWA members – lost their jobs. During this time, there was a major realignment of the caste-based politics of Gujarat: with a decline in the once-dominant Congress party (representing the lower castes and Muslims) and the rise of the Bharatiya Janata Party (BJP, representing middle and upper castes and Hindu nationalism). Over this period, Gujarat in general and Ahmedabad in particular faced many episodes of civil unrest associated with what in India is called 'communal violence.' This was particularly pronounced in the early 1970s, mid-1980s, and early 1990s and culminating in a tragic outburst of BJP government-sponsored communal violence (Hindu versus Muslim) in 2002. All of these major economic and political events have had not only short-term but also long-term impacts on the livelihoods of SEWA members.

In Ahmedabad city, the closure of the textile industry has had a dramatic impact on the local economy. It took nearly three decades for the city economy to recover through a shift to large-scale manufacturing on the periphery of the city as well as finance and banking in the modern part of the city. Meanwhile, well over 100,000 textile mill workers lost their jobs: of which, one-quarter 'retired' or left Ahmedabad City; and three-quarters found work of some kind (Breman, 2004). Of those who found alternative work, only 30 per cent found jobs in other factories or power-loom units. The rest – around 75,000 workers – ended up in the informal economy, competing for opportunities in home-based manufacturing, service-repair jobs, street trade, and transport (ibid.). The net result is that in contemporary Ahmedabad City, once widely known for its textile industry including an organized and protected workforce, well over 75 per cent of the workforce is engaged in the informal economy (Rani and Unni, 2000).

The closing of the textile mills affected not only the local economy but also the local polity. To begin with, the decline of the textile industry was accompanied by the breakdown of two civic organizations that had played important roles in promoting inter-communal engagement, the Textile Labour Association and the Ahmedabad Mill Owners Association (Varshney, 2003). Secondly, the retrenched workers, who had once worked alongside each other in the textile mills, found themselves competing for the few alternative economic opportunities in the overcrowded informal economy (Breman, 2004). Thirdly, the retrenched mill workers became alienated not only from regular secure work but also from public services and institutions and mainstream society in general (ibid.).

Whether or not increased competition in the informal economy has contributed to increased violence in the city, it is clear that the successive waves of communal violence in the city, culminating in the tragic Hindu-Muslim violence in early 2002, have contributed to increased risk and uncertainty in the informal economy. Each wave of civic unrest or violence leads to the suspension or closing down of many occupations, at least for the duration of the unrest or violence. For those who do not earn a salaried income, these temporary closures have severe consequences for daily livelihoods and longer-term economic prospects. Also, in many of the recent waves of violence, countless businesses – especially those run by Muslims – have been looted or burned.

In addition to these man-made disasters, several natural disasters in Ahmedabad City have also undermined the livelihoods of SEWA's members and other working poor. Prolonged and widespread droughts in Gujarat in the late 1980s and 1990s gave rise, in the short-term, to a hike in prices for certain goods as well as a slump, in the medium-term, in the state economy. Nearly 20,000 people died in the earthquake of 2001, which also created a major shock to the economy, associated with a boom in construction in rural Gujarat (to repair and replace affected houses) and a bust in the construction industry in Ahmedabad City (as the industry adjusted to its damaged public image and new government regulations). Also, the 2001 floods in Ahmedabad city resulted in the destruction of many slum households and the loss of livelihoods for many categories of the working poor: for example, the paper pickers of Ahmedabad could not collect and recycle the waste that had become water-logged; the cart pullers and pedal rickshaw pullers could not ply the streets for several days; and the flood waters destroyed the stored goods or raw materials of many households and businesses.

In response to the so-called natural disasters, some of which could have been prevented or better managed, SEWA has developed its own disaster-response strategy. There are several distinctive features of SEWA's response to such disasters.[6] First and foremost, SEWA's response focuses on employment or livelihoods. From the perspective of SEWA's members, who often have few possessions to lose, the loss or temporary suspension of employment is what affects them most deeply. For example, when parts of Ahmedabad City were severely flooded in 2001, aid agencies focused on the damage to houses. But Raji-ben, a SEWA member who collects waste paper for a living, saw the problem differently, even though her home was under several feet of water:

> The slums were flooded and many of the houses collapsed. But the real crisis for us was that we had no work. Because of the flood all the garbage was wet. ... With SEWA we approached the Municipality and got them to agree to pay us to clean up our own locality. (Rajiben Parmar, waste collector, SEWA 2002 Annual General Meeting, cited in Vaux and Lund, 2003)

For SEWA, then, all disaster interventions are seen as a way of helping its members return to secure work: immediate medical or childcare services should help people get back to work and reconstruction efforts should be designed to provide local employment. In other words, SEWA does not believe that relief should be followed by rehabilitation: rather, it believes that relief efforts should create employment for – and thereby rehabilitate – affected persons (Vaux and Lund, 2003).

When SEWA began relief efforts after the 2001 earthquake, the affected households asked SEWA if they had some work for them. SEWA immediately began distributing cloth, thread, and needles to its members and other local residents who make embroidered crafts and garments for a living. As the women returned to work, they required childcare, a place to work, and a safe place to store their goods. Although more than a million houses had collapsed during the earthquake, 'shelter' *per se* was not the most immediate concern of many local residents. No rain was expected for months and people could keep warm with blankets. What they needed instead of tents and plastic sheets, SEWA learned by asking, was a basic temporary structure with four walls, a solid roof, and a door that could be locked: that is, a secure place to store what few possessions they had. After they were able to again earn a living, the local residents wanted their homes rebuilt in the local style that provided work as well as living space (ibid.).

Gujarat suffers frequent droughts and floods. During droughts, or other periods of 'scarcity,' the main response of government is to set up special public works schemes in which people are paid in food or cash to clear and widen roads, or dig water-collection pits. Based on its experience, and the perspective of its members, SEWA has been trying to persuade the local state government that, instead of digging pits or widening roads, people should be paid to do craftwork or other work using traditional skills. SEWA's other drought-related proposals to government, based on ideas from their members, include: a fodder security scheme for livestock-owners, employment around water conservation, rainwater harvesting for homes, and plantations for drought prevention (ibid.).

Further, because SEWA promotes local organizing and develops local teams to carry out all of its activities, it has a decentralized grassroots intelligence and response system in place. Local members and leaders of SEWA in the earthquake-affected areas began travelling around these areas soon after the earthquake struck, talking to affected persons and identifying their priority needs. Because they were in the area for the long term, not just for relief and rehabilitation, they were interested in building long-term capacity and reducing future vulnerabilities (ibid.).

During the drought and earthquake responses, SEWA worked closely with the State Government of Gujarat. SEWA was appointed a member of the Advisory Committee on the Gujarat State Disaster Management Authority. With the Government of Gujarat, SEWA secured a large grant from the International Fund for Agricultural Development for relief-rehabilitation efforts after the 2001 earthquake. About a year into this collaboration, the Government of Gujarat stopped releasing the grant funds and started harassing SEWA: accusing SEWA of unspecified and unverified financial irregularities and calling for special audits. Eventually, to clear its name and be able to act independently, SEWA decided to withdraw from all of its collaborations with the Government of Gujarat, not just the earthquake relief project.

Because it had worked closely with government on many of its projects, SEWA was suddenly strapped for funds. SEWA began to cut costs in all programmes and at all levels; none of the SEWA organizers claimed their salaries for nine months; and local members began donating rice and other grains. At the height of the crisis with the State Government, the members of SEWA reassured the organizers of SEWA: 'This is just one more disaster like a drought or earthquake – don't worry.'

The crisis with the Government of Gujarat represents a major turning point for SEWA, which has always chosen to work closely with government. SEWA has weathered the crisis, finding strength and solidarity from its members, but there are challenges ahead and SEWA will need to rely increasingly on that strength and solidarity. Fortunately, the membership of SEWA has continued to grow during the crisis. Also, in the past year, SEWA has been officially recognized as a national trade union and has been invited to be a founding member of the International Trade Union Confederation. In short, while SEWA's strength in numbers and in solidarity was being tested at the local level, it was being officially recognized by the trade union movement at both the national and international levels.

The strength of SEWA has been severely tested in the past several years. But SEWA, like a spreading banyan tree, has been able to sink its roots deeper and spread its branches wider to withstand prevailing winds. But, like a banyan tree, if it is going to continue to flourish, SEWA will require water (alternative sources of funding) and sunshine (an end to the persistent campaign by the Government of Gujarat to discredit it). To sum up, SEWA has demonstrated its capacity to increase well-being and incomes and reduce risks and vulnerability while at the same time building the capacity of its members to manage and sustain its intervention.

Endnotes

1. The most recent history of SEWA, full of telling stories and profound insights, has been written by Ela Bhatt (Bhatt, 2006). Two earlier, also engaging, histories of SEWA were written by Jennefer Sebstad (1982) and Kalima Rose (1992).
2. SEWA organizes regular Exposure-Dialogue programmes designed to expose selected outsiders to the realities of the lives and work of its members. I have taken part in two of these Exposure-Dialogue programmes with SEWA. In January 2004, I spent two days and two nights with Kamla-ben in Kheda District, Gujarat together with Ravi Kanbur of Cornell University and two SEWA facilitators, including Jyoti-ben. The following year, in January 2005, I had the opportunity to spend a day and a night with a construction worker-cum-SEWA leader in Ahmedabad City together with Arjan de Haan of DFID and two SEWA facilitators, Ramila-ben and Darshita-ben.
3. Harijan ('children of god') is the term Mahatma Gandhi gave to the lowest caste groups called Scheduled Castes by the British. The Vankars are a weaving sub-caste among the Harijans or Scheduled Castes.
4. SEWA's membership includes women workers who are a) fully independent self-employed; b) semi-dependent self-employed; c) dependent wage workers; d) casual wage workers who do not have a fixed employer; and e) sub-contracted workers who are paid by the piece. None of them are salaried workers and few of them are fully dependent wage workers, hence SEWA's choice of the term 'self-employed.'
5. As of now, there is no single database of SEWA members. While the Union tracks the membership as a whole, the different parts of SEWA maintain separate lists for the services they provide. However, the SEWA Union is currently issuing identity cards – with a designated membership number – to each of its members. Using these membership numbers, SEWA plans to create a single database with merged lists so that they can analyze and understand what share of its members, from different geographical areas

or different occupational groups, participate in the various activities and services of SEWA.

6. For a comprehensive account of SEWA's strategies to deal with recent widespread crises, see Vaux, 2002; and for a summary analysis of SEWA's approach to crises see Vaux and Lund, 2003.

References

Bhatt, E (1992), *Cooperatives and Empowerment of Women*, speech delivered in Ahmedabad, India.

Bhatt, E. (2006) *We are poor, but so many*, Oxford University Press, New York.

Breman, J. (2004), *The making and unmaking of an industrial working class: Sliding down the labour hierarchy in Ahmedabad, India*, Oxford University Press, New Delhi, India.

Chen, M. and Snodgrass, D. (2001) *Managing resources, activities, and risk in urban India: An impact assessment of the SEWA bank*, Assessing the Impact of Micro-Finance Services (AIMS) Project, USAID, Washington, DC.

Rani, U. and Unni, J. (2000) *Urban informal sector: Size and income generation process in Gujarat: Part II*, SEWA-GIDR-ISST-NCAER Contribution of the Informal Sector to the Economy, Report No. 3., National Council of Applied Economic Research, New Delhi, India.

Ranson, M.K., Joshi, P. and Shah, M. (2003) *Assessing the reach of three SEWA health services among the poor*, SEWA Social Security, Ahmedabad, India.

Rose, K. (1992) *Where women are leaders: The SEWA movement in India*, Vistaar Publications, New Delhi, India.

Sebstad, J. (1982) *Struggle and development among self-employed women: A report on the Self-Employed Women's Association, Ahmedabad*, USAID, Washington, DC.

SEWA Academy, et al. (2002) *Parivartan and its impact: A partnership programme of infrastructure development in slums of Ahmedabad City*, SEWA Academy, Ahmedabad, India.

Varshney, A. (2003) *Ethnic conflict and civic life: Hindus and Muslims in India*. Yale University Press, New Haven, CT.

Vaux, T. (2002) *Disaster and vulnerability: SEWA's response to the earthquake in Gujarat*, Experience Learning Series No. 18., Disaster Mitigation Institute, Ahmedabad, India.

Vaux, T. and Lund, F. (2003), 'Working women and security: Self-Employed Women's Association's response to crisis', *Journal of Human Development*, 4(2): 265–287.

Author's note

I first visited SEWA in 1979. Since then, I have worked closely with SEWA in several capacities: as a donor in the early 1980s, when I was Oxfam America's field representative in India; as a researcher in the late 1980s and 1990s, when I carried out research in one of the villages where SEWA began its rural operations and in Ahmedabad City on the impact of the SEWA Bank on its urban clients; as a Visiting Professor at the SEWA Academy in the early 2000s, when I carried out overview analyses of all impact assessments of SEWA and all studies on SEWA's membership. For the past 10 years, I have also worked closely with SEWA in another capacity: as a colleague and ally in a growing international movement of organizations of informal workers worldwide inspired by SEWA.

Over the years, I have had the privilege and pleasure of interviewing many of the members and organizers of SEWA and working closely with Ela Bhatt (SEWA's founder), Renana Jhabvala (SEWA's National Coordinator), and other senior SEWA organizers. This case study draws in equal measure on my first-hand knowledge of the organization and my research on the membership, operations, and impact of SEWA. The case study represents, in effect, a synthesis of all that I have learned about SEWA over the past three decades.

The working poor women who make up the membership of SEWA are examples of people who, because of their gender, have been neglected or discriminated against in their own communities, who because of their caste and class, have been neglected and discriminated against in the wider society and polity and who because of the nature of the work they do, have been neglected and discriminated against in the economic plans and policies of their country. Against these odds, they have been able, with SEWA's support, to build a remarkable community of interest and identity: the first and largest trade union of informal workers – all of whom are working poor women.

Much has been written about SEWA. It is known for its contribution to Gujarat State, India, where it was founded and is headquartered, and to India where it now operates in several states and has had significant impact on national policies. It is also known for its influence worldwide on the women's movement, the microfinance movement, and the labour movement. Most recently, Ela Bhatt, the remarkable founder of SEWA, has written a history of the organization entitled *We are Poor, but So Many*. Hopefully, this case study will contribute to an understanding not just of communities of interest and identity, but also of the unique nature and operations of SEWA itself.

I would like to thank all of the SEWA members and organizers who have shared their experiences and struggles with me over the years. More specifically, I would like to thank Jyoti-ben Macwan who is featured in the case study and who is now the General Secretary of SEWA for presenting the case to the forum of authors and contributors in Thailand in June 2007, and for commenting on an early draft. I would also like to thank Reema Nanavaty, Director of Economic and Rural Development at SEWA, for her comments on the early and final drafts.

CHAPTER 9

People's institutions as a vehicle for community development: a case study from Southern India

Alison Mathie

Abstract

This chapter profiles the work of Myrada from the perspective of people living in two villages in Southern India. Myrada has been at the forefront of the self-help group movement in India and has focused on assisting groups among the poorest, particularly among women, in order to build their capacity for savings and credit. These 'people's institutions' are a vehicle for group members to build their assets, assert themselves in the larger community, and have a voice in local government. The case illustrates the impact these people's institutions have had on the livelihood of individuals and groups, and their influence locally. It also draws attention to the importance of policy instruments and institutional mechanisms to ensure that the most disadvantaged have access to opportunities to save, borrow, and build their assets.

Introduction

Nidhana w pradhana? Nidhaanavé pradhaana?
(Gradual change yields the strongest results)
– Kannada proverb

The villages of Sagare and Kankana Halli are located in the *taluk* of HD Kote, which was identified in the early 1980s as the most 'backward' among the 7 *taluks* of Mysore District in Karnataka State in Southern India. Myrada, one of the largest NGOs in India, has been active in the area since then, focusing on its signature strategy of building 'people's institutions' as a foundation for the most disadvantaged to lever themselves out of poverty. Examples of such institutions include the Self-help Affinity Groups (SAGs) for savings and loans and Watershed Development Associations (WDAs) to protect land and water sources.

Now that Myrada is phasing out, Sagare and Kankana Halli offer contrasting settings from which to learn about village capacity to sustain these people's institutions independently. This case study therefore elaborates on how people in these villages, once 'backward,' have gathered the momentum to move decisively forward. It explores the role that people's institutions have played in this process, showing how they can act as a vehicle for people with few apparent resources or 'assets' to bring about positive change in their communities. This is particularly evident if principles of self-help are aligned with government policy, economic opportunity, village-based assets and NGO practice based on a firm belief in people's capacity. Through SAGs in particular, people like Mahadevamma (Box 9.1) have been able to mobilize financial assets to increase their livelihood options, and strengthen their voice in local public affairs, both a solid demonstration of 'agency'. Building complementary institutions to ensure that self-help groups have access to banking services, Myrada is demonstrating the 'bankability' of self-help group

---

Box 9.1: Sagare village: Mahadevamma's story

When I first joined a Self-help Affinity Group (SAG) 14 years ago, I lived in a mud hut and tried to eke out a living on one acre of land, growing millet and lentils. There were five of us who knew each other as friends and decided to form a SAG. We urged others to join us so that eventually we had 20 of us in the group. We started by saving Rs5 per week each, and the first loan for a group member was for Rs100.[1] Initially there was resistance from the men, but eventually they learned to respect us and we built up our confidence in our own ability to do things.

In my own case, after saving for five years, I took out a loan of Rs10,000 and bought an additional quarter acre of land and started growing cotton and coconuts. By using a pump to access water from the irrigation channel, I planted 40 coconuts, which began to yield after six to seven years. I later took a loan of Rs50,000 and bought another quarter acre. Since I have run a pipe from the irrigation channel, I am now able to access sufficient water to grow greens. I sell a harvest of greens to another SAG member for Rs200 which she then sells at the market, making a Rs40 profit after deducting her expenses. So now I have one and a half acres, with coconuts on one plot and greens on another. I have also leased four acres for Rs80,000 for three years (I have done this three times) and grow padi rice.

In one year I earned Rs85,000. I invested it in gold and also took out a life insurance policy. I have savings of Rs9,100 in the SAG and Rs20,000 invested in animals. My three children are in school: two boys (in Form 7 and 9) and one girl in Form 10.

Compared to our starting point, our SAG has come a long way. Our weekly savings have risen from Rs5 to Rs50 per week. The first loan 13 years ago was for Rs100. Today, the minimum is Rs5,000 and the maximum is Rs50,000. Now I am confident I could manage a loan of Rs100,000!

Many others have asked to join our group even though we already have the maximum of 20 members. So we say to them, 'You can't join us, but if you start a group we'll support you.' Three new groups have formed under our guidance.

I represent our group at the SAG federation meetings at the Community Managed Resource Centre (CMRC) office. All the SAGs are represented at these meetings, and we have become quite competitive with one another to be able to save the most! It would have been impossible for me to attend meetings outside the village 14 years ago, but now I have meetings with the CMRC manager, the *gram panchayat* officials, bank staff, and *taluk panchayat* officials.

membership to government and the private sector. The idea of self-help is therefore positioned in a chain of interlocked institutions that are designed to protect against slippage backwards and to encourage continued forward movement.

Before the experiences of Sagare and Kankana Halli villages are outlined, an overview of developments in India's state, market, and civil society sectors lays out the context for the emergence of self-help groups. As a civil society actor, Myrada's role is then discussed in some detail as it has played a decisive role in building the capacity of people's institutions to take an active role in civil society themselves. Finally, this case study reflects on how people mobilized and built their assets through these institutions in the particular cases of Sagare and Kankana Halli.

The state, market, and civil society: an emerging enabling environment?

Since the early 1990s, when it opened up its markets to international trade, India has experienced rapid economic growth and now enjoys the status of an emerging global economic power. The question of who is enjoying the benefits of this growth has been hotly debated, pitting the 'trickle down' theorists against those who see state intervention as essential for redistribution. NGOs like Myrada, long established in an expanding civil society sector, have positioned themselves as mediators between the state and the market, paying attention to protecting disadvantaged groups from further exploitation, and helping position people to take advantage of opportunity. In this scenario, people's institutions like those being promoted by Myrada have to be able to thrive, resisting the polarizing effects of economic growth.

State-level institutions

The 1993 amendments to the Indian constitution prescribed a three-tier system of district, *taluk*, and village-level governments in an effort to decentralize control of planning to local decision-making bodies. This was a decisive departure from the centralized state planning and highly bureaucratized delegation of programme delivery that had characterized national and state level governments since independence. Under these amendments, Karnataka, like other states, had to take measures to prevent local elite domination with the result that women are now required to constitute a third of elected members in all local government bodies (and to hold one third of council presidencies and vice presidencies), while scheduled castes and tribes are required to hold positions in proportion to their local population. These policy changes have not immediately translated into a disintegration of traditional power structures, but they have sent strong message about the roles that the traditionally marginalized can aspire to, and provide leadership experience for those thrust into positions of responsibility in public life (Blair, 2000; Isaac and Franke, 2002). Moreover, 20 per cent of taxes raised at the village level have to be spent on programmes that benefit the most disadvantaged (for example, food for work programmes).

Since land access is of particular relevance to this study, two state policy changes are of note. First, the Wildlife (Protection) Amendment Act of 1991 placed strict regulations on the use of forest land, establishing boundaries and restrictions where there had previously been fluidity and rights of access for those people living in or near protected forested areas. In regions close to forested areas, the act has precipitated individualized land tenure arrangements. As land values have increased, more intensive use of landholdings has occurred, making watershed protection and development an imperative in HD Kote project areas. Associated with the act, fuel wood use has also been restricted and a corresponding subsidy on liquid petroleum gas has been introduced to promote its use as a sent alternative.

On the question of land, it is also important to note that the Karnataka State Amendment to the Hindu Succession Act specifically addressed women's insecure right to land. However, according to Brown, Ananthpur, and Giovarelli (2002), the intended benefits are still not reaching the neediest women even under this more progressive legislation, and ownership and control of land continues to be mediated through male relatives. The fact that women in the SAGs in the two villages of this study have been able to acquire and control land in their own names is therefore no small achievement.

Market trends

In the last 25 years, liberalization of the economic and regulatory environment has affected the asset base of rural livelihoods directly through agricultural policy and indirectly through growth in urban employment and urban markets. In general, economic growth has tended to favour urban over rural populations, although with sufficient levels of investment in rural infrastructure and in education these differences have been shown to have been mitigated by access to services in small towns (Fan et al., 2005). Investment policy and the consequences of economic growth are, however, uneven in their effects. Agricultural policy has, for example, shifted from public investments in extension and credit services for farmers to a privatization strategy requiring heavier investment on the part of farmers themselves in high-yielding seed varieties, fertilizer and pesticides, inevitably tending to favour wealthier farmers. The rural banking sector has also been liberalized and decentralized, with local banks now expected to cover their costs through more high-end lending at the local level or through amalgamation.

In Karnataka State, economic growth in urban centres such as Bangalore and Mysore stimulated by trade liberalization and investment in high-tech industries has generated employment opportunities as well as market opportunities for rural producers. However, the rise in land values in neighbouring rural areas, such as the Sagare area, has put an additional pressure on the poorest sectors of the population, either because the prospects for the poor of breaking into the land market are slimmer, or because those who do own land are under increased pressure to sell during periods of crisis. As will be described later, institutions that can help them access and protect those assets are essential.

Civil society

The history of volunteerism and charity in India is of interest to this study because it helps to explain the prevailing service orientation of the civil society sector as a whole. It also sheds light on the precedents of the SAGs that Myrada has been promoting. Both Hindu and Buddhist religions have traditionally expected followers to be of service to the less fortunate, inspiring the emergence of service-oriented and welfare-oriented organizations. In addition, according to Srivastava et al. (2004: 157–169), the organization of artisans into guilds (since the 'Buddhist period') was a significant development in that these early member-based organizations played both an economic and regulatory role by determining wages and standards, but also played a social role by providing for widows, orphans and the elderly.

Pre-independence nationalist movements added a new dimension to the character of civil society not just in India, but all over the world, notably in terms of the Gandhian emphasis on social reform and empowerment of the poor. However, in the years immediately following independence in 1947, the government (and foreign donors, which had a predominantly welfarist orientation during this period) tended to prioritize social services both through public sector programming and through direct funding of non-government social service organizations. With further expansion and diversification of its funding base, the NGO sector has begun to shift towards a larger role in policy advocacy and political education, although to this day India's civil society sector continues to be dominated by social service activity. The NGO sector's role as an advocate has, in fact, already experienced a backlash: The government's pride in India's position as 'the largest democracy in the world' has prompted questioning about the legitimacy of the NGO sector as a voice representing the interests of the poor. Nevertheless, Myrada has a well established independent reputation in India. By focusing on the task of institution-building, it has created a niche that complements rather than threatens the role of government, particularly in the provision of microfinance services for the poor (Satishchandran, in Fernandez, 2001). With faith in the strengths and abilities of people as individuals, and in the exponential possibilities when they combine their strengths to work as a group, Myrada's ideas for people's institutions have more in common with the principles behind guilds – members organizing to maximize economic advantage while taking care of their own members – than with the welfare and service organizations that have dominated the civil society sector and its donors.

Sagare village

Sagare village, located 15 km from HD Kote, comprises a dense network of streets surrounded by parcels of intensively-worked padi rice fields, millet and lentil plots, and banana groves. It is home to 900 families, 450 of whom are members of scheduled tribes (ST), and 100 of whom are scheduled caste (SC) members. The remaining families belong to *gowda* (farmer caste), *shetty* (trader caste), *medar* (basket weaver caste), and other smaller castes. Of those 900 families, 700 are below the official poverty line,[2] the poorest relying on occasional or precarious work as agricultural labourers, sometimes as bonded labourers, paying off debt.

The village is situated within 5 km of a reservoir dammed in the 1940s. The construction of the dam was accompanied by canal construction and those wealthier farmers who were able to invest in the basic technology required to access water from the canal were able to irrigate their land. Around the same time the first primary school (Grades 1 to 4) opened in Sagare, but it was rudimentary: few of the boys who attended acquired anything but the most basic of literacy skills.

Apart from these changes, situated in the most remote of Mysore district's *taluks*, without road access to marketing centres, Sagare lagged behind others in terms of infrastructure and social developments until the 1980s when the first boreholes were constructed. Connections to these boreholes had a dramatic social and economic impact: the work of women was reduced by providing access to water at six hand pumps in the village, and irrigation became a possibility for those who could build connecting pipelines. Today, people's responses to the question, 'How much land do you have?' reveal that their sense of security and opportunity is closely tied to the proportion of wetland relative to dry land in their possession. Nonetheless, all land is scarce, with landholdings averaging three to four acres, and it is a most valued resource. Nobody sells land unless he or she is desperate.

Myrada began its involvement in HD Kote in 1982. A fieldworker was posted to Sagare and helped to form a village development committee as the local decision-making body for distributing donor resources for housing and water supply in keeping with the 'basic needs' priorities of aid agencies at the time. By the 1990s, however, Myrada had taken the position that such heavy investment by a donor agency was potentially harmful. Staff members recall that the Village Development Committees (VDCs) became focal points for competition for resources, rather than a mechanism for equitable distribution, let alone preferential treatment of the most disadvantaged. There was also concern that Myrada's services ran parallel to, and sometimes in competition with, government service delivery. A longer term sustainable strategy had to be devised. The basis of this was capacity-building of individuals and groups through Self-help Affinity Groups (SAGs). Through these, even the poorest could begin to save and strategize for developing better livelihoods.

Myrada staff members began to realize that in their earlier efforts to encourage inclusive and representative groups along the lines of the VDCs, they had been neglecting the obvious – existing social groups had the relationships of trust that could serve as the basis for people to save and access credit. So, rather than insist on broad-based and inclusive membership, these 'affinity groups' were identified as the base from which people could build financial security and identify opportunity, 'constituting what could be called traditional social and institutional capital' (Fernandez, 2001: 5) There were no requirements to include particular people – the groups were formed entirely on the basis of existing functional relationships such as extended family groupings, caste groupings, or women who collect water together. Groups could be gender-specific or mixed.

Through these SAGs, people began to save money. At first, this could be as little as Rs5 per week. Over time, savings that accumulated in the Common Fund would be the basis of the security required for individuals to take small loans, topped up by external funds from banks and financial institutions. The SAGs would decide whether to loan money to the individual, based on their own risk assessment of the purpose of the loan and the reliability of the borrower. No restrictions were placed on the use of the loan. It could be for consumption or production; the only consideration was whether the borrower was likely to be in a position to repay the loan. This decision was critical because the SAG had to take collective responsibility in the event of loan default.

According to a local proverb, 'gradual change brings the strongest results.' The impact on women's lives has been slow, steady, but cumulatively dramatic. For example, one woman described her transformation from a bonded labourer to a bank agent. Released from bondage 20 years previously, she and her husband eked out a precarious livelihood on a small plot of dry land, that at one time had to be mortgaged. She joined a SAG with other women members of her caste and began to save in very small increments, gradually building up the confidence to take a loan. She then learned tailoring through the SAG and began to earn a small income. Now 13 years later, she acts as an agent for the bank, collecting savings for people to deposit. Her income has allowed her to take back possession of the land and buy an additional half acre, paying for it in instalments (personal communication, 2005).

Although Myrada had encouraged affinity groups to form irrespective of gender, over time it became clear that the women's self-help affinity groups were the most sustainable. There are several reasons for this. Men were more likely to travel outside the village for labour or trading, so the routine of weekly SAG meetings and savings was problematic for them. Women, on the other hand, were more likely to be village-based. Tolerant of slow but steady improvement in their status and livelihood, women were motivated to maintain the discipline required to keep the groups going. Also, trust developed in an atmosphere less mired by leadership rivalries than in the groups with men (personal communication, 2005).

Since Myrada recognized the role of women in the household and their potential as entrepreneurs, it saw the potential of the SAG as a vehicle for both awareness-raising and skill-based training. Health, education, entrepreneurship and leadership skills were therefore introduced as subjects for discussion at weekly meetings. In the initial stages, Myrada staff would attend these meetings and assist with group formation and bookkeeping, but the SAGs subsequently managed each of these activities themselves.

Infrastructure developments in the 1990s moved Sagare out of relative isolation. Bridge and road construction, coinciding with India's surge in economic growth in urban centres such as Bangalore and Mysore, provided Sagare village with ready access to markets in the *taluk* centre of HD Kote and in Mysore, 80 km away. Those farmers who could afford the fertilizer and pesticide inputs could now participate in maize and cotton production using high-yielding hybrid varieties. Trading and small business opportunities opened up for those with the means to respond. A post office opened in the village as well as a 'fair price shop,' offering government-subsidized commodities. Improved roads and a bus service made the high school and hospital 15 km away more accessible, although it was not until later in the 1990s when a Primary Health Unit in the nearby town of Sargur was established that immunization rates reached acceptable levels. Around the same time, the first phone was installed. Rural electrification made its appearance. A district-wide water and sanitation programme, financed by the World Bank, enabled local government to put in place village-wide drinking water supply and sanitation facilities. With constitutional amendments, local government decentralization mandated inclusive participation in local decision-making, along with the reservation of elected positions specifically for scheduled castes and tribes and women.

Mahadevanayaka, a 35 year-old leader from a scheduled tribe, tells how he was able to take advantage of these changes, explaining how 'if you work hard, there are many opportunities':

> From the age of ten, I worked as a bonded labourer for 10 years. Once released, I went to school, working after school to save money. Afterwards, I got involved in the youth group and became its president for five years. I was then elected as a leader in my *nayaka* (ST) community. Because of this community work and the contacts I made through selling coconuts, I became well known in Sagare and got elected onto the *panchayat*. (personal communication, 2005)

Now he earns a living from diverse sources: from selling betel leaves grown on his quarter acre of land, from selling other people's coconuts, and from the 'sitting fees' earned as an elected representative on the local *panchayat*. Thus, in his life, schooling was a major breakthrough, opening doors for a person of lowest caste status to demonstrate leadership potential. Without major setbacks in health, he was able to solidify his position through hard work and reputational capital earned through trading connections, so that he is now in a position to influence events at local government level. Now he debates whether to save for the future or purchase a television to keep him informed, and whether to stay in Sagare or move to Mysore for greater employment opportunity. These are life choices beyond the bounds of possibility for a bonded labourer.

In more recent years, the SAGs formed in the early 1990s are reaching a level of maturity. Now 33 in number,[3] with a membership of 493 out of 900 families, they are able to leverage loans from the microfinance institution *Sanghamithra* at the level of twice the amount of their total savings. They access this credit service, along with the information, advisory and auditing services of Myrada through a Community Managed Resource Centre, 4 km away. Serving 120 SAGs and 27 WDAs in 50 villages, the CMRC has also provided a venue for SAG 'federation' meetings with two members from each SAG attending on a regular basis to address issues such as reporting progress of groups, understanding and influencing bank policy, resolving conflicts, and promoting new affinity groups (Fernandez, 2001). Since 2002, SAGs have been paying fees for these services, collectively contributing to 50 per cent of the CMRC manager's salary.

Beyond their savings and loans function, SAGs have matured into people's institutions with wide-ranging activities and roles in village life. Their members' level of awareness of social and economic issues means that SAGs, for example, have begun to influence the priorities of local government expenditures. This is either because SAG members have been elected to the local *panchayat* (6 out of a total of 14 *panchayat* members are also members of SAGs) or because they have found a confident voice to press for change. One female member recounts how her SAG gathered the support of other SAGs and raised the issue of sanitation at the local *gram sabha*. As a result of this unusually strong voice from women at the *gram sabha*, Sagare *panchayat* has become a 'clean village' and recommended by the Government of Karnataka for an award under a Government of India award scheme known as *Grama Puraskar Yojane*. (D'Souza, personal communication, 2007). As one young man noted:

> [Having village-wide toilet facilities] has made it easier for women who used to have to wait till after dark, and for all of us scheduled caste members whose houses were so far away from where we were permitted to defecate. Before, I had to walk two kilometres. (personal communication, 2005)

SAG advocacy for community-wide toilet facilities has therefore had the effect of reducing inequalities, challenging even the geographic confines associated with caste. In another example of SAGs enacting a citizenship role, SAGs routinely use their Common Fund for the public good, including prizes for school children, contributions to tsunami relief, or for religious functions.

The most visible aspect of recent change in Sagare has been the establishment of a high school in the village, serving several villages in the vicinity. The high school, with its high rate of enrolment and 0% drop-out rate (D'Souza, personal communication, 2005), is in many ways a culmination of a number of trends over the last 25 years. With limited land for expansion, and with the availability of family planning, low levels of infant mortality (less than 20 per 1,000 live births), and high level of uptake of birth control (51 per cent of couples), family size is smaller (averaging two children, as compared to five or six children 20 years ago) (Shivakumar, personal communication, 2005). Families aim for a more diversified livelihood for their children, one that is not so dependent on agriculture and may involve employment elsewhere. They also talk about the importance of education to reach a level of awareness that will make them less vulnerable to exploitation, and better able to take advantage of opportunities. Many also recognize that it is through schools that other changes in village life are also introduced. Sanitation in schools, for example, is said to be the best predictor of uptake of toilets in students' homes.

Investment in children since the 1980s, particularly as a result of PLAN's involvement with Myrada since that time, is therefore producing results: greater awareness of the importance of education, combined with increased awareness of what constitutes quality education. Smaller family sizes and investment in education both indicate a longer term shift in livelihood strategy. Also, the fact that Sagare boasts a 100 per cent tax collection rate suggests not only a capacity to pay but also the potential capacity of local government to redistribute revenue to benefit the most marginal, smoothing the way for their participation in a sustainable means of livelihood. Ensuring that decisions are made to do so will depend on whether these people's institutions are strong enough to act as a voice for their membership, and for those still beyond their reach.

Kankana Halli

With 49 families and a population of 218, Kankana Halli, nestled in the hills at the edge of recently protected forest land, stands in contrast to the bustle of Sagare village. Yet the central concern of the community is similar: What options do rural, remote communities have in the face of land use pressure and volatility of agricultural product markets?

The first settler families of Kankana Halli arrived in 1965, forced out by drought in Kanakapura, near Bangalore. Traditionally self-employed as charcoal sellers, they established themselves as farmers, cutting down forest to make way for fields of millet and lentils, with charcoal production as their principal source of income. Once settled, they encouraged others – of their own caste and other castes – to join them and thus provide additional labour. The settlement became legally sanctioned, first by the issuing of licenses to sell charcoal, and second by the granting of land title to the already settled lands.

From the start, schooling for children was a priority. Mobilizing the support of neighbouring villages, the initial settler families appealed to the government

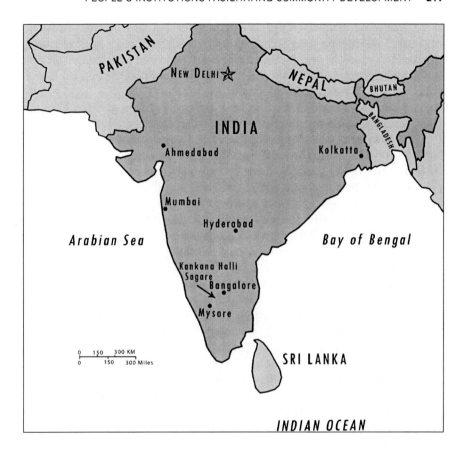

to establish a school. Families contributed funds, land, and labour to construct a one-room school, staffed by one government-funded teacher. Opened in the mid 1970s, the school soon had over a hundred pupils and the original building was outgrown. Today the village has a newly built, government-funded school with two teachers, and the child-focused emphasis of the HD Kote project has built upon that initial investment in children made by Kankana Halli families themselves.

Included in the project area, the village had similar experiences of Myrada's programmes in Sagare village. Village Development Associations (VDAs) were formed initially to ensure broad-based participation in decisions related to infrastructure development. However, once again, it became clear that these were not appropriate for building financial capacity and livelihood diversification through savings and credit. Thus, Self-help Affinity Groups were introduced as a means for groups to form more naturally and organically, organized around shared responsibility for savings and loans.

The SAG formed here was among women; as in Sagare, SAGs are less popular and less successful among men. However, by the end of the 1990s, there would be a more compelling reason for both men and women to organize. Forbidden now to encroach upon the adjacent protected forest area, the land belonging to people of Kankana Halli fell within a designated area for watershed development. Each village within this area had the opportunity to collaborate in Watershed Development Associations (WDAs) to significantly expand the area under cultivation and increase productivity. For Kankana Halli, this affected 45 acres of land.

Two WDAs formed, made up of both men and women who occupied adjacent lands and could therefore benefit from mutual collaboration. An example given by one of the WDAs was as follows: by each of the 14 members saving Rs10 per week, the threshold sum of Rs14,000 was accumulated in less than two years, sufficient to take a two *lakh* loan for a group to purchase small irrigation pumps. In the time taken to save for this technology, the water table in these watershed areas would have risen as a result of a combination of new farming practices: embankment formation, land levelling, and pond construction. Technical support through Myrada provided WDA members with experience in participatory data collection techniques (such as mapping, wealth ranking, and transect walks) on which to base planning decisions. Members of WDAs helped each other in the construction of embankments, levelling of land and water collection on each individual family's land, recognizing that they were mutually dependent on each other for the maintenance of the whole system.

Under this system, each participating family's land would benefit from increased productivity because land that had not been productive in the past, due to lack of water or excess soil erosion, could now be farmed. Without expanding total land area, productivity could be increased especially when combined with judicious plantings on the embankments (such as fruit trees), organic composting and manure, and since cattle could now be watered at ponds on the farm site rather than being taken to more distant watering holes. Farmers could begin planting two crops in succession in a year, rather than just one. So productive and diversified has agricultural production become that a village elder was able to proudly comment, 'Everything but salt and kerosene are grown here' (personal communication, 2005).

Living on the boundary of protected forest land means that measures have to be taken to protect farmland from wild animals, including elephants. Traditional methods had been reasonably effective but labour intensive (such as camping out at night in a 'blind' in a tree ready to launch firecrackers to frighten the animal and rouse support from family members). More effective has been the use of electric fencing. The WDAs are now finding ways to mobilize funds for solar electric fencing with solar energy tapped through photovoltaic cells installed at the old school house in Kankana Halli.

All told, as one grandfather explained, there has been a transformation in land use practices in this village from an extensive system requiring continuous encroachment into forest areas to an intensive, carefully managed, and organic system:

> We used to cut down the trees to make fields, but now this is not allowed. Now we irrigate the land and our land is more productive. We used to grow cotton using government-issued fertilizer, but now we farm organically. (personal communication, 2005)

Similarly, a woman commented not only on the importance of the new skills learned for ensuring sustained tree growth, but also on a strengthened capacity to collaborate:

> We have learned about bunding and levelling, about planting on the bundings, and about saplings. Grazing is easier now. But most important is the fact that we have got used to working in collaboration [to ensure watershed protection]. (personal communication, 2005)

Collaboration has also extended to advocacy. A 2 km stretch of tarred road now runs through the village, the result of a successful campaign, working through the local *gram panchayat* member.

As in Sagare, WDAs and SAGs access services through the CMRC. Located 11 km from Kankana Halli, this centre has 94 SAGs and 46 WDAs in its service area. Services include: regular SAG assessments, on the basis of which training needs are discussed; access to financial services such as auditing; linkages to various government departments and programmes; access to subsidized liquid petroleum gas; training programmes of various kinds, such as health, leadership, and income-generating skills training; exposure visits; and access to *Sanghamithra* banking services. Services specifically designed for the landless include training in income-generating activities such as establishing vermi-compost units, dairying, sheep rearing, leaf plate-making, etc.

Agricultural developments have taken an interesting turn in Kankana Halli. From one perspective, the push to promote mono-cropping in the 1980s reinforced a dysfunctional, individualized tenure system. People constructed embankments but only on their own plots, limiting their effectiveness in preventing run off and soil erosion. Some areas, for example, were deliberately left unprotected to make way for the rented tractor. Under the Myrada-HD Kote programme technical support has effectively reversed some of these tendencies, by raising awareness of the fragility of the environment and local ecosystems, and has also demonstrated the productivity gains of watershed management when families live adjacent to one another and cooperate to develop more intensive organic farming practices.

Building sustainable institutions: Myrada's footprint

Myrada and the self-help group phenomenon

Myrada has now had close to 30 years experience of building people's institutions in India and elsewhere in South and South East Asia. According to its director, it currently employs 450 staff to work directly with 1.5 million of the region's poor. To give an idea of scale, Sagare and Kankana Halli are two villages among 448 within the Myrada-HD Kote project in Mysore District, which in turn is one of 15 major projects in three Indian states that are managed by Myrada. It also has staff working for government agencies in three other states, and conducts regular training visits throughout the country (Fernandez, 2005). Myrada is credited with initiating the Self-help Group (SHG) movement in India, with several government and non-government initiatives modelling self-help groups on the Myrada prototype of Self-help Affinity Group or SAG.

In India as a whole, the total number of SHGs now stands at 3 million with 25 million members (Wilson, 2006). These SHGs have provided savings and credit services for members otherwise excluded from the formal banking system, and they have also taken on important social and political roles in village life.

Along with admiration for this phenomenon come questions about the contradictions inherent in outside organizations ushering in 'self-help,' the level of dependency of SHGs on NGOs, and the capacity of SHGs to self-replicate and become a truly sustainable movement while still catering to the poorest groups (Wilson, 2006). As recent studies have shown, there are 'lights and shades' in terms of their financial and social functions (ibid.), and a recognition that probably the single greatest factor in making or breaking movement out of poverty is health (Krishna, 2007: 66–79) and access to affordable health care. SHGs as a movement are therefore part of a larger web of interconnected factors influencing positive and sustainable change.

Myrada's approach

Myrada itself has always been clear about recognizing self-help at its 'rawest' (in coping and survival strategies, for example), moulding that capacity in a shape and form that can facilitate poor people's access to financial services and improved livelihood options, and putting institutional mechanisms in place to ensure sustainability. This, however, takes time, and one of the challenges has been resisting donor pressures to bring about quick results:

> Our position is that, to build capacity, we may have to go at a slower pace than donors expect. We do not want to be constrained by time-bound results in the initial stages....It takes six months to two years to 'mobilize' a village. (Fernandez, personal communication, 2005)

Protecting the space for villages to move at their own pace does not mean to say that Myrada is not itself influenced by the agenda of its donor partnerships. In the case of PLAN, for example, Myrada would not have taken up child-focused programming without the insistence of PLAN. Yet Myrada was able to demonstrate that this external assistance would not be effective without concurrent investment in building the capacity of people's institutions to manage these inputs.

While Myrada has promoted several people's institutions (SAGs, WDAs, children's clubs, youth clubs, etc.), the SAGs are the most vibrant and widespread. Most significantly, they have provided the impetus for the design of other institutions, such as the Community Managed Resource Centres (CMRCs), and *Sanghamithra*, to guarantee the sustainability and up-scaling of these village based institutions.

It is important to stress the thinking that underlies this vast capacity-building project. When first conceived, 'affinity groups' were a deliberate departure from the cooperative society model with village-wide membership and elected leadership. The affinity groups model, now well-accepted by the microfinance sector, is based on the recognition that relationships of trust have already been established among various informal groupings in the community. Financial accumulation and effective group action depend on these relationships of trust. In the case of women, for example, the affinity group provides a safe space to build their asset base independently of the often exploitative social relations of village or domestic politics. With regard to leadership, SAGs do not have formal elected leadership positions where one member is elevated to represent the rest; instead, leadership responsibilities are rotated and decision-making is by consensus. In this way, each member is helped to develop the capacity needed for record keeping, interaction with banks, and representing the SAG at CMRC meetings. All members participate as a group in decisions about loan use and capacity to repay of individual members, based on an insider assessment of risk.

These practices are significant because they reflect the confidence Myrada has shown in the existing strengths and capacities of the poor, which is the cornerstone of Myrada's work. Indeed, perhaps the most vivid illustration of Myrada's attitude is its discovery of this hitherto unrecognized capacity: 'The affinity groups were unpolished diamonds sitting under stones, some of which we ourselves had placed; we just happened to kick these stones by accident' (Fernandez, 2005: 4).

An ability to notice such 'diamonds' meant that Appreciative Inquiry methods came naturally to Myrada staff, and were integrated into fieldworker training. Focusing on strengths and capacities meant that relationships of dependency between the SAGs and Myrada could be more deliberately avoided. In keeping with this principle, a clear strategy was devised to ensure that SAGs could link directly with institutions such as banks and government agencies so as to be able to function independently.

SAGs operate as follows. Members pay a weekly sum, based on their ability to contribute, and this is deposited into the SAGs Common Fund. The SAG has an account at the nearest bank, thanks to Myrada's influence on National Bank for Agriculture and Rural Development (NABARD) policy, and that of the Reserve Bank of India, which now permit banks to loan to groups as groups without asking for the purpose in advance, and even if they were not formally registered.[d] Group members can borrow from this Common Fund, and can use this as leverage to borrow a larger loan from the bank, through the SAG.

As of 2007, for example, the SAGs in the entire HD Kote project area (now numbering 2122) have mobilized their savings to leverage 2.57 the amount of their savings in loans from *Sanghamithra* and local banks. (D'Souza, personal communication, 2007).

Myrada's involvement at the early stage was for a fieldworker to attend meetings of the newly formed SAGs and to facilitate linkages with the banks and other institutions. Raising awareness on issues such as health, education, leadership, and training opportunities has also been made available through the SAGs. SAGs have thus come into their own as 'credit plus' microfinance institutions. Myrada itself, however, has been at pains to point out that it has never been, nor intends to be, a microfinance institution itself, preferring to exert pressure on the existing banking system to cater to the banking needs of the poor.

Sustaining the SAGs through building institutional linkages

Despite concessions by the banking sector, Myrada argued that the banking needs of the rural poor were still not being met. Some of the reasons for this were the inadequacy of services in remote areas (liberalization policies had led to restructuring and amalgamation of rural banks), the cumbersome transactional requirements of the banks for SHGs and a dragging of feet by some banks to fully embrace the new policy. Most significantly, and because of these weaknesses, in order for Myrada to withdraw from its programming areas, of which HD Kote/PLAN is one, it had to be confident that SAGs could link to financial institutions completely independently.

Based on these considerations, the idea for *Sanghamithra* (meaning 'Group Friend/Friend of Groups') Rural Financial Services was born, and established as a not-for-profit institution under Section 25 of the Companies Act in 1995. *Sanghamithra* is a microfinance institution independent of Myrada, but with Myrada staff members on the board, it has been designed to cater to the needs of the expanding SAG market. When it exists in close proximity to other rural banks, it is intended to provide the healthy competition required for rural banks to improve their services to the rural poor; once this has been achieved, *Sangamithra* can move on. Thus, it is positioning itself as a 'friend' to rural banks as well as the groups, by demonstrating the creditworthiness of SAGs (already at 97.5 per cent recovery rate), and showing the way forward in terms of product design and customer services.

The Community Managed Resource Centres are relatively new institutions providing a critical link in Myrada's sustainability strategy. Emerging in the year 2002, and now numbering over 53 across all Myrada project areas, they were conceived as centres that could provide services to SAGs and other community-based institutions for a fee, performing the functions that Myrada used to provide with no charge (Fernandez, 2004). Their membership is comprised people's institutions (such as SAGs), not individual members, and a fee for services is paid by each, entitling it to a range of basic services such

Elected representatives of a Self-help Affinity Group in Sagare village perform transactions on behalf of their group at a local bank.

as SAG advice, bank linkages, and access to training opportunities. A manager with several years experience at the village level works with a Management Committee elected from the membership. A measure of the success of these CMRCs and the SAGs they serve is that over the last four years SAGs have maintained payment of the annual fee for service and their combined payments contribute 50 per cent of the CMRC manager's salary

Included in these services is a linkage role: the CMRC links SAGs to a range of government programmes, to *Sanghamithra* and to commercial banks. It also acts as a quasi executive for the still informal 'federation' of SAGs which meets regularly. To be developed further, according to Fernandez, are ways to offer specific support to farmers who, given the relative neglect of this sector, need access to quality inputs, technological and marketing information, and re-orientation towards a more entrepreneurial approach to diversifying agricultural production and livelihood strategy (personal communication, 2005).

This section on Myrada's institutional footprint would not be complete without commenting on its collaborative role with government. Collaboration is now seen as a 'strategic link in [Myrada's] efforts to upscale...as well as to initiate policy change arising from experience in the field, especially in programmes where government and NGOs work' (D'Souza, personal communication, 2005). Before, government officials attempted (and often failed) to plan, select, deliver and inspect services (resulting in numerous delays and cost escalations). Now with 'community participation' expected in decentralized planning, communities are encouraged to mobilize financial contributions, labour contributions, skills and expertise (in planning, site selection, monitoring, and inspection, for example), as well as to scrutinize contractors. Myrada's role has been to inform and encourage productive relationships, ensuring that people understand their entitlements and obligations, and positioning institutions like SAGs and WDAs so that they can negotiate, mobilize, and leverage resources in a demand-driven local government system.

The case of Sagare and Kankana Halli villages: changes in the asset base

What has been the significance of the changes that have occurred in the lives of people in these two villages over the last 20 years? In this section we highlight assets that have been built and how these have combined to enhance people's capacity to be in control of their livelihoods. The emphasis is on the perspective of SAG and WDA members, the more disadvantaged in the village as a whole, giving an indication of the redistributive effects of the changes that have occurred.

Physical and human assets

When asked about significant changes over the last 20 years, people in both Sagare and Kankana Halli tended to focus on roads and schools. A road connection is high on rural people's priority list since it allows economic integration with the outside world, and more effective service delivery. Infrastructure associated with irrigation and water supply also signals dramatic change: the productivity gains from the conversion of wet to dry land, the reduction of workload for women, and the health gains from a potable water supply. In Sagare, the arrival of rural electrification was a further boost for the establishment of small enterprises and was also associated with improved health care facilities and schools. In both villages, health indicators were positive, reflecting uptake of accessible immunization and primary health care services, the decline of water-borne disease, and the absence of malaria.

In Kankana Halli, the importance of children's education was the first reason that villagers became organized after they settled in the area. In Sagare, the new high school is a great source of pride, a physical embodiment of the slow but steady savings and investment strategies of the SAG membership and their hopes for a future less dependent on agriculture, as well as less exploited by others. As one man noted:

> Education means we have access to information. With access to information, we can get out from under oppression. There is no more deception. Before all

the benefits would go to literates because they know all about government services. (personal communication, 2005)

Active encouragement of girls' education suggests that they will also 'get out from under oppression' at the household level.

Financial assets

SAG membership has increased women's access to, and control over, financial resources and this has enabled them to invest in other assets. Most common were investments in agriculture such as land, seed or other agricultural inputs, equipment and technical assistance for building embankments and fencing, or an irrigation pump. Investment in micro enterprise was also common. A woman might buy provisions for her husband's trade store or buy bangles or spices wholesale and sell them at local markets. Finally, although it is discouraged, some women might also invest in social relationships through marriage or dowry payments.

The loans would at first be very small but would gradually increase, as this woman explains:

At first I hesitated to join a group. Then I joined and paid Rs5 per week. Gradually the weekly sum became higher, going up to Rs10–15 per week. Now I can save up to Rs50 per week. I have confidence that I can get a loan and pay it back. I already have a loan of Rs10,000 which I am using to irrigate dry land. (personal communication, 2005)

Loans were therefore not only an instrumental means to purchase productive assets but also, over time, a way in which women could express their confidence in their capacities as investors and entrepreneurs.

Social assets

Women frequently mentioned how the experience of membership in SAGs and WDAs has resulted in deeper and wider *social* relationships. As one woman commented: 'Before the SAGs, there were no support networks. I was lonely. I could only work inside the home, not outside' (personal communication, 2005).

Wider social linkages were often associated with a stronger sense of active citizenship whether through contributions to relief efforts, paying for school prizes, or actively encouraging the formation of new groups. In addition, the notion of public service is seen to be closely related to election to public office:

I have been a SAG member for the last four years. Before, I had been doing voluntary social work in the community. I was then elected as a representative at the SAG federation level and I am now on the board of directors of the CMRC. All this gave me good experience and helped me to become known by many people. Now I am a *panchayat* member. (personal communication, 2005)

In addition to the benefits to individuals and communities of active citizenship encouraged by SAG membership, separate mention should be made of the liberating effect of accessing financial resources through the self-help groups rather than the moneylender. People spoke frequently of getting out from under oppressive relationships:

> Before, we would be exploited by moneylenders. We didn't even know how to sign or where to sign. Now that I have learned to save, I am more secure, and I also have the courage to talk to officials. I am not dependent on others to speak for me. (Male SAG member, personal communication, 2005)

This confidence goes hand in hand with a greater degree of connectivity with the outside world. Remembering their fear of interacting with people outside their own families, members of one women's SAG operating in Sagare for eight years identified a long list of linkages made with government officials, banks, life insurance agents, product marketing agents, hospital workers, NGO services, and the federations and organizations of which they were members such as the SAG federation and the CMRC.

Diversifying and managing assets

Among poorer families, increasing the overall asset base has been matched by an increased diversification of livelihood to spread risk. As William D'Souza, Program Officer for the PLAN/HD Kote District Office pointed out, 'the poor need security and opportunity' (personal communication, 2005). Diversifying their asset base (and their investment portfolio) so that they are neither so dependent on agriculture, nor one source of employment, nor one form of investment, provides them with that security. With a sound risk management strategy in place, they are in a better position to respond to opportunity. For example, a young female member of a scheduled tribe, whose husband had deserted her, was encouraged to join a SAG. To do this, she first had to save money in order to catch up to the savings level built up by other members. Having done this, she borrowed money from the SAG to lease land to grow vegetables. Through the SAG she found an opportunity to work part-time as a cook in the local school, enabling her to repay her loan promptly.

Above all, women have choices about how to spend their time. Keen to take advantage of income-earning opportunity, women in one SAG reported that they now manage their time with 'more discipline' and 'dedicate maybe [only] 25 per cent of our time to our husbands and children and use the other time to do other things, such as selling bangles, or cloth, or packing spices' (personal communication, 2005).

Internal agency: local capacity to organize and act

Traditionally, different caste communities have been organized through the informally elected leaders of each caste. To this day, it is caste leadership that organizes religious ceremonies, marriages, and other traditional functions. Women have no decision-making role in these rites.

The *panchayat raj* system of local governance is designed to decentralize *and* democratize decision-making. Specific constitutional provisions have been made to counteract caste-based and gender-based social divisions by guaranteeing places for women and scheduled tribes and castes as elected representatives. Without these provisions, entrenched positions would tend to be sustained and politicized. Thus, for all its flaws in implementation, the *panchayat raj* system is a means by which local priorities can drive the distribution of government funds. New organizational forms in civil society are an important part of the overall picture, whether in the form of youth groups, cultural groups, or SAGs. The dynamic of 'internal agency' is in a state of flux: traditional forms of organization (such as family or caste) are disappearing or adapting, and new associational groupings are emerging.

Self-help Affinity Groups

SAGs are the most obvious example of the new associational groupings. Based on relationships of trust they have deepened the trust internal to the group and have also built relationships of trust with other SAGs through the federation, or with other SAGs at the village level. According to William D'Souza, the decision to shift from a representative village development committee model to an affinity group model was initially met with criticism:

> At first, we were criticized for 'dividing' the village. But affinity groups are more natural groupings, and many cut across caste lines. As we reorganized in this way, we noticed how much more vibrant these groups were. (D'Souza, personal communication, 2005)

As an illustration of the effects of this vibrancy, women and men spoke of how women's status in the community and in the household had risen as a result of membership in the SAGs. They agreed that there was more shared decision-making in the household, and more male participation in household chores. 'Just the fact that women are sitting here on the porch discussing with you, while men are standing and looking on – that shows how much things have changed here,' said one woman (personal communication, 2005). Another claimed, 'Now I can take full responsibility to maintain the family while my husband travels outside the village to trade' (personal communication, 2005). All members of the SAGs are taking responsibility for managing the SAG, rotating leadership roles so that each woman gains leadership experience, rather than propelling one into a position of responsibility over others.

Reminiscent of how traditional craft guilds fostered an ethos of community-building among their members, SAGs and women members are increasingly matching their economic role with a citizenship role acting for 'the public good.' There are several ways they have done this. Individually, many SAGs use Common Fund resources to make donations to various charitable causes, whether to support tsunami or earthquake victims, or to purchase books as prizes for schools. Collectively, they have petitioned the *gram sabha* to take a stand against drinking alcohol, so that now its sale is prohibited in the village. They have also combined to propose particular priorities for *gram sabha* expenditure, as in the case of the village-wide toilet construction in Sagare village. Some of these decisions arise from federation meetings.

Individual women are assuming roles reserved for them in local government. Six out of the 16 places on the Sagare *gram panchayat* are reserved for women SAG members. A local Sagare woman, now standing for election at the *taluk* level, described her efforts to form a SAG and how her skill in bookkeeping earned her employment in other SAGs. She also works as a cook at the school and as a trainer for Myrada, and acts as an agent for a private insurance business. She persuaded her husband to take out a loan to build a flour mill. Their combined assets now include the flour mill, an acre of wet land, life insurance, post office savings, and jewellery. Her SAG savings are a form of security she can fall back on should her income from other sources fail and she becomes unable to pay the recurring costs at the flour mill. Through encouragement from Myrada she has been active in promoting groups, and in helping those who cannot form groups to set up savings accounts in banks.

Myrada's withdrawal from villages in HD Kote is premised on the development of sufficient linkages among and between people's institutions and external agencies, and so that village development is effectively shifted to local agencies SAGS, WDAs, youth groups and children's clubs all combine to build that interconnectivity and the capacity to hold local government to account and to leverage external resources.

Leveraging external assets

SAGs and WDAs have demonstrated their capacity to leverage funds through the government rural banking system and through the more recently formed *Sanghamithra* microfinance institution. If capacity to leverage is one side of the coin, worthiness of investment is the other: repayment rates among SAG are, according to the bank manager of the Cauvery Grameena Bank, at a rate of 95 per cent. Apart from financial investments in them by banks, SAGs also attract credit-plus activities in villages where they are a significant part of the fabric of village life. PLAN, for example, directed its housing grants, health awareness, and child rights awareness through the SAG system because it constituted a proven organizational base through which education and awareness could gather momentum. Similarly, government training programmes and service delivery are more effective because of the enlarged social network and its capacity to mobilize community participation. For example, SAGs are consulted in water and sanitation programmes which require community expertise (regarding site selection, for instance), community labour, community financial contributions, and community monitoring.

The role of external agency

To discuss Myrada's role means discussing it in relation to the villages where it works, the government with which it collaborates, and its donors. Each of these aspects is instructive. Its changing role at the village level has already been discussed, but perhaps its choice to encourage natural 'affinity' groups – building on existing associational networks, rather than artificially creating socially representative groupings – is particularly instructive. Its emphasis on attitudinal change in the training of its own fieldworkers is now carried on through its training of government workers. This has instilled a pride in the capacity to support others: 'a hand up, not a handout.' Without this, Myrada staff members feel the technical aspects of their work with SAGs could easily have floundered.

Shifting from an active presence in each village to playing an intermediary role through the CMRCs is consistent with Myrada's confidence in the capacity of SAGs. It is also a deliberate sustainability strategy. As it withdraws, Myrada will want to know whether the SAG mobilization efforts have become self-sustaining as mechanisms for people to access assets to improve their livelihood options by financial means. They will also want to know if building capacity to influence local decision-making has also improved the potential for accessing assets through means of political representation. The question will also be raised about whether new SAGs will self-replicate among the poorest, or whether, without active encouragement to form new groups, the 'poorest' will become poorer.

In Sagare village, perhaps 500 of the 900 families are involved in SAGs. For many of the poorest, however, forming or joining a SAG appears impossible. For example, a woman working as an agricultural labourer for extended periods outside the village (at the coffee plantations in Tamil Nadu, for instance) would have to pay a fine to the SAG for each week of absence. For some, the fine is worth it. Other women or families have reached a crisis point. Living close to the precipice, they lack the confidence and the social capital to take the initiative to form or join a group.

One such woman from Sagare village described her situation. Although encouraged to join a group years ago, she did not, partly because her husband discouraged her from doing so. She and her husband are both agricultural labourers. Her husband had an accident six months previously. To pay for hospital expenses they leased out their one acre of dry land, and also sold their cattle. Her earnings are Rs25 per day, which is less than half the official minimum wage rate and less than the rate her husband could earn if he were well.

During Myrada's active phase this family might have been helped by encouragement to form a group, or Myrada's social safety net opportunities, such as food for work, could have smoothed this family's entry into a position of being able to save. Now the incentive to form groups is the Rs5,000 revolving fund offered as a start-up to newly formed groups under a government scheme, as well as the demonstrated effect of the success of other SAGs. The local *panchayat* has taken up the role of providing 'smoothing' opportunities: 20 per cent of tax revenue, for example, is redirected into food for work programmes such as village cleanliness activities that are supposed to be offered to help people in this situation. Yet the woman in this case claimed she was not aware of these. As a vehicle for information and as a voice at the *panchayat* level (to ensure enforcement of minimum wage rates, for example), SAGs can be a force to prevent slippage of the poor into destitution. Will the example set by existing SAGs be sufficient for new groups to form? Or is it at that level that Myrada or another external agency will still need to intervene?

Such cases will test the commitment of 'people's institutions' to the new poor and poorest in the quest for institutional sustainability, and test the quality of collaboration between Myrada and government to ensure the continuation of the services required for people's institutions to thrive.

Conclusion

The concept of 'self-help' is a controversial one. Critics have pointed out that the promotion of self-help can be a means by which development is depoliticized: government abdicates its responsibilities to redistribute wealth with an attitude of letting poor people look after themselves, leaving their fate in the hands of leadership in existing power structures. Berner and Phillips, for example, argue that while the self-help debate has helped to create respect for the poor's capability and resourcefulness, and a certain degree of humility on the part of 'expert' and top-down interventions, it is important not to overstate the case:

> The opposite extreme, namely relying completely on their own latent capacities, will likely prove to be just as futile. The idea that poor communities can 'develop themselves' – if it means that heterogeneity and inequity within communities can be glossed over, if it means that the macro structures of wealth and power distribution can be ignored – is flawed to the point of being harmful. (Berner and Phillips, 2005: 27)

Self-help in the context of Myrada lies between these two extremes. The commitment to building people's institutions is not only so that the poor can diversify their livelihood options themselves (through the SAG savings and credit functions), but also so that a demand-system is created for better governance and a private sector with a pro-poor agenda.

As the examples in Sagare and Kankana Halli demonstrate, Self-help Affinity Groups and Watershed Development Associations have not only strengthened the innate capacity of individual members, but have also demonstrated their power to mobilize, organize, influence, advocate, and leverage as a group – in other words, to assume control over their own livelihoods and to effectively influence the direction of village development through local government. Most of these are women's SAGs, and most are from scheduled tribes and castes. To the extent that SAGs have succeeded in enabling their membership to build up their assets and move out of poverty is evidence of profound transformation in political life both within the household and within the village.

For people to move forward, risk must be tempered by a level of security, and opportunity must be mediated by relationships of trust. For those most at risk, and especially where caste identity places severe restrictions on livelihood prospects, those conditions can take many years to emerge. Viewed from a livelihoods perspective, a sense of security is possible if one has access to, and control over, essential assets in sufficient quantity and diversity so that risk can be managed and crisis can be avoided. These assets may be tangible such as cash savings or jewellery, land, or a road connection to outside markets. Equally important are the intangible assets such as good health, particular skills, leadership qualities, and relationships of trust with others. With opportunity, people have a reason to mix and match those assets, and to mobilize them to meet opportunity in a calculated risk for improved prosperity.

As Bebbington (1999) has argued, assets are more than instrumental to the owner, they also give the owner identity, and with that identity, a capacity to act. For the individual group member, self-help means building an asset base that generates the capacity to make choices. With that capacity comes 'agency.' In conjunction with other interventions by the state and the market, Myrada's role has been to facilitate this shift in capacity, withdrawing once these dimensions of asset-based development – assets and agency – converge in the people's institutions it has nurtured.

Endnotes

1. 1US$ is equivalent to approximately Rs40 (Indian Rupees) at 3 March 2008.
2. Below Poverty Line (BPL) is determined by a composite index of land holding, housing type, and annual income. The cut-off is Rs12,000 per year, which is equivalent to US$260 at the time of writing.
3. Nine of the SAGs are men's groups, and eight are government-initiated.
4. The SAG-Bank Linkage Model was launched in 1992. According to Fernandez, 'There is no better example, to my knowledge, in the history of anti-poverty strategies, where a small initiative was picked up and supported by NABARD, a government financial institution, and built up... with NABARD taking the lead over a period of 15 years, during which it changed policy at the national level' (Fernandez, 2005: 26).

References

Bebbington, A. (1999) 'Capitals and capabilities: A framework for analyzing peasant viability, rural livelihoods and poverty', *World Development*, 27(12): 2021–2044.

Berner, E. and Phillips, B. (2005) 'Left to their own devices? Community self-help between alternative development and neo-liberalism', *Community Development Journal*, 40(1): 17–29.

Blair, H. (2000) 'Participation and accountability at the periphery: Democratic local governance in six countries', *World Development*, 28(1): 21–39.

Brown, J., Ananthpur, K. and Giovarelli, R. (2002), *Women's access and rights to land in Karnataka*, RDI Reports on Foreign Aid and Development No. 114, Rural Development Institute, Seattle, WA.

Davies, R. and Dart, J. (2005) *The 'Most Significant Change' (MSC) technique: A guide to its use.* Available from http://www.mande.co.uk/docs/MSCGuide.pdf [Accessed 3 August 2007].

Fan, S., Chan-Kang, C. and Mukherjee, A. (August 2005) *Rural and urban dynamics and poverty: evidence from China and India*, Food Consumption and Nutrition Division Discussion Paper No. 196, International Food Policy Research Institute (IFPRI), Washington, DC.

Fernandez, A. (2001) *Putting institutions first – Even in microfinance*, Myrada, Bangalore, India.

Fernandez, A. (2004) *Sanghamithra: A micro finance institution with a difference.* Myrada, Bangalore, India.

Fernandez, A. (2005, March) *Self-help affinity groups (SAGs): Their role in poverty reduction and financial sector development*, Paper presented at the International Conference on Microfinance in the Global Strategy for Meeting the Millennium Development Goals hosted by Concern Worldwide, Dublin, Ireland.

Isaac, T. and Franke, R. W. (2002) *Local democracy and development: The Kerala people's campaign for decentralized planning*, Rowman and Littlefield, Lanham, MD.

Krishna, A. (2007) 'The stages-of-progress methodology and results from five countries', in Moser, C. (ed), *Reducing global poverty: The case for asset accumulation*, Brookings Institution, Washington, DC.

Srivastava, S.S., Tandon, R., Wojciech Sokolowski, S. and Salamon, L.M. (2004) 'India', in Salamon, L.M. and Wojciech Sokolowski, *Global civil society: Dimensions of the nonprofit sector* (Vol. 2), Kumarian, Bloomfield, CT.

Wilson, K. (2006) 'Foreword', in *Self help groups in India: A study of the lights and shades*, EDA Rural Systems Private Ltd. Available from http://www.edarural.com/documents/SHG-Study/Executive-Summary.pdf [Accessed 2 July 2007].

Glossary

gowda	Farming caste
gram panchayat	Local government body at the village level in India
gram sabha	Persons registered in the electoral rolls of a village within the area of the *panchayat*

lakh	Unit in the Indian numbering system; equal to 100,000
medar	Basket weaving caste
panchayat raj	A decentralized form of government in which villages are responsible for their own affairs; advocated by Mahatma Gandhi and adopted by state governments in post-independence India
Sanghamithra	A microfinance institution meaning 'Group friend/Friend of Groups'
shetty	Trader caste
taluk	A city or town serving as a headquarters within a larger district

Author's note

Although our priority for this book was to focus on examples of community-driven development where there had been little external assistance, we also realized that there was a place for stories of communities that had been helped by an external organization in such a way as to enable communities to take ownership and responsibility for 'changing the course of their own development.' Myrada has a long-standing reputation for stimulating sustained poverty reduction through self-help organizations and 'people's institutions'. For this reason, we were interested in looking closely at communities that were sustaining these people's institutions successfully and continuing to see an improvement in people's livelihoods. In addition, the Coady Institute had been following Myrada's work with interest for a number of years, particularly its use of innovative participatory techniques, such as appreciative inquiry. As an external agency fostering community-driven development, we assumed there were lessons to be drawn from the way in which Myrada interacted with people at the community level. At my request, William D'Souza, project manager for HD Kote-PLAN, identified two contrasting villages in the project area, Sagare and Kankana Halli, for exploratory case study research.

While both villages had been within Myrada's orbit, I emphasized throughout the fieldwork that I was interested in the perspective of community members on change in general, without restricting it to their work with Myrada. In both villages, active SAGs were invited to discuss the 'Most Significant Change' in their villages over the last 30 years, using a modified version of Rick Davies' and Jess Dart's 'Most Significant Change' technique (Davies and Dart, 2003). To explore the main themes emerging from these discussions, follow up interviews were conducted with individual SAGs (five in Sagare, two in Kankana Halli) and with individual SAG members (10 in total). In Sagare, three were women's SAGs and two SAGs had both men and women members. In Kankana Halli, community members gathered as a group to discuss both the experience of WDAs and SAGs, and follow-up interviews were conducted with two family groups. Interviews were also conducted with older people in both communities to provide a historical context for village activity.

Fieldwork took place in November 2005, assisted by the translation services of Mr Ravi Shankar. In addition to interviews with villagers, interviews were conducted with Myrada staff in Bangalore (Aloysius Fernandez and Vidya Ramachandran) and those staff at Myrada-HD Kote with responsibility for programming in these two villages, including the two managers of the CMRCs (Mr Mahadevaiah and Mr Channappa). Particular thanks go to William D'Souza, and Rajappa for facilitating the interviews, answering questions, and making documents available.

Government officials interviewed included local government officials at both the *panchayat* and *taluk* levels, including Dr Shivakumar, the medical officer for the *taluk*. Mr Mahesh Babu, the bank manager of the Beechanahalli Branch of Cauvery Kalpatharu Grameena Bank, was also interviewed.

Following the field research, interview data and data from secondary sources were combined and analysed to produce this case study. Saleela Patkar was kind enough to review an earlier draft, and William D'Souza reviewed the final draft for factual content.

CHAPTER 10

Jansenville Development Forum: linking community and government in the rural landscape of the Eastern Cape Province, South Africa

Susan Wilkinson-Maposa

Abstract

As a philanthropic funding agency, Ikhala Trust's work with the Jansenville Development Forum has recognized the full extent of the 'horizontal philanthropy' operating at community level in Jansenville and has worked to support and strengthen this. The careful balancing act of helping communities strengthen themselves without creating dependency is discussed in the larger South African context of striking the balance between rights or entitlements that South Africans have fought for, and opportunities for people to build sustained independent livelihoods, reinforced by traditions of mutual self-help.

Introduction

We are different from other donors. We are more interested in sharing in your journey than telling you what to do. We try to put a value on what people do for their own development. (Bernie Dolley, Director, Ikhala Trust)

This chapter illustrates how local associations bound by principles of mutual self-help came together under a community-based mechanism – the Jansenville Development Forum (JDF) – to strengthen their capacity and access external resources. Their shared goal and vision was to advance out of adversity and seek greater opportunities. This story is set in the township area of Jansenville, a small town of 6,000, located in the sheep and goat farming area of the Eastern Cape province, in the Ikwezi Local Municipality, the 'mohair capital' of South Africa.

It offers a rich example of how community assets and agency created a demand for organization and self-strengthening that resulted in the emergence of a community-based intermediary non-governmental organization (NGO). The JDF not only incubated civil society, but acted as a focal point for local government consultation with community in municipal-level planning processes.

The JDF story began in 2000, when a group of ten community-based organizations (CBOs) came together, including a burial society, a women's income-generation group, and an advice office (providing information on rights and responsibilities related to various issues including labour laws, social grants, and access to basic social services). Some CBOs had been in existence for 10–13 years, while others had been in existence for less than two years, but all had the mutual desire to 'move' (forward). Increased access to external forces – networks, training, and funds – was sought in order for the groups to grow. Sharing what they had, such as volunteer time, basic office infrastructure, knowledge, and experience, the CBOs set out to improve the contribution they could make to local community development. To make this happen, they drew on, tapped into, and leveraged local norms and practices of self-help – pulling together, caring, and sharing.

Several institutional actors are involved in this story. The protagonist is the JDF as an umbrella body of CBOs. The supporting cast consists of Ikhala Trust, a community grant-maker based in Port Elizabeth, and local government, the Ikwezi Municipal Council. Each actor plays a distinct role.

First, JDF, a mobilizer and organizer, emerged from within the community and incubated the capacity of the associational life and energy that already existed. It did not introduce new associations. Strong and capable leadership nurtured a common interest: the desire to 'move.' JDF tapped into the support systems built into the norms and culture of township life. It also linked civil society efforts, rights, and needs to the government's mandate to engage more closely with local communities for fuller participation and responsiveness. Second, Ikhala Trust, an external grant-maker, is a facilitator. Through its support of JDF, it created a space for the organization and its members to 'discover' themselves. Ikhala did not lead from a donor perspective, but rather 'lifted up' existing capacity through advisory support to close gaps. It prepared and qualified JDF to increase its access to new resources and opportunities. The technical, advisory, and financial support provided by Ikhala came with its own reputational capital that JDF leveraged to link with external support and resources.

Third, local government, the Ikwezi Municipality, is a strategic collaborator. The government and civil society dichotomy was not overplayed. JDF is a 'watch dog,' but it also contributes to the council's ability to carry out its mandate to promote community participation in local government planning processes and the provision of basic social services as a right of citizenship. For its part, the council is serious about people's participation and good governance. It has begun to adapt how politicians interact with the community and has established various fora to strengthen communication, including monthly meetings with civil society.

The roots of JDF began in shallow, yet fertile, soil. In 2002, adversity – unsustainable funding, a lack of coordination and limited resources – brought fragmented groups together. Yet it was the practice of self-help, such as a willingness to share and work with the small things they had, including a phone, fax machine and office space, that kept them together and allowed collective advance toward a more viable existence.

JDF operated 'out of nothing,' having to 'beg' for small things, including ink for the printer or a ream of paper. In August 2002, a grant of R20,000 (or 2,534 USD, since 1 USD is equivalent to approximately 8 South African Rand, at 3 March 2008), followed by a second grant of R13,000, were awarded by Ikhala Trust. These were used to purchase a telephone and fax, as well as stationery, allowing JDF to produce funding documents and communicate with the outside world. Members were excited but disciplined: they showed up for work at 8 a.m. to discuss programmes, talk about the previous day's activities, and share problems. They relied on volunteer labour; as well, they brought their own furniture and cleaning materials from home. Then, in 2003, Ikhala Trust brought a computer: this was a turning point. In addition, JDF received its first funds from government in June of the same year. The National Development Agency (NDA) provided a grant of R887,000. Intended for one year, it was extended to three. This allowed JDF to move forward and grow.

In the seven years since its inception, JDF has developed considerably. While there was one staff member at the start, there are now eight. From its beginnings in a one-room building, the organization is now housed in an 11-room building. Funding has increased from a first round of start-up funds in 2002 to a solid funding relationship with government. Volunteers are now wage-earners. And, building on its origins as a group of disparate CBOs, JDF is now a leading organization, recognized locally, regionally, and provincially. During this time, the Jansenville community has, in fact, 'move' forward. The magnitude of this achievement should not be underestimated. In the words of Judy Chalmers, Member of Parliament:

> To know how far they have come, you have to know where they came from. This is an example of a community that works together with good leadership. Twenty years ago, it was a war zone – a terrifying place, especially for young people trying to resist under apartheid. A few weeks ago, there was a fair where you saw 'two days of happiness' – a genuine mixing of races eating together, dancing, etc. I have worked here since the 1980s and it is a wonder to see how this town has progressed. Jansenville has very [few] natural resources, including water, so it is exciting for me to hear the stories. This place is a fantastic symbol of the new South Africa. (personal communication, 2007)

This account told by an activist and passionate advocate of social justice and transformation is poignant. It portrays a lived reality that broadly frames the South African experience and sets a backdrop to appreciate the Jansenville story.

This case study tells the Jansenville story from the JDF perspective and in the context of a newly democratic country. It unpacks Jansenville's experience and achievements by placing them in the framework of self-help and mutual assistance – local assets and agency – as well as the institutional framework of an intermediary organization able to satisfy demands from 'below' (community associations) as well as from 'above' (government). Attention is drawn to interesting insights for development practice, including the conundrum for community-driven development that lies in the tension between entitlement and empowerment, or rights and responsibilities.

Insights for community-driven development

The JDF experience highlights two critical dimensions of community development that are flagged here and developed more fully in subsequent sections. One is the recognition and strengthening of help traditions and norms as a community asset and indicator of agency. The second is the inherent tension between citizen rights and citizen responsibilities in achieving sustainable community development.

Local systems of self-help

The Jansenville case demonstrates the potential or promise of community assets and agency as a developmental tool. That is, the practice and norms of people helping one another were the 'seed' that JDF nurtured to bring the community together. This seed was germinated, through CBO incubation, to facilitate community-driven development and promote movement away from adversity.

What is so special about this? The conventional lens tends to guide the eye along a vertical line of resources flowing up and down, from people and communities of high net wealth to those of low net wealth. The Jansenville example shows what is visible through a less frequently used lens. JDF's gaze is set on side-to-side or horizontal flow of tangible and intangible resources, among and between people and associations within a community. Organizations came together of their members' own volition, sustained by drawing on, and pooling together, the contributions of each group. These contributions ranged from skills, knowledge, and experiences, to fax machines and telephones, to plastic chairs and loaves of bread. JDF operated like this – reliant on its own commitment, vision, and resources – for three years prior to any significant financial assistance.

Rights and responsibilities

This case also brings to the surface the tension between citizen rights and claims on the state for social services (constitutionally enshrined in South Africa), and the responsibility of citizens to do things for themselves and generate their own opportunities. JDF has successfully brought the community to the point of movement with access to social services and social development funds. However, there is now a dire need for enhanced employment and livelihood opportunities. A critical question emerges: Will the community, largely dependent on social grants, see this development as a job for the government or will it embark upon the process of creating its own opportunities?

For JDF, a relevant issue is how to facilitate access to 'rights' in a way that does not create dependency and expectation, but rather retains a community's sense of its own autonomy and ability to generate opportunities and a longer term vision for the future. This issue has become a reality in 2007. JDF is currently moving into a new phase, building on its success in incubating civil society, while simultaneously incubating entrepreneurship, to help the community make a transition into enterprise and employment creation for more robust and sustainable livelihoods. This will not be easy and there is no silver bullet. However, potential links exist, including fostering the connection between social entrepreneurship and economic development. This issue of livelihood promotion is revisited in the conclusion with some preliminary thoughts on the potential for JDF's commitment to asset-based social development to evolve into asset-based economic development.

The need for this shift is exemplified in the discussion in the section 'National realities' below, as the national and local reality of high unemployment, low levels of entrepreneurial activity and high levels of dependency are detailed.

The context

The particular relationships of help that brought CBOs together in the small town of Jansenville can only be fully appreciated when the contradictory realities of the new South Africa are taken into account. This section explores these contradictions, setting the scene at national and local levels.

National realities

The trauma of the apartheid years, and the euphoric idealism that followed, fuelled the creation of a stridently progressive Constitution in 1994, one that was committed to 'a better life for all' through reconciliation, redistribution and transformation. A newly enfranchised black electorate could now expect to enjoy the material, social, and political benefits of citizenship, enshrined in a Bill of Rights which included access to an array of social grants designed to lift the poorest groups from destitution. Meanwhile, a growing economy would offer broad-based opportunity for employment.

Yet the legacy of apartheid has been slow to change. Although a middle-income country in Gross National Product (GNP) terms, South Africa continues to have one of the highest levels of income inequality in the world (with a Gini coefficient of 0.58), with hardship deepening among black South Africans in many areas. Inequalities in land ownership and housing stock continue to follow the contours of racial layering (Kuljian, 2005). A growing economy has not significantly budged current unemployment levels of 26.7 per cent (Statistics South Africa, 2006) because the labour force is relatively unskilled. Inexperience of entrepreneurship in the apartheid years has meant that black South Africans still have relatively low levels of entry into entrepreneurial activity. A recent Global Entrepreneurship Monitor (GEM) report placed South Africa with a Total Early-Stage Entrepreneurial Activity (TEA) index of 5.29 per cent, which is considerably lower than the global average of 9.43 per cent. The TEA index measures the percentage of individuals between the ages of 18 and 64 who are involved in starting a new business (Maas and Herrington, 2006). Also, participation in the workforce has eluded many because they have been compromised by the devastating blow struck by HIV/AIDS, infecting one in six adults (AVERT, 2007) which the South African government has only recently officially recognized and begun to deal with. A social grants system unique in the developing world – almost 50 per cent, or 49.7 per cent, of South African government expenditures were related to community and social services (Statistics South Africa, 2006) – acts as an effective safety net, but the dignity assured by effective education and meaningful employment has still to take hold.

As an emblem of the achievement of political freedom, South Africa has made a constitutional commitment to democratize development by establishing mechanisms for broad-based citizen participation in local government. The boldness of this undertaking should not be underestimated, given that during the apartheid regime there were separate public services for each racial group. Under the new constitution, these separate and exclusionary services were dismantled and their roles amalgamated into one inclusive public service for all, which was no small task. Now, local government not only has a responsibility to deliver services (water, electricity, roads, etc.), but also has a mandate to help build democracy and promote socio-economic development. It is expected to share decision-making with the private sector and community groups, a role without precedent in the centralized, top-down delivery system under apartheid (Chikulu, 2000).

However, given the impact of the economic aspects of apartheid, people in South Africa have tended to judge local government more on its performance in essential service delivery than on its efforts to provide a democratic space for citizen engagement (Mattes et al., 2003). Inevitably, until there is a connection between the merits of consultation and visible results of wealth redistribution, the value of participation will not be fully appreciated. It therefore falls to organizations like the JDF to make the benefits of democratic space real for people, as demonstrated in its partnership with local government in poverty assessments, and its participation along with other stakeholders in the formulation of an Integrated Development Plan (IDP) required of all municipalities. (In Ikwezi Municipality's 'Vision 2011', a Masithethisane – 'Come, let's talk together' – programme is planned, whereby every three months, councillors and municipal officials visit each community in order to report on government programmes, answer questions, and listen to input from community members.)

Local realities

Jansenville is located in the municipality of Ikwezi in the Eastern Cape Province. The Eastern Cape is one of the poorest provinces in South Africa with the highest levels of unemployment in the country at 29.6 per cent (Statistics South Africa, 2004), which has implications for the revenue base from which to draw on for the backlog of service delivery commitments, as well as the potential for employment. The population density is small in these rural areas. The terrain around Jansenville is comprised of vast tracts of dry savanna bushveld; its tenuous vegetation supporting extensive sheep and goat farming. According to a recently commissioned report for the mohair industry, 61 per cent of world mohair production is based in South Africa, with the Jansenville area a major contributor to overall production. Large sheep and goat farms, owned by white Afrikaans farmers for generations, have been major employers of black and coloured labourers. In the nervousness associated with political transition, and uncertainty about the future of the industry, sheep and goat herds are reported to have declined (personal communication with a commercial farmer and Notizi Vanda, April 2007), and some farms have been converted to game farms for high-end tourism. However, a recent resurgence of confidence is now reflected in the Ikwezi municipality staking much of its future on the promise of increased production of mohair, greater opportunities for value-added production (e.g. tanning and mohair processing), and greater participation of black farmers in the industry through its 'emerging farmer' programme.

Ikwezi municipality as a whole has a population of 10,000, with Jansenville's population approximately 6,000. The municipality is relatively racially integrated with approximately 10 per cent of the population white, 55 per cent coloured, and 35 per cent black (Statistics South Africa, 2001). As the statistics from the last census show, the rate of unemployment is devastatingly high at 46.35 per cent, with a corresponding high level of dependency on social grants (between 65 per cent and 70 per cent). In Jansenville, approximately 46 per cent are registered as unemployed; 32 per cent have withdrawn from the workforce or are not looking for work; 21 per cent are employed full-time; and 1 per cent are employed as seasonal workers (estimates based on the 2007 Ikwezi Local Municipality Draft IDP). Lack of employment means that a large proportion of the Jansenville population relies on government social grants as the main source of revenue. Social grants are provided by the government to residents who are unable to sustain themselves. Grants range in size from R200 per month for a Child Support grant to R870 per month awarded to those eligible for the Old Age Pension, the Care Dependency grant, the Disability grant or the War Veterans grant. To position these in terms of their contribution to people's livelihood, the minimum wage guide for farm workers, a typical employment opportunity in Jansenville, ranges from R885 to R989 per month, depending on the season (South African Department of Labour, April 2007).

While social grants have the potential to build the local economy by injecting financial resources, much of the grant money is spent in neighbouring towns or externally run businesses, and therefore does not stay within the community. With the exception of a few *spaza* shops (general stores) there is very little evidence of local trading. On social grant day, a flea market operates, but the majority of the vendors reside outside of Jansenville, moving from town to town. As they move on, local monies circulate out of the immediate economy and are not retained.

The government is addressing this issue through business grant schemes that promote small business, but in a country where the Global Entrepreneurship Monitor (GEM) ranking is deteriorating, it may be an uphill battle (Maas and Herrington, 2006). The GEM study looks at rates of entrepreneurship in a country, including the impact on national economic growth and factors that encourage entrepreneurship; its 2006 report tried to isolate some factors that explain why South Africa's position in the GEM rankings has deteriorated over time despite improved macro-economic conditions in the country. One of the most important findings is that potential entrepreneurs lack the mindset and skills to become true entrepreneurs. Although a positive entrepreneurial culture is starting to form on a macro level, entrepreneurship on a micro level is not showing any signs of growth. International markets are not penetrated, employment creation is not encouraged, and innovation is under pressure. The low levels of educational qualifications may be an important factor in explaining why this discrepancy persists. The challenges of starting a new business are many, given the short supply of skills and business acumen, including an entrepreneurial mindset, which is not surprising, given a legacy of apartheid.

For the municipal government, the alleviation of poverty has been its first priority. Personal communication with the mayor of Jansenville highlights that local government has been preoccupied with delivering the services expected since the Bill of Rights was introduced, and with trying to bridge the gap between income from its own limited revenue base of roughly R11million, and additional funds of R21 million required from national, provincial or private sources to fulfil its commitments. Since 2000, significant progress has been made in terms of infrastructure development, such as improvements to local housing, water collection tanks, toilet installation, and electricity in the township area, but huge backlogs remain.

Employment has been generated by the expansion of public services and by this intense period of infrastructure development. However, in the longer term, these short-term employment opportunities will have to be replaced by a sustainable means of livelihood for those making the shift from: a) employment in public works, and b) unemployment or destitution, assuming that they are enabled by social grants to seek work or take risks in self employment.

The challenge ahead

In many respects, therefore, Jansenville, and the Ikwezi municipality of which it is part, is at a transition in terms of its future. Will social grants be the way people in this community maintain their current livelihood base, or will there be sufficient redistribution of assets and restructuring of the economy to ensure that the income poor can grasp new opportunities and move beyond the limitation of their current livelihood situation? JDF played a role in bringing the Jansenville community to where it is today. It can be anticipated that the organization's contribution will continue into the future.

JDF's story

An account of JDF's development needs to start with an appreciation of the organizations that formed it. This includes local associations that emerged independently through norms and practices of self-help and were later further assisted by JDF. Two stories – The Ikwezi Edu-care Story (Box 10.1) and The Khayalesizwe Burial Society (Box 10.2) – are told here. They are prime examples of local associations that emerged organically within the community and drew on local resource mobilization, priorities, and commitment. In the case of Edu-care, membership in JDF skilfully leveraged government funds to pay for children's attendance fees. This support validated a community service and strengthened what the community was doing for itself.

Box 10.1: The Ikwezi Edu-care story: Jolene Kolobile, Director

In 1987, I noticed that there were many children roaming the streets of Jansenville, so a friend and I decided to gather them and run a day-care service for them. We called a meeting to discuss this with the community and explained what we were going to do. Soon, a committee was formed. At first, we started at the church hall, and then moved to another church hall, and then another hall. To keep things running, we would ask banks, businesses, parents, etc. for support. Parents were very supportive and would give us anything we needed (pots, food, and clothes). They still do that today. Finally, in 1993, the municipality gave us the building we are in today and in 1994 we started receiving a salary.

Now the parents are starting a community garden to grow food that will be used to feed the children. The agricultural department gave us the seeds and fertilizer for this. Since we have a water tank from the municipality and one from JDF, the garden is possible. We have become a member of JDF and they work closely with us, providing fax, phone, and typing services. Through them, we are able to access funding from NDA. There is also talk of opening a second-hand clothing store in our compound that will provide a salary for one of our volunteers.

We now have 85 kids. It costs R30 per month per child, but the department of social services covers this for 60 of the children. I often visit the other schools and check on the children who have gone through us. Those children who did not start here are struggling.

Similar to the Edu-care experience, the story of the Khayalesizwe Burial Society tells how access to a one-time grant through JDF strengthened the community's own priorities. An external grant purchased a body fridge. This asset allowed the society to offer a 'community mortuary.' This service contributes to the sustainability of the society by creating further revenue streams. Again, self-help was not displaced, but strengthened.

The experience detailed in Box 10.2 offers a strong example of how a strategic and well-thought-out grant can reinforce a community's own asset base and ability to act without creating dependency or detracting from local priorities and needs.

To continue with the JDF story, attention now turns to its organizational development and interplay with other institutions. From an organizational development perspective, JDF started out as an incubator for CBOs and emerged into an intermediary organization that satisfies civil society as well as local government. JDF went through four stages of growth: start-up, take off, growth, and transition, as described in the next section.

Box 10.2: The Khayalesizwe Burial Society story

Perched on top of a hill with the graveyard in distant view, is a simple white, cement block building with a tin roof. Neatly kept, it sits on the edge of a township and is secured with a simple wire fence. Inside are two rooms. One contains coffins, and one in particular, with varnished wood and polished handles, sits on the floor next to a simpler dark wooden box. In the other room is an imposing body fridge that can hold six corpses. Inside an old lady 'lies sleeping.'

This Burial Society was established 16 years ago. The idea was introduced by a society in a neighbouring town. Its leader guided them in how to set up and run operations; once 50 members were secured help was no longer needed.

Today the society has 500 members, and it provides a vitally-needed service to the whole community (black and coloured alike), especially in a context of a high HIV/AIDS death rate, and in the absence of a local mortuary facility at the state hospital. The society owns, and conducts operations from, a building purchased from the municipal council. Members pay a monthly fee of R20. The funds are collected by volunteers and recorded in a booklet.

In 2004, through its membership in JDF, the society received a one-time external grant. With this, a three-tier body fridge was purchased. Membership fees are used to run and maintain this equipment – electricity, for example, costs approximately R300–400 a month – as well as provide services to members. Provision of a mortuary facility increased membership and allowed the society to sell services including space in the fridge, as well as transport from the home or hospital to the mortuary and then to the cemetery. Furthermore, the relevance and reputation of the society also increased through a relationship of respect and cooperation with the local hospital.

In terms of benefits, a member is entitled to a simple coffin – with an estimated cost of R1,000 – upon his or her death. Members are also entitled to a dug grave; help to lower the coffin into the grave with ropes if the member can't afford the machine; seven days in the fridge and a further three days if needed at a charge of R25 per day; food and refreshments for the funeral for R140; a bus from church to cemetery for R280; and a contribution toward a hearse to pick up the body for R60.

Start-up

In 2000, a disparate group of CBOs pooled and shared their limited resources to 'keep going.' They did their best with what they had collectively and drew on local norms and traditions of pulling together and sharing. This strength was leveraged to network with others – including the Eastern Cape NGO coalition – as well as to develop a relationship with Ikhala Trust. Ikhala's advisory support was instrumental in helping CBOs frame their vision and objectives. Furthermore, JDF drew on Ikhala's own networks and reputational capital to access funding through the Strengthening Capacities for Transforming Relationships and Exercising Rights (SCAPE) programme. (SCAPE is a civil society capacity-building programme coordinated by CARE South Africa-Lesotho.) This allowed the municipality and CBOs to be trained, and made it possible for JDF to conduct its own field survey and come up with a Jansenville livelihood assessment. The results of this study informed the mission and objective of JDF: to share limited resources; carry out fund-raising; guard against duplication; and organize civil society. JDF lobbied for space and was awarded a house by the local municipality as its office premises.

Take off

In November 2002, funding came from Ikhala Trust. A small, but significant, grant allowed JDF to organize access to a telephone, fax machine, and computer. This was 'gold.' It enabled communication with external agencies and allowed JDF to focus on writing proposals and developing programmes.

Growth

In 2003–2004, JDF received a substantial operating fund from the NDA, which enabled JDF to implement its programme plan for that year. (NDA reports to Parliament through the Minister for Social Development. It is mandated to grant funds to Civil Society Organizations (CSOs) to meet the developmental needs of poor communities; strengthen CSOs for long-term sustainability; locate funds for the NDA; and support consultation, policy debate, research, and publications.)

The NDA funds allowed all CBO members to run their own projects and receive training. Furthermore, JDF began to operate like an established organization and volunteer staff could now be paid. In this period, the district and provincial governments also provided funds to renovate the office premises. From 2003 onwards, things 'really moved' and the JDF centre was busy. Over time, the CBO incubation process bore fruit as members registered independently with the Department of Social Development and accessed funding directly. Grounded in their emergent strength, CBOs no longer required 'hand holding.' This has allowed JDF's role to evolve.

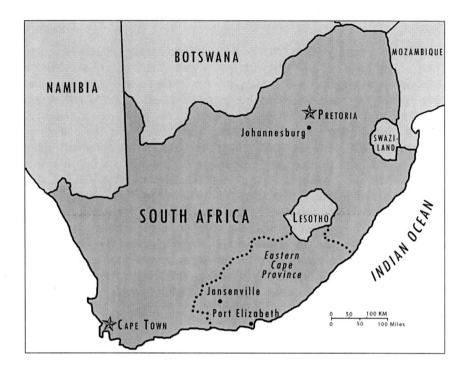

Transition

Over the 2006–2007 period, JDF's role has changed. It has met its initial objective and has taken all of the initial CBOs to a point of independence. At this juncture, the emergence of new CBOs has come to a halt and an 'incubator' is no longer needed. JDF has completed its task and has built up local civil society. As such, JDF finds itself at a turning point. What its role will be in the future remains uncertain.

What is certain, however, is that members have grown to a level where they no longer need JDF for financial and technical support. The networking connections, bonding social capital created among the organizations, and ability to leverage the name of a well-respected organization such as JDF continues to benefit those involved.

The JDF focus is no longer simply that of supporting civil society members as much more work is being done in coordination with government, including local government. For example, the Premier's Office for the Eastern Cape awarded JDF funds to train civil society in neighbouring towns on local economic development (LED). Further, JDF monitors selected government projects with, for example, the Department of Agriculture and the Department of Social Development. Also, JDF has trained and organized the volunteers sitting on area committees (designed to facilitate citizen participation in local planning), including the representatives from various units that work with the Ikwezi municipality.

On the 'shop floor,' JDF now has a training centre and new activities are 'more like a business.' Financial support from a large bilateral donor has been used to set up a tele-centre which will provide a service to the community as well as generate an income stream for JDF. Also through a public-private partnership between the department of Social Development and Smart Byte, a small internet service provider based in Port Elizabeth, youth receive computer training. The idea is for them to train others and generate 'business.' While the future for JDF is not yet clear, a new role is currently being forged.

On top of the organizational development trajectory detailed earlier in this section, different institutional roles and their interplay can be layered, deepening the story, and highlighting the significance of JDF as an intermediary organization.

Institutional interplay

From an asset and agency perspective, opportunities were created by various associations and institutional players, including CBOs and government coming together for mutual benefit. The range of assets that each brings to the table is diverse – monetary and advisory assets, as well as contributions of volunteer time and goods in kind – and the ability to act expresses itself in many ways: at its most fundamental, CBOs came together under one representative structure. They also share a central office block or premises. There is also inter-institutional collaboration facilitating resource flows (such as funding, access to information etc.) among and across JDF, Ikhala Trust, and various arms of government. Through this inter-institutional engagement, opportunities are created to achieve a range of interests and mandates, and serve the mutually beneficial interests of improving Jansenville.

Figure 10.1 illustrates the JDF intermediary experience and shows that within its institutional framework, JDF has to satisfy demands placed upon it, both from below, by the community, and from above, by government.

As the figure shows there was pressure for JDF to come into being, as local associations – a group of ten CBOs – had a need for organization, mobilization and strengthening. JDF's emergence as a higher level, or umbrella body, resolved these demands and developed member capacity along with the ability to access resources. The CBOs are diverse, including groups for hospice care, early childhood education, provision of legal and rights-based advice, emerging farmers, and various income-generating initiatives. Some are more formalized than others, with some receiving external funds and others reaching into their own pockets, and relying on goods in kind and voluntary labour from members and the community.

There is also pressure from above. JDF's existence satisfies the government's need for scale as it requires larger and professional organizations through which to channel social service delivery. Also, the presence of JDF facilitates

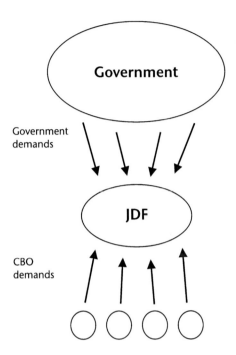

Community Based Organizations

Figure 10.1: JDF: an intermediary organization

Ikwezi Municipal Council's mandate and obligation to serve community in an engaged and responsive way, particularly in local planning decisions.

Notizi Vanda points out that there is a history of unsustainable local government projects and a tendency on the part of government officials to say, 'here is the money – you organize.' However, she notes that JDF has contributed to reversing this and fostering a stronger relationship. It is significant to note that in 2006, the government, in an unprecedented move, decided to build new offices in Jansenville. This decision was informed by a concerted effort to service the community in a more effective and coordinated way. The new government complex, which will contain the Department of Social Development, the Department of Agriculture, and the Department of Public Works, is being constructed right next to JDF – on the same plot. The practice of government erecting new premises so close to the township community is unusual, if not exceptional, and indicates a deliberate effort to establish an effective relationship between government and civil society.

In summary, JDF emerged in response to a civil society demand for organization and eventually found itself also satisfying the government's need for scale and professionalism. This raises a key question. What does this duality mean for JDF? Two things stand out.

Angora goats – the basis of the mohair industry – wind their way home through the township of Jansenville. Government grants in the post-apartheid era have resulted in improved infrastructure (including water and electricity) and improved housing.

First, it means that the Director, Notizi Vanda, has had to expand her role to bridge the gap between associations and institutions, and between citizen volunteers and local government. Notizi is a strong leader who wears many 'hats.' When she says 'we,' sometimes she is talking about her role as the coordinator for JDF, sometimes she is talking about her role as a part-time councillor on the Ikwezi Municipal Government Council, and sometimes she is talking about 'we' in the sense of her membership of the community as a whole. Her multiple hats involve multiple accountabilities. Excerpts from an interview in Box 10.3 recount her personal story.

Notizi Vanda is a striking figure and personality. Her story, her achievements, as well as the respect she visibly commands, confirms her credibility and authority as a leader. This ingredient is arguably a quintessential feature of JDF's achievements and success.

Second, JDF is member-based. It is 'instructed' from below by the members and recognized by government. Members shape the agenda and decision-making processes of JDF, and also appear to be instrumental in Notizi's participation in local government. Bernie Dolley, Director of Ikhala recalls that:

Box 10.3: Notizi Vanda: an inspiring leader

Wearing two hats

I am now a Councillor with responsibility for Infrastructure and Service Delivery in Ikwezi Municipal Government Council. I work part-time at this, paid by the municipality; so I spend the mornings at JDF and the afternoons at the municipal offices. My JDF income is now used for incentives for volunteers.

If you know the South African constitution now, [you will know that] it is very much in love with community participation, so it is easy [to play these two roles]. Whatever is happening at JDF is a joint programme with the municipality. Also, our municipality is not well-resourced [and] JDF has some resources that [the municipality doesn't] have, so for me to do some of the things the government cannot...is easy because I am part of JDF.

Taking up a leadership role in the community

I was born in Jansenville and trained as a teacher. After teaching outside Jansenville, I came back here in 1987 and taught maths and science. Then I took a leave of absence to become a facilitator for the Quality Schools Project, developing materials for maths and science courses in the surrounding schools. But you know, in small places, if there is a phone and a fax people will all flock there. They don't care if [the office is for] education or health or whatever. So the corner that I was using ended up being a community corner, instead of focusing on schools. Then it went so far that people came from the income-generating activities and business, coming here for faxes and phone and all those things. That's why we came together as a community-based organization. I never went back to teaching because I began to see myself as a development worker.

Leadership in the post-apartheid period

In 1995, things began to change. I was asked to stand as a candidate for mayor in the first local government elections. I was elected! I wasn't even trained in how local government operated. No one was. It was all so new. I couldn't take it! People were expecting miracles. So I resigned in 1996 and then started to study local government and how it operated. At that time the capacity of local government councillors was very low. [So that is when I got back into community organizing work.] We came together as community-based organizations with different tasks and programmes. Bernie [now the Director of Ikhala Trust] assisted us. We had the objective of sharing limited resources, gathering together for fund-raising, guarding against duplication, and organizing civil society.

In 2001–2002 we were really struggling. I think I was the only one who wasn't really struggling because I had savings from when I was teaching. I was running JDF mostly on my own money, but with a small grant from Ikhala Trust. But we had a team and [members] understood the whole project. They hoped that down the line we would be funded one day. And eventually, after Ikhala Trust, came NDA.

Then last year I was approached again by the Province. There is a mandate for 50 per cent representation by women on local government councils. So I agreed to become a councillor. So now I divide my time between JDF and local government, though of course there is a lot of overlap. As NGOs, as much as we are watchdogs of the government, we also want to assist on what government is unable to do because we are on the ground. Because of our small municipality and lack of manpower we are allowing ourselves to be of assistance.

She has declined this position (councillor) before, because she was trying to build JDF, but I think she got to the point where the community was pressuring her to accept it. This is how it is and the community will hold you to account, so I never picked up that there is a problem [or conflict of interest]. (personal communication, 2007)

Attention is drawn to the reality that in a small community, resources, including leadership, are scarce and will be mobilized and utilized to best advantage. The community sees Notizi Vanda as a valued and critical resource, and illustrates a determination to maximize this strength.

To conclude this appreciation from an asset and agency approach, the JDF model is one example of how an intermediary organization successfully used a community's 'bonding capital' (i.e. the ties that hold a group together) to leverage bridging capital (extended asset provision and acquisition through linkages with organizations and networks beyond the community). That is, JDF strategically used what the community already had to access more.

A multi-directional framework for development assets and agency

In 2003, development workers from a group of international foundations expressed their concern that foreign models of community grant-making assistance, including the community foundation model, were being introduced and used in Southern Africa with little consideration for what was already happening locally. The Ford Foundation took up this concern and funded the Building Community Philanthropy project at the Centre for Leadership and Public Values, Graduate School of Business at the University of Cape Town, to develop a systematic understanding of local norms and traditions of self-help and mutual assistance that exist in poor African communities. Research was conducted in four countries over a three-year period (2003–2005). The findings found in *The poor philanthropist: how and why the poor help each other* detail what people in poor communities consider to be help, the content of transactions, the actors involved, why people help each other, as well as what 'rules' or codes of conduct they follow in a decision to help or not help (Wilkinson-Maposa, et al., 2005).

The research has made a significant contribution to how we can think about resource flows. It generated the concept of horizontal philanthropy or philanthropy of community (PoC). This idea tells us that resources move 'side to side.' It also points out that people who are poor are not only the recipients of development assistance; they also give to one another for self-help and mutual assistance. In this case, resources are 'internal' to the community. In contrast, there is 'vertical philanthropy,' or 'philanthropy for community,' (PfC). In this case, resources flow 'up to down' from the rich, or those of high net wealth, to the poor, or those of lesser financial means. Resources are external to the community being served. This is the case in development assistance and charity.

Figure 10.2 offers a framework to conceptualize the relationship between different sources of help. Horizontal help is on one axis and vertical help on the other. An arc is drawn between them. Each is briefly explained.

Aligned with horizontal help is the idea of responsibility for mutual self-help, based on relationships of reciprocal obligation and cooperation through which people draw on their own agency: the ability to bring about change and create opportunities within a localized face-to-face context. Philosophically, mutual self-help is a melding together of giver and receiver as 'co-determined bearers of humanity reflected in the [Ubuntu] axiom, "I am because we are"' (Wilkinson-Maposa et al., 2005: 101).

Aligned with vertical help is the resource flow from institutions and people of higher net wealth to those of lower net wealth: 'help' motivated by charity, altruism, patronage or generosity and given by choice. In addition to these are resource flows from government through which wealth is redistributed, not as an act of charity, but as an expression of obligation to citizens, based on the notion of rights and entitlements. Resource flows arising out of entitlements of citizenship are therefore an expression of cooperation and 'self-help' within the state, with the state mediating redistribution of wealth, but without expectations of reciprocity.

The arc connects vertical and horizontal help. This is done to illustrate that they do not act in isolation. Rather, they exist simultaneously. It is not a matter of choosing one or the other; they can co-exist.

Placing the arc onto this illustration also draws deliberate attention to the fact that very little is known about the horizontal and vertical interplay: that is, their relationship and effect on one another. An intervention or support placed at equal distance from the vertical and horizontal axis illustrates that vertical help stimulates horizontal self-help and suggests that a balance has been achieved between 'rights and responsibilities.' Placement left of centre, toward the vertical axis, would indicate a movement toward dependency, and placement right of centre toward the horizontal axis indicates unsustainable self-help and (or) limited growth and leverage of it.

In short, the arc, and the continuum of interplay that it represents, directs attention to how the introduction and use of external resources in a community impact on local asset mobilization and community agency. Do those resources support, distort, or strengthen agency? Do they increase or diminish community autonomy and agency; and do they decrease or increase dependency? Is the resource flow from government (a right) interpreted differently from the resource flow from philanthropic sources (a gesture of help), and as such, do they have different impacts on community autonomy and agency?

If applied to the case of Jansenville, JDF would be placed somewhere on the arc. This positioning would shed light on the potential and contribution of an intermediary organization to negotiate the space between external and internal resources and 'set the rules' so that external resources do not 'corrupt' or distort the community's own asset base and weaken its autonomy.

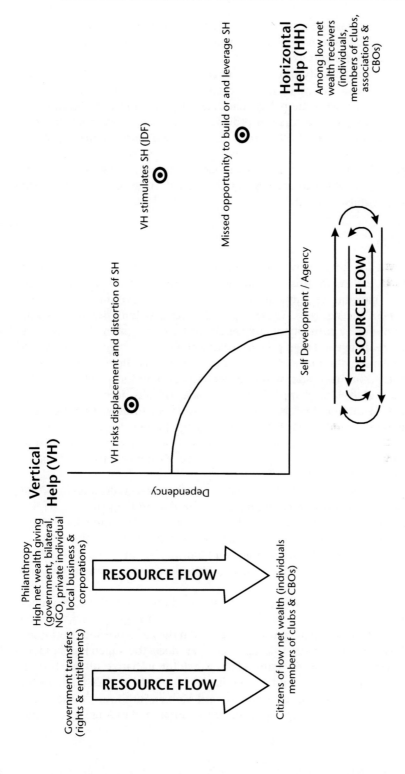

Figure 10.2: Multi-directional framework

As recounted earlier in this chapter, JDF has been particularly instrumental in mediating the interplay between what the community can do for itself and what the state and external development assistance can do for it. JDF has built up the capacity of CBOs to engage with such agents. In addition, it has provided a bridge to facilitate and link community needs, rights, assets and agency with the policy mandates, services, and facilities that the state and development actors can provide. In exercising these roles, JDF has brought the community to the point of 'movement' and has met its initial objective. However, as noted earlier, a reorientation is under way. JDF's focus has begun to shift from social to economic development since employment and improved livelihoods are desperately needed in Jansenville. To remain relevant, JDF must readjust.

Conclusion

JDF faces a looming irony. Two approaches – the intermediary approach mentioned earlier in this section, in combination with a rights-based approach – have successfully linked the community to government funds and disbursement mechanisms. These approaches have skilfully walked the fine line of community entitlement and community empowerment. However, the conundrum these two forces present for dependency on external support still looms as Jansenville moves into the future. At risk is the expectation that government, business, and/or the development community will create the economic and livelihood opportunities that are critically needed.

To traverse this terrain, it is likely that JDF will need to address a critical and challenging question: What is the right message to send regarding what the state or government can do for communities, what civil society can do, and what communities can do for themselves? Specifically, what is the balance and what does the strategy look like?

In effect, three key strategic considerations emerge for consideration to inform a framework for continued community mobilization and organization within an economic development and livelihoods agenda (Market Umbrella, 2000):

1. Expand local opportunities for micro and small enterprises: the potential for micro-entrepreneurs to trade and hawk at the monthly flea market, currently dominated by non-resident business people, is an obvious and potential start.

2. Link micro and small business, the not-for-profit sector, and government support programmes: the information technology project offering computer training to youth, operated from the JDF office and mentioned elsewhere, illustrates this approach, as does the emerging farmers' project on Hardwood farm. (This is a joint initiative of the Eastern Cape Department of Agriculture, Ikwezi Municipality, SAMIL, a mohair supplier and processing company, and Mohair South Africa. It consists of a training centre for emerging farmers interested in Angora goats and

mohair production, offering instruction in all facets of management over a three-year period.)

3. In its intermediary role, JDF could facilitate a multi-layered and integrated approach with government and civil society to tackle the complex issue and tenuous terrain of a social grant system and viable livelihoods, including key elements of the rights and responsibilities question. The LED and the IDP process and various related financing mechanisms position this discussion.

Support for livelihood development in Jansenville will not be easy. Hurdles should not be underestimated. Economic opportunities are limited, yet not non-existent. The infrastructure for small and medium enterprises (SMEs) is also underdeveloped, although investments can be made and SMEs can benefit from the range of infrastructure projects already begun by government including a major road works initiative. Finally, people tend to seek jobs and wage employment or receive social assistance as their source of livelihood. Small enterprise is neither of these and requires a different mindset. As stated earlier, dependency on social grants remains high – at 65–70 per cent – and the entrepreneurship ranking in South Africa is steadily decreasing. The magnitude of this shift cannot be overemphasized. A shift from the deficit mindset of dependence on social grants and the enterprising nature and confidence needed for business ownership would represent a significant leap forward.

Past achievements can craft future success

JDF has been a key player in social development in Jansenville and has the potential to continue its intermediary role in the promotion of local economic development and more sustainable livelihoods. In making this transition, its leadership, incubation model and asset-based approach are strengths to draw upon in the steep climb toward local economic development. Strategic shifts, however, will be required. For example, JDF's commitment to asset-based social development could give way to asset-based economic development. That is, instead of focusing on building up CBO capacity to access and attract external dollars to the community, an asset-based economic development activity would set out to create an asset that will, over time, generate many incomes (Market Umbrella, 2000). Furthermore, JDF's incubation of CBO capacity to access services would make way for the incubation of micro-enterprise businesses within the community to create and benefit from economic opportunities.

In summary, the Jansenville community and JDF have many challenges ahead of them, but also many achievements and successes behind them. As they continue to 'move,' they do so from a solid foundation: one of pride and hope, as well as respect and trust from external actors. All are arguably fundamental to sustainable community-driven development.

References

AVERT (2007) *South Africa: HIV and AIDS statistics*. Available from http://www.avert.org/aidssouthafrica.htm [Accessed April 24, 2007].

Chikulu, B.C. (September 2000) Building a peaceful and sustainable future: Democratic governance, decentralization and reconstruction in Southern Africa: A South African perspective. Paper prepared for International Development and Research Centre research workshop, 'Building a Peaceful and Sustainable Future: Democratic Governance, Decentralization and Reconstruction in Southern Africa', Johannesburg, South Africa.

Ikwezi Local Municipality (2007) *Vision 2011*, Ikwezi Local Municipality, South Africa.

Ikwezi Local Municipality (2007) *Draft integrated development plan (IDP): 2007–2012*. Available from http://www.ikwezi.gov.za/images/IDP2007-2008.pdf [Accessed 28 August 2007].

Kuljian, C. (2005) *Philanthropy and equity: The case of South Africa*. Available from *Global Equity Initiative website*: http://www.fas.harvard.edu/~acgei/philanthropy_pubs.htm [Accessed 25 July 2007].

Maas, G. and Herrington, M. (2006) *Global entrepreneurship monitor: South African report*. Graduate School of Business, University of Cape Town, Cape Town, South Africa.

Market Umbrella (2000), *Pastabilities: From public assistance to private enterprise*, Green paper published by marketumbrella.org, Yolola University, *New Orleans*, USA. Available from: http://www.marketumbrella.org/uploads/file/gp_2000_pasta.pdf [Accessed 12 March 2008].

Mattes, R., Keulder, C., Chikwana, A.B., Africa, C, and Davids, Y.D. (2003) *Democratic governance in South Africa: The people's view*, (AfroBarometer Working Paper No. 24). Institute for Democracy in South Africa, Cape Town, South Africa.

South African Department of Labour. *Basic guide to minimum wages*. Available from http://www.labour.gov.za [Accessed 25 July 2007].

Statistics South Africa (2001) *Census 2001: Primary tables Eastern Cape 1996 and 2001 compared*. Report No. 03-02-05 (2001). Statistic South Africa, Pretoria, South Africa.

Statistics South Africa (2004) *Provincial profile 2004: Eastern Cape*, Statistics South Africa, Pretoria, South Africa.

Statistics South Africa (2006) *South African statistics 2006*, Statistics South Africa, Pretoria, South Africa.

Wilkinson-Maposa, S., Fowler, A., Oliver-Evans, C. and Mulenga, C.F.N. (2005) *The poor philanthropist: How and why the poor help each other*, Centre for Leadership and Public Values, University of Cape Town, Cape Town, South Africa.

Author's note

In exploring potential communities for this collection of case studies, the Coady Institute was keen to include a case that offered insights for donor or philanthropic organizations. At the CIVICUS conference in Glasgow in June 2006, Dr Alan Fowler drew Alison Mathie's attention to a research monograph that he and I authored, entitled *The Poor Philanthropist: How and Why the Poor Help Each Other.* As a 'pull-out' to highlight, Alison identified the idea that poor communities do not just receive development assistance but also give, by mobilizing their own resources internally to address need within the community.

I was then approached to identify a South African case study. I turned to my colleague Bernie Dolley, Director of Ikhala Trust, community grant-makers in the Eastern Cape, for advice. She immediately proposed JDF, an Ikhala grantee that she has worked with since its inception. Coincidentally, the Coady Institute had previously explored working with Fort Hare University in the Eastern Cape and knew of Bernie through her involvement in the East Coast NGO Association (ECNGOC).

JDF was selected because it had made unique and impressive achievements in community mobilization in order to access government services and other grantmakers. JDF's members were ready to tell others about this. But more than this, JDF was also at a turning point. Its members wanted to reflect on where they had come from, what they had accomplished, and where they were heading. The opportunity to recount their story came at just the right time. As well, we thought the case could serve as an inspiration to others. The Jansenville community has been able to accomplish something that many other communities in South Africa are struggling to do with varying degrees of success – that is, work effectively with local government to access assets, including rights and entitlements of the community.

Within a few short months the research team (Susan Wilkinson-Maposa, Alison Mathie, Brie MacMahon) was addressing a meeting convened by JDF's director and founder Notizi Vanda. Over 30 people attended. This turnout of civil society and government representatives was unprecedented. Even the African National Congress (ANC) Member of Parliament, Judy Chalmers, attended. Over the next week, we interviewed upwards of seven key informants, made at least ten site visits including community based organizations and government projects as well as institutions (municipal offices, the police and the local hospital). We also sat down and heard the chronology of events from JDF's inception to date, as told from the perspective of Notizi Vanda and Bernie Dolley, an external advisor. Board members of Ikhala Trust were also interviewed to gain a fuller understanding of the principles guiding their work.

Conducting this case study was a privileged experience. The research process was more than a retrospective recollection and account of the past. For Notizi and Bernie in particular, it was an opportunity to engage with the past in order to reflect on, inform and craft a future vision and direction for JDF. It was exciting to be part of their thoughtful journey.

The chance to contribute this chapter has afforded me a valued opportunity to shed some light on local norms and traditions of self-help, as a distinctive dimension of community assets and agency that deserves to be recognized and appreciated in community development theory and practice.

SECTION II
ABCD in Ethiopia, Kenya and the Philippines

The following three cases explore the experiences of Oxfam Canada and partner NGOs in Ethiopia; CREADIS in Kenya; and SEARSOLIN/Xavier University in the Philippines. To different degrees, all applied an Asset Based Community Development (ABCD) approach in their programming and the cases trace the changes that have occurred in the communities where they worked.

In the Kenya case, the application of an asset-based approach comes after a demoralizing period in Kenyan history. A corrupt political regime, economic decline, cutbacks in public expenditure and the onslaught of the HIV/AIDS crisis have resulted in out-migration, depleted resources, and a strong sense of entitlement to external assistance. The ideal of self-help inspired by 'Harambee' now rings hollow. In this context, an asset-based approach facilitated a transition by farming households to a more diversified range of commercial crops, and helped community groups make incremental steps from rotating savings schemes to accessing loans and other services from local government and private sector institutions.

In the case of SEARSOLIN/Xavier University, ABCD has been applied in various rural communities and the case discusses how a shift of thinking from 'deficits' to 'assets' has affected motivation on the part of both fieldworkers and community members. The complementarity of an ABCD approach with the shift to organic agriculture is also highlighted – both encourage valuing indigenous knowledge as well as adapting and innovating (socially and technically) to meet new opportunities in local and global markets.

The Ethiopia case study is a description and analysis of the experiences of five communities that applied an asset-based approach over a three-year period and the role of the three NGOs as facilitators of this process. Building on past success in community organizing for local development, these communities were able to identify opportunities to improve household and local community economies. The case raises the possibility that when an outside facilitator (in this case an NGO) steps back, this action can spur local associations to undertake community development activities on their own.

CHAPTER 11

Stimulating Asset Based and Community Driven Development: lessons from five communities in Ethiopia

Gordon Cunningham

Introduction

Rural communities in Ethiopia have a long history of driving their own development, particularly in terms of how people band together to create local governance structures and help each other deal with crises. While they vary from region to region, clan associations and other groups wield considerable influence. Clan elders are custodians of societal norms and arbiters of conflicts; in some regions, they still administer traditional social welfare systems. One of the most common traditional associations in rural Ethiopia are the *idirs* or burial societies. There are also a variety of other groups, such as *iqubs*, or rotating savings and credit associations, *senbetes*, whose members celebrate after church services, and *mahabers*, or rotating feast groups. In some regions there are also traditional self-help associations or communal labour groups. For hundreds – perhaps thousands – of years these traditional institutions have helped rural communities in Ethiopia survive and thrive.

Yet in the past several decades many rural communities in Ethiopia, especially in drought-stricken areas, have developed a dependence on outside agencies for survival. Today the population of Ethiopia exceeds 75 million, with an annual growth rate of 2.9 per cent. Nearly 44 per cent of the population is under 15 years of age, compared with just 3 per cent over the age of 65. Close to 85 per cent of the population is still living in rural areas, including more than seven million pastoralists. Between seven and eight million people are recurrently deemed 'food insecure,' with more than three million people receiving food aid in 2006. According to Stephen Devereux of the Institute of Development Studies in the UK, not enough is being done to alleviate people's reliance on such aid. As he states in a discussion paper for the Department for International Development (DFID): 'Given the fragile natural resource base and climatic uncertainty, current policy emphases on agricultural intensification are misguided, while institutional constraints such as inflexible land tenure and ethnic federalism perpetuate this unviable livelihood system. Inappropriate food aid interventions by donors add another layer of dependence' (Devereux , 2000).

Despite this, many multilateral and bilateral donors have joined with the Ethiopian government in a food security coalition to move from emergency humanitarian aid to what has been called a productive and protective safety net system. The government of Ethiopia has termed this move a 'paradigm shift' (World Bank, 2004). But Lucie Goulet, Country Director for Oxfam Canada from 2003–2006, says that in Ethiopia, where chronic emergencies have necessitated emergency interventions, 'humanitarian aid and longer term development work has been defined by a traditional top-down model...where NGOs are seen as gap fillers to deprived and voiceless communities. This has led inevitably to a progressive disempowerment of communities' (personal communication, 2005).

Weary of a development process that places NGOs as the active drivers and communities as the passive recipients of development projects, Oxfam Canada began looking for ways to help rural Ethiopian communities reclaim the ability to drive their own development. In the spring of 2003 along with three partner NGOs, staff members of Oxfam Canada set out to test a different approach. They were influenced by the work of John McKnight and Jody Kretzmann (Kretzmann and McKnight, 1993) on asset-based community development (ABCD) and by Alison Mathie and Waad El Hadidy (CDS and Coady Institute, 2002) on community-driven development in Egypt. The question Oxfam Canada staff members asked themselves was this: is it possible for outside agencies to stimulate community development using an asset-based approach? Staff members hypothesized that an adapted ABCD approach – one that helped people to reflect on previous endeavours and to identify community assets – would motivate them to undertake new community-driven activities.

This case study analyzes the experiences of three Ethiopian NGOs from March 2003 to February 2006 in terms of: the changes in the communities' asset base over the three years; the role of internal and external agency in mobilizing and building community assets; and the degree to which this new approach has been internalized by the participating communities and NGOs. Fieldwork for the case study took place in February 2006, conducted by a team of five researchers from the Coady International Institute and Oxfam Canada. The interviews and community meetings were organized into themes to facilitate in-case analysis and to ensure consistency across all sites.

The Ethiopian context

The state, the market, and civil society

Ethiopia is unique among African countries in never being officially colonized by a European power. Except for a brief occupation by Italy (1936-1941) the Ethiopian state has survived, with various territorial expansions and contractions, for more than two millennia. In the past half-century Ethiopia has transformed itself from a long-standing feudal society, to a centralized communist state, to a nominal Democratic Republic, based on a form of 'authoritarian ethnic federalism' (Ayenew, 2002: 130–146). Yet the modern era shares with the past a constant tension between authoritarian rule from the centre and traditional forms of decentralized governance in the regions.

Imperial rule in Ethiopia, which ended with the reign of Emperor Haile Selassie, formed an unbroken chain that stretched back to biblical times. The last two emperors had attempted to assimilate Ethiopia's 79 ethnic groups into a united state by mandating the use of Amharic as the official language and promoting Abyssinian Orthodox Christianity (Habtu, 2005). But their rule was overthrown in 1974 by a highly centralized communist regime known as 'the Derg.' The Derg established central ministries that set rural development quotas for such activities as terraces, roads, schools and health clinics. Yet it will be remembered most for the 'red terror,' a wave of repression used to impose the will of the central state on the population. The Derg was overthrown in 1991, by a coalition of guerrilla forces known as the Ethiopian People's Democratic Front.

Over the last decade, the current regime began to decentralize authority, both to accommodate rebellious ethnic groups and to promote socio-economic development. A federal state structure was adopted, with nine ethnically based regional state governments and two special administration areas for the country's two largest cities, Addis Ababa and Dire Dawa. Each region has a separate constitution, elected assemblies, the right to use its language in schools, administration, and courts, and the authority to mobilize resources, draft budgets, and implement socio-economic development activities. Within each region, there are three additional levels of government which decentralize government authority even further: zonal, *woreda* and *kebele*. Since 1974, *kebeles* (often composed of a number of 'clusters' or villages) have become the lowest administrative unit in the formal state sector in Ethiopia. The *kebele* administration collects taxes and debts, maintains law and order, runs a social court, and provides various administrative services. With limited resources, *kebeles* depend heavily on *woredas* for both financial and technical support.

Ethiopia's 556 *woredas* are autonomous self-governing units with elected councils, executive committees and administrations. With an average population of 100,000 in each, they have a host of responsibilities, including primary education, primary health care, agricultural extension, infrastructure development, and the promotion of cottage industries. As such, they are a locus of decentralized socio-economic development activity in Ethiopia. However, there is a critical shortage of trained local government personnel, particularly women. Local governments also lack sufficient revenue to fulfil their myriad responsibilities, and are unable to raise additional revenue locally. That leaves them dependent on higher levels of government for funding, and allows zonal and regional governments to exercise tight control over them. All of these factors hinder the effectiveness of local government. A report by the United Nations concluded that '*woredas* and *kebeles* have been given too many responsibilities and functions without the necessary financial and resource capacity to undertake development at the local level' (UN-HABITAT, 2002).

While the relationship between higher levels of government and *woredas* could be described as 'under-resourced,' the relationship between government and civil society organizations (CSOs) is characterized by resentment and suspicion (Graham, n.d.). Although Ethiopia's Ministry of Capacity Building has stated its desire to see such organizations working hand in hand with government and the private sector, many civil society organizations in Ethiopia are distrusted by the government. NGOs, in particular, are seen as competitors for the resources from international donors and some are perceived as politically motivated and unaccountable to any local constituency. When political tensions rise in the country, the government tends to react by trying to exert more control on the NGO sector.

Land remains the property of the state. The current regime re-established state ownership of land in 1995 (Adal, 2004). Although they do not own land, farmers enjoy some usufructuary rights to traditional plots, including limited inheritance rights, as well as the right to lease out land for short periods of time. The household head has possession of the land. This usually means that men control decisions of access to, or control over, individual plots. Although women who head households have the same usage rights as men, customarily it has been only the male sons or descendants who are allowed to inherit, with the eldest son being first in line.

Men tend to be the economic decision-makers, except in households headed by women. Generally, women are responsible for cooking, including gathering fuel and carrying water, childcare, and working in subsistence gardens. Unmarried men tend to support the household in cash crop production, herding, and cutting wood, while unmarried women tend to support their mothers, fetching water and collecting firewood. Some landless youth support themselves through sharecropping, animal rearing, and some off-farm employment, but farming opportunities for young people continue to decrease through land fragmentation and soil erosion.

Religion is another important facet of most Ethiopians' daily lives. Sixty-two per cent of Ethiopians report themselves to be Christian with thirty three per cent declaring themselves to be Muslim (Habtu, 2005). This makes Ethiopia somewhat of a religious success story; a country split between devout Muslims and Christians who co-exist relatively peacefully. While a small minority still practises traditional religions, the fastest-growing religion is evangelical Protestantism.

Yet there are other pressing challenges, such as the government's tight control over the private sector. In the banking sector, for example, no foreign investment is allowed. Recently, there has been a move toward limited deregulation in some industries, partly spurred by Ethiopia's bid to join the WTO. The Ethiopian economy is growing rapidly, but is still heavily dependent on foreign aid. In 2006, the country received US$ 1.9 billion in foreign aid, but earned only US$434.6 million in export revenue. That same year, real

GDP grew by more than 8 per cent though inflation hovered around 12 per cent (The Economist Intelligence Unit, 2007). Although no figures exist, remittances from the Ethiopian diaspora, sent home to family members, are also thought to be a significant source of foreign exchange. There are currently estimated to be 350,000 Ethiopians in the Washington, DC area, 96,000 in Los Angeles, and more than 10,000 in New York (Mekonnen, 2007).

Background on the action research

Oxfam Canada invited three Ethiopian NGOs to take part in ABCD action-research and all three agreed. The Oromo Grassroots Development Organization (HUNDEE) and Kembatti Mentti Gezzima (KMG), both small NGOs, were already using traditional culture, practices, and institutions as an entry point in communities and the methodology proposed by Oxfam seemed consistent with these approaches. The leadership of the Relief Society of Tigray (REST), Ethiopia's largest indigenous NGO, and a service-delivery organization rivalling regional government in the size and scope of its programmes, saw an opportunity to strengthen community-level practice and enhance its reputation as an innovative development organization.

The ABCD approach: methodology, tools and timeline

Much of the initial training of NGO fieldworkers involved getting their acceptance to try an ABCD approach. This approach required field staff to shift from a 'needs-based' focus, that often led to NGO-driven projects or programmes, to an 'asset-based' focus that could result in community members mobilizing their own resources. Most NGO field staff workers had formed the habit of initiating relationships with communities by identifying problems.

Instead, the ABCD approach required field staff to begin by asking community members about past successes in undertaking local development activities without outside direction or resources. Building on the positive energy that resulted from this appreciative interviewing, fieldworkers helped a core group to identify and make an inventory of assets, after which an economic analysis tool was introduced to help members of the core group mobilize these assets for development. Once people in the community began to undertake their own development activities, usually within six months of the initial facilitation, fieldworkers were asked to step back and become brokers or intermediaries, connecting community members to outside organizations and resources, or lobbying local government or NGOs on behalf of local community initiatives.

The community experience with ABCD

This case study follows the experience of five communities in applying an ABCD approach over a three-year period: Ilu Aga in Oromya (Hundee), Adis

Alem in Tigray (REST) and three communities in the Hobicheqa area of SNNP region.

Ilu Aga, Oromia

Ilu Aga is located in the Ejere district of Oromia region, with a population of approximately 3,720 (620 households), consisting of two Oromo clans, the Elu and the Aga. The Oromo people are well known for caring for one another, developing traditional support and safety net systems to share agricultural labour and pool community resources to look after the destitute, the disabled or the elderly. The primary source of income in the community comes from mixed agriculture, with crops of wheat, barley and beans, while animal rearing is a supplemental income source. A growing number of landless youth are engaged in off-farm income-generating activities. During the past decade and a half, over-harvesting and over-grazing have resulted in severe deforestation and topsoil erosion.

Hundee (meaning 'root' in Oromo), also known as the Oromo Grassroots Development Organization, was established as an NGO in 1995. It focuses on food security in Oromia by establishing village cereal banks, seedling nurseries, and civic education programmes, and at the same time, it works to enhance women's empowerment. Hundee's philosophical approach to development is to start with the 'culture' of the community. For all its forward thinking, Hundee has not always had a good relationship with local government, in contrast to REST, a more established organization. Though tension between Hundee and the government has lessened recently, from time to time Hundee staff have been detained under suspicion of political organizing.

In the spring of 2003, Hundee used the cereal bank association as its entry point for introducing the ABCD process in Ilu Aga. Over the next few months, a core group of community members, who had undergone the ABCD process, fashioned a development agenda that integrated environmental and economic concerns. The group's ten-year vision involved increasing community income, diversifying income sources, reducing dependence on chemical fertilizers, and addressing the loss of soil and water resources. To realize this vision, members agreed they should revive practices used successfully by their ancestors, such as terracing, composting, and crop rotation fertilizing with animal manure. They also agreed that any savings would be invested in improved livestock varieties and in the irrigation of communal land. The group also decided to plant a mixture of commercial and indigenous, nitrogen-fixing species.

The ABCD process in Ilu Aga

The ABCD process in Ilu Aga began when a Hundee fieldworker named Teshome asked for a meeting with the cereal bank association. At that meeting Teshome explained that he had come to discover community successes and strengths. He asked people to tell him, and each other, about occasions when the community had undertaken development activities without direction or help.

Teshome gathered a number of community stories, such as a tale of the construction of paths to transport grain to the cooperative store in a neighbouring community and the story of a river diversion scheme, completed more than 20 years before, to irrigate communal agricultural land. There was a recent story about a community member who had visited a relative who was making a good profit on potatoes. The community member also began to grow potatoes in Ilu Aga, and sold them in the local market for a good price. Many other people in Ilu Aga had become interested in growing potatoes, not only on homestead plots but also on some communal land. Though Teshome had been working with the cereal bank association for two years, he had never heard these stories. When he pointed this out, one farmer replied: 'you came and reminded us what we have accomplished in the past. We've never even talked about these stories with our youngsters' (personal communication, 2006).

Out of this appreciative interviewing process a group of about 50 villagers decided they wanted to form a 'core group' to undertake community development on their own, as their parents and grandparents had done. Teshome helped facilitate a process to uncover community assets. Over a three-day period this group worked to identify the skills of individuals, list formal and informal associations that could be mobilized, describe relationships the community had developed with government and non-government institutions and identify physical assets and natural resources.

The group uncovered more than 60 different skills possessed by community members. The inventory included conventional farming skills, such as sowing, threshing, and animal-rearing, and less conventional farming-related skills, such as the construction of small-scale irrigation schemes, and flood protection. It also included construction, artisan, and business skills. The inventory also included categories such as cultural, civic and health skills. After the skill inventory the group set about listing all the formal and informal associations in the community. The few formal associations included government-promoted associations for youth, farmers, women and household clusters. The newest formal association was the cereal bank association created by the community with the assistance of Hundee. The informal associations included more than 45 burial societies (*idirs*), several traditional rotating savings and credit schemes (*iqubs*), and traditional religious and marriage festival groups (*senebets*, *mahabers*, etc.) or mutual cooperation associations, and even a new environmental protection association. The cereal bank association was seen as the most important association in any community-driven initiative because of its dynamic leader, Abera, and the fact that its members included the heads of most of the informal associations in the community. Abera had at one time been the head of a national union of farmers, and he had returned home to farm in Ilu Aga. Several of the informal associations, particularly the *idirs*, were seen as key to mobilizing people, resolving conflicts, and raising financial resources within the community.

The final step in identifying community assets was the construction of a detailed community map. The group used it to list assets which included institutions, physical assets, and natural resources. Once the core group had assembled a list of community assets, Teshome facilitated a session on the economic analysis tool called the 'leaky bucket.' This exercise pointed out the significant household spending on social festivities and alcohol. This point had previously been raised by local government officials; however, due to the political tension between the community and the government, many community members felt offended by being told how to spend their money and chose to continue their spending practices almost as a form of civil disobedience. The 'leaky bucket' session allowed community members to see for themselves how much money was leaking out of Ilu Aga and to envision what the local economy might look like if this money were reinvested in productive initiatives.

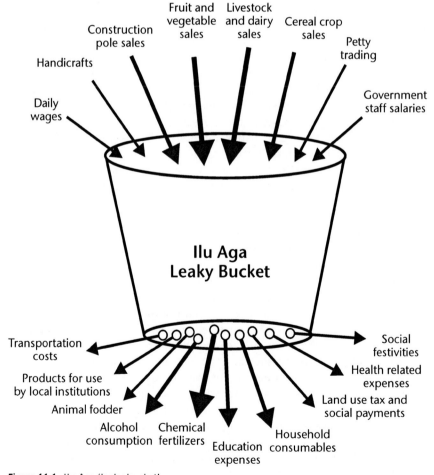

Figure 11.1: Ilu Aga 'leaky bucket'

The most striking result of the leaky bucket session was a discussion among local farmers about money spent on chemical fertilizers. Many farmers felt that they were currently worse off than they had been a decade earlier because they were spending almost as much to produce their crops as they were earning in harvest sales. The group agreed they should revive more cost effective and environmentally sustainable practices such as terracing, composting, crop rotation and using animal manure for fertilizer (instead of simply using it for fuel and house floor sealant). They also agreed that any savings they realized would be invested in improved livestock varieties. In addition, the group decided to plant a mixture of commercial species, such as eucalyptus, for eventual harvest and sale as construction poles, and indigenous, nitrogen-fixing species, such as acacia, to provide windbreaks and retain soil on sloped land.

The core group then gathered all the villagers together, using the map to illustrate how the community might look in ten years if ideas from the ABCD process were implemented. Two men who were not members of the core group suggested that a grinding mill should be a priority instead, but group members pointed out they had identified activities that could be carried out without reliance on outside resources. The community might be in a better position to undertake a grinding mill initiative once income had increased, and expenditures, as well as environmental degradation, had decreased. Others wondered about reviving the idea of constructing small dams and river diversion schemes for irrigating communal land, allowing them to grow potatoes on a larger scale. The community elders agreed that this idea should be added to the core group's plan.

The community action plan ultimately focused on four activities. Organic crop and soil improvement could be managed through composting, manuring, and crop rotation, while tree planting, along with terracing and irrigation, would be possible with small-scale river diversions. The community had the labour along with most of the tools and skills, as well as the natural resources needed to carry out these activities. All they needed from outside the community was some legal advice to demarcate areas for tree planting, technical assistance with irrigation from the *woreda*, and some help from a Hundee-supported community nursery to access large numbers of tree seedlings.

Compost-making and terracing began immediately after the action plan was devised. Although the *woreda* had not yet delineated land for tree planting, several individuals decided to grant slightly less than one hectare each for this purpose. The Hundee-supported nursery agreed to supply the seedlings. The community also undertook seven small river diversions which gave most people access to irrigated land. The local *woreda* sent three government officers to provide assistance for the irrigation schemes. Because land is fragmented, individual households take turns to divert water to their plots. Over time, the resulting increase in irrigated land has allowed villagers to diversify into vegetable production. A household plot with a crop of potatoes on the newly irrigated land has resulted in additional annual income of roughly 1,000 *birr* (or ETB, equivalent to approximately US$106 at 3 March 2008), with buyers from Addis Ababa purchasing Ilu Aga vegetables at local markets.

While the community of Ilu Aga did not undertake all of the opportunities identified during the ABCD process, some individuals may have been stimulated by the process to carry out other activities. And anecdotal evidence suggests that a reduction in expenditure on festivities and alcohol is happening in some households. In addition, a local woman, Ayaletch led an effort to bring clean, potable water to the community. After living in Addis Ababa for many years, she returned home to Adis Alem, and was shocked at the quality of the drinking water. After talking to people about the issue, she began lobbying the local *woreda* office but got no response. After attending ABCD meetings in 2003, she organized a group of people to successfully restore a local spring. This time the *woreda* government responded by agreeing to provide materials for several new dug wells, not just in Ilu Aga, but in three surrounding villages. Over the past three years Ayaletch has also helped form an *idir* for female petty traders and for those involved in a communal vegetable garden.

Perspectives of community members

Community members in Ilu Aga identified three significant changes that had occurred two years after the ABCD process was introduced: an increased tendency for people to work together; improved income management in households, and the perception that Ilu Aga was leading the way for other communities.

Box 11.1: Yilma's story

The change in our community is not complete but we are starting to get organized...We sell our grain together through the cereal bank. We have a group of farmers trying a backyard composting system, and no longer using chemical fertilizers, we are working together on construction projects, and many of us have changed our habits of spending and saving. We didn't used to harvest winter water, but now we know it is an important asset and so we harvest it. Instead of our animals grazing freely, we manage their grazing seasonally to make best use of the land – another asset. Even our children make their own vegetable gardens to contribute to the household income and cover school expenses.

After the ABCD training, we began to plan our households. We would first look at our income and plan what should be spent on specific expenses. We diversified our income through gardening and fattening of our animals... To live tomorrow, we needed savings today. The chairman of the cereal bank and the members of the *kebele* even participated in many different activities to diversify their income.

We now teach others what we learnt. Those who participated in the ABCD training came from different villages within Ilu Aga, and when they returned to their villages they transferred knowledge to family and friends. We learned a great deal from the ABCD training and still remember it. If we had the maps with us, there are so many new things we could add now. In my *idir*, we had a plan to purchase a pumping machine (for 3,000 ETB) to use for irrigation. In another group I belong to, we plan on purchasing some good potato seeds rather than the traditional ones to bring a new variety of potatoes to our area.

A number of community members involved in the irrigation initiative suggested that the motivation of participants in such projects was steadily increasing in Ilu Aga. As Ambasa observed: 'Ten bags of salt can be a heavy load for one person, but it is easy for ten people' (personal communication, 2006). He suggested that the more people see the benefits of collective action, the more they want to become involved in group activities. For him, the most important change was that of people being willing to help each other.

An increased tendency to work together was important, people contended, because it had allowed them to carry out a number of small initiatives that, taken together, greatly improved life in the community. One group purchased plastic tubes for tree seedlings and sold the trees for income generation. As well, an addition was built onto the school with all of the money (over 10,000 ETB) and labour coming from the community. And people credited the leaky bucket tool with helping them to increase savings, reduce unnecessary expenditures, like alcohol, and diversify their livelihoods. One man pointed out that he had learned the importance of paying closer attention to his income and expenses, and that he had started discussing financial decisions with his wife: 'Composting is an example of one of the changes we decided...I also feel I shouldn't drink alcohol, since there are other risks involved, like making bad decisions and contracting AIDS. I would rather spend the money to send my children to school so they can improve their lives' (personal communication, 2006).

Ilu Aga seemed to be emerging as a role model for other *kebeles* in the *woreda*. Several community members recalled people from neighbouring villages asking them how it was that households in Ilu Aga were able to save money and reduce their consumption of alcohol. They concluded they were working more cooperatively within their households:

> ... Before the ABCD training, only men were making household decisions [but] the training we received from Hundee taught us to practise sharing our household assets....Now when we want to sell a horse or a cow, we discuss this with our wives and even our older children. Adjacent *kebeles* are not as involved in such things, but we are teaching them. (personal communication, 2006)

Others recalled neighbouring communities inquiring about the women's *debaree* group – which had swelled to more than 60 members. They pointed out that this positive feedback from neighbours further motivated them to work together to develop their community.

Perspectives of outsiders

Hundee staff members felt there were three significant changes in Ilu Aga over the past two years: the villagers had developed a clear vision of what kind of changes they wanted to achieve over the next decade; associational leadership had initiated and sustained community-driven development activities; and the local government had become much less suspicious of both associational leadership and Hundee fieldworkers. As a result, those in local government were not only more supportive of Ilu Aga's development, but were beginning to see it as a model community within the *woreda*.

What most impressed Hundee staff about Ilu Aga's development agenda was that it integrated economic and environmental concerns. As Teshome Assefa commented: 'All of the interrelated activities...promote their vision of a green community and provide income generation potential for community members...perhaps most importantly, they can be started with the assets the community has now' (personal communication, 2006). Particularly effective in helping the community conceptualize the interconnectedness of the local economy and natural environment was the 'leaky bucket' tool. The subsequent community vision involved increasing income, diversifying income sources, and supporting biodiversity.

Hundee fieldworkers also felt that several local associations had developed strong leaders willing and able to drive the community development process. Although this process had begun long before, it had, nevertheless, accelerated. Fieldworkers singled out Ayaletch, the woman who had led the effort to get potable water in the community, and Abera, the head of the cereal bank association. Both of these leaders had developed skills and confidence from working in larger centres, that helped them as leaders in Ilu Aga. While Ayaletch had been confrontational at the outset of the ABCD process, demanding Hundee supply the community with a new well, she had learned to mobilize local resources when restoring the spring after seeing others do it. Abera had been so effective in developing the cereal bank and supporting the ABCD process that Hundee hired him to work as its agent in Ilu Aga when Teshoma moved to another Hundee project area. Teshome recalled how much easier it was for Abera to introduce new ideas because of his personal connections to villagers and local government officials through kinship, clan, and the *gada*, or traditional governance, system.

An atmosphere of better relations between Hundee and the local government was identified as the third most significant change. Zeguye, the Executive Director of Hundee, remarked on how the government's attitude towards Hundee had improved: 'Initially, the government would try to take over our meetings...[thinking] we were bringing people together for political reasons. Now it is more appreciative...ABCD brought about concrete physical outcomes and increased the potential of the people. This is in line with what the government wants' (personal communication, 2006). This shift in attitude had an impact in creating the environment needed for true community-driven development, allowing associations to access government resources to enhance and sustain their activities.

Kebele officials, several of whom were either part of the ABCD core group or members of the irrigation group, stated that people were now coming together in groups, both for their mutual benefit, and for the benefit of the larger community. In the view of *kebele* officials this was very important. It meant not only that groups in the community were initiating activities but that many of these activities fit very well with the development agenda of the *woreda* which made the job of mobilizing people much easier.

Similarly, *woreda* officials suggested the most significant change that had occurred in Ilu Aga during the two years was that the community was more organized and better able to carry out development activities. They attributed this change to the combined efforts of Hundee and the *woreda* government, noting that Hundee's work with the community had an impact on community members' attitudes. They pointed to the reduction of harmful traditional practices such as female genital mutilation and the noticeable improvement in household management. They also gave credit to their own programmes, such as the Farmers' Training Centre and the Health Post, yet they pointed out that Ilu Aga's success would leverage further investment from government. Specifically, they mentioned plans to expand the school by two grade levels, extend the irrigation system, develop a new tree nursery plot, and construct additional roads. Interestingly, *woreda* officials did not see a difference between community-initiated projects and those initiated by the government. Since *woreda*-level resources are limited to the provision of technical assistance and materials not available locally, communities have to mobilize skills, labour, and local materials even for government-promoted projects. For this reason, the officials suggested that all activities at the community level are, in a sense, community-driven: 'it is the community [members] who choose what projects to undertake. They are the ones driving development. We may give advice, but the community makes the final decision and puts in the effort' (personal communication, 2006). It seems clear that local government officials do not see a link between the changes they have described in Ilu Aga, such as villagers' increased capacity to organize and work together, and the fact that these activities were initiated by the community.

Adis Alem, Tigray

Adis Alem is located in Tigray's Central Zone within the District (*woreda*) of Degua Tembien. The citizens of Adis Alem have a long history of resilience in the face of adversity. In the 1980s the community lost one quarter of its citizens as a result of war and famine. Today, Adis Alem is predominantly a farming community of just under 1,400 people. Most households survive through crop production, animal rearing, off-farm activities such as masonry, wage labour and food for work programmes, and more recently, beekeeping. Large numbers of young men migrate out of the community in search of wage labour.

Due to its prominent role during the years of struggle against the Derg, much of it in exile, REST (Relief Society of Tigray) was well-positioned to become the leading development NGO in Tigray under the current regime. REST has developed such close relationships with national, regional and local governments that to outside observers it is often difficult to tell the difference between REST staff and government officials at the community level. Many people in Tigray still refer to REST as *Maret*, 'the Saviour,' and this has both positive and negative implications. On the one hand, it shows how important REST has been in the lives of Tigrayans over the past two decades. On the other hand, its evolution into a service provider has meant that individuals and communities have become dependent on it.

The ABCD process in Adis Alem

In the summer of 2003, REST fieldworkers introduced the ABCD approach to elders in Adis Alem. The elders liked what they heard but worried that both REST and the government were trying to reduce their support to the community. Over the next several months, REST fieldworkers facilitated a process of discovery for a core group of community members – beginning with appreciative interviewing. People not only talked about how they had mobilized their skills, labour, local materials, and money to build a church, they also recalled working together to terrace hillsides, plant trees, establish new water sources and maintain existing ones. They also took great pride in describing how their ancestors had managed a local forest.

A subsequent stage of asset identification involved making inventories of: individual skills; the various formal and informal associations in the community including their relationship to local and external institutions; and the community's physical assets and natural resource base. Once all the diagrams, inventories, and maps had been hung in the farmer's training centre, community members took pride in showing them to visitors – particularly to members of nearby communities.

During this part of the process community members identified clear differences between formal and informal associations. Formal associations such as the farmers' association, women's association and youth association were not spontaneous expressions of local initiative but vehicles encouraged by and used for working with local government. In fact the regular contributions collected by members of these associations were required to be sent to the *woreda* office (so that these funds can leverage additional funds from higher levels of government). In contrast, a local elders association has recently been formed spontaneously and this group does not forward any of its money to the local government. This was a point of pride for its leader, Walgocose: 'there are people in other *tabias* who are interested. When we meet informally at the festivals or forums we tell them what we are doing and they ask us in detail how we managed to set up our own fund this way and about the space [we have created] between our association and the *woreda* administration' (personal communication, 2006).

When analyzing the community economy with the 'leaky bucket' exercise, people were amazed at the amount of money that households were spending outside the community on agricultural inputs and household consumables such as coffee and liquor. It also confirmed what they already knew but had felt powerless to act on, that elements of their natural resource base, such as soil and water, were being depleted and that their future human resource base – youth – were leaving for better opportunities elsewhere.

The discussions led to an action plan to mobilize assets at the household, association, and community levels for increasing income, decreasing unnecessary expenditure, retaining soil and water, and providing opportunities for youth to remain in the community. Households could decrease their purchases of food from outside the community by more effectively retaining seeds for their crops and by adding small homestead vegetable gardens. Composting and manuring, which had been done in the past, could be undertaken to reduce expenditure on fertilizers. Most households also had the skills and available labour to construct small homestead ponds to capture rainwater. Families could use some of their increased savings from reduced expenditures to purchase forage seedlings to further reduce expenditure on feed.

At the association and community levels, core group members felt it made sense to take advantage of recent government programmes. For example, members of the youth association agreed to take advantage of a government programme to develop apiculture cooperatives. The core group also agreed to mobilize people for participation in government programmes such as health care and sanitation, agroforestry, terracing, improvement of rangelands through planting of fodder, enclosure of some areas, and gulley reclamation.

Two years after the introduction of ABCD in Adis Alem, the results are impressive. More than 65 households have created homestead ponds, started small vegetable gardens, undertaken compost and manuring activities and planted more than 2,000 forage seedlings. The notion of the 'leaky bucket,' initially introduced as a community-level tool, proved very popular at the household level. It has passed from community member to community member, and is reportedly now being used by households in neighbouring communities without the involvement of REST or the government. More than 30 households are now recording their monthly income and expenditures. At the community level more than ten hectares of land has been terraced (labour provided by 120 households), more than 95 hectares of rangeland have been enclosed (labour provided by 225 households) and more than 5,000 multi-purpose seedlings have been planted on communal land through a community agroforestry initiative.

Community members also began to use their existing assets more efficiently. Land reclamation of gullies increased available farmland so that it could be distributed to landless youth, as an incentive for them to remain in the community. A group of them subsequently formed a beekeepers' association, which was granted permission to use a piece of common land to build a honey cooperative. The group now exports honey outside the community, and membership has increased to 55 members. As well, animal waste was once left lying where it fell. Now animals are kept enclosed so that dung can be gathered in one place. It is kept for composting and this has led to higher

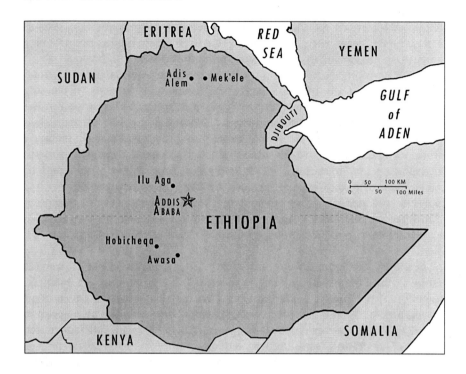

soil fertility. Water is now harvested in household ponds; this has allowed the creation of small vegetable gardens around the ponds. Soil erosion has been reduced by the planting of trees and the construction of terraces. Local trees are pruned to promote growth and the branches are used for firewood.

Woreda officials and REST staff see evidence of an increased willingness to embrace government-led initiatives that fit the community's priorities. They were also impressed by efforts of the local community to bring youth into the mainstream of economic development: in this case by involving landless youth, both in reclaiming degraded land and by encouraging cooperative enterprise.

Perspectives of community members

In February 2006, two groups of community members from Adis Alem were asked to list the significant changes that had occurred in their community during the previous two years. Both groups independently identified 'attitudinal change in the way community members looked at the local economy' as the most important shift in thinking by far.

People had begun to focus on ways of increasing inflows, or revenue, and decreasing outflows, or expenditures, in the community. They had also begun to examine their own household incomes and expenditures. A woman spoke of how she now manages her household differently: 'Personally, I have saved 650 *birr*. I have kept more grain, rather than selling and being short later. I have minimized expenditures, and increased my savings, [which] go to purchase goats. Now I keep animals enclosed at home and I also have a pond. This has increased my sense of security' (personal communication, 2006). Ato. Wolde Kansay said 'I used to sell my produce in the market and then take the money to purchase alcohol. After the leaky bucket exercise I realized that I was spending money against my family. I have now quit this habit and my household is much more harmonious. The important change was a change of mind' (personal communication, 2006).

Another attitudinal change identified by both groups was an increased openness to new ideas both from inside and outside the community. Community members felt confident that they could initiate their own

---

Box 11.2: Aiya's story

I am a farmer and live in Adis Alem with my wife and two small children. I rent 0.5 hectares of land – a 30 minute walk from my home – and I split the earnings from the land with the owner. I [also] have 0.5 hectares of land where I grow forage and elephant grass for animal feed, as well as sunflowers and a local flower called *hohot* to provide pollen, as I am involved in a local beekeeping association. For household consumption and income generation, I grow vegetables... [watered by] my backyard pond. My land also allows me to raise many cattle and poultry protected from the sun by the barn I built [together] with a local brick mason I hired using my savings.

Since the ABCD programme began, I have improved upon many of my activities. I now water my vegetables more regularly and...have increased the quantity and quality of the produce. I have begun fattening my animals, allowing me to make a profit when I sell them at the market. I sell about four cattle per year, and make 100 ETB profit on each one. It is this type of income diversification that has led to my family's food security. My household is increasing its inflows and decreasing the expenditures. This is now happening throughout the whole community: people are drinking less alcohol, spending less on festivals, and coming together for communal work.

My wife and I are both active in the ABCD project...facilitators contact me when they need to call a meeting, and I mobilize the rest of the community in my area. I also mobilize [people] when we need to organize communal work such as gulley reclamation, clearing livestock ponds, and soil and water conservation work. I was chosen...because I can cooperate with people easily and because I am respected...as I am very active and hard working. The community is easy to mobilize...[because people] have seen the benefits of ABCD within their own households.

ABCD has brought a great deal to our community, but I do not think it has yet reached its full potential. Within the community, it is most often only one person from each household who goes to the ABCD meetings – usually the head (the man). I think it would be better if both [husband and wife] were involved in ABCD because then we could achieve optimal improvement within the homes and our community. My wife and I are members of the core ABCD group, and so we can make good decisions about income and expenditure at our household level. ABCD should continue in our community, especially through capacity-building training on agriculture, management of income and expenditures, and income diversification.

development activities without direction from either the government or REST. They were also willing to embrace government-led initiatives that fit with the community's priorities.

Finally, community members reported a shift in their attitudes towards working together. Although the community has a long history of communal work, it is now more organized. Community groups and teams meet monthly, and in some cases weekly, to decide on activities and discuss issues. The results are clear to everyone: 'working in a group has allowed us to better manage both our time and labour. It allows us to mobilize the resources of ten people together rather than separately' (Ato. Araya Adhara).

Perspectives of outsiders

During the same period in February 2006, the REST fieldworkers and one head office staff member came to the same conclusion as that of community members – the most fundamental change was one of attitude and behaviour. First, they noted the way in which the community had shifted from being dependent on both REST and the government to initiating local development activities. In this respect REST staff members felt that Adis Alem was markedly different from other communities in the area: 'previously these people had a "culture of dependency" syndrome, looking most of the time for outside help…[and] community meetings with REST used to be about people expecting funds, but now we can meet about other purposes' (Tesfaye, personal communication, 2006). REST staff members felt that one of the reasons for this shift was that there were 'more lively' local associations in Adis Alem than in other communities.

Second, they sensed a new receptivity, among community members, in terms of taking advantage of selective government and REST programmes. Most of the activities undertaken by the community are the same types of activities promoted by REST and the government in Tigray. Yet the degree of uptake and the enthusiasm with which community members embraced certain initiatives impressed REST staff and *Woreda* officials. REST staff members felt that the main reason for this increased receptivity to government programmes was probably the way in which the 'leaky bucket' analysis had resonated with the community. One of them, Daniel, observed: 'In the past, farmers resisted these types of activities when they have been introduced from the outside, but now that it is coming out of a community-driven process the results may be different. They are now active partners with REST' (personal communication, 2006).

Third, they identified the emergence of a sense of responsibility among community members with regard to helping neighbouring communities. Several examples were cited in which groups of citizens from Adis Alem had travelled to nearby villages, without any direction or remuneration, to promote asset-mapping or the 'leaky bucket' analysis. Part of this was attributed to efforts by the government and REST to promote Adis Alem as a model

Group of women in Hobicheqa.

community, but REST staff also acknowledged the sense of accomplishment that had emerged from people having successfully undertaken community-driven development activities.

Officials from both the *kebele* level and *woreda* level were also asked to identify the most significant changes in Adis Alem over the previous two years. Both groups of officials cited 'increased motivation' to change the community's circumstances. From the perspective of *tabia* and *woreda* officials this motivation to change its circumstances had led the community to engage in a variety of activities, both community-driven and government-led. The officials pointed out that even in the government-led initiatives the community had embraced these programmes to a greater extent than other villages in the *woreda*. The *kebele* chairman, himself an ABCD facilitator and a member of the apiculture group, sensed greater appreciation for the accomplishments of his ancestors and a willingness to look first to 'what resources we have and what we can do with them' (personal communication, 2006). *Woreda* officials were also clearly impressed with the changes in the community. They pointed out that Adis Alem now ranked first among *tabias* in the *woreda* because of soil and water conservation activities, construction of household ponds, and prompt repayment of credit: 'what we notice about the people in Adis Alem as compared to other [*kebeles*] is that they seem to motivate each other. The members of the honey cooperative love their organization and are committed to it...Adis Alem is among the best because farmers are receptive to new ideas' (personal communication, 2006).

Part of the reason why *woreda* officials are so supportive may be the strategy REST used to begin the ABCD process. Staff members began with a workshop for a dozen *woreda* officials, emphasizing how the process would help the government in its goal of weaning communities off food aid. Self-reliance at the household and community level could be promoted by getting people to initiate development using local resources first. *Woreda* officials were further encouraged to support any community-driven activities that emerged from the ABCD process partly because this would be a very efficient use of government resources and would enhance community self-reliance over the long term.

While both REST staff members and *woreda* officials were glad to see people in Adis Alem take advantage of government programmes, they were sceptical about the ability of community members to initiate or sustain initiatives independently. REST staff members saw a need for their intensive involvement in Adis Alem for years to come. At senior levels of REST's management there is a clear belief that the organization is as important to the development of rural communities in Tigray now as it was during the struggle for political independence in the 1970s and 1980s. At the field level, it is clear that REST staff members are critical for guiding development and even keeping Adis Alem on track. As Daniel comments: 'they may go back to the old ways again unless there is follow-up with REST and the work is institutionalized' (personal communication 2006).

Hobicheqa, Kembetta

The Hobicheqa area is approximately 400 km south of Addis Ababa. Most of the 22,000 people living in this area are from the Kembetta ethnic group, known throughout Ethiopia for its high rate of literacy. The majority of the population is Protestant Christian, with small minorities of Muslims and Orthodox Christians. Hobicheqa, which in the Kembetta language means 'lions' forest,' is today one of the most densely populated rural areas of the country with no lions and very little forest. The main livelihood is subsistence agriculture and the raising of livestock, which is often complemented by agriculture and livestock sales, and, occasionally, petty trading. Partly due to a growing land shortage, both seasonal and permanent migration for work is common, particularly among young men. A common destination for seasonal work is the sugar cane factory in Metahaha, several hundred kilometres away. In addition, a legacy of one of the Hobicheqa area's most prominent sons, who at one time was the Ethiopian Ambassador to South Africa, is a small, but influential diaspora in South Africa. The remittances, and increasingly, the investments, from the Hobicheqa diaspora have become important sources of income and capital for many Hobicheqa area families.

Kambatti Metti Gezzima-Tope means 'women of Kembetta pooling their efforts to work together.' It is also the name of a small indigenous NGO established in 1997 by Bogaletch Gebre, a local Kembetta woman who was the first female member of the science faculty of the University of Addis Ababa. KMG's mission is to empower women and their communities to build on their positive traditions such as *gezzima*, or self-help, to eliminate harmful traditional practices such as female circumcision. Over time, KMG has utilized a development approach it has called Community Conversation and Enhancement (CCE) which, like Hundee's approach, facilitates community reflection and discussion on both positive and negative traditional practices.

KMG has been active in the Hobicheqa area since 1998. The focus of its work there has been to use CCE to engage elders, youth, women, government officials, NGO workers, teachers, and traditional and religious leaders in discussions meant to raise awareness about both harmful traditional practices and HIV/AIDS. In 2002, these conversations led to the first marriage – in Hobicheqa – of an uncircumcised woman in the Kembetta Tembaro Zone. Abdisa Abosa and Genet Germa's story was documented by KMG and made national and international news. As a result of KMG's intense campaigning on this issue a bylaw was written at the district level to prevent the practice of female circumcision.

The ABCD process in Hobicheqa

Unlike REST and Hundee, which tested the ABCD approach in only one community each, KMG decided to pilot ABCD in three Hobicheqa area *kebeles*: a small town (Hobicheqa 01), a peri-urban community (Hobicheqa PA), and a rural village (Doreba PA). KMG settled on communities that were accessible to the KMG office in Durame and represented the diversity of communities in Hobicheqa.

In May 2003, KMG identified four people from each community and approached them to see if they would be willing to be facilitators of a different kind of community development process. The potential facilitators identified by KMG, with the assistance of *kebele* administration officials, were evenly divided between women and men, and were all well respected members of their communities (although not, in most cases, formal leaders). KMG then worked with the *kebele* administration and the new facilitators to identify approximately 50 people in each community to form a core group. Once formed, each core group was asked to decide on whether to accept the facilitators selected and trained by KMG or to choose other community members for this purpose, since KMG had agreed to train any new facilitators selected by the community. Only one of the facilitators selected by KMG was not accepted by this core group. All three community core groups came together at the school in Hobicheqa town to be introduced to the ABCD process.

Each core group began by looking for past community successes in initiating and sustaining community development activities that had not been supported by outside agencies. The elders spoke of community efforts to build the school in which they were meeting, pointing out the importance of having a place where all six *kebeles* in the Hobicheqa area could gather for meetings and celebrations. They also spoke of how the three communities mobilized, occasionally, to build bridges. They offered recent examples, too, such as building houses for the elderly, helping each other with farming activities, helping those who lost livestock, holding weddings, accompanying sick people to the clinic and taking suspected criminals to court. This spirit of cooperation had been institutionalized to some degree in the local *idirs*, the main vehicle for people to help each other, particularly in times of crisis. Community members enjoyed the opportunity to reflect on past successes, pointing out how it rekindled self-reliance and pride.

They went on to identify skills in their respective communities. The most common skills were either related to agriculture, or to handicraft and artisan work. Agriculture skills included a long list related to growing a variety of crops, animal fattening, poultry and beekeeping. Handicraft or artisan skills were related to such activities as weaving, sewing, and basket-making. There were a number of other skills, ranging from construction to traditional healing. In addition to all of these, there were additional skills, such as those needed for professional disciplines, such as teaching, or for small enterprises such as vehicle repair and hairdressing. According to Ayeleche, an interesting result of the process was the inclusion of skills that had not been previously valued, at least publicly: 'we also realized that blacksmith and pottery skills were an asset, where before these skills were not respected and people who did them were outcasts within our society' (personal communication, 2006). In Hobicheqa, blacksmiths and potters tended to be descendants of a clan of landless people who were seen as having the 'evil eye' and often shunned at social events.

The most important associations included *mahabers*, *idirs*, *iqubs* and an association called *debo*, a mutual aid society to help men undertake labour-intensive tasks. Other associations, more recently established, and formally sanctioned by government, included women's associations, youth associations, and, in the town of Hobicheqa, an Anti-AIDS Club and an association to combat harmful traditional practices. Churches were the most important institutions for mobilizing people for activities. The main government agencies – with a *woreda*-level presence –included the Departments of Agriculture, Education, Justice and Health. A number of NGOs worked in all three communities: World Vision, KMG, Gogata Care, Red Cross and AMAZ. The only private sector institutions were a handful of cooperative flour mills.

Next, core groups drew maps of their communities, identifying physical assets, such as roads, buildings, and land use patterns. The maps were not considered complete until everyone in each core group was satisfied. At a subsequent meeting, each core group drew a straight line through their maps, and members then walked their respective transect lines, developing detailed cross-sectional diagrams. One of the highlights for community members was the number and size of limestone deposits identified, of which the KMG staff member had been unaware.

The main sources of revenue coming into the communities were from sales of cash crops, livestock, and timber. Other important sources of household income were wages for daily labour, and remittances and investments from family members working outside the area. In Hobicheqa town there were additional income streams for handicraft production, poultry and egg sales, and revenues from petty trade and small retail shops. Money was spent outside the communities on such things as clothing, furniture, medication, fertilizer, kerosene, and agricultural implements. People realized that they could increase inflows and decrease outflows by replacing chemical fertilizers with organic fertilizers, improving their management of the natural resource base – particularly limestone deposits and remaining forests – and reducing expenditures on social festivities and the consumption of alcohol.

As in the cases of both Ilu Aga and Adis Alem, individuals in the Hobicheqa area also began changing their saving and spending patterns almost immediately. They reduced spending on coffee, alcohol, and social festivities. In Doreba, a committee was formed to advise families about reducing wedding expenditure. Abebe explains how reducing household expenditure had an impact on his family: 'I used to spend over 100 ETB on *Meskelle*, which coincides with the beginning of the school year...I used to have to take out loans to cover [it], but now I only spend ten ETB on the holiday. All of these changes...allowed me to send my children to school. I see investing in my children's education as an investment in the future' (personal communication, 2006). While reducing expenditures on non-essential items seems like common sense community members reported that the leaky bucket exercise made them see exactly how much of a difference it could make – and where they might invest the savings to increase their incomes. Several community members also pointed out that in the past people had reacted negatively to government campaigns to get them to reduce non-essential expenditures because they resented the government telling them what to do in their households.

Core groups then met with their respective communities to develop visions and action plans. In contrast to planning in Adis Alem and Ilu Aga, that of the three Hobicheqa communities seemed to be based on longstanding community aspirations for basic services and infrastructure rather than on opportunities identified through the 'leaky bucket' analysis. In the town of Hobicheqa, for example, the main community vision was to have access to electricity within ten years. In both rural *kebeles* the main community vision was to gain access to potable water, although in Hobicheqa PA the vision also included building a school, reforesting degraded lands, and improving several local roads and bridges. While the community action plans got off to a good start, group members in Hobicheqa town (01) realized, within months, that their action plan was too ambitious. Driven largely by the more elite members of the core group, the dream of electrification came to be seen as a long-term goal. Although the group was successful in raising more than 12,000

ETB in cash and one million ETB in future pledges, the group hoped that this could leverage a much larger commitment from government. When this did not happen, members looked at smaller projects that were achievable, and decided to support poultry, bee-keeping and embroidery activities.

To pursue their identical goals of improving access to potable water, both the Doreba and Hobicheqa PA core groups began to mobilize local funds, labour, skills, and materials to clean, protect, and improve access to three springs. While road repairs and the construction of small bridges did improve access to water, the distance to these springs meant that daily water collection in both *kebeles* was still arduous. The core groups decided to approach the Bureau of Water and Mines for technical assistance in assessing other potential sources and technologies for potable water.

At this point, two intriguing events occurred. Due to a personnel shortage at KMG, fieldworkers were forced to curtail visits to the ABCD communities. Because Hobicheqa 01 was closest to the KMG office, and was changing its action plan to concentrate on small, income-generating projects, fieldworkers decided to focus attention there. The consequence was that core groups in Doreba and Hobicheqa PA were left alone for several months. During this time, a number of spontaneous group activities began to emerge. Arising out of conversations between core group members and others in the two rural communities 16 small 'ABCD' groups were formed. Activities included the growing of vegetables and apples – a new commodity – for sale, the making of rope as well as the making of baskets and mats from enset leaves, the initiation of a small grain bank, the setting up of two types of simple insurance schemes, as well as the establishment of a house construction group and a labour-selling group. None of these activities were part of formal community action plans.

The second event was even more surprising to KMG and Oxfam Canada staff members. People in Zatosahodera, near Durame, had been approached to see if they would agree to Oxfam Canada training new KMG fieldworkers there. Villagers agreed to participate in appreciative interviewing sessions, asset-mapping exercises, and the application of the 'leaky bucket' tool. When a KMG fieldworker visited Zatosahodera by chance several months later, he was astonished to find that community members had formed a savings club and created a communal vegetable garden as a direct result of the training activities and with no follow-up from KMG staff.

Had the absence of KMG fieldworkers in these villages – where people had learned to identify assets and opportunities – been the real catalyst to community-driven development? Oxfam Canada staff members noticed that in Adis Alem, Ilu Aga and Hobicheqa 01 the activities mentioned in the action plans fairly closely mirrored the interests and programmes of the facilitating NGOs. But in Doreba, Hobicheqa PA, and Zatosahodera, where KMG fieldworkers had not influenced the process, the communities had mobilized to undertake myriad activities unrelated to the interests of the NGO.

Perspectives of community members

Community members from Hobicheqa 01, Hobicheqa PA, and Doreba were able to reach a consensus on the most significant changes that had occurred in their communities over the previous three years. They described the first change as very simple and yet very powerful: the ability to recognize individual and community assets. Tadesse Gichamo, an elder from Hobicheqa 01, put it this way: 'We used to think that only the rich had assets, but now we see that we too have assets... our health, our land, our knowledge, and different kinds of natural resources' (personal communication, 2006).

Aster describes the empowering effect this change in thinking has had on her: 'After I joined the ABCD group I learned how to process enset by-products to make baskets and ropes and quickly began making money... I [also] gathered the butter from those who bring small amounts to the market... I put together all of the butter I collected and sold larger amounts to make a profit... I am now able to cover my household needs and no longer need to wait for money from my husband' (personal communication, 2006).

While the recognition of assets was important, people also noted that they had also begun using their assets more efficiently. They had started exploiting existing resources effectively, wasting less, and diversifying their activities so

---

Box 11.3: Emmanuel's story

After attending the ABCD training sessions, two other members of the ABCD core group and I thought about how we could put what we learnt into action to improve our livelihoods. We approached our local *idir* members and discussed... possible activities we could become involved in together. Twenty-eight members of the *idir* (six women and 22 men), agreed to join our group. Over time, we came up with the following goals: to help members in times of need; to save the lives of the members if ever they were ill; to help members out when they lost an ox; and to help provide adequate shelter for members. To date, we have carried or driven six members to the clinic in time to prevent their deaths. We have replaced two oxen and three cows. We have also been able to give money to one member to build his home.

Initially, we began our savings by contributing 20 cups of grain each and five ETB during the rainy season. The grain was used by the members in times of need. They were expected to give back double what they took at the next harvest period. We now have 30 quintals of grain saved. At the end of each season, we sell the remaining grain to make a profit for the group. The profit is then given out on a credit basis to members of the group. Those who receive credit are expected to give the money back within six months with a 50 per cent interest rate.

Since we formed [our group] we have added to our vision. We now also want to ensure that every member's child gets to attend school, and we want to deal with the issue of the lack of potable water. If we are able to achieve this, we hope to start a group apple farm as an additional source of income... The community is surprised to see all that we have achieved in such a short period of time... I think that the lesson of increasing savings and decreasing unnecessary expenditures will be something the community continues doing. People within the community are saving money through their new found household management skills and teaching this to others.

that they were less vulnerable to negative shocks, such as weather, diseases, and prices that could affect their livelihoods. Ayeleche, from Hobicheqa PA, described how she has re-allocated household assets: '...In our house we began making many little changes...Now I buy the eggs of the hybrid [chickens] and add them to the local chickens so that I can get some hybrid chicks. I have decreased the money I spend on my children's clothing...[And] I have begun growing vegetables...for household consumption...The water used for washing our clothes [is also used] to water the vegetables' (personal communication, 2006).

Besides helping themselves, people also noticed their increased willingness to help each other. In some cases, the motivation to do so was for the betterment of the whole community. An example was given of how a local *idir* changed its rules to allow savings to support local students with higher education. In other cases, cooperation was seen as mutually beneficial, as in the case of a labour-sharing group in Doreba. The group found that when individuals sold their labour they received two ETB per day. When ten people sold labour together they could get 45 ETB per day, practically doubling their earnings. Aster suggests that this increased cooperation was influenced by the process: 'ABCD is a mirror that has allowed us to see ourselves. We have changed ourselves and we are changing each other. Water trickles down slowly, but it brings change' (personal communication, 2006).

One other change that seemed significant to several individuals, though it was not named by the community groups, was the way in which gender relations had become more equitable, at least for some families. For example, some households had shifted to joint decision-making: 'before this training I would get angry when my wife asked where I had been...[I] would spend a lot of the money on alcohol...We now discuss...how much money we spent, and on what...it has created a forum to discuss other issues and our relationship has become more open and full of love' (Korkore, personal communication, 2006).

A more open relationship between couples often stemmed from a new appreciation for what women could contribute to household finances, given the opportunity. In the case of Aster, membership in a self-help group helped her engage in new ventures on her own. She didn't tell her husband of her work, wanting to wait until she had made real progress. At Christmas, she was able to buy clothes for her children using her savings: 'My husband saw the clothes and questioned where they came from. He was very happy when he saw what I was able to achieve. Although it is not [part of] our culture to show appreciation for what another is doing, I think my husband [told] others how proud he is' (personal communication, 2006).

This shift in gender relations arose out of a new sense of self-confidence on the part of women, an appreciation of their contribution by menfolk, and the increased leverage of women in household decision-making as a result. Interestingly, the isolation experienced by many women in their marriages had been related to the issue of dependence. Now, there are two trends:

women's collaboration with other women in self-help initiatives, and a more collaborative relationship with their husbands.

Perspectives of outsiders

KMG fieldworkers all agreed that the most significant change was the number of ABCD groups that had formed spontaneously, particularly in the two rural communities. What was particularly shocking for them was that they did not even know that many of these groups existed until early in 2005.

The other important change was the way in which communities approached local government for assistance. The core group in Hobicheqa 01 had collected significant contributions and pledges before asking for government support for electrification. Lombamo Handiso, the *kebele* administrator for Hobicheqa 01, stressed this community mobilization effort. He felt that represented a change in thinking, since people now believed that electrification was no longer a matter of 'if,' but of 'when.' Similarly, in Doreba and Hobicheqa PA, when people approached the Bureau of Water and Mines for help, it wasn't to demand a well; rather, it was for advice on alternative sources and technologies for accessing potable water. This change in approach was seen as one that enabled the communities. And with such an approach they could get

---

Box 11.4: The Hobicheqa diaspora in South Africa

There are some people from the church who are in South Africa and have been sending money back for the church. There are also individuals who send money back to their families. Additionally, the Ethiopian Ambassador for South Africa, Tesefaye Habiso realized that there was a great deal of work available in South Africa. He helped people from our region to get work there. Four boys from one family went there and within a very short time, they all had vehicles. Unless God helps us in some other way, this is something we could never expect to afford.

Within the past three years over 40 vehicles have been bought by those from our area who are in South Africa. Three years ago there were only 5 vehicles between here and Hosana. There are now 70. Some of these people return from South Africa with their cars and some send money back. Some even invest in other people's businesses such as buying livestock. If the livestock were purchased for people outside of the family, the family were expected to follow things up to ensure the person who received the cattle were doing their part of the deal [i.e., paying back a share of the offspring].

All of our support systems used to be very informal, but now deals surrounding money are becoming more formal and sometimes require contracts. Some lend money to poorer friends and family...Those who do go to South Africa often sponsor others from the area to go. If someone living abroad dies, money from the Edir is given to their family. Money is also given by the community to people who are leaving the Kebele to help them. This helps to ensure they will send money back to support us. The action plan for the electrification project of Hobicheqa 01 has included collecting financial contributions from the diaspora both in and out of Ethiopia. It was the role of the committee to contact these people. I have heard that the diasporas wanted a detailed proposal before giving any money to the community.

Excerpt from an interview with Lolamu Kabissa (personal communication, 2006).

more support from local government than if they demanded that to which they felt entitled. Bushalo, Chairman of Doreba *kebele*, observed that through this 'people [had become] more active in their own development' (personal communication, 2006).

Bushalo also explained that although *idirs* had always been around, people were now forming themselves into many different types of associations. Both the existing *idirs* and the new associations had begun undertaking grain trading, labour sharing, and house construction. He described the healthy competition that had developed between the 13 sub-areas of the *kebele*, suggesting that when one group did something innovative, it motivated other groups. However, the *woreda* administrator, Biranhu, stated: 'the reality is that a few people working for the *woreda* cannot change the lives of the people – the community members must do that' (personal communication, 2006). This reaction highlights one of the challenges of an asset-based approach. Instead of seeing community-driven activities as points of leverage for government investment, local officials may instead see community initiative as a substitute for state involvement.

Results and analysis

Changes in the community's asset base

Between 2003 and 2006, all five communities (Adis Alem, Ilu Aga, Doreba PA, Hobicheqa 01, and Hobicheqa PA) experienced significant increases in physical, financial and social assets, as well as a reduction in the degradation of, and in some cases a small improvement in, several natural assets.

All five community action plans included building or improving specific physical assets or infrastructure, though electrification did not materialize in the town of Hobicheqa (01), all three Hobicheqa area communities were able to mobilize to make improvements. Three roads – ranging in length from 5 to 15 km – and eight bridges were constructed, and 19 springs were cleaned and restored. In Adis Alem, more than 10 ha of land was terraced, more than 95 ha of rangeland was enclosed, and more than 65 households dug small ponds, allowing the creation of vegetable gardens. In Ilu Aga, seven small dams were built to irrigate areas of common land that were used previously only for grazing.

While some of the community action plans did specifically include savings, in all five communities significant amounts of money were mobilized at the group and household levels. This was due mainly to reductions in expenditures on social festivities, and on regular consumption of such items as coffee, sugar and alcohol. Small associations also accumulated savings. Some of these were formed so that people could save money for building materials, such as corrugated iron roofs. Other associations saved money to provide livestock insurance or emergency medical assistance to group members. Still others used group savings to purchase inputs for income-generating activities. Villagers in

Ilu Aga completed an addition to the local school with 10,000 ETB raised through contributions from individuals and groups. And grain banking helped individuals and groups to save money. In the Hobicheqa area, an association saved grain for sale for times when prices were high. The success of this effort led to the formation of three similar groups by members of the same *idir*.

Complementing the increase in savings, there was a marked increase in household income in all the communities. Households attributed their increased income to investing savings in new, or enhanced, activities such as vegetable production, beekeeping, animal-fattening, poultry-rearing, and seedling and timber production. People described annual increases in household income from several hundred to several thousand ETB. In Adis Alem, the largest source of new income was from honey production: the beekeeping association reported an income of just over 42,000 ETB in its first year. In Ilu Aga, vegetable production on newly irrigated land was the largest source of increased household income (roughly 1,000 ETB annually). Seedling production and animal fattening (up to 2,000 ETB in four months) were also significant. In the Hobicheqa area, increases in income were spread across the widest range of activities, including honey production (up to 800 ETB), poultry-raising, and a host of smaller income streams such as embroidery, basket-making, renting out labour (as a group), and apple production. Several community members pointed out that getting involved in new activities made them less dependent on one or two main income sources and helped spread their income over the year. Another way in which households attempted to lessen vulnerability was to invest in upgrading their houses, constructing water catchments, building small shops for petty trade, purchasing additional livestock or seedlings, and sending their children to school.

Community members reported an increased trust in each other and in their leadership. In Adis Alem, members of the beekeeping association pointed out that they could now leave equipment outside without fear of it being stolen or damaged. Others pointed out that where they once used to hire people from outside the community they now try to find people with the same skills within their communities. They also reported an increased willingness to share their skills with others even if it meant competition. One farmer in Doreba described how a fellow group member showed him how to make beehives, an economic activity that is now his largest source of income. People remarked on an increase in mutual assistance for timely ploughing, or for community-level improvements such as terracing. The reduction in household spending on social festivities raises the question as to whether spending less on social activities may weaken social bonds. Could an increase in one type of asset, that of household savings, lead to a decrease in another form of community asset, that of social capital? A closer look, though, shows that social festivities are not being eliminated or even scaled back; rather, people are finding less expensive ways of participating.

People in the four rural communities – all except Hobicheqa 01 – which is largely urban – made concerted efforts to rebuild their natural assets. They concentrated on protecting soil, water, and trees. Their renewed interest in composting came as a result of seeing, first-hand, how the overuse of chemical fertilizers was destroying their soil. Terracing, reforestation with multi-purpose seedlings on communal land, and gulley reclamation were undertaken as strategies to prevent flash flooding and soil erosion. Increased rainwater harvesting in Adis Alem, and small dam construction in Ilu Aga, have also been adopted as a way of increasing community access to water resources. Many of the efforts mutually reinforced each other, such as reforestation and terracing – a combined strategy to reduce water runoff and soil erosion. In Ilu Aga, the community began using reforestation as a form of terracing, using trees instead of stone walls. These initiatives have built support with local government officials who feel pressured by higher government directives to get communities involved in such activities.

Internal agency: ownership, leadership, and associational life

People's ownership of the process of change seems greater and more authentic in the Hobicheqa communities where the NGO inadvertently removed itself after brief, intensive facilitation. Internal agency appears weakest in Adis Alem, where REST fieldworkers never really shifted from facilitation to accompaniment. Where internal agency appeared to be strongest, people spoke of the struggle they had had in motivating others. Aster, from Hobicheqa PA, commented on how difficult it was to call meetings of the ABCD group which she led, since people were not paid to attend. Group members wondered why they should stop work for as many as five days to focus on mapping their assets without being paid. She stressed that 'we convince them by telling them it is for their own development...that poverty is not just a lack of resources, but a lack of management of those resources' (personal communication, 2006). While at the outset it was a tremendous challenge for leaders to get community members to work together for their own betterment once this was accomplished fostering internal agency became easier.

It is hard to determine the degree to which all members of the communities were included in the ABCD process. In Adis Alem, there were no women among the facilitators and contact committee members. In Ilu Aga, the process began only with the members of the cereal bank association, and in the Hobicheqa area, only leaders of local associations were selected. As the ABCD process evolved, though, it seems to have become more inclusive. This usually happened through the emergence of new leaders who distinguished themselves through small group activities. In Adis Alem, for example, a number of landless youth were drawn into the process through participating in beekeeping and reclaiming gulley land. In Ilu Aga and Hobicheqa PA, strong women leaders, such as Ayaletch, and Aster, brought other women into the ABCD process. There is also evidence that, at least in some households – in all communities – husbands are including wives, and even grown children, in financial decisions. In Hobicheqa 01, the ABCD core group was initially dominated by educated, affluent community members who pushed the agenda of electrification. Once it became clear that this was too ambitious, these members became less active, while those less accustomed to leadership spearheaded groups concerned with poultry, beekeeping, and embroidery initiatives.

It is this informal leadership – individuals leading through action, rather than position – that was regarded as central to success. Community members pointed to leaders who had spent time elsewhere and who had returned with new ideas or those whose skills had developed through work in church groups or *idirs*. Leaders were seen as visionaries who proposed new ideas and motivated others to believe in these ideas. Unafraid to stand up for their beliefs, they were also considered to be objective, open to other points of view, and willing to ask for advice. In each community, people recalled associations that had failed because the leadership lacked these characteristics. Good leaders, people observed, often had strong family backgrounds that led them to become influential. They were usually educated and able to speak well in public. In Ilu Aga, it was pointed out that such people could be identified while they were young, so they could be mentored into becoming leaders.

The ABCD process was also helping to redefine associational life. In Ilu Aga, people pointed out that the formerly strong Oromo tradition of gathering to discuss issues had been revitalized by the ABCD process. As well, there was more coordination between groups. ABCD core groups had become, to some extent, 'associations of associations,' comprised of representatives from informal associations. In Adis Alem, this has been formalized through small contributions to the ABCD committee by other associations. In Oromia and Kembetta, such formalization was seen as too politically risky. Perhaps the most powerful way associational life changed was that existing associations had been adapted for new purposes. In Ilu Aga, a horse riders' association is now a farmers' group. Members are pooling savings to purchase an irrigation pump for 3,000 ETB and have invested some savings in a community micro-credit scheme.

External agency: catalytic facilitation and accompaniment

The ABCD approach forced fieldworkers of all three NGOs to think differently about their roles. Once a given community began driving its own development, the role of the fieldworkers, at least in Ilu Aga and Hobicheqa, turned to one of accompaniment. Sometimes they provided advice, but more often they helped the community develop relationships with outside institutions, primarily local government. For NGOs to make the shift from providers to catalytic facilitators or brokers was easier for some than for others. Certainly, fieldworkers from all three NGOs found that entering the community by way of appreciative interviewing was a powerful experience. Teshome, from Hundee, pointed out that he found it liberating to tell the community that he had come 'as a student to learn, rather than as an expert to teach' (personal communication, 2006). Fieldworkers could also remember moments when the communities took charge of the process. In Hobicheqa PA, this happened when the core groups presented results to the larger community. Getatchew points out that 'it was at that point I realized that KMG was no longer the facilitator' (personal communication, 2006).

REST fieldworkers, however, expressed doubts that the ABCD process would continue successfully if they stepped back. Despite this, REST's special relationship with government allowed fieldworkers to link the beekeepers' association in Ilu Aga to a programme that supports apiculture development in Tigray, and to help the association get *woreda* approval to use common land for hives and building. Community groups have been connected, by REST, to government-sponsored initiatives in soil and water conservation, agroforestry, and pasture improvement. REST fieldworkers also helped convince local government to provide a cement water tank in Adis Alem. However, fieldworkers at Hundee and KMG managed to make real strides in the transition from facilitation to accompaniment. In Ilu Aga, Hundee fieldworkers were able to help the community negotiate permission from the *woreda* to dam and divert streams for irrigation of common land for potato production. They are also helping the community identify organizations that could provide technical assistance on strengthening irrigation channels. Similarly, KMG is currently trying to link Hobicheqa PA with an international research institute that specializes in water issues.

Internalization of ABCD by the participating NGOs

While the action-research process appears to have had little impact on the approach of REST, it has significantly shaped the ongoing work of Hundee, KMG, and Oxfam Canada. Members of REST's senior management were never really involved in the process while the executive directors of both Hundee and KMG were closely engaged. Zegeye X, the Executive Director of Hundee, observed: 'Before ABCD, Hundee's role was that of holding the power, but through the ABCD process, we had to transfer that power to the community... this should be done in all of our projects' (personal communication, 2006). Hundee is now using the ABCD approach in five new communities in separate *woredas*. KMG also plans to expand ABCD work to six additional communities in Kachabira *woreda* where large committees of elders, women and youth have been mobilized. However, Bogaletch Gebre, the Executive Director of KMG sees a potential danger in creating expectations and promoting ABCD if governments are not prepared to invest in the community initiatives: 'development workers need to be asking how can we truly develop self-reliant societies which demand accountability from their governments? At the moment, these villages are just surviving, so how can we go beyond survival? To improve ABCD we should ensure that when we see a community pulling itself up...it is supported and does not fall back' (personal communication, 2006).

Oxfam Canada has recently integrated the ABCD approach into its work in community-based risk management with pastoral communities, developing a five-year programme to consolidate and expand the approach for NGO and community relationships in Ethiopia. Mindful of the challenge posed by Bogaletch, it has included mechanisms to give community initiatives long-term impact. A small community innovation fund allows Oxfam Canada to support promising initiatives in select communities that have the potential to increase in scale. The organization is also building relationships with national and international agricultural research institutes and technical colleges in the hopes they will be interested in community innovation and share research and technology with new communities. This new network may help create a more enabling policy environment for asset-based and community-driven development within Ethiopia's current limiting realities. In a country where NGOs can draw negative attention, Oxfam Canada regards ABCD as a liberating approach that helps build citizen power.

Conclusion

Much has been learned from the first phase of ABCD action-research in Ethiopia. It is indeed possible for an NGO to stimulate people to become actively engaged in their own development by encouraging them to appreciate successes and build on existing strengths in the community. When NGO fieldworkers facilitate – rather than drive – development becomes an 'inside-out' instead of an 'outside-in' process.

It might be suggested that the facilitating NGOs sometimes exerted too much influence over the process. Occasionally, people may have been swayed in their choice of community activities. As well, there may have been a bias toward economic issues. Yet this raises the question of whether an ABCD process, facilitated differently, and with different tools, might stimulate other types of activities, such as a community-driven response to the prevention of (or care of those with) HIV/AIDS.

Nevertheless, the ABCD approach as it has been developed in Ethiopia is clearly a catalyst for economic development – for many, it is a journey of discovery, analysis, and action. Community members, both in groups and in their own households, start accumulating savings by reducing expenditures. In Ethiopia, this process has been aided by a long tradition of informal savings through *iqubs* and *idirs*. The savings realized through expenditure reductions are then channelled into investments, through individual or group income-generating activities. These, in turn, result in increased incomes which feed into savings and into the acquisition of additional assets, creating a virtuous spiral.

A similar virtuous spiral seems to occur with respect to both internal agency and the relationship between community members and outside agencies. With each small success in undertaking locally determined development activities, communities increase their capacity to act. And the leaders who emerge from the process begin to look for different kinds of relationships with outside agents.

The capacity of outside agents to respond to this opportunity for partnerships and investment will be critical to the success of ABCD in Ethiopia. Given the degree of government decentralization in Ethiopia the *woreda* level administrations are increasingly acquiring the ability (if not the resources) to either support or thwart community-driven initiatives. NGOs that see their role not as 'builders of' but 'builders on' local capacity seem to welcome this approach at the community level. Their challenge is in finding donors to fund a process that cannot predetermine outcomes and results and accepts a larger degree of uncertainty. NGOs with a role of service delivery have much more difficulty with this approach. For most NGOs and local governments, using an ABCD approach will mean finding a balance between being responsive to community-driven initiatives and at the same time retaining a role of providing important services or entitlements to these communities. If they can achieve this balance, they can shift from being 'gap fillers' in voiceless communities to 'gap bridgers' – helping communities with an active and engaged citizenry look for new relationships with outside institutions.

References

Adal, Y. (April 2004) *Access to land in rural Ethiopia: A desk review* (Draft), Submitted to: Sustainable Land Use Forum, Addis Ababa.

Ayenew, M. (2002) 'Decentralization in Ethiopia: Two case studies on devolution of power and responsibilities to local authorities', in Bahru Zewde and Siegfried Pausewang (eds) *Ethiopia: The challenge of democracy from below*. Nordic Africa Institute, Uppsala/Addis Ababa.

Centre for Development Services, Egypt and the Coady Institute (2002) 'Extended case studies', in *Asset-based community development: Success stories from Egyptian communities*. A manual for practitioners. Available from: http://www.coady.stfx.ca/resources/abcd/CDS_manual.pdf [Accessed 20 February 2008]

Devereux, S. (October 2000) *Food insecurity in Ethiopia: A discussion paper for DFID*, Institute for Development Studies, Sussex, UK.

Economist Intelligence Unit, The (2007) *Ethiopia country report*. Available from: http://www.eiu.com [Accessed 22 August 2007]

Graham, J. (n.d.) *Whither NGOs in Ethiopia? NGOs and the state: Part II*. Available from: http://www.addistribune.com/Archives/2003/04/18-04-03/Whither.htm [Accessed 22 August 2007]

Habtu, A. (2005) 'Multiethnic federalism in Ethiopia: A study of the secession clause in the constitution', *Publius: The Journal of Federalism*, 35(2): 313–325.

Kretzmann, J. and McKnight, J. (1993) *Building communities from the inside out: A path toward finding and mobilizing a community's assets*, Institute for Policy Research, Northwestern University, Evanston, IL.

Mekonnen, A. (February 2007). *Ethiopia diaspora, please come home!* The Reporter. Available from: http://www.ethiopiareporter.com/modules.php?name=Newsandfile=articleandsid=12082 [Accessed 22 August 2007]

UNHABITAT (2002) *Local democracy and decentralization in east and southern Africa: Experiences from Uganda, Kenya, Botswana, Tanzania and Ethiopia.* Nairobi, Kenya.

World Bank, (2004) Presented by T. Haque. and A. Dabalen (AFTH3), (March 16). *Ethiopia: Moving from humanitarian assistance to a productive safety net.* Location: J7-044. Sponsored by: Social Safety Nets in Social Protection Anchor, World Bank, Washington, DC.

Author's note

I would like to dedicate this case to Allison Maddison, a Coady youth intern in Ethiopia in 2001 who first connected the Coady Institute to Oxfam Canada in Ethiopia and started the conversation that led to the action-research profiled in this case. On 31 December 2004, Allison lost a courageous battle with cancer at the age of 27.

I would also like to acknowledge the work of several dedicated field staff at REST (Tesfaye, Tewedros, and Daniel), Hundee (Teshome and Yosef) and KMG (Getatchew), without whose dedication to documenting the ABCD process as it unfolded in the communities, none of this would have been possible. I also want express my thanks to Megan Foster and Brie McMahon who, while working for the Coady Institute, pulled together much of the documentation from three years of action research prior to the community visits made by the research team in February 2006. Most importantly I would like to thank the community members of Adis Alem, Ilu Aga, Hobicheqa 01, Hobicheqa PA and Doreba, as well as the *woreda* officials who work with these communities, for being so generous with their time and insights.

The research team consisted of three Ethiopians (Samuel Molla Degaga, Mengistu Gonsama, and Semalegn Belay – all with Oxfam Canada) and three Canadians (Lucie Goulet with Oxfam Canada, Marilyn Struthers with the Trillium Foundation of Ontario, and myself).

As a *ferengi*, or foreigner, in Ethiopia (or any other developing country) I have always found it very awkward to be present in a small village setting when people are talking about development. Villagers tend to assume that you are the donor or at least a senior person with an NGO. Talk invariably turns to community problems or needs as villagers try to anticipate what the foreign guest wants to hear. What I found so refreshing about my time visiting the five Ethiopian communities in researching and writing this case is that people were eager to tell their stories, they were proud of their accomplishments and they were not trying to second-guess what the outsiders wanted to hear.

In contrast, I remember well my first visit to the community of Ilu Aga, several months before Hundee began using an ABCD approach there. The first reaction to our visit was that a community member stood up and spoke of the problem of lack of access to clean water. After hearing her out, a member of the Hundee staff introduced us and said we were not coming with any ideas or projects, but that we wanted to learn from their past successes. He asked the roughly 50 community members assembled to describe what they were most proud of in their community. After a few seconds of silence people started whispering to each other and then began stepping forward with stories of small initiatives that they, their parents or grandparents had undertaken. The person who had stood up and talked about the lack of clean water in Ilu Aga was Ayaletch, who three years later was the woman in the case who mobilized her neighbours and the *woreda* administration to build a new well in Ilu Aga.

CHAPTER 12

Reviving self-help: an NGO promotes Asset Based Community Development in two communities in Kenya

Alison Mathie

Introduction

Community Research in Environment and Development Initiatives (CREADIS) is a small NGO operating in western Kenya since 2000. Its director, a graduate of the Coady International Institute in Canada, was an enthusiastic adopter of Asset Based Community Development, known as ABCD, and returned to Kenya eager to apply it. She was concerned about the environmental degradation in her district and the despondency of local communities in the face of years of political malaise and economic decline, compounded by health challenges (primarily HIV/AIDS) and natural disasters (such as El Niño). Some people, especially young men, were migrating in the hope of finding a better life elsewhere; others were simply trying to cope. There was anger at the failure of the government to deliver services, uncertainty about markets for their agricultural products, frustration at the arbitrary nature of NGO assistance, and an expectation that 'handouts' should flow from NGOs. People felt increasingly powerless to stay in control of their own livelihoods. Now with the prospect of a new political regime, and the possibility of economic recovery, CREADIS saw an opportunity to 'prime' communities for a different experience of development with an asset-based approach.

The two communities where the ABCD approach was applied are in Bungoma District, close to the Ugandan border. Bisunu is a small, rural, dispersed settlement of 328 households, 22 km by dirt road from the district centre of Bungoma town. Ndengelwa is peri-urban, located on the main inter-provincial highway, 12 km from Bungoma town. It is relatively large – comprising four villages, and about 1,200 households. The mainstay of people's livelihoods in both places is agriculture. Ndengelwa's location means that government services are reasonably accessible and opportunities exist for small roadside enterprises, and access to urban markets and employment. Bisunu, on the other hand, lacking these advantages, has been characterized as being 'in the development shadow' (Nabiswa, personal communication, 2007).

CREADIS promoted the idea that people in communities *can* drive their own development, even if this takes place very gradually, as in 'individuals interacting with other individuals to bring about change, one step at a time' (Narayan, 2000: 279). For this to happen, however, there are sometimes psychological barriers to be overcome so that people regain confidence in themselves as agents of change, proactive rather than dependent in their relationships with external organizations. Simultaneously, a shift in the thinking of external organizations has to happen so that they see people in communities as having 'agency,' a capacity to act in which investment should be made. This case study is about an NGO's effort to revive the damaged reputation of self-help while working in a social and political environment scarred by disillusionment. The change brought about by CREADIS' work is modest, but significant in terms of a shift in thinking on the part of fieldworkers with respect to community members, on the part of men with respect to women, and on the part of farming households with respect to their role as managers of a diversified livelihood base.

The case begins with an overview of Kenya's post independence history. This sheds light on some of the reasons for the disillusionment just described and on people's experience of mobilizing, or being mobilized, for self-help.

Post-independence political and economic change in Kenya

With resentment and rebellion mounting against land appropriation by British settlers, Kenya gained political independence from colonial rule in 1963. Leaning towards an 'African Socialist' model, planning under the new government was centralized and promoted economic growth through heavy investment in the public sector, while also encouraging both smallholder and large-scale farming, invigorated by land redistribution in the immediate post-colonial period. In an initial ten-year period of optimism, the economy grew steadily and rapidly, but faltered in the late 1970s, due in part to the global oil crisis, and went into reverse during the 1980s. Part of this decline was attributed to adverse terms of trade and stiff structural adjustment measures that cut public sector expenditure, but the corruption tolerated and perpetuated by the Moi regime (1978–2002) was also significant: external donors and private sector investors simply lost confidence.

In the 1980s, domestic and international pressures to decentralize power resulted in new powers being legislated for the districts. However, economic decline set in just when decentralization policies were put in place, immediately jeopardizing the potential of local government authorities to act. Whether because of cutbacks in expenditure or because of corruption, the 'supply' of public funds for local development was limited. Economic growth continued to plummet in the 1990s, compounded by the suspension of aid by major donors. At the same time, the HIV/AIDS epidemic since the early 1980s and El Niño in the 1990s were crises that increased demands on an already emaciated public sector. Local and international NGOs multiplied to fill the breach, although their impact and effectiveness was piecemeal and uneven.

When the country finally returned to a multiparty system and the National Rainbow Coalition (NARC) government came into power in 2002, an economic recovery strategy was put in place, designed to nurture good governance and restore economic growth. Now growing at a rate of 5.8 per cent nationally, there is measured optimism about the economy, according to an article by Tom Mubusu entitled 'Investors upbeat about year, promise increased business' published in *The Standard* on 3 February 2007. However, efforts to restore trust in local governance have had mixed success. District authorities report being caught between central planning prescriptions and district level consultative planning. Also, there are now discrete funding streams that bypass district authorities, such as the Constituency Development Fund, a discretionary fund for national members of parliament to disburse in their constituencies. A recent survey by the Kenya Institute of Public Policy Research and Analysis (KIPPRA), through the Democratic Governance Support Program (DGSP), in advance of a nationwide campaign to render government more accountable at all levels, revealed that while most of the population was aware of free primary education, few knew about, let alone had access to, these decentralized funds such as the Constituency Development Fund, the Local Authority Transfer Fund, the Road Maintenance Levy Fund for road construction, the HIV/AIDS Support Fund, the Constituency School Bursary Fund and the Rural Electrification Fund (KIPPRA n.d.). Until that time, therefore, access to those funds had tended to be limited to those who were well-informed, well-organized, and well-connected.

Communities being mobilized or communities self-mobilizing?

In some respects, ABCD echoes the call to 'self reliance' heard in the early days of Kenya's independence. Cooperatives and credit unions were promoted to further rural development policy in the coffee and dairy industries, while self-help projects to build infrastructure such as roads and schools were encouraged under the banner of 'Harambee' (meaning 'pulling together' in Swahili). Integrated into the government's nation-building and national development strategy, the self-reliant spirit of Harambee translated into cost-sharing between the government and community members (the latter contributing labour). Later, communities themselves began to initiate projects: fund-raising for schools and health centres, for example, were carried out on the understanding that government would match-fund these community-led initiatives. Later still, however, during the Moi regime (1978-2002), Harambee became tainted by political patronage and corruption, and was even co-opted by the President, calling for contributions to a project of his choice. By contributing to Presidential Harambees, business people were widely reported to be able to 'buy' protection from claims against them for sub-standard work, or to secure government contracts (Osendo and Gachucha, 2003),

Since the 1960s, the self-reliant spirit of community mobilizing for Harambee has been frequently invoked by government and NGOs alike. The formation of Community Based Organizations (CBOs), for example, is a requirement for accessing government funding or for NGO assistance, on the assumption that CBOs are a space for community members to share in decision-making and share the benefits of these relationships with outside agencies. Unfortunately, in Bungoma District at least, this type of 'participation' has often meant little more than contribution of money or labour or a tokenistic 'taking part' in decisions made by government and non-government agencies alike who have steadily (perhaps inadvertently) eroded community capacities to mobilize around their own agenda (Nabiswa, personal communication, 2007). In many cases, CBOs that registered to participate in a government or NGO project subsequently became redundant, with little genuine social capital built up in their membership.

Frustrations with both government and non government services have led to a degree of cynicism about the value of investing time and effort into organizing to respond to NGO or government projects. At the same time, some NGOs are, by reputation or fact, distributing material benefits to some communities. Those who are not at the receiving end of this develop expectations and resentments. Government and NGOs now complain about a 'handout mentality' in communities.

Yet, it goes without saying that self-help is the *modus operandi* of much of rural village life. Whether they are clan-based work groups, burial societies, or savings clubs, traditional clan-based mechanisms for organizing are age-old, although many are under considerable strain given the HIV/AIDs crisis and general economic downturn. Some have endured and evolved over time into associations. For example, 'table-banking' or 'merry-go-round' associations are vehicles for small-scale savings and loans, and sharing of ideas within communities, and are the building blocks on which more formal savings and credit services can build.

Life in rural communities in Bungoma district

Bungoma district is the second largest in Kenya and among the most densely populated districts in Kenya. This is reflected in intensive agricultural production on smaller and smaller plots, with two hectares being the average 'small' farm size and seven hectares the average 'large' farm size. Only 15 per cent is under forest cover, providing firewood to the 84 per cent of the population dependent on firewood as its main fuel source, a vulnerability underscored by the fact that (at the time of writing) British America Tobacco Company required tobacco producers to cure tobacco leaf (using fire wood) before sale.

The fragility of the environment under current land use practices is one among many challenges facing farmers. Given the proximity to major trucking routes to Uganda, Bungoma District has been hard hit by the HIV/AIDS pandemic, which in turn has had a major impact on farming household productivity[1] and strained extended family care mechanisms. Also pervasive has been the impact of a systematic failure by the previous government to deliver on its commitments for public financing of services and infrastructure. An environment under stress, depleted government services, and limited alternative employment have all combined to result in a rate of poverty of 56 per cent in the district. This is higher than the Kenyan average of 48 per cent (Republic of Kenya, 2001).

As elsewhere in Kenya, agriculture is in a state of flux. Economic liberalization policies have brought agriculture out of government protection and control, affecting the pricing and marketing of the local staple, maize. By August 2008, the COMESA (Common Market for Eastern and Southern Africa) agreement (protecting local industries from cheaper imports) will end and the importation of cheap sugar from the region is likely to undercut the reputedly less efficient sugar production in Bungoma District. Agricultural diversification (in terms of both agricultural products and their markets) has been emphasized as the strategy for small holder farmers to minimize risk. This shift, however, is more than a shift in what farmers grow – it is a radical departure from a 'farmer as producer' model to a 'farmer as owner-manager' model. One implication is that extension agents, once providing technical assistance for production of one or two cash crops in a vertically-integrated commodity chain, must now link farmers to appropriate services for diverse crops and products, whether farmer training, advice on production and marketing, sustainable land use practices, access to credit, or technical advice on value-added production. Farmers have to show more resourcefulness as they operate in markets that have become less predictable.

The deterioration in government services during the 1990s caused both escalating levels of poverty and mistrust in government. According to Nabiswa (personal communication, 2007), Bungoma District was particularly hard hit between 1991–2002 because of local support for the opposition party during the Moi regime. For many families the forces affecting them were overwhelming. At the same time, the number of NGOs multiplied in the district during this period, many of them competing for donor funds, and therefore unable to move the sector forward in a concerted effort. Rumours of money destined for the poor being siphoned off to benefit NGO staff were rampant. The erosion of trust in external agencies of all types meant that people became reluctant to respond to government or NGO programmes unless material incentives were provided.

CREADIS

CREADIS is a young NGO, with the attendant challenges of establishing its credibility at the community level, while building a reputation as a dependable vehicle for donor funding. Given the level of mistrust just described, these challenges have been no small matter. However, even with very few resources, it has earned a strong reputation for its expertise in improved small-scale

---

Box 12.1: What is an ABCD methodology?

The principle behind ABCD is that when communities and external institutions recognize and value community assets (including, for example, social assets found in associations and a history of collaborative activity, and the individual strengths and skills of members of the community) communities are able to regain the confidence to mobilize their assets for a common purpose. Over time, that activity demonstrates local capacity that can be used as leverage to attract further investment or support.

Typically the process begins with simple storytelling in the tradition of 'appreciative inquiry.' Interviews with community members generate stories of success and an explanation of the reason for success – reasons as broad as particular leadership styles, skills or favourable policies that stimulate people to act. From this point forward, the community is encouraged to make a more rigorous appraisal of its assets, beginning with individual assets and moving through an inventory of associations and institutions, and natural and physical assets. An analysis of the local economy is then carried out using the popular education tool – 'the leaky bucket' – to identify opportunities for increasing inflows of resources into the community and ways to minimize outflows. At each phase of the asset-mapping or listing, the community comes together to review and comment on the assets identified. Finally, with all this information at its disposal, the community sees how to link assets with opportunities and formulate a plan that will take it towards a realistic goal.

NGO fieldworkers facilitating this process often undergo an 'aha' moment themselves, especially the first time, when they recognize skills and capacities in the communities that they had never before appreciated. Their change in thinking about the communities with which they work is critical to the success of the methodology.

---

agricultural production. CREADIS works closely with the Kenya Agricultural Research Institute (KARI), emphasizing affordable technological improvements such as improved seed varieties, animal husbandry, and measures to improve soil fertility such as crop rotations and the use of green manure. It promotes the use of local varieties (*Amaranthus*, for example) and hybrid varieties (such as the Vitamin A-enriched sweet potato) that offer greater protection to the compromised immune systems of People Living with HIV/ AIDS (PLWHAs). Farmer research and experimentation has been a hallmark of its work.

As is typical with newly formed NGOs, CREADIS has been operating on project funds, and is only now poised to secure core funds, including a vehicle. Its initial staff – the director, three extension agents, and a financial officer – were housed in rudimentary offices in Bungoma. Transportation to the field was by public transport and sometimes staff members worked voluntarily because of funding shortfalls.

The rationale for adopting an ABCD approach had several dimensions. First, CREADIS wanted to be part of the solution to the general malaise in rural agricultural development. Without a different way of working with communities, the prospects were not good. New economic opportunities were beginning to present themselves for farming households, but this required farmers and communities to be proactive. Self-help itself now had to be self-driven, with NGOs like CREADIS linking communities to the institutions and services that could help people sustain and extend the incremental steps they were making towards better livelihoods.

Implementing ABCD

The first place where CREADIS tried the ABCD approach was Bisunu, with appreciative storytelling, mapping and organizing techniques taking place over a nine-month period between September 2003 and June 2004. In Ndengelwa, this took place over a period of nine months from March to December 2004. In Bisunu, the pace was slower and the results less impressive than in Ndengelwa, but the initial circumstances put them at a significantly greater disadvantage at the outset, so this is not surprising. In both communities, groups mobilized their existing assets for small-scale income-generating projects, with technical advice and linkages provided by CREADIS. The key elements of the process were: method, message, maximizing participation, and maintaining momentum.

In terms of *method*, CREADIS made full use of the entire range of 'ABCD' tools, and made additions of its own, notably in conducting a gender analysis of access to and control over various community and household assets. After each phase of asset identification and mapping, communities met to validate the data gathered. These activities represented a heavy investment of staff and community time, especially in the early stages, but were justified as a process of raising awareness, sharing information, building a sense of solidarity and internalizing an asset-based way of thinking. After the initial six-month phase, marked by the development of a community or group action plan, CREADIS fieldworkers continued to follow up on a monthly basis.

The *message* that CREADIS conveyed was that the community should not expect material support, but that CREADIS would take people through a process which would help them to identify and mobilize assets, and help link them to 'institutional assets.' This message was reinforced by the shoestring operation that CREADIS ran at the time. Because of funding shortfalls, fieldworkers were sometimes working in a voluntary capacity. Without an office vehicle, they used public transportation to go to the field, and later used a motorbike. These were inconveniences, but it showed that this NGO was different, not flush with funds from outside donors like some NGOs, but committed to maximizing its own limited resources.

CREADIS' objective was to provide an opportunity for *all community members to participate*. They expected interest to be keen at the beginning, then tail off, but to increase again if the initiatives of a few groups proved to be successful. To maximize participation, meetings were scheduled during the daytime, partly because CREADIS wanted to invite government officials as 'added value' to the meetings, and partly because travel to and from meetings would not be feasible at night for either NGO staff or for dispersed rural households. As expected, numbers were high at the beginning (Bisunu: 80; Ngengelwa: 140). People had to walk up to 4 km which meant a considerable investment of time and effort, but the early awareness-raising, asset-mapping phases were interactive and fun, attracting much interest.

Given that the ABCD process was initiated without secure project funding, it is a credit to the tenacity and dedication of the staff that, against all odds, it was able to maintain momentum throughout the initial six-month period. The harder part was maintaining the momentum after the action plans were put in place. Fewer people stayed engaged in the self-initiated group activity that followed, but their progress was closely observed by others in the community, and many benefited at the household level from the activities carried out by group members. However, it was harder to sustain momentum in Bisunu than it was in Ndengelwa.

The experience in Bisunu

Bisunu's overriding concern was access to water. The nearest year-round boreholes were over two hours walking distance away. Tree cover was sparse because of pressures on cultivable land and demand for charcoal for tobacco curing and domestic cooking needs. As a result, land quality was suffering, the water table was getting lower, and river beds and boreholes were drying up. In the past, water had been piped via a gravity-feed system from Mount Elgon about 20 km away but deforestation had caused the lowering of the water table to a level below the point at which gravity could pull water down to Bisunu.

Taking the community through an ABCD process, this concern was so paramount that the initial idea for a community project was to raise funds in the hope of securing match-funding for borehole construction. Yet without a guarantee of funding support, or of government commitment to addressing the water supply problem, CREADIS' strategy was to encourage more modest initiatives that had a greater chance of early success. With an average plot size of one hectare, any improvement in agricultural productivity would make a difference in terms of household income. Discussions among farming households and CREADIS fieldworkers over several weeks had revealed a wide range of specific farming knowledge and skills, as well as farming groups that had experimented with new ideas, and 'merry-go-round' groups pooling savings and rotating loans.

Eventually, four groups formed to come up with an action plan that CREADIS would help them implement. In each group, table banking was started, which meant that small loans for individual members could be generated. A typical trajectory for individual members was as follows: the initial loan was used to purchase a chicken; from the revenue from eggs and chicks, a pig was purchased; from the sale of the piglets, school fees were paid; and so the accumulation of assets continued.

One group decided to lease land from one of the richer members. They planted new 'commercial' crops. Oxen, needed for planting, were rented at a concessionary rate from another of the group members. CREADIS contributed its expertise in improved agricultural techniques using local resources, and offered low or no-cost planting material from the Kenyan Agricultural

Research Institute. Income from the sale of groundnuts or soy beans from group plots could then be shared among members and further invested in small livestock.

For the most part, women benefited more directly than men from these activities because new 'commercial crops' were a natural extension of the food crops women were already responsible for, and small livestock had also typically been women's rather than men's responsibility. Without rights to land, surplus food production and assets in livestock were the means by which women were able to earn an income. In addition to direct sales from their commercial crops, group members also realized value-added opportunity. The women started to sell porridge, chapattis, cakes, and biscuits at local markets. In this way, farms of the group members became more diversified and their households more food-secure. One young woman explains how her own farm has become more productive:

> Even though my farm is very small, I am now able to make as good a livelihood as those who have larger farms. I plant groundnuts and I fertilize them with manure so they grow well. I have some food and I am making an income. I am proud of my small farm. (Foster, 2005: 6)

This strategy has been effective irrespective of size of landholding. The farm plot belonging to a wealthier group member illustrated below (Figure 12.1) was the typical pattern of diversification people were now adopting. From exclusive maize production, farmers are diversifying into beans, groundnuts, potatoes and napier grass (sold as livestock feed). Farmers benefit not only from the spread of risk in a diversified system but also from the increase in yields per acre from the sustainable practices now being encouraged (for example, crop rotations and organic fertilizer.)

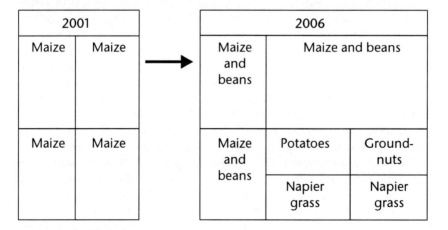

Figure 12.1: Diversification of a four-hectare plot

Comments were made about changes in the gender division of labour in the household. From dependence on maize, and cash crops such as sugar cane and tobacco for which men were the income earners, there was evidence of a shift to a wider variety of food crops and commercial crops associated with women's participation and their economic independence. A male farmer was able to observe that: 'Women can provide for their family in this way and they don't have to depend on the husband. We now have fewer conflicts in our household.'

Despite these positive outcomes, many people, particularly men, voiced disappointment at the pace of change, and the fact that their fundamental problem – their water supply – was still no closer to being solved. In the face of this disappointment, the sustainability of the groups was by no means certain. Later in 2006, however, one group decided to make the commitment to formally register as a CBO, a move that was required if they were to be eligible for government or NGO programmes. The CBO has called itself *Luma*, which means 'Work hard without giving up.'

The experience of Ndengelwa

In contrast to Bisunu's location off the beaten track, Ndengelwa is on the main highway, a location that has proven to be one of its main assets. Public transportation runs frequently, and the journey to Bungoma town is well within range of the ubiquitous bicycle or *boda boda* (bicycle taxi) for those with employment there, and the opportunities for micro-enterprises on the highway are several.

Small-holder farming is the main livelihood activity. The proximity of Nzoia Sugar Company is a reason for farmers to grow sugar cane as a cash crop under contract, but returns on sugar have been low and unreliable for reasons related both to the market and to the dysfunctional management of the sugar company. Farming households now supplement sugar with various commercial crops for sale in local markets, as well as crops grown for basic subsistence. Men have tended to focus on cash crop production, with women concentrating on food crops for household consumption and sale in local markets. Farm plots are four acres on average, larger than in Bisunu, but they are decreasing in size due to population pressure. Small enterprises add to the base income from agriculture. These enterprises include trades such as masonry, carpentry, welding, bicycle repairs, and small retail stores. Their profitability has ebbed and flowed with seasonal income flows in the sugar industry and with the varying fortunes of the sugar company over the years.

CREADIS' involvement with Ndengelwa began in 2004. Rather than taking the whole community through the ABCD process, fieldworkers worked with four different groups of men and women, taking each through the sequence of activities, culminating in the preparation of a group action plan. The groups organized themselves on the basis of location, so that travel to meetings could be minimized. A volunteer village development facilitator (VDF) was selected and trained by CREADIS to help each group identify its assets.

As in Bisunu, CREADIS facilitated a gender analysis of the assets identified in order to draw attention to differences in women's and men's skills, capacities, contributions and access to resources, to stimulate discussion about the consequences of these differences, and to encourage activities that took these differences into account. Participants were asked to identify who had access to, who had control over, and who benefited from different assets such as water, timber, agricultural produce, education, livestock, marketing opportunities, business enterprises, the grinding mill, land, farm equipment, transportation, sand harvest, and fish ponds. Leadership was also discussed as a gender issue.

This exercise was important for several reasons. First, it highlighted assets that had not even been considered assets before – men's and women's unique skills and experience, for example. Second, it highlighted sectors of the rural economy where women were excluded, such as in the activity related to fish ponds or sand harvest. Third, it raised people's awareness of gender differences and raised questions about the appropriateness of these differences given current economic and social realities. This awareness would prove important as women began to take advantage of new opportunities, and both men and women began to see for themselves the appropriateness of increasing women's participation in decision-making, reducing their workload, and gaining title to land (a referendum on land reform had failed to endorse proposed legislation). The 'leaky bucket' exercise provoked much discussion since it required people to think about what money was coming in and what money was leaking out of the community. The leakage of household finances to alcohol consumption (and the fact that this diverted resources away from education, etc.) was a sobering lesson for men to learn. The four groups compared their results, challenging each other on the net economic gains and losses. Together they generated new ideas for plugging leaks and increasing flows of money into the community.

For many, it was the first time they had understood how the local economy worked. For example, they began to consider value-added activities such as making sunflower oil, rather than selling sunflower seeds to traders. One inspired young leader (a recent graduate in agricultural engineering) came up with a proposal for a pedal-operated, sweet potato slicer which he himself could make using local materials. In each case, the groups came up with plans to collaborate on activities that either plugged the leaks (increased domestic food production, organic rather than purchased fertilizer) or increased inflows (food processing, livestock rearing, diversifying into commercial crops). These were goals that CREADIS was well-placed to assist them with, given its own expertise and its links with government ministries and NGOs such as Heifer Projects International, Kenyan Agricultural Research Institute and the Sustainable Agriculture Centre for Research and Development in Africa (SACRED Africa).

As in Bisunu, the message was consistent: look to your own assets and resources and mobilize these first. Local knowledge about the natural resource base and indigenous agriculture was highlighted, as was the potential for incremental savings and investment through the table-banking scheme.

In November 2005 and May 2006, the groups were asked to comment on significant changes that had occurred since CREADIS fieldworkers had been working with them. Approximately 30 people were involved in the discussion on each occasion. Once again, group membership was shown to have positive results for individual households, because it provided access to training and technical advice especially in agriculture and livestock production. The story of one farmer, Philemon (see Box 12.2), illustrates the kind of transformation that has been possible for individuals who have accessed the ABCD experience through a group. Like the community members in Bisunu, people interviewed in Ndengelwa commented positively on working collaboratively in groups and were beginning to see cooperation among farming households for marketing purposes. Men acknowledged a greater respect for women's contribution to income generation and household decision-making.

Improvements in agricultural productivity were made using local assets for the most part. They adopted organic technologies to maximize the short growing season associated with the short rains and used locally available plants and techniques to improve pest control and soil fertility. By pooling and rotating their own savings, they were able to purchase chickens and progressively move 'up' the livestock ladder, thanks, in part, to favourable purchasing arrangements through the NGO Heifer Projects International. The sum total of these activities has given them confidence to diversify into commercial crop and livestock production for local markets and to spread their risk over a wider range of food crops for domestic consumption.

As in Bisunu, the changes that people are making in Ndengelwa are small-scale, yet significant at the level of the household, though not yet at the level of the group. It is also apparent that relatively well-off group members are able to take advantage of new opportunities at a faster pace than the less well-off, although this does not mean to say that the former are exploiting the relatively poor. Instead, they have been willing to share their resources by leasing out land and equipment at non-commercial rates to group members, and have assumed leadership roles because of their experience, education, and general levels of confidence.

In one group, for example, the leader is a woman who gained experience as a poultry farmer in the 1980s. Her group had initially tried to grow soy beans and potatoes during the short rains, but hail destroyed the crop (hailstones as large as golf balls are not unusual and the impact of such storms, while localized, can be devastating). The group decided on a poultry project instead and financed the initial purchase through a table-banking scheme in which members contributed KSh70 monthly and took turns to use KSh50 to purchase poultry (the remaining KSh20 used to purchase poultry vaccines and refreshments for group meetings).[2] Initially, income would come from egg sales, but would eventually be earned from the sale of chickens also. The leader of this group, the wife of a local schoolteacher, had previous experience in poultry rearing and was able to give advice to other members. Meanwhile, she was able to increase her flock of chickens and has now invested in a small retail business at Ndengelwa market, an initiative she attributes in part to seeing a business opportunity after participating in the 'leaky bucket' exercise.

Another group was mainly composed of women (18 women and 10 men). They had no prior experience of working together, but had been encouraged by elders in the village to form a group and participate in the activities being promoted by CREADIS. One reason for this was that among those 18 women were ten widows, without any source of income, who were therefore dependent on their husband's family (HIV/AIDS has resulted in a high dependency ratio). Yet the group also included people of means and influence. One member had been elected to the Constituency Development Fund committee for this village, and another had been working as secretary to a water supply project to be administered through LATF (Local Authority Transfer Fund). By May 2006, this group was able to report modest achievements: table banking had yielded sufficient loan funds to enable each member to purchase one or more chickens; complementary training enabled people to continue to build up assets in small livestock, and generate income from fodder crops (napier grass). As a result, an elderly lady could report that 'even though I am old, I am not just sitting doing nothing; I don't depend on anyone.' Not all were successful, however. Two group members reported that their chickens had succumbed to disease or had been killed by animals, and it was also noted that the table-banking scheme was only operational in post-harvest periods. For many, there was no surplus to pay monthly dues during periods of food shortage. As a group, they have been able to pool land and obtain seeds for a group groundnut plot, with the stated intention to raise the money from the sale of groundnuts for registration as a group. A group poultry scheme is also planned.

A third group (in which the chief and sub-chief are members) had similar stories of modest improvements in agricultural production and some value-added processing such as sweet potato cakes sold at church and local markets.

Finally, another group with 19 members reported that only nine remained active. The many widows in this group were unable to pay back the loans they took from the group table-banking scheme – they were not able to translate the loans into individual micro-enterprises because of their lack of access to other assets.[3]

One of the Ndengelwa ABCD groups has registered as a formal CBO with the Ministry of Social Services, as *Sinani* Community Based Organization. *Sinani* means 'pooling efforts towards a goal.' Others may not follow this route. For them, these groups have served a useful but limited purpose. The question is whether capacity to self-mobilize has been stimulated as a result of this activity. For example, farmers with commercial crops, like Philemon, are organizing new production groups. They grow specific crops on a large

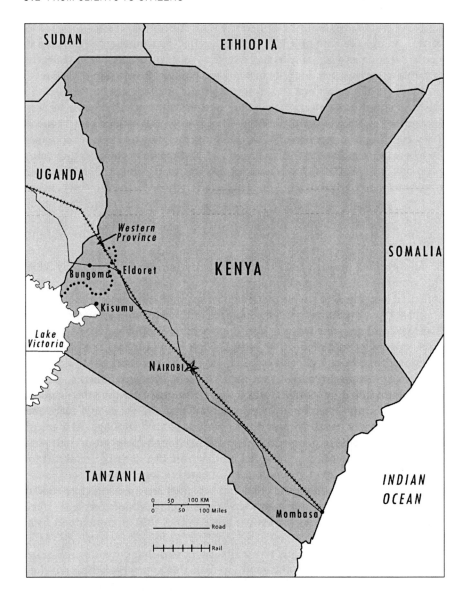

enough scale, and market them as a group, using marketing information from organizations such as Kenya Agricultural Commodity Exchange (KACE) and the Ministry of Agriculture.

With or without the influence of CREADIS, Ndengelwa's proximity to Bungoma District headquarters means that government, non-government, and private sector services are more readily available. NALEP (National Agriculture and Livestock Extension Programme) had been influential in Bungoma District, for example, and Ndengelwa had been one of its pilot sites for its 'extension pluralism' model. Several NGOs were working there, including three offering microfinance services, Heifer International and another offering support to people living with HIV/AIDS. The difference that the work of CREADIS has made is in helping to make these links and in building the capacity of groups to seek out these services.

Summary: reviving self-help?

In both Bisunu and Ndengelwa, the ABCD process has shed light on existing assets that can be drawn upon to generate income: indigenous knowledge and agricultural expertise have been applied to improve production at little or no

---

Box 12.2: Philemon's story

'Before, we were just complaining. Now I believe power is in our hands. With money, you command respect. You become an honourable member' (Philemon, personal communication, 2005).

At 2.5 ha, Philemon's landholding is a little larger than average in his village. Like other farmers, he has been growing sugar cane under contract to Nzoia Sugar Company. The company provides planting material and fertilizer, and organizes harvesting groups to cut the cane at maturation. His earnings consist of what is left over after the company deducts these costs from the value of the harvest. The relationship with the sugar company and the companies to which it outsourced credit and service delivery operations has been fraught with difficulty. Like all farmers, he sometimes waited years for payment, especially during the period 1998 to 2003 when the crisis in the sugar industry was at its worst, suffering from mismanagement, failure to adapt to the liberalized economy, inefficient operations and widely reported corruption.

With uncertainties in the sugar industry, Philemon was ready to diversify. Inspired by early enrolment in the ABCD groups, he began trying local and improved varieties of food crops and 'commercial crops.' Building on local agricultural expertise, he has now experimented with soybeans, sweet peppers, hot peppers and napier grass, all of which can be sold in local markets. These are in addition to the maize, bananas, and kale that have been staples for domestic food consumption and sale. He has also planted trees for firewood, shade, protection from hailstone damage, and water conservation. He has 'rediscovered' plants that prevent plant disease and insect infestation, and has learned ways of intensifying production with minimal use of purchased inputs.

How has this made a difference in his life? In several ways: by his account his income has increased by 50 per cent. He is now accessing local markets to sell his commercial crops, using the price information provided via mobile phone by the Kenya Agricultural Commodity Exchange (KACE). Diversification has not only reduced his risk, it has also contributed to improved soil management. Most significantly, Philemon now feels himself a manager, making his own decisions, rather than relying on contracts from the sugar company. Sugar cane ('the lazy man's cash crop') still occupies half his land, but it takes up to two and a half years to mature. Commercial crops that produce over shorter periods can generate five times the income. It is harder work but, as long as he can access markets, worth his while.

Philemon speaks proudly of his achievements and the wisdom of maximizing traditional agricultural knowledge and blending this with organic innovations from the Kenyan Agricultural Research Institute. He sees himself as a researcher and an innovator, rewarded for his efforts.

cost; specific plant varieties have been selected for their pest resistance or their nitrogen-fixing qualities; and organic waste has been used as an alternative to purchased fertilizer. 'Women's' crops have become more marketable in diversified commercial production and along with the product of small livestock husbandry, their contribution to household well-being is being reassessed and their status enhanced as income earners. People have gained confidence in their capacity to participate in the diversified agricultural production now necessary for economic survival. Also, by including gender analysis in the ABCD process, both women and men had to acknowledge that control over assets is unequal and that by reorganizing and redistributing assets the household and the community as a whole could benefit. Small but significant changes have been observed, such as men sharing with their wives the income from their sugar cane sales and discussing as a couple how to manage household finances, but changes of deeper significance have been noted with respect to women's increased economic opportunities from diversified crop and livestock production.

Being mobilized or self-mobilized

Writing about *Active Social Capital,* Anirudh Krishna (2002) showed that sustained community self-mobilizing requires both a propensity to organize (or experience of successful organizing in the past), incentives to continue organizing, and leadership to bridge the two. These are useful distinctions on which to base a discussion of the work of CREADIS in these two communities.

CREADIS wanted to demonstrate confidence in community capacity to work independently of outside institutions and strengthen that capacity, especially given the erosion of trust in government and non-government agencies. It attempted to do this by invoking memories of successful organizing in the past and to recreate those positive experiences – in other words reinvigorating 'a propensity to organize' around common interests. The danger, as they saw it, was to engage with external agencies too quickly in case community activities became channelled towards fulfilling the outside agency's agenda rather than their own. CREADIS is satisfied that in the three-year period, group activities have served to benefit individual farming households especially in terms of income generation, spreading of risk through diversification, and improving women's position as decision-makers in the household. In fact, it is worth considering whether the lack of 'handouts' was a disincentive to some men, while women were more modest in their aspirations and saw opportunity to derive some economic independence. Whether these groups have emerged as community assets in their own right, ready to mobilize in order to leverage access to a broader asset base through institutional linkages, is less clear. Two groups ('Work hard without giving up' and 'Pooling efforts towards a goal') have formally registered as CBOs, while members of other ABCD groups have gone on to regroup in other ways, as Philemon has done for the purpose of marketing.

The initial incentive to organize in these two communities was the opportunity CREADIS presented to access the training opportunities CREADIS had to offer, and see what community members could accomplish through their own efforts. In the case of Bisunu, there were small successes, but the real incentive was lacking – the promise of a water supply they so badly needed. As one man explained in his interpretation of 'the glass half full' analogy: 'We have filled one half of the glass; now it is your [external agent] turn to fill the other.'

The trend, however, is that with devolved funds, local government expects communities to be proactive in a 'demand-driven' model of service delivery. Government officials are spending less time intervening in community affairs and offering their services, partly because public sector cutbacks have meant that their numbers have not kept pace with population growth, but partly as a deliberate strategy for encouraging stronger community participation in local decision-making. For communities like Bisunu and Ndengelwa, this means that traditional attitudes of deference to authority have to give way to a more assertive stance – people must organize and ask for what is being offered (Peters, 2005). As this goes to press, CREADIS reports that the Bisunu group has now successfully lobbied government to attend to its critical need for water.

Leadership

According to Nabiswa, chiefs and assistant chiefs in the community are regarded as the link between government and communities, yet many chiefs and assistant chiefs are ill-equipped for this role, unable to conceptualize what real development means in terms of sustainability, people's participation, or even knowing the root causes of the challenges faced by their people. They have frequently assumed an autocratic style. Under new policies, these chiefs are now being trained to adopt a more democratic style of operation and are encouraging citizen participation, but in order to make this happen, communities would be well advised to organize to influence these changes.

While formal leadership at the village level is exclusively male, as is land ownership, women have demonstrated leadership potential as informal leaders. The experience of CREADIS in these two communities has borne this out in the ABCD groups that have formed. Typically, these informal leaders are the wives of formal leaders, well-educated women, or women carrying high positions in the church. According to Peters and local government officials, among those who consistently participated in the ABCD process were 'young, hardworking women' in the community (Peters, 2005: 15). They regularly outnumbered men at meetings.[4] Although women were excluded from formal leadership positions, some had completed farmers' training sessions that left them with some new skills and some leverage over men from the community. Three women were elected as chairpersons to lead their groups toward successful completion of their action plans.

As Peters points out, leaders require a social entrepreneurial orientation. They often emerged later in the ABCD process, once they had built up confidence, and had the inspirational qualities of fresh ideas and the enthusiasm to match:

> As the process continued, other leaders emerged from among those who attended sessions regularly. One was a young woman who attended regularly, was initially very shy, but gradually gained confidence, internalized the approach and offered to become a VDF. (Peters, personal communication, 2005)

Unfortunately, while leaders might emerge gradually in this way, many people with leadership qualities, especially men, are seeking employment elsewhere. For example, a recent agricultural engineering graduate, fired with enthusiasm about opportunities for value-added production and improved yields in Ndengelwa, was participating actively in one of the groups until a position as an agricultural engineer drew him away.

Leaders who combine work experience outside the community with a commitment to their home community are the ones who can bridge the gap between community capacities and outside opportunities. In Ndengelwa, the Area Agricultural Officer (AAO) was an excellent example. He had fresh ideas. Others in the community might participate but they had no experience on which to base suggestions other than ideas people had tried before or ideas suggested by the CREADIS staff. Through the AAO, opportunities through the Ministry of Agriculture were made available and some farmers have received training under this programme as a result (Peters, 2005: 11).

In summary, emerging leaders in Ndengelwa are typically men and women in the 20–30 age group with agricultural expertise who are generally respected and well-connected in the community. They are enthusiastic in their uptake of new ideas, relatively well-educated, less deferential to traditional authority, and underemployed. People with these characteristics have time to attend meetings and confidence to participate actively. They have a personal stake in their community's development, and appreciate the opportunity to participate in educational and training opportunities.

External assets and agency: readiness to respond

The ABCD approach, as applied by CREADIS, was designed to stimulate self-help by mobilizing assets to build the confidence and reputation to link with external agencies and programmes. One asset-mapping activity was a comprehensive survey of local institutions, including churches, schools, training centres, government institutions, commercial enterprises, retail shops, flour mills, cash crop buyers, and NGOs. For this exercise, information was gathered about the programmes and services of these institutions, the type of people eligible for services, their physical facilities, and the linkages to other institutions and services. The purpose of this exercise was to build awareness among community members about the institutional assets in their immediate community and in surrounding areas and encourage them to seek out these resources. What is remarkable about the inventory is the wealth of 'assets' in each of these institutions that go above and beyond their primary function, and the potential for mobilizing these assets for community-initiated activity. The institutional mapping exercises ultimately gave community members a clearer understanding of the institutional resources available to them and the more active members and groups then took steps to link with these institutions. Farmers in Ndengelwa, for example, are making use of the nearby agricultural training centre offering tips on how to diversify and improve production, and are also linking with the Farmer Field School umbrella network which provides additional information on improved crop varieties and technologies.

Another result of the ABCD activities, however, has been the linkages made with new NGOs working in the area. For example, individuals and groups in Bisunu that have gone through the ABCD process have presented themselves as organized, innovative, and showing initiative. NGOs that have responded to these groups and individuals include Western Kenya Region Christian Community Services, SACRED Africa, Small and Micro Enterprise Programme (SMEP) of the National Council of Churches of Kenya and the Ecumenical Church Loan Fund (ECLOF). Some are working with groups as a whole, while others are working with individuals from these groups.

Of interest also are devolved funds through government channels that provide an incentive for communities to organize formally as CBOs. These include the Constituency Development Fund (CDF), the Local Authority Transfer Fund, the Community Development Trust Fund and the Kenya Roads Board Fund. Access to the relevant information and access to decentralized funds is uneven. However, in the two communities described here, a community group in Ndengelwa has successfully accessed CDF funds for a start-up electricity supply for their roadside market area. Bisunu, despite the slow pace of organizing, has recently managed to get the government's attention and plans for a borehole are under way.

Reflections on the process: the perspective of field-level workers

The role of internal versus external change agents

Fieldworkers claim that the groups in both communities have a stronger appreciation of their own capacities and expect fewer handouts or immediate solutions; they see that external change agents can only boost, not replace local internal efforts. They claim that this reflects an internalization of ABCD principles. This shift is not complete, particularly in Bisunu, where progress has been slower and the situation graver with respect to basic services: 'They accept ABCD, but they do not believe. They will engage, assuming the handouts will still come' (CREADIS fieldworker, personal communication, 2006).

If, as fieldworkers, they are not 'providing handouts', they believe their effectiveness is in their ability, first, to build confidence and capacity of community organizations to be independently proactive and, second, to play a bridging role between communities and external agencies. They see their role as supporter and coach rather than as provider or problem solver.

Strengthening the ABCD process

At a more detailed level, CREADIS fieldworkers discussed how they had applied an ABCD approach and drew a number of conclusions. First of all, while acknowledging that the process is labour-intensive, they claimed that the period of appreciative storytelling, discussion, asset mapping, and identification of opportunity was essential. It proved to be a constant reference point as the groups pushed forward, sometimes requiring reassurance and encouragement. As with all heavily-facilitated processes, however, the challenge was in maintaining the momentum once the initial period of intense activity had ended and groups were starting work on their action plans. They concluded that some of the vulnerability lay in the formation of groups. Rather than build on a pre-existing associational base, fieldworkers encouraged the formation of new groups and these were having growing pains just as CREADIS moved into a maintenance role rather than an active role in these communities.

In the early stages, groups with more women tended to be more successful as 'women are more patient and committed' when it comes to attending meetings regularly and contributing small incremental savings to table-banking schemes (Munoko, personal communication, 2005). However, men's access to land and the combined agricultural expertise of men and women was beneficial to the success of experimental plots. Undoubtedly, the agricultural expertise that CREADIS had to offer was a key resource for these groups.

Group composition was influential for other reasons. It was important to have a sufficient number of farming households involved who could take on more of the risk of the group activity than others. For example, those farming households that have the resources to diversify production and have family members in non-farm employment were least vulnerable to vagaries in economic opportunity and to unpredictable weather and more willing to experiment and lend their land or other resources for experimentation by others.

This is not to suggest that the income and asset differential is particularly high in either of these communities, but that a certain level of diversity is advantageous to the group's survival. One group composed of a high proportion of widows simply could not survive despite the leadership of more established farmers. For some of these widows even the minimal requirements to contribute to group savings in the table-banking scheme were too onerous.

Fieldworkers have a responsibility to help the groups be realistic in their expectations while providing consistent encouragement, and striking this balance was, undoubtedly, sometimes a challenge. One suggestion made

Assessing progress – an ABCD group in Ndengelwa, western Kenya.

was that acceleration of the group activity could be achieved by providing incentives rather than simply linking communities to organizations that operate with incentives (the EU-funded water and sanitation schemes, for instance, where communities have to contribute 15–30 per cent of the total cost). For example, increasing the pace of capital accumulation through revolving funds could be achieved by topping up the revolving funds so that loans could be larger.

Nevertheless, the survival of the group is not necessarily the be all and end all, especially if the momentum generated in the initial phases of the process can be transferred elsewhere into groupings that may make more sense to particular individuals. In fact, over time, those at CREADIS see this as one way in which an attitude of opportunity and possibility spreads to a threshold from which the larger community can combine its efforts for more ambitious goals. In the meantime, managing expectations, maintaining a long-term view, and balancing community effort with advocacy for entitlements from government are the tasks at hand.

Conclusion

Has CREADIS been able to revive a spirit of self-help through the ABCD approach? The evidence suggests that it has, but not in the fashion so tarnished by Harambee. The spirit of self-reliance is being seen at the household level in the adoption of agricultural practices that maximize the knowledge and resources of farming households, and a renewed confidence in the principle of diversification on which sustainable farming systems are based. It is also being seen in the stronger position of women relative to men as they take advantage of income-earning opportunities. Whether or not the gender analysis and profiling contributed to this is hard to say for sure, but women's willingness to accept slow-paced incremental improvements in livelihood and their capacity (given their pre-existing roles in food production) to take advantage of opportunities in commercial crop production mean that they have made income gains that have in turn enhanced their status.

The results of organizing in groups have been mixed. The group has been a vehicle for trying out new ideas and innovation; it has also been the point of entry for government and NGOs to communicate with communities. Sometimes the groups have been formalized into CBOs, which can then access other services, or individuals have transferred the experience in the ABCD groups to membership of new groups and associations, such as marketing groups. All of these shared experiences build social capital and expand the base of active leadership in the community. Nevertheless, it requires tenacity and patience to secure the basic services from government, and to secure opportunities for people to save, access credit, and access markets. There is no quick fix, but the attitude that ABCD represents in communities is a strategic shift. Some people made the shift quickly, others more slowly, and a few did not make it at all. The prevailing environment of other NGOs and politicians giving handouts meant that managing expectations was an ongoing challenge.

The other part of the equation, however, is in the mindset and capacity of external institutions and their field staff. Attitudes towards small-scale farming households can only be respectful if fieldworkers and the institutions they represent fully appreciate the knowledge, experience and capacities that precede their arrival. The impact of the ABCD approach on those fieldworkers and their institutions in terms of their own learning about the communities with which they work should not be underestimated.

Ultimately, a shift in the community's perception of itself as having capacity to initiate change relies in equal measure on external agencies upholding their part of an unspoken social contract by providing the services that communities can reasonably expect. The revival of self-help (over and above strategies for survival) is intimately related to a restoration of relationships of trust with external institutions. A more liberalized agricultural sector may benefit local communities if they can become managers of their own livelihoods, but they have to connect with services and opportunities, with the confidence to make local government work for them. Self-help, yes. Neglect by government, no.

Endnotes

1. Estimates of HIV/AIDS prevalence are highly variable. The Bungoma District Development Plan, 2002–2008 gives a prevalence rate of 20–30 per cent among the general population and 8.3 per cent as the figure for antenatal mothers (2001 figures, down from 12 per cent in 1992). More recent community surveys carried out by Moi University put the figure for Western Province as a whole at 14 per cent, with swathes of higher incidence along the Trans Africa Highway (Mabel Nangami, personal communication, 2006).
2. 1 USD is equal to approximately KSh70 (Kenyan Shillings) at 3 March 2008.
3. Note that women have no rights of land inheritance. The referendum for these rights resulted in the 'No' vote prevailing. The argument against was that it would further subdivide land into non viable units, and that allowing women to inherit land would enhance their economic power, making them too independent, thereby encouraging divorce cases. Against this, was the argument that daughters could sell to their brothers and thereby release funds for their own well-being if widowed.
4. The Area Agriculture Officer said he could only get the elderly women to attend his meetings.

References

Foster, M. (November 2005) *Trip report: Kenya*, (Internal document) Coady International Institute, Antigonish, Nova Scotia, Canada.

(KIPPRA) Kenya Institute for Public Policy Research and Analysis *EU-DGSP (democratic governance support programme) and the pilot project 'promoting public participation in local governance.'* (n.d.). Available from http://www.kippra.org/dgsp.asp [Accessed 5 September 2007]

Kenyan Agricultural Research Institute (2005) *Agricultural innovations for sustainable development: Strategic plan 2005 – 2015*, KARI Publications Unit, Nairobi.

Krishna, A. (2002) *Active social capital*, Columbia University Press, New York.

Narayan, D. (2000) *Voices of the poor: Can anyone hear us?*, Oxford University Press, New York.

Osendo, C. and Gachucha, W. (December 2003) 'Harambee: Patronage politics and disregard for law', *Adili News Service for Transparency International Kenya*, Issue 50.

Peters, B. (2005) *Review and summary of ABCD action research documentation for Ndengelwa*, (Internal document) Coady International Institute, Antigonish, Nova Scotia, Canada.

Republic of Kenya. (2001) *Bungoma district development plan 2002–2008*, Ministry of Finance and Planning, Nairobi, Kenya.

Author's note

The Kenya case is one of three case studies that draw on action research of 'Asset-Based Community Development' (ABCD) initiatives conducted by partners of the Coady Institute. Gladys Nabiswa, the director of CREADIS, was a graduate of the first Certificate in Asset-Based Approaches to Community Development at the Coady Institute in 2001 and was keen to apply an ABCD approach. On the Coady Institute's part, we were interested in following how this approach would be applied in a situation of severe social, economic and environmental stress by a very young NGO with few resources of its own.

Without providing direct financial support for the ABCD fieldwork, the Coady Institute supported the documentation of the ABCD initiative, spanning a three year period from 2003–2006, during which time, Carolyne Munoko documented her reflections on the ABCD process that she and her colleague Herbert Masengeli had introduced in Ndengelwa and Bisunu. Brianne Peters, a youth intern from the Coady International Institute who spent five months at CREADIS in 2004–2005, assisted with some of the documentation and produced a summary review of the ABCD work in Ndengelwa. Additional information was drawn from interviews conducted in the communities on annual follow-up visits by the Coady Institute. During this time, the Roncalli Foundation contributed to the documentation of the action research.

In May 2007, I carried out field work for this case with John Kennedy Obisa (a Coady graduate) to focus on the significance of the changes brought about by applying an 'ABCD' approach, and to set these changes within the context of political, social and economic changes in Kenya. During this seven-day period in the field, we conducted interviews with CREADIS board members and staff, local government officials, and community members in Ndengelwa and Bisunu, using an adapted 'Most Significant Change' format to structure the inquiry. John Kennedy Obisa's insights into CREADIS's work in these communities as well as his careful overview of the various funding streams available through government were valuable contributions to this case study.

I would like to thank the community members of Bisunu and Ndengelwa who were so willing to be interviewed, and to acknowledge the contribution of Gladys Nabiswa, director of CREADIS, who has generously given her time to support her staff in the action research initiative, and who has provided many additional insights into the case herself. The diligence and dedication of Gladys and her co-workers in very difficult times in western Kenya is as impressive as the forbearance of community members themselves.

CHAPTER 13

From DCBA to ABCD: the potential for strengthening citizen engagement with local government in Mindanao, the Philippines

Alison Mathie

Introduction

'Before, people were always waiting for development. So people would always wait for me. With ABCD I started to feel less of a burden. I gave my leadership role to others' (Carmen, extension worker, personal communication, 2006).

'Sometimes we let the country's dark and miserable situation overwhelm us and freeze us into pessimism, cynicism, or worse, inaction or indifference' (Fr Nono Alfonso, S.J.)

The South East Asia Rural Social Leadership Institute (SEARSOLIN), based in Cagayan de Oro City, Philippines, has been running training programmes for the civil society sector for over 40 years. Since 2000, it has integrated the principles of an Asset Based Community Development (ABCD) approach into its leadership training and outreach programmes (Mercado, 2005b). What appealed to SEARSOLIN about the approach was its focus on assets and community capacities. It was seen as a positive and motivating alternative to the more conventional focus on problems, weaknesses and needs, and the relationship of dependency and powerlessness this had inadvertently created. With its characteristic penchant for acronyms, SEARSOLIN refers to its new direction as a shift from the Deficit Community Based Approach (DCBA) to an Asset Based Community Development (ABCD) approach (Mercado, 2004).

SEARSOLIN trains social development leaders from Asia, the Pacific, and Africa, so the context for its training is not based on the Philippines experience alone. While, in the beginning, the curriculum was geared towards economic and agricultural development, current emphasis on local government decentralization in many countries has led to a demand for courses on democratization of economic opportunities and participation in local governance, while concerns about environmental degradation have prompted interest in courses on ways to ensure natural resource protection. Fortunately, the experience of the Philippine NGO sector in these struggles provides much to share with leaders elsewhere. Because an ABCD approach offered both a theoretical and practical way to discuss these issues at the community level, SEARSOLIN integrated ABCD in its core courses in community organizing, sustainable agriculture, cooperatives and micro-enterprise, volunteerism, peace-focused approaches to development, media advocacy, and peri-urbanization.

This chapter explores how SEARSOLIN and its sister organizations applied the ABCD approach in three different communities on the island of Mindanao in the Philippines. It examines the effectiveness of this approach in complementing NGO efforts to work with communities to restore or strengthen a base for people's livelihoods and to deepen citizen engagement with local government. The first site, Midkiwan, is a rural community of mostly tenant farmers situated 15 km from Cagayan de Oro City. Further south is the *barangay* of Tongantongan in Bukidnon Province, which is working in partnership with the local municipality and Xavier University to promote organic agriculture in the vicinity of Valencia City, an area that underwent land reform in the 1980s. The third site is a community of mainly landless indigenous *lumad* peoples near Kitaotao, further south in Bukidnon province. Running through the accounts of each of these communities are some common themes: the question of access to, and control over, land, which is so fundamental to a rural livelihood base; how to engage most effectively with local government to access services and entitlements; and how to make the most of existing assets to improve livelihoods in the short term.

Country context

To understand how these local experiences fit into the context of social and economic trends in the Philippines as a whole, some historical background is necessary. Ever since colonial times, power and economic growth have been concentrated socially and economically in the dominating elite, and geographically in the capital city, Manila (Tumbaga and Sabado, 2003). The inequalities associated with this centralism were accentuated by corruption (itself a feature of centralization and lack of transparency), which was at its most extreme during the period of Martial Law under President Marcos (1972–1986). In the post-Marcos period, commitments to decentralization, land reform, and liberalization of the economy created a climate of cautious optimism about political and economic change. Policies were introduced to democratize the political system and usher in a period of more evenly distributed economic growth throughout the country. Yet, despite these strategies, a recent World Bank study gives legitimacy to what civil society organizations have been arguing for decades, namely the 'inability of public institutions to resist capture by special interests and thus promote the common good' and 'a frail social contract between the state and its citizens' (The World

Bank, 2006). Under these circumstances, civil society has a vital role to bring political promises to fruition.

Throughout its own history, SEARSOLIN has contributed to the strengthening of civil society by training development leaders and implementing development projects on Mindanao with the other outreach arms of the College of Agriculture of Xavier University, run by the Society of Jesus of the Catholic Church. When SEARSOLIN was established in 1964, poverty in the Philippines as a whole was escalating in both urban and rural areas. Both the Catholic Church and NGO sector were promoting labour unions, cooperatives, and credit unions as an alternative for the poor in the face of communist expansion throughout South East Asia (Carino et al., 2004). SEARSOLIN's founder, Fr William F. Masterson S.J., had been influenced by the work of Rev. Dr. Moses Coady in the Canadian Maritimes, who, 30 years earlier, had promoted producer cooperatives and credit unions as a middle ground between the excesses of capitalism and the appeal of communism during a similar period of social tension. Five years after the Coady Institute was launched in Nova Scotia, Canada, in 1959, its training programmes in social leadership for the cooperative movement became the model for the social leadership training programme at SEARSOLIN (Mercado, 2005b).

During the 1970s and early 1980s, the Marcos regime tightened its grip, but the Philippine civil society sector grew steadily more expressive, and was actively supported by the Roman Catholic Church. During these turbulent times, NGOs characterized themselves as 'the people's alternative,' working to raise people's awareness and challenge an unresponsive government, resulting in the famous 'People's Power Revolutions,' which succeeded in ousting two corrupt presidents: first Marcos, then Estrada (Association of Foundations, 2005). Meanwhile, under the second Director, Bishop Antonio Ledesma, S.J., SEARSOLIN continued its training in social leadership, carefully promoting community organizing and participatory approaches, inspired by the social teachings of the Church. These teachings were interpreted to mean addressing issues of social justice with agrarian reform, upholding the integrity of creation through sustainable agriculture, and promoting the human rights of women, children, and indigenous communities.

With the transition to liberal democracy under President Aquino (1986–1992), NGOs were encouraged to evolve from political activism into a 'pioneer' role, providing innovative strategies for community organizing and poverty reduction at community and national levels. With strong backing from the NGO sector and progressive members of Congress, the Aquino Administration passed landmark pro-people legislation such as the Comprehensive Agrarian Reform Law (1988), the Cooperative Code of the Philippines (1990), and the Local Government Code (1991). It also laid the groundwork for the Indigenous People's Rights Act that was approved in 1997 under the Ramos Administration. With these laws in place, NGOs had the legitimacy to help strengthen citizen capacity to engage with local government and to participate in development planning.

It is in this context that SEARSOLIN, during the directorship of Dr Anselmo Mercado, saw the promise of ABCD. As an approach, it built upon the principles of community organizing, and would therefore help communities to reassert themselves as active citizens with skills, assets, and capacities. Included as assets were the specific laws that people could now invoke to protect their claims over their other assets such as land, social services, and democratic governance. Encouraging citizen engagement with decentralized local government, the extension worker became less the paternalistic provider 'at the service of all,' and more the link between communities and local institutions. This paved the way for communities to access services and economic opportunity.

In total, SEARSOLIN has tried the ABCD approach in about 98 rural communities in Myanmar, Cambodia, Vietnam, Laos, Indonesia, India, and the Philippines. The communities of Midkiwan, Tongantongan and Kitaotao are illustrative of the different ways ABCD has been interpreted and applied in the Philippines.

Midkiwan

Midkiwan is a community of approximately 75 households, located 15 km from Cagayan de Oro City. Settlement dates back to the 1960s, when five households established themselves on land designated as a logging area. Over time, basic infrastructure was established – a school, a road, electricity, and rudimentary water supply – mostly with 'sweat equity' of community members. In the 1990s, organized action against illegal logging in upland

---

Box 13.1: A note on ABCD

Community development work is often motivated by the need to address poverty or disadvantage. For this reason, NGOs and government agencies tend to view communities as full of problems. As a consequence, people in the community may internalize this view and begin to present themselves to outside organizations in terms of their deficiencies, or, as Mercado (2005c: 96) describes, with a 'mendicancy mentality'. In this way, often unintentionally, relationships of dependency on outside assistance are reinforced rather than weakened. An ABCD approach takes a different view and adopts a different strategy. In this approach, rather than focusing on needs and problems, communities are encouraged to recognize the full range of assets within their grasp. These include social assets such as the capacity to organize, strong leadership, support networks, and shared knowledge for survival and innovation. These in turn are the means by which more conventional assets can be marshalled for economic activity – labour, finance, savings and investments, natural resources, and infrastructure, for example. The ABCD approach uses a wide range of popular education tools to help people identify these different types of assets as well as explore opportunities. The process of mapping and recording these assets and opportunities tends to mobilize communities to draw upon these assets. Challenging outsider perceptions of their deficiencies, communities can then begin to take a proactive role as agents of development, mobilizing their assets to meet economic opportunity and mobilizing themselves to access assets (health care, education, and other basic services, for example) to which they are entitled by virtue of citizenship.

areas resulted in the government designating 550 hectares of land to 400 families in the area (including Midkiwan) for an Integrated Social Forestry programme. Subsequently, this was strengthened in 1995 when a 'Certificate of Stewardship Claim' of 1.6 ha was awarded to each farming family (Polestico et. al., 1998).

Despite formalized obligations to protect the natural resources on which these families depend, and the economic opportunities afforded by close proximity to a major city, their livelihood base has remained tenuous. Farming is dominated by the cultivation of corn as a mono-crop, with a variety of vegetables also grown for the urban market. However, in the absence of effective local government support services to ensure compliance with the conditions of the stewardship awards, the sale of firewood offers more lucrative and quicker returns, and little has been achieved in terms of reversing the deforestation trend. According to Polestico et al., forest cover had been reduced from 80 per cent at the time of settlement in the 1960s, to approximately 18-20 per cent by the mid-1990s. The water table has lowered as a consequence of forest depletion. This, in combination with the lack of investment in more sustainable agricultural practices, has led to a decline in agricultural production, and farmers have been unable to compete with growers who have easier access to urban markets and more productive resource endowments.

These constraints can be attributed in part to the tenure arrangements. Approximately half of the farming households are tenant farmers with obligations to pay a third of their produce in kind to the land owner. Although share cropping is technically illegal, it coexists with other tenure arrangements in a complex web of overlapping claims, and this has inhibited sustainable land use practices. Why make an investment in contour farming if land may have to be surrendered under land reform legislation? The selling of trees for firewood offers short-term profits, but with the uncertain future of land tenure arrangements, why invest in planting?

Uncertainty about land tenure and about the quality and quantity of land for future generations makes the investment in children's education a priority. People simply see no future for their children in agricultural production or in minimum wage employment in Cagayan de Oro: families reported that half of the daily wage of those working in town was spent on transport.

The *barangay* council is limited in terms of its resource allocation and its tax base. On the basis of an April 2005 survey, 91 per cent of the population is below the poverty threshold, and only 25 per cent have access to potable water. Historically, for a variety of reasons to do with the capture of political power by the land-owning elite, community members are very cautious in pursuing land-ownership issues with government officials. The community members have learned to live with the situation by not advocating for absolute ownership, but assurance for continued use of the land under mutually beneficial terms. They have learned to side with the winning political party so that their requests for social services like road repairs, provision of electricity, etc. can be approved by the local government.

SEARSOLIN's involvement with Midkiwan began in 2001, when the community was invited to participate in an exercise conducted by students of the institute's diploma programme as part of their training in ABCD. 'Appreciative inquiry' was used to discuss success stories from Midkiwan's past which, in turn, laid the foundation for identifying the resources and assets that the community could continue to draw upon. A resource map and transect walk identified physical and natural resources, a social map identified the active associations in the community, a Venn diagram showed the relative importance of linkages with external institutions (government, non-government, and private sector organizations), an income and expenditure tree prompted a discussion of financial assets and opportunities, and a demographic profile gave an indication of the community's human capital resource base. SEARSOLIN was also able to show how even communities that are poor in the conventional sense have power as a voting block, an asset unheard of during the era of dictatorial rule.

Following the review of assets and opportunities, options for action were discussed and prioritized, and action plans developed that would link these assets with opportunities (see Figure 13.1). The plans reflected a vision, discussed at length, of a community where material well-being was matched with spiritual and social well-being. Thus, Midkiwan intended to develop a strong community organization; diversify livelihoods and increase income through raising livestock (an activity that did not require addressing the land tenure question); promote early childhood education; and hold seminars to discuss and strengthen spiritual values in the community.

The Midkiwan Community Development Association (MICODA) was established in 2001, with membership open to all households. Until this time, while the organized action against illegal logging mentioned earlier in this section involved large numbers, typical organizing for sustained community activity involved small groups rather than the whole community. For example, traditional forms of shared labour in the *bayanihan* system involved several households. There was also a small association called the Basic Ecclesial Community (BEC) related to the Catholic Church. There were two retail cooperatives, each with approximately 30 members. The decision to organize a community-wide association was therefore ambitious, and initiated in full knowledge of the work that lay ahead reconciling different interests. Divisive elements existed here, as in all communities – different religious affiliations, rival informal leaders, and an underlying tension that arises from the dependence of tenants on the good graces of landowners.

The construction of a community meeting centre was a decisive step taken by the association to forge a sense of unity. Drawing upon the awareness generated by the ABCD process, MICODA members were encouraged to mobilize their skills and assets towards this common purpose. Local carpenters volunteered their time and expertise, and other households contributed a quota according

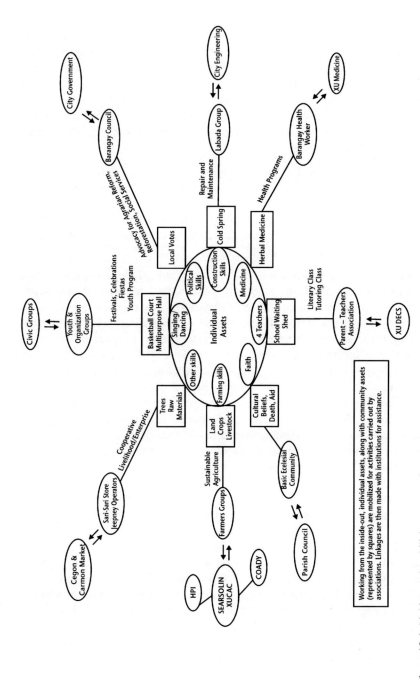

Figure 13.1: Linking and mobilizing community assets
Source: Rachel Polestico, based on fieldwork in Midkiwan, 2001.

to their own particular skills and assets. A membership fund was started to raise funds (membership dues and fines paid by members in lieu of labour contributions). Records were kept of different members' contributions. One of the community leaders took the initiative to ask for second-hand corrugated iron roofing as a donation from the City Council, and limestone from a nearby quarry was transported with support from the local government. One man and one woman emerged as informal leaders, reflecting the active membership of both men and women. During the course of the following year, a meeting centre was built, water tanks were constructed to collect run-off water, and a tree nursery was established, all at the initiative of the association. According to one MICODA member, the fact that the community was organizing such projects of its own accord was significant:

> This was the way we did it – coming together for work and pooling our resources. But this was different. Before, formal leaders like the *barangay* officers used to be the ones to tell us what to build, where to build and what resources were needed. [Because there was no sense of ownership] people didn't care about these structures and so sometimes they were destroyed. (personal communication, 2006)

SEARSOLIN's role was two-fold in this embryonic phase. First, it provided training for community leaders. Second, it facilitated linkages with two NGOs offering opportunities for communities trying to link their own assets with realistic prospects for action. Heifer Project International (HPI) had a 'pass on the gift' programme by which small livestock loans were repaid by giving one of the offspring to the next-in-line recipient. The Christian Children's Fund (CCF Taiwan) was interested in promoting children's welfare, rights, and development through their child sponsorship programme and was exploring ways of investing in early childhood education in community-managed day-care centres, a departure from its child sponsorship programme. Day-care centres are equivalent to kindergarten and are considered almost a necessity for children to succeed in primary school, yet for very young children the few government-run centres that do exist are often at too great a distance, and attendance has consequently dropped.

One avenue for support by CCF was through parent associations. Communities with an active and viable association could qualify for assistance with a one-room facility for early childhood education, built with the volunteer labour of parents, and staffed by a community member. This broadened the relevance of MICODA for all members of the community. Its membership expanded to 71 members, representing almost all the households in Midkiwan, and has since become the model for other communities in the expansion area of CCF's early childhood education programme. It is CCF's intention that, over time, these parent associations will federate into a larger body and address children's issues in the context of broader community development through more effective links with local government.

Community members now view the association as a vehicle for accessing local government and other services. They have assumed a more proactive stance, as this MICODA leader reports:

> Now we don't wait to be approached – we approach external organizations ourselves. When we wanted a meeting hall, we talked to the *barangay* for permission. Then we talked to the City officials and asked them for limestone, and approached the Department of Natural Resources for tree seedlings. (personal communication, 2006)

Interestingly, local government sees MICODA as a vehicle for more effective community relations, or as some have suggested, an asset of the *barangay* council rather than of the community. Just as leaders of the association note the increase in the confidence of community members, recently so cautious of outsiders, local government officials report that people are more willing to attend meetings, are more socially active generally, and are able to articulate their concerns effectively at *barangay* council meetings. Local government officials even noted that the health survey conducted in April 2005, was a case in point since people were more willing to be surveyed, an observation that speaks volumes about the suspicion with which people regarded government officials in the past.

According to Bona Anna's evaluation research conducted in 2005 (Anna, 2005), and interviews conducted for this study in 2006, MICODA members reported that the experience had heightened their appreciation of their own capacities and strengths, particularly their capacity to organize as a group to make incremental improvements to household assets (improved agricultural practices, and investment in small livestock) and community assets (a community centre, and improved water access points). They also commented on their ability to link effectively with outside agencies to access additional resources (the activities of MICODA and the link with CCF for early childhood education, for example). On the other hand, attempts to address the deforestation issue and its attendant long-term consequences have been frustrated. So long as the *barangay* council is ineffectual in enforcing the ordinance to replant on land with stewardship claims, the tree nursery will make little difference, and the association does not yet have the will of its membership behind a concerted effort to forgo short-term gain from firewood sales.

It is perhaps not insignificant that the choice of metaphor for MICODA is the life-giving tree, as illustrated in Figure 13.2, most at risk under current livelihood strategies. As Visitacion Bargamento, President of MICODA, notes:

> We like the symbol of the tree because a tree gives life, supports us, counteracts pollution, shades us and provides us with food. The church is the main root... MICODA also includes many other families with many other ideas – we are a much larger association now. The lateral roots are our local assets. The trunk of the tree is MICODA. The branches of the

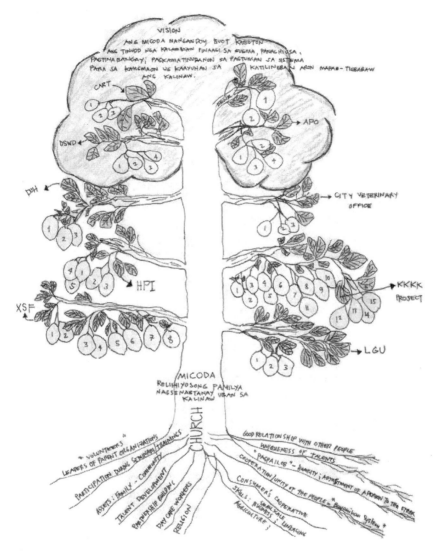

Figure 13.2: MICODA 'vision tree'
Source: Midkiwan Community Development Association.

tree represent outside organizations and the leaves of the programme are the programmes that [it] offers in our community... the top of the tree is our vision for MICODA and the community. With all our activities we have a sense of responsibility to one another. We view success through our children. We want them to be educated: to go to school, which we did not have the chance to do. We dream of a bright future for them. (personal communication, 2006)

Despite a positive evaluation of the ABCD experience in Midkiwan, Anna cautions that an ABCD approach could contribute to a potential de-politicization of development, serving a neo-liberal 'do-it-yourself agenda.' The test of this is whether the approach has, in fact, contributed to effective engagement with local government to ensure that it fulfils its responsibilities, especially in tackling the issues of land reform and environmental conservation. At this stage, as Visitacion says, education is the focus of MICODA: an issue of importance to all parents as an investment for the future. It is also a safe goal, requiring no confrontation, and an acknowledgement that rural life cannot support an expanding population, particularly given the existing distribution of resources. This metaphor could be taken further to envision a tree that becomes a forest, or a federation of associations like MICODA. A group of associations may be in a better position to address the more intransigent issues of land reform and resource protection, so that the investment in children's education is not only a means to a life outside Midkiwan, but also a means to deriving a livelihood from sustainable agriculture and forestry.

Tongantongan

The Tongantongan case illustrates the application of an ABCD approach on a wider scale – at the *barangay* level – integrated into a pre-existing programme promoting sustainable agriculture. Tongantongan is one of 31 *barangays* in the municipality of the City of Valencia, Bukidnon province, Mindanao. With approximately 1,300 households and a population of 8,000, it is situated astride the flat plains to the east of Valencia City, providing the ideal environment for paddy rice production, and the hilly upland areas, given over to timber concessions in the 1960s and devoted to upland farming systems. Coinciding with rapid forest depletion by the logging industry exploiting these concessions, the 'Green Revolution' in the 1960s ushered in a new era of mono-cropping in both areas. This system was heavily dependent on chemical fertilizer and pesticide (for corn in upland areas and rice on the plains), favouring large-scale farmers who could afford the necessary inputs and enjoy the economic benefits of scale. During the 1980s, however, land ownership changed dramatically under the Comprehensive Agrarian Reform Program (CARP), signed into law in 1988 by President Aquino. In the upland areas, a 25-year lease arrangement was put in place as part of a Community Based Forest Management (CBFM) scheme, integrated with upland farming systems. In lowland areas, land ownership was transferred to landless farm workers, lessees, or share tenants (Polestico et al., 1998).

Under the regulations of this programme, to prevent the land reverting to wealthier farmers, land could not be sold for ten years. In the period since these restrictions on sale were lifted, however, only 106 families out of the original 1,100 have retained ownership of their land. The cost of inputs and the deterioration in the soil structure made these intensive and chemical-based systems unaffordable, unsustainable or unprofitable, forcing many to sell their land and revert to lessee status. In other words, 'land to the tiller' has often been reversed as financial constraints have driven 'land to the teller' (Polestico, personal communication, 2006).

Since 2001, the *barangay* of Tongantongan has been implementing a ten-year development plan, known as Community Based Sustainable Agriculture (COMBASE).[1] A five year moratorium on the use of GMO (Genetically Modified Organisms) products, including rice (City Ordinance of 2001), was one of a series of policy instruments put in place to create a favourable environment for COMBASE. A local ban on rice burning, to encourage farmers to plough rice debris back into the soil, was another. Institutional arrangements that would link community interests to municipal level government departments was also significant: COMBASE required the convergence of the development plans of 15 different stakeholders, including representatives from *barangay* and city governments, provincial government line agencies, national government line agencies, the Sustainable Agriculture Center of Xavier University College of Agriculture, and community-based associations. An ambitious project, it has required implementing joint plans by informal groups, community-based associations, the local *barangay* council along with its various committees, and a Stakeholders' Assembly. The latter brings together the combined ideas and resources of *barangay* and municipal governments, the private sector, and community members.

An evaluation conducted in November 2004 by the Sustainable Agriculture Centre of Xavier University's College of Agriculture showed that just three years into the COMBASE development plan, many successes were evident (College of Agriculture Complex, Xavier University, 2004). A 5 km farm to market road had been built resulting in lower transportation costs (PHP5 per sack of rice compared to PHP12 per sack).[2] The road allowed public transportation access to the community, and facilitated the return of many people to set up residence in Upland Tongantongan. Two new provision stores had opened and another two were under construction. Land value had also increased.

Also, sustainable agriculture had become established in the community. Forty-five per cent of farming households were practising sustainable agriculture to varying degrees and 15 per cent were practising exclusively organic systems. Over a thousand organic backyard gardens had been established. These and the organic paddy rice fields were supported by a training pool of local farmers and the Tongantongan Organic Farmers' Society for Sustainable Agriculture (TOFSSA), an association established to disseminate best practice and facilitate marketing of produce. Finally, two community-managed 'Learning Centres' were established in Upland and Lowland Tongantongan, to offer training to farmers across Mindanao, the Philippines and South East Asia.

The success in the *barangay* of Tongantongan has encouraged Valencia City to formulate a Sustainable Agriculture and Organic Rice Development Master Plan for all 31 *barangays* under the guidance of 'Task Force Organic.'[3] (COMBASE, n.d.) Under consideration is the formation of cooperatives to facilitate marketing, especially of organic produce. Following a 'One Town,

One Product' Department of Trade and Industry policy for organic product certification for the export market, rice is likely to be the focus for Valencia City.

Integrating the ABCD process

Lowland and Upland Tongantongan had different experiences of ABCD. In Lowland Tongantongan, ABCD was integrated into COMBASE two years after sustainable agriculture systems had been piloted, and a core group of interested farmers paved the way for a community-wide programme. Essentially, some of the techniques of ABCD, such as asset-mapping, were introduced when the programme began to scale up, reinforcing principles of an asset-based approach that had already been unconsciously (or intuitively) implemented (Foster, 2001). In Upland Tongantongan a more classic application of an ABCD approach was applied.

Lowland Tongantongan

Sustainable agricultural practices had been introduced in Lowland Tongantongan area by a group of 11 farmers trained at the Sustainable Agriculture Center (SAC) of the College of Agriculture, Xavier University, in 1999. These early adopters were able to demonstrate that farmers could maximize their yields using their own resources rather than purchasing inputs. For example, local seed varieties were resistant to pests, local *guano* could substitute for chemical fertilizer, dividing plots into smaller units would be rewarded by higher yields, contrary to conventional wisdom. 'The other farmers thought we were crazy – they were always trying to amalgamate plots, not divide them,' reported one farmer in Lowland Tongantongan (personal communication, 2006). Other farmers began to experiment with these ideas, particularly women, who then persuaded their husbands.

Once these farmers were convinced that these techniques were effective, the next step was to make a case for complete conversion to organic production. Going organic required farmers to maximize every potential asset. They saved household organic waste and scrupulously collected manure from small livestock. They composted rather than burned field waste. They cultivated herbal ingredients for organic fertilizer and pesticide production near the house. They stored different seed varieties for various crops so as to maintain bio-diversity and grew leguminous crops in the boundaries between plots. They maintained irrigation water at its most efficient levels, filtered the water through water hyacinth and recycled it into fish ponds.

Gradually, more farmers started taking an interest, learning from these early adopters, often by unconventional means of diffusion. In one case, for example, a farmer who had planted *Madre de Cacao* on the boundary of his farm noticed that the leaves had been pruned:

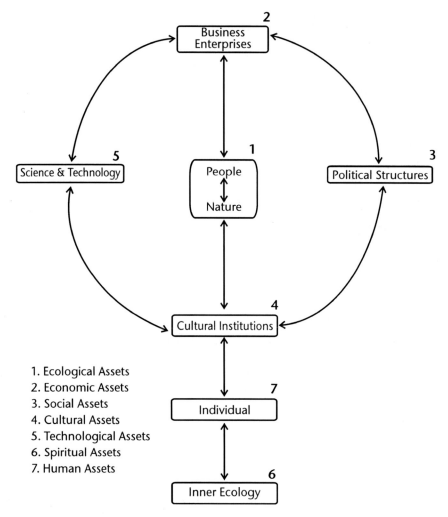

Figure 13.3: The asset-based sustainable agriculture development framework
Source: Adapted from Galario et al., 2005

I later learnt that the leaves of this plant are used as a fertilizer and that the culprit was my neighbour. This was a defining moment for me. Thanks to him, I am now practising organic farming. (personal communication, 2006)

COMBASE added muscle to those demonstration and diffusion effects by providing an institutional support mechanism to encourage farmers to make the conversion. Two to three years of cropping cycles would be required to regenerate soil that had been subjected to heavy use of chemical inputs. To tide farmers over this period of lost income, a PHP20,000[4] 'conversion' loan fund was granted by the bank and guaranteed by the city government. Combined with the moratorium on GMO seed varieties and local legislation to manage solid waste and encourage maximum use of composting, this financial package provided the incentive to 'risk' conversion. Further encouragement came from the community leadership. One of the early adopters was the *barangay* captain herself, who had gone entirely chemical-free in 2000.

Seeing the complementarities of an asset-based approach to COMBASE's objectives, Mr Vic Tagupa, the coordinator, integrated and improvised elements of the approach. Following the sustainability principle of 'finding internal solutions to internal problems,' ABCD could potentially link internal problems with the internal assets that could be used to find internal solutions. In keeping with 'systems thinking,' the idea of a sustainable bio-resource flow for agricultural production was similarly extended to the idea of a web of interconnected assets sustaining community development, as illustrated in Figure 13.3 below.

In the initial stages of the programme, the coordinator had carried out extensive surveys to identify problems in the community that could be addressed by COMBASE. After exposure to ABCD, he began to design a new survey that specifically explored community assets, skills and resources that could be mobilized to address those problems, particularly in the area of sustainable agriculture in Lowland Tongantongan. Representatives from the *puroks* were given basic training in ABCD and in how to carry out a household survey. These volunteers were introduced to the wide range of assets to be identified, such as individual skills and talents, the capacities of associations, or other more conventional material assets such as land, water, finances, etc. Following the training, 800 of the 1,300 households were surveyed. The Stakeholders' Assembly then used the results to identify the potential of community assets to achieve the pre-existing goals of the community. As one community development worker commented: '[They realized that] there are so many assets that they have that are not used!' (Mars, personal communication, 2006). The principle of 'internal solutions to internal problems' translated into a question posed each and every time a planning decision had to be made: 'Can we achieve this without using external assets?'(Tagupa, personal communication, 2006). The results of the survey were consulted to find out if, indeed, community members could achieve it.

In this way, action plans were developed and verified by the local community. Backyard gardens were established and a training centre built. From this point on, an ABCD 'attitude' was integrated into the day-to-day running of the programme. Among farming families, one consequence of this was greater interest among farming households in human and social asset development rather than an exclusive focus on physical and tangible benefits of the COMBASE programme. Fieldworkers from SAC observed that when people only focus on what is coming in from the outside, they also only focus on external institutions for assistance at the expense of strengthening their own associations. When this happens, 'They are dependent. They are missing the things that they have – they aren't using them' (Tagupa, personal communication, 2006).

If the first principle of sustainable systems is to find internal solutions to internal problems, an equivalent challenge for social systems and organizations is to ask the practical question: How do you know what you need until you know what you already have? The local *barangay* council, whose captain continues to be a staunch supporter of this approach, reported that exposure to asset-based thinking resulted in members of the Stakeholders' Assembly realizing that even among themselves they did not know what programmes, resources and other 'assets' were available through their respective institutions or associations. To mobilize those assets required creativity in organizing, whether at the level of farming households or coordinating household and institutional activities through committees and the Stakeholders' Assembly.

Upland Tongantongan

Based on the effectiveness of integrating the ABCD approach in Lowland Tongantongan, the Stakeholders' Assembly then decided to apply an ABCD approach in Upland Tongantongan, in the *purok* of San Roque, comprised of 30 households. Here the approach was applied differently, partly because the relatively small population allowed more community-wide interaction in the process, and partly because, unlike in Lowland Tongantongan where ABCD was initiated after the start of the programme, an asset-orientation could be used from the start in San Roque. Within the overall COMBASE programme, this sub-programme became known as Asset Base and Sustainable Land Use in Marginal Upland (AB-SLUM). After a comprehensive group exercise in asset mapping and planning, a number of ideas were generated. These took into account the existing array of assets in the community in terms of knowledge, skills and organizational capacity and the availability of training opportunities through COMBASE: contour farming for sustainable and diversified crop production; small livestock production, production of organic fertilizer, establishment of a seed-banking system, marketing of organic products, and solar electrification.

Reflecting on changes since AB-SLUM, community members identified three related outcomes of significance. First, they identified the results of sustainable agriculture practices for their own livelihoods. Second, they noted their increased capacity as managers and organizers. Third, they assessed the combination of these practices and capacities in the construction and running of a training centre for local farmers, similar to the training facility in lowland Tongantongan. According to local farmers, the use of sustainable agriculture practices has rejuvenated soil structure, increased fertility, and encouraged more diversified production. Not only has this increased food security but it has also encouraged production in sufficient volume for sale in Valencia City, especially now that the new road access has halved the costs of transportation. Men reported that they are less likely to hire themselves out

as plantation labour, since they see greater benefit from managing their own plots. As a Lowland Tongantongan farmer commented: 'before [we shifted from chemical-based to sustainable practices] we had higher yields but more debt. Now we have lower yields but no debt. On balance we are better off' (personal communication, 2006).

Explaining their renewed confidence as leaders, researchers, and managers of their own production, they emphasized their capacity to organize as a group. In fact, in the initial ABCD mapping exercise, the *bayanihan* system of organizing cooperative work groups was recognized as an asset to communities in its traditional form, and ways of adapting it as a renewed asset for the current situation began to be discussed. The adapted *bayanihan* tended to be more inclusive, involving whole families rather than just men on certain projects, depending on whose skills and assets were needed.

The evolution of the *bayanihan* system warrants further discussion because it also sheds light on the question of 'agency.' As noted, the system existed traditionally as a way in which male members of extended families would pool their labour for house construction, land clearing and other agricultural activities. In more recent times, however, before the introduction of COMBASE, *bayanihan* became the mechanism for 'Food for Work' programmes organized by the *barangay* council. In return for community work, such as road maintenance or grass cutting, the *barangay* would provide rice to the *bayanihan* group. Meanwhile, under mono-cropping regimes, farming became more individualized, weakening the traditional *bayanihan* as a unit of self-mobilized cooperation and production. Since COMBASE, the original concept of *bayanihan* as a self-mobilized production group has been reinvigorated as community members experience the value of cooperative endeavours. Five groups are functioning actively, approximately three days per week, working on members' farms on a rotational basis with one member of each household required to be present. *Bayanihan* groups have built the ridges for contour farming on hill slopes.[5]

The *bayanihan's* role also expanded into other community-wide activities. Having contributed volunteer labour for the construction of the training centre in Lowland Tongantongan, community members in the *purok* of Upland Tongantongan saw no reason why they should not have their own training centre. One family agreed to donate land, and work proceeded with all families (including women and children) contributing labour and materials according to their skills and capacities, in newly formed *bayanihan* groups. On their part, the *barangay* council provided food for the *bayanihan* groups as encouragement, but refused to provide galvanized iron sheets for roofing, rejecting expectations that an in-kind or financial grant would be automatically forthcoming.

Discouraged, community members left the structure without a roof for several months, until the COMBASE programme arranged for the *purok* leader to visit a community cooperative building in another part of the province where roofing had been made from locally available materials (*cogon* or bamboo). Inspired by this visit, the *purok* leader urged the people of Upland Tongantongan to do the same. Having completed the basic structure themselves, including constructing a roof from local materials, they were successful in securing a donation from city government to enable them to expand the building and improve the kitchen so that the facility could accommodate farmers coming for training courses. The centre is now operational, offering training opportunities to farmers in the area and revenue-earning opportunities to the trainers and caterers.

This experience is interesting because it illustrates how the idea of communities organizing first, in the expectation of later outsider investment (in this case local government), can be problematic. Local government doesn't want to set a precedent (other requests for iron roofing will follow), yet people have grown used to these quid pro quo arrangements in 'food for work' or 'counterpart' funding. But once the community stretched itself further to build the roof themselves, the rewards came in the form of support from the city. The difference is in the discretionary nature of the response, and it is where the idea of the expectation of quid pro quo (an 'entitlement') is replaced by a more discretionary arrangement ('an investment').

Negotiating expectations and obligations in the relationships between local associations and local government is likely to take on increased importance in the creation of new forms of organizing that are consistent with decentralized, community-driven processes. As government-led forms of organization give way to organizational forms that are a genuine expression of self-mobilizing, the capacity of communities and their local governments to adapt and innovate will be tested.

Nowhere is this more urgent than in the organization for marketing of farmer produce. Farmers throughout Tongantongan who have persisted with organic agriculture are members of TOFSSA, which now has 83 members (45 upland farmers and 38 lowland farmers). Their objectives, as a group, are to promote common interests and motivate and help each other in organic production. Based on current trends in urban markets, the demand for organic produce is likely to rise, especially if certification of organic rice is accomplished, as is the intention. Even without certification, and no increase in the selling price, farmers maintain that they have increased their income because of lower costs of inputs. Valencia City has some plans to promote cooperatives, but the record of government-driven cooperatives is that they have tended to stifle genuine self-mobilization and become over-dependent on government (Mercado, 2005a). Creating institutional forms of community-driven development in producer cooperatives that can respond promptly to the vagaries of agricultural produce markets will require further negotiation between the private sector, the various government agencies, and local communities.

The role of assets and agency in Tongantongan

The principles of sustainable agriculture have been applied to sustainable community development: look first for internal solutions to problems in the assets that already exist. It is here that an 'ABCD' approach has been integrated to strengthen the effectiveness of a shift in thinking away from dependence on external solutions. In the process, there has been a reaffirmation of the farmer in the roles of manager and researcher, and a reaffirmation of community organizing capacity through an adapted *bayanihan* system.

Without reconfiguring these social assets, technical innovation might not have taken hold.

At another level, cooperative effort is required in the roles and responsibilities of membership in TOFSSA, and through representation in the Stakeholders' Assembly. It is here that linkages are made to external opportunities through government and private sector agencies represented in the Assembly. Without a doubt, the energetic leadership of the *barangay* captain has been a key factor in Tongantongan's success. She regularly attends *purok* meetings, and maintains a wide circle of connections that ensure easy access to government circles, guided by a personal commitment to 'Listen to your people, link with other agencies, and maintain positive relationships with those officials and agencies' (Pugado, personal communication, 2006). For this reason the community presents itself at Stakeholders' Assembly meetings as organized, capable of fulfilling bureaucratic requirements and with the leadership necessary to ensure proper disbursement of funds. As one government official commented, when explaining why Tongantongan was 'the best' of 31 *barangays* in the municipality, he explained: 'Over the last 15 years, when we call for a *Barangay* Assembly, there is 90–100 per cent attendance at Tongantongan. This is much higher than other *barangays*' (personal communication, 2006).

Kitaotao

The *lumad* of Mindanao constitute 6 per cent of the island's population (Muslim, M.A. and Cagoco-Guiam, R., 1999). These unassimilated indigenous peoples identify with neither the waves of immigrants who came from other Visayan islands of the Philippines beginning in the 1950s, nor the Moro (Muslim) peoples of western Mindanao. Their livelihood and lifestyle has been greatly disrupted by land expropriation on the part of plantation owners and new settlers, and by logging concessions granted particularly under the Marcos regime. Logging has stripped most of the forests which only 40 years ago covered the island and provided the *lumad* with their traditional hunting and gathering way of life.

Beginning in 1986, the *lumad* began asserting their claims to ancestral domain land, a right that was legitimized under the People's Rights Act (1997). However, this legislation has often proved ineffectual in the face of other laws such as the Philippine Mining Act (1995), which also gives multinational companies rights over *lumad* territory. Because of the failure of *lumad* to secure rights to ancestral domain, many communities remain fragmented and dislocated, with few opportunities for establishing a livelihood. Moreover, they have experienced discrimination and prejudice at the hands of dominant groups with whom they have had contact. It is not surprising that communities describe themselves as lacking motivation, with many individuals dependent on alcohol and frustrated by a deep sense of alienation.

Amy Patriarca, a recent graduate of SEARSOLIN's certificate programme in Asset Based Community Development, was employed as a community development worker in several *lumad* settlements. She was tasked with identifying training priorities for skills training. A dynamic personality, she applied an ABCD approach with enthusiasm and persistence, beginning in July 2002. Married to a *lumad*, and with his continued support of her efforts, she was able to break down suspicion and resistance towards outsiders in the settlement, while at the same time paving the way for constructive linkages between the people living in the settlement and those in local government.

One of the *lumad* settlements where she worked was situated on the outskirts of Kitaotao. One member had inherited 0.7 ha of ancestral domain land on which he had planted sugar cane. All the other households were landless and relied on waged labour on nearby sugar plantations for their livelihood.

Recognizing the precarious livelihood base of people in this settlement, her goal was to rebuild lost confidence in their own capacities and to help them build assets to expand their livelihood options. She also recognized that the key to their success would be acknowledgement by local government of their responsibilities to *lumads*. As with the other settlements, she visited the Kitaotao settlement once a week for six months, often staying overnight. She went through an ABCD approach systematically, beginning with interviews to draw out success stories and then conducting a variety of popular education techniques to draw out community assets and strengths.

Throughout the six months, she had high expectations. Between her weekly visits she would, for instance, expect community members to complete the mapping of community assets or the household-by-household charts of strengths and skills. Among the assets they identified was a small piece of land that one of them had inherited as part of the ancestral domain of his father, a *Datu*, or tribal leader. They also identified the general skills in settled agriculture they had learned through working as plantation labourers. They saw opportunities, but realized they would need more specialized training if they were to have a chance of generating income from farming activities.

According to Dr Andreas Lewke, coordinator of the training, the common perception was that indigenous peoples (IPs) would not be able to be trained alongside other groups because of their lack of confidence and lack of basic experience and capacity. Ignoring this advice, he held five-day training sessions and watched how the IPs gradually gained confidence and participated more actively. Not having had experience of the ABCD approach himself, what impressed him about people from this community was that people were already 'ready.' They were not providing wish-lists. They were organized, motivated, aware of their assets, and ready to volunteer what they had in the way of resources and skills. In particular, they were aware of themselves as assets.

After the training courses in improved agricultural techniques, the idea of a group-run vegetable garden came up. An association was formed. The member who had inherited land agreed to let his land be used for a period of five years. Everyone offered what they could: the newly acquired skills of individuals, their labour to work as a group, and material goods, such as bamboo and wood for fencing. Clearing of land began, each household being allocated 300 square metres, and the soil was prepared for the planting of an array of vegetables for sale in the local urban market. The goal of the group was to use minimum chemical inputs to maximize cost effectiveness and soil quality.

The garden would require frequent watering. The programme coordinator linked the group to a small grant fund to enable the purchase of a water pump and plastic sheeting to line a water reservoir. The reservoir was built by the group members themselves. The compensation to the owner of the land for leasing his land to the group for five years would be these inputs: the reservoir, pump, and fencing. According to Andreas Lewke, the programme coordinator: 'In all of the 11 years I have spent here, I have never seen anything like it as when I saw these families combining their labour to build the reservoir' (personal communication, 2006).

Each family agreed to dig an area 72 cm x 72 cm x 3 m deep, and they did so at the same pace. This was important because if any family lagged behind the others, it would hold everyone up. Once the reservoir was completed, the association allocated land to each family group in the association. With skills learned by members in the training and a carefully managed production and marketing system, the association has been successful in raising the incomes of its membership. As one Kitaotao woman points out: 'Now we can meet our daily harvest needs. Now our time is all spent here [rather than on sugar plantation]. We didn't know how to assess our assets here but now we do. Our ideas are our assets' (personal communication, 2006).

Contrary to the pervasive negative image that is painted of indigenous people's character and capacity, this settlement now has a thriving cooperative horticultural enterprise that has surprised the local authorities (the observations themselves are revealing of pervasive attitudes). As the Vice Mayor observed:

> Before the IPs were lazy and content to eat only once a day. They didn't get health care and just worked on sugar farms for 70 pesos a day. Now the 20 members of the garden project are a model for the other 40,000 people in Kitaotao [municipality]. They don't have to depend on large landowners – their income is from the vegetables. Before, they had no choice but to work for low wages. Now these people control their prices. (personal communication, 2006)

Controlling prices has been achieved by the association through cooperative ownership and control of its own labour. The recognition of members' skills and ideas as assets is a remarkable change, especially since they were once marginalized and discriminated against. Members of the Vegetable Growers' Association report that the experience has been transformative in other ways too. Without land, people had limited means to build a livelihood other than by working as labourers on sugar cane plantations. Now people have skills and experience in horticultural production and an organizational capacity to collaborate on a jointly owned and managed initiative. Wage labour does little to forge a sense of community, partly because people have to spend long hours away, but also because there is little need to cooperate – they work as individuals. The vegetable garden has provided a reason to collaborate and a reward for effective organization and management. A young woman, for example, commented on the dedication of the group 'to motivate, develop and grow with one another' (personal communication, 2006), a sentiment clearly shared by others. As another member of the association attests: 'The garden has inspired me; I have been so busy there that I didn't have time or interest to drink; I enjoyed the atmosphere at the garden and spending time with friends there' (personal communication, 2006).

While the struggle continues for *lumad* groups to secure their ancestral land rights, a jointly managed initiative has helped build organizational as well as livelihood capacity. In the process however, it has also 'cracked open encrusted structures' because people have questioned traditional authority and developed a new association with its own independent leadership structure. The local tribal leader, resistant to (and suspicious of) NGO activities, has been undermined by the success of this initiative, particularly since local government authorities now recognize this success and support the association's work. Two opposing views have emerged: on the one hand, members of the association believe that the *lumads* cause is enhanced by the success of this vegetable project and the positive relationship with local government. On the other hand, the traditional leader claims that the cause is harmed by the possibility of being co-opted by the authorities.

It is clear that leadership is now becoming more diffuse. The owner of the ancestral domain land where the vegetables are grown has emerged as an informal leader in the process. Because he works part-time with local government, people in the community approach him with conflicts or issues that they feel may need to be channelled to the *barangay* level. Another leader who has emerged is a woman who had never held a leadership role before and is now the president of the local association that manages the garden. In contrast to the leadership approach of the traditional leader, whose autocratic style has alienated many within the community, she leads with a sense of respect for the contributions and ideas of each member. As one community member put it: 'before we only looked to one leader and couldn't express ourselves. Now in the group we can meet and discuss [things]' (personal communication, 2006).

From the point of view of the programme coordinator, the linkages established with local government have been strategic. A 'win-win' situation has been created so that: 'Members of the association say, It's our project; local government officials also say, It's our project. Both are taking responsibility and pride in it, which is good.' (personal communication, 2006)

Once viewed as 'lazy', *lumads* are now treated with respect by local government officials here as a result of their interaction on matters relating to the vegetable project. If carefully nurtured, this change in attitude could strengthen the *lumad* hand in their bid to regain ancestral lands. New leadership may be able to demonstrate that finding ways to integrate more effectively

Members of the Kitaotao Vegetable Growers' Association transplant seedlings on land lent by one of its members for a five year period.

in mainstream society may be more than a stop-gap measure. Rather than weakening the resolve of the *lumads* through cooption, the respect earned from these successes may be the more powerful base from which to launch a bid for land claims.

Reflections

How has an ABCD approach been applied?

ABCD has been applied quite differently in the different sites. In Midkiwan and Kitaotao, popular education tools were introduced to identify community assets, and community members were taken through visioning and planning exercises to come up with a realizable community initiative. In the case of Kitaotao, the application was more rigorous. Here, asset identification and mapping took place over several weeks, with community members completing the maps and inventories themselves after the visit by the extension worker. In the case of Tongantongan, an asset-based approach was complementary to the principle of 'internal solutions to internal problems' associated with sustainable agricultural practice. An asset-based attitude and sustainable agricultural practice were therefore mutually reinforcing. In Lowland Tongantongan, a household survey was used to identify what assets could be drawn upon by the community to achieve their existing plans of identifying 'internal solutions to internal problems.' In Upland Tongantongan, a more rigorous form of community asset mapping and mobilizing was used, resulting in a renewed appreciation of the livelihood potential of natural resource endowments if these were managed in a sustainable way and a reassertion of the community's organizational social assets. In all sites, assets were built and strengthened as a result.

Assets were also reassessed in the process. As Vic Tagupa observed, in Tongantongan as a whole, the COMBASE programme and the ABCD approach contributed to a reassessment of existing assets for smallholders: land is not just 'something to be mortgaged or used as collateral' (personal communication, 2006). As well, farmers came to regard themselves as researchers and managers, not simply producers within a tightly controlled supply chain of mono-cropped rice or corn. And women are early adopters and innovators in sustainable agriculture, not followers. For people in Midkiwan and among the *lumad*, who understand what it is to be without land or the confidence of a long lease, human and social assets become paramount. Hence, a high value is placed on cooperation and collaboration, and on the investment in children's education in the hopes that landlessness will not be the constraint for them that it has been for their parents.

What has changed in terms of people's 'agency'?

If agency is 'the state of being in action or exerting power' (Stein, 1984: 25) and 'capacity to act' is a reflection of people's assets and identity with those assets (Bebbington, 1999), agency has been strengthened across all sites. Observable and reported changes include shifts from negative to positive self-image, from an attitude of dependence to self-reliance, from isolation to connection and collaboration, from passive to active participation, from monopolized to shared leadership, from beneficiary to decision-maker or manager, and from fragmentation to cooperation. To varying degrees these shifts were reported not just by community members in their generalizations about the community as a whole, but by less influential groups within the community, such as upland farmers relative to the more affluent lowland farmers, women in relation to men, or *lumads* in relation to mainstream society.

Capacity to act is, however, most powerfully expressed in the associations that were built or strengthened through the ABCD activities. In Midkiwan, MICODA was a revival and strengthening of a church group. In the case of Kitaotao, a new association emerged, developing from the core group of community members who participated in the asset-mapping and inventory activities, which allowed them to see possibilities for collaborating on a joint economic activity. In both Midkiwan and Kitaotao, these emerged independently of local government but, in terms of associations, people saw themselves in a stronger position to engage with local government as a result of their community activities. In Tongantongan, local government was at the centre of organizing efforts while encouraging associational forms for different activities, some of which emerged independently such as the revived transformed *bayanihan* production groups. In the case of the latter, as indicated earlier, the ABCD approach was more of a complement to the COMBASE programme, rather than an independent catalyst.

Sustaining a community-driven process will depend on how these organizations fare in the future. In Midkiwan, MICODA was three years old at the time of writing and at an 'emergent' stage (Stage 2 of 4 stages defined by CCF). In the case of Kitaotao, the future of the vegetable growers' group is uncertain after the five-year lease period has ended. Whether the group will be able to use this experience to strengthen its case for the realization of *lumad* land rights is difficult to say. At the very least, this experience of collaborative effort is a base of cooperative and entrepreneurial experience that members may replicate independently or in different groups at the end of the five years.

In the case of Tongantongan, the institutional framework for cooperative and community driven development exists through various associations and the Stakeholders' Assembly. Its legitimacy rests on the base of participation and cooperation at the level of farming households and new forms of *bayanihan* groups. Its future will depend on leadership to reinforce the mechanisms for participation. Thus far, the *barangay* captain has been exceptional in this respect.

An important indicator of 'agency' (or community capacity to act) is the way in which extension workers relate to that community. Extension workers reported a change in their role and relationship with communities. As one worker notes, a readiness to 'give [the] leadership role to others' rather than shouldering responsibility for solving community problems (personal communication, 2006). Emphasizing the capacities of community leaders, affirming individual talents, and encouraging the resolution of conflicts, workers noticed a shift in their own (and their organization's) approach from one of paternalistic service to a linking role, bring people together, providing access to information, and helping expand relationships with external agencies so that communities can diversify their relationships as well as their livelihood base. As another of SEARSOLIN's fieldworkers commented: 'ABCD brings out a more positive approach. It makes a big difference. People are taking ownership more. People are taking charge' (personal communication, 2006).

Conclusion

In terms of 'agency,' the ABCD approach has been reflected in a capacity to be both reactive and proactive. For example, communities have organized to react to an opportunity, often evoking previous organizing efforts where sweat equity was provided in return for government services. It is in this context that the term 'counterpart' is often heard, even as a verb, as in 'the community "counter-parted" its labour.' In contrast, showing a more proactive capacity, some communities were able to take on one self-mobilized activity after another, leveraging external assistance. They see themselves more as attracting investment than attracted by external incentives. The members of MICODA, the vegetable growers' group, and the TOFFSA have all taken a proactive role, finding now that as a more organized voice, they are all better-positioned now to take up issues with local government or other external institutions.

It is still difficult, but necessary, for members of communities to think of their access to land, social services, and participation in governance as their rights to be claimed rather than as favours to be earned through loyalty or subservience to the powerful. In fact, it is the duty of the Department of Environment and Natural Resources to assist the people of Midkiwan to reforest the land obtained through the Community Based Forestry Management instrument. It is part of the policy of the government as signatory to Agenda 21 to promote sustainable agriculture and to provide the necessary infrastructure, like roads and schools, for the beneficiaries of the Comprehensive Agrarian Reform Program. It is a provision of the Indigenous People's Rights Act that *lumad*s get protection and support from local government even when they are displaced and not living in their ancestral lands. The ABCD process should therefore include awareness of rights and advocacy strategies for claim-making.

Finally, no matter how well-intentioned, effective development practice can stand or fall based on the spirit and understanding of the fieldworkers and the effective support of those fieldworkers by their NGOs. Training in an asset-based approach has been shown here to inspire fieldworkers to recognize the assets and skills of communities, and to help people mobilize those assets over which they have control. Fieldworkers who are effective do not see themselves as 'doing ABCD to communities' but as catalysts for communities to organize and lead their own community development. It is then the role of the NGOs and local governments to support those fieldworkers and those communities by advocating for an accelerated pace of change so that asset creation and asset-building can continue.

Endnotes

1. The full title is Community Based Sustainable Agriculture – Strategic Agriculture and Fisheries Development Zone – Comprehensive Land Use Plan (COMBASE-SAFDZ-CLUP).
2. 1 USD is equivalent to approximately 45 PHP (Philippine Pesos), at 3 March 2008.
3. TFO, created by City Ordinance number 03-2005, is composed of COMBASE committee chairs, and of representatives from Xavier University, the City of Valencia, and civil society organizations.
4. Approximately 440 USD.
5. Of the 37 households practising Sloping Agricultural Land Technology, 18 are in San Roque.

References

Anna, B. (2005) *Implementing asset-based community development: A case study from the Philippines*, Unpublished thesis for the Masters in Philosophy in Development Studies, Massey University, Palmerston North, New Zealand.

Association of Foundations (2005) *Philippine NGOs in the 21ˢᵗ century: Searching for renewed relevance*, Association of Foundations, Quezon City, Philippines,

Bebbington, A. (1999) Capitals and capabilities. A framework for analyzing peasant viability, rural livelihoods and poverty, *World Development*, 27 (12): 2021-2044.

Carino, L.V., Racelis, R.H., Fernan, R.L., Sokolowski, S.W. and Salamon, L.M. (2004) 'The Philippines' in *Global civil society: Dimensions of the nonprofit sector*, Kumarian Press, Bloomfield, CT.

College of Agriculture Complex, Xavier University (2004) *Support for food security, sustainable development and promotion of the culture of peace activities of the college of agriculture complex*, Fifth Interim Report to Danchurchaid Xavier University, Cagayan de Oro City, Philippines.

COMBASE. (n.d.) *Sustainable agriculture and organic rice development master plan in Valencia City: Asset-based rapid participatory rural appraisal and mapping manual*, Xavier University, Cagayan de Oro City, Philippines.

Davies, R. and Dart, J. (2005) *The 'Most Significant Change' (MSC) technique: A guide to its use*. Available from http://www.mande.co.uk/docs/MSCGuide. pdf [Accessed 3 August 2007].

Foster, M. (2001) *Report on pilot phase of ABCD in Midkiwan and Tongantongan* (Internal document), Coady International Institute, Antigonish, Nova Scotia, Canada.

Galario, J.M. Jr, Salvan, G.F., MGA and Tagupa, V.I. (2005) *Local government initiatives to promote organic agriculture: Tri-sector partnerships for sustainable agriculture and organic rice development master plan in Valencia City, Bukidnon*, Paper presented to the 2ⁿᵈ Organic Agriculture Conference, Bureau of Soil and Water Management, 6 December 2005, Quezon City, Manila, Philippines.

Mercado, A. (2004) *The 'ABCD' approach*, Paper presented to the ICRA Asian Forum, 29 November – 3 December, 2004, Taiwan.

Mercado, A. (2005a) 'The Government and the cooperative movement', in Mercado, A. (ed.) *Readings on cooperative-ism and cooperatives*, SEARSOLIN and College of Agriculture, Xavier University, Cagayan de Oro City, Philippines.

Mercado, A. (2005b) *The SEARSOLIN story: 41 years*, SEARSOLIN and College of Agriculture, Xavier University, Cagayan de Oro City, Philippines.

Mercado, A., (2005c) 'The 'ABCD' Approach to Sustainability of Cooperatives' Philippines Federation of Credit Cooperatives: Northern Mindanao League Annual General Assembly and Educational Forum SEARSOLIN, Xavier University, Cagayan de Oro City, 7 May 2003, in Mercado, A. *Readings on Cooperative-ism and Cooperatives*, pp95–98 SEARSOLIN/College of Agriculture, Xavier University, Cagayan de Oro City, Philippines.

Muslim, M.A. and Cagoco-Guiam, R. (April 1999) *Mindanao: Land of promise*. Available from: http://www.c-r.org/our-work/accord/philippines-mindanao/promised-land.php [Accessed 3 August 2007].

Polestico, R.V., Quizon, A.B., and Hildemann, P. (1998) *Agrarian reform in the Philippines: Status and perspectives for 1998 and beyond*, German Agro Action, International Institute of Rural Reconstruction and Y.C. James Yen Center, Silang, Cavite, Philippines.

Stein, J. (ed) (1984) *The Random House College Dictionary*, Random House, New York.

Tumbaga, L.C. and Sabado, M.M. (2003) *Propelling growth, managing costs: A challenge to local governments*, Ateneo Center for Social Policy and Public Affairs, Quezon City, Philippines.

World Bank, The (2006) *The World Bank country assistance strategy for the Philippines 2006–2008*, The World Bank, Washington, DC.

Glossary

barangay   The smallest local government unit in the Philippines
bayanihan   A spirit of communal unity or effort to achieve a particular objective
lumad   A group of indigenous peoples of Southern Mindanao, the Philippines
purok   A village, district, or ward
Datu   Title for ancient tribal chieftains and monarchs in the pre-Hispanic Philippines

Author's note

As explained in this chapter, the relationship between SEARSOLIN and the Coady Institute goes back over forty years. In 2000, an article in the Coady newsletter about ABCD piqued the interest of Dr Mercado at SEARSOLIN. Around the same time Vic Tagupa from Xavier University attended a course at the Coady Institute and had informal conversations with Gordon Cunningham about ABCD. From that point on, Vic Tagupa began applying some of the principles of ABCD in work he was doing promoting organic rice production in Tongantongan, Valencia City, and Rachel Polestico and Luther Labidad began introducing the ABCD principles in their training at SEARSOLIN. Subsequently, they adapted the approach in several different settings on Mindanao and encouraged graduates of their programmes in the Philippines and elsewhere as they experimented with this approach.

This case study focuses on three sites – Midkiwan, Tongantongan, and Kitaotao. Because of the contrasting land tenure arrangements, and their different experiences with local government they provided contrasting settings in which to explore the potential of an ABCD approach. With funding support from the Comart Foundation, SEARSOLIN was able to document its experience using this approach, which could then be reviewed for the production of this case study.

Megan Foster assisted with data collection and document review in early 2006, building on her reporting on the early work in Tongantongan and Midkiwan in 2001, all while employed by the Coady Institute. Alison Mathie and Megan Foster then carried out field research in February 2006. In each site, three days were spent interviewing community groups and individuals, beginning with a modified version of Rick Davies' 'Most Significant Change Technique' (2003). Separate interviews were conducted with extension workers and programme directors, with agricultural officers, and local government officials. Following a review of all data, a preliminary set of findings was discussed with programme staff and a deeper level analysis explored in this group setting. Megan Foster's insights on leadership have been particularly helpful, and are now being analyzed further for her thesis research for a Masters in Adult Education.

Rachel Polestico, Dr Anselmo Mercado, Luther Labidad, Andy Lewke of SEARSOLIN, and Mr Vic Tagupa of Xavier University facilitated the research and were generous with their time and knowledge, as were extension workers Carmen Oblimar, Marcelo R. Sialongo, and Amy Patriarca. Leileen Abachin and Mericris Omahoy provided able translation services, and Lindy Daclag provided photographic documentation.

In particular, thanks must go to members of the communities of Midkiwan, Tongantongan, Maramag and Patag for graciously sharing their stories and answering questions. Barangay Captain Ms Deody Pugado was particularly helpful in facilitating the research in Tongantongan.

It is always a humbling experience to try to capture in 20 pages what has taken place over years of hard work and involved the passion and dedication of so many. I am grateful to Rachel Polestico and Vic Tagupa for their help in getting three complicated stories straight and to Jay Ross for his comments on an earlier draft.

CHAPTER 14
Conclusion

Alison Mathie and Gordon Cunningham

The [local informal] affinity groups were unpolished diamonds sitting under stones, some of which we ourselves had placed; we just happened to kick these stones by accident.' (Fernandez, personal communication, 2006)

The case studies in this book are a testament to the power of people working as a community (of place or of identity) to change the course of their own development. Not only can these communities serve as inspiration to others but they also present the possibility of citizen-driven development as both a starting point and an objective of development practice. Seen in this light, the cases reveal 'unpolished diamonds' to be uncovered in many places: leadership; social networks that connect people to resources, information and mutual support; a long history of technical and social innovation; and diverse and complex livelihood strategies that balance maintaining security with exploring opportunity. These riches may not be sufficient in all communities for sustaining broad-based movement out of poverty, but recognition of them does provide the basis for leverage. NGOs and governments that for decades assumed the role of primary agents of community development are shifting their ground in response to a well-organized community, where people are confident of their experience and achievement. In this concluding chapter, we review some of the common threads running through these cases. The intention is to inspire new community leaders and external agencies to stimulate and support citizen-driven development elsewhere, to discover similarly successful communities, and 'to imagine and practice development differently' (Gibson-Graham, 2005: 6).

Leadership that motivates people to act

In these case studies, people in communities have been motivated to collaborate, whether to respond to a crisis, or to protect their interests, or to meet opportunities. Yet the real motivators are not the crises or opportunities themselves but the leadership that is able to stimulate the sense of pride in the community's history, the sense of hope or possibility, and often the sacrifice needed to realize longer-term goals. Typically, leadership is found not in formal leaders but in committed activists, social innovators and entrepreneurs who achieve legitimacy because of their reputation as 'doers' in the community. The young leaders in the Egypt case, for example, are given the blessing of traditional leadership and allowed full rein to act on their vision, earning recognition as leaders by their capacity to mobilize youth and other resources in the community, and by their ability to negotiate astutely with government. The social entrepreneur in the Vietnam case was an innovator twice over – in his ability to transform the previous political era's collective ideal into a private sector enterprise, and doing this without compromising either the need to make a profit or the commitment to provide locally based employment. The different leaders in Conjunto Palmeira who inspired community action first in protest, then in building the local economy are further examples.

Sometimes provided by leaders in the community, sometimes by leaders outside the community, the bridge to information and support beyond the community is a critical element in these cases. Jamal in the Morocco case, for example, is the bridge that links the opportunity presented by the migrants from France with the pre-existing capacities and motivations of their villages of origin. Ela Bhatt, the driving force behind SEWA's growth, draws upon her experience of union organizing and her professional legal background to inspire self employed women to organize and to connect them to the information and advice they need.

Women's leadership pervades these cases, but sometimes in subtle ways. In some cases women were at the vanguard of change – as in the case of SEWA's leadership, for example, or Rosa in the Jambi Kiwa case, Deody Pugado, the *barangay* captain in the Philippines case, Notizi Vanda in the South Africa case, or Marinete in the Brazil case. In other cases, women's leadership was the result of a different way of working at the community level – building slowly on existing resources rather than promising large and sudden change. The women leaders of Community Based Organizations (CBOs) in Jansenville, South Africa, are a case in point. The Kenya case is another: the ABCD approach introduced by the Kenyan NGO promised no quick fixes, but women recognized that they could gain from the incremental steps offered through 'assisted self-help' (while some men took a more disdainful view of such a slow pace of change). The same response came from women in Ethiopia who at the start of the ABCD process stood back, but were recognized over time as the force behind changes they were able to orchestrate in their communities. Similarly the South India case demonstrates how a slow but steady approach to group savings and lending increased women's group assets far faster than the men's groups and paved the way for women's influence at the SAG federation and local government levels.

The inspiration of individual leaders notwithstanding, the recurring theme of these cases is dispersed leadership (Tapia et al., 2003). Implicit in the ability to mobilize is the leadership of many, working in complementary ways. Where this stands out most is in the Brazil, Ecuador, Canada, South India, SEWA, and US cases, with the latter providing a particularly vivid example of Latino immigrants realizing the collective breadth of their experience that could be channelled towards a common purpose. Their belief in their collective capacity helped each and every one to 'hang in there' when external agencies were slow to respond. As in other cases, rather than leading from the front of the group most of the key individuals were 'connectors' whose magic lay in bringing people together, seeing the potential in their friends and acquaintances, and asking them to lend a hand.

Dispersed leadership in these cases is less about relieving the burden of leadership of a few, or about diluting the concentration of power in their hands, and more about the power to act being spread widely. This spreading of power is possible in communities where the associational base is strong because in each association or informal network leadership skills are being practised. Nonetheless, inviting new leadership can be a challenge, particularly where economic opportunities have drawn younger community members away. Addressing this, the Brazil case showed how the Residents' Association recognized the importance of nurturing a new generation of leaders, by stipulating this responsibility in its bylaws. The Jambi Kiwa cooperative in the Ecuador case and SEWA, both member-based organizations, provide examples of deliberate nurturing of leadership through the ranks and rotating leadership at the top.

Motivation to lead, and to act collectively or cooperatively, was in all cases undergirded by a well articulated set of values. Whether the Gandhian principles of SEWA, or the responsibilities to others imbued in Islam, or the traditional sentiments of *ubuntu* in South Africa ('a person is a person through other persons...my humanity is bound up inextricably in yours...'), or the principles of social justice in humanist traditions, or 'loving thy neighbour' in Christian traditions, religious faith is invoked as the reason for caring and sharing, and also for forgiving and directing energy towards the future. As Rosa in the Ecuador case says of her attitude towards a painful past and a more promising future, 'The challenge is not to be bitter...the way forward is for us all to come together.' (Guamán, quoted in Cunningham, this volume).

Innovation from blending local knowledge with new ideas

Leadership has also played an important role in preparing the way for innovation. Not just a new idea or a new technology, innovation also has to do with the climate that permits the development of new ideas. Leaders therefore have to be innovative in the way they disseminate and discuss new ideas with the wider community as well as open to new ideas themselves. For example, to improve prospects of future survival and prosperity, the villages in the Moroccan Souss required 'hardware' in the form of infrastructure for irrigation and electricity. Effective and affordable technical solutions required the melding of local skills and imported expertise. At the same time, the discussion involved in reaching these solutions became the forerunner of innovative social arrangements (the 'software') to manage the infrastructure, again building on and adapting the traditional forms of community resource management. Without the collaboration of traditional leadership with the leadership of returning migrants, and the ability to resolve the tensions inherent in the fusion of old and new, appropriate social and technical innovation would have been difficult to accomplish.

The blend of technical and social innovation was also found in other cases. In Ethiopia, traditional burial societies became the vehicle for organizing a grain bank, a house construction group, a labour sharing cooperative, and an oxen insurance scheme. In Canada, the residents of St Andrews adapted a share scheme meant for joint stock companies to finance their curling rink. Similarly the 'technical' innovations in member-owned savings and credit in the South India case could be applied to adaptations of pre-existing affinity groups, and so on.

Pretty notes that 'throughout the history of modern agricultural development, local groups and institutions have rarely been recognized. As a result, external institutions and governments have routinely suffocated local institutions during agricultural modernization' (Pretty, 2001: 281). The Philippines case illustrates this and its counterpoint. Here, 'modernized' agriculture introduced in the 1980s reorganized farmers so that mono-cropping of high-yielding varieties of rice or corn was individualized and streamlined into larger and larger plots, while marketing was 'cooperativized' through government. Now, with the adoption of diversified organic agricultural production, dormant (rather than completely suffocated) local institutions have since re-emerged as an adapted *bayanihan* system of shared research, knowledge, and labour on the smaller, more intensively worked plots. At the same time, farmers have resumed their role as organizers and managers of agricultural production, not just producers of agricultural commodities, and some have additional responsibilities as stakeholder representatives in deliberations about the project itself with local government, university, and private sector actors.

There is no glossing over the fact that crafting these innovations and adaptations can be fraught with conflict: resistance to new leadership, resistance to women's participation, resistance to the ideas of returning migrants, resistance to inclusion of people of the lowest caste have been dealt with in several different ways and have sometimes taken years to resolve. Resolution has come about either because the positive contribution of those previously excluded has been recognized, or because of the skilled mediation of community leaders, or because community approval of the activities of individuals and groups renders them immune to political manoeuvring by an old guard. Often it is those who have left the community and who return with new ideas based on experience elsewhere that trigger change, and those, like the young leaders in the Egypt case who can do this with the full blessing of traditional leaders, are the most likely to be successful.

Inherent in any opportunity for innovation is a potential trade-off that community members have to weigh. For example, in both Ecuador and

Vietnam, people's efforts to come together to reclaim indigenous knowledge (medicinal and aromatic plants in Ecuador and the bamboo trade in Vietnam) resulted in the formation of new enterprises. These emergent firms and some of the member-owned MFIs featured in this collection constantly struggle with whether they are businesses or social enterprises. In both cases there is a reluctance to grow the businesses (an increase in assets) if doing so requires a loss of control over decision-making (a decrease in agency). Innovation in these examples not only requires taking a risk, but being accountable for the consequences; so the way people organize to share that accountability and manage risk becomes crucial for community cohesion.

Balancing risk: the need for security as well as opportunity

At the household level, new livelihood strategies require a similar weighing of risk. As the South India case makes clear, 'people need security and opportunity,' to move out of poverty and a position of inferiority. Incremental savings, and opportunities to take loans through the SAGs, allow members to gradually build up assets, and this in turn influences their motivation to meet opportunity, such as investing in a lease of land to grow commercial crops. The SEWA case similarly shows that for women in precarious self-employment, insurance and protection against unfair employment practices are the first priorities in a livelihood strategy. In both cases, these associations are the vehicle for individual women to build security and identify opportunity, and at the same time they constitute a secure base for poor women to act as a group to further their interests and advocate for their rights, whether in their dealings with government or in their dealings with the banking sector.

Several of the cases emphasize how gradual this process of building security is. Although the sequencing may vary, the establishment of basic infrastructure and health and educational services (South India, Morocco, Egypt) is typically the first priority. Then, through pooling financial assets, greater financial security can be achieved through savings and investment (South India, SEWA, Ecuador). In the Brazil case, the Residents' Association realized that the very security they had fought for in one generation was not affordable for the next unless serious efforts were made to increase opportunities for income generation. Part of the solution was to issue local currency that could only be used in participating businesses in the community as a way of preventing leakage of local spending power.

Balancing rights and responsibilities

Permeating all these cases is the question of what people in communities take pride in doing for themselves, and what are considered social and economic obligations of the public sector. Many of the cases here demonstrate that rights and responsibilities are intertwined, that citizenship is as much about mutual support and collective effort as it is about occupying a space to claim rights from the state. Most of the cases in fact show how these two dimensions of citizenship can overlap or mutually reinforce each other, and how it is community initiative and community innovation that sets the terms of engagement with state actors rather than the other way round.

The Canadian and South Africa cases are two examples of the way in which communities have helped redefine the notion of entitlement from the state – and in so doing empowered their citizens. The Canada case demonstrates the leverage a community can pull with local government if it can first demonstrate that government investment will yield sustained results. The community had already built a community centre and curling rink without seeking government assistance. This put them in a strong position to convince the government to support a community-initiated, non-profit, affordable housing scheme for senior citizens. In the South Africa case, we are witness to a delicate balancing act: community leaders struggle with the issue of how to facilitate access to long fought-for rights (in this case, social grants) in a way that does not undermine motivation or capacity to act for themselves. Through negotiation, this tension may be resolved through various forms of 'co-production' of services such as pre-school education, road maintenance, or home-based care of the sick (Goetz and Gaventa et al., 2001), but such solutions are likely to be highly contextualized in time and place, varying with people's changing expectations and local government capacities to deliver.

And so, the way communities engage with the state has much to do with the historical and political context. For this reason, the cases illustrate a variety of strategies used to get attention from state actors. Sometimes these strategies are confrontational, as in the early period of the Brazil case and the protests organized by SEWA. By contrast, in several country contexts, such as in the Egypt case, such strategies would have been counterproductive and a more conciliatory approach was required. Interestingly, in the US case, while some community leaders were keen to use tactics inherited from community organizing during the civil rights movement, other leaders prevailed in the choice of a more patient strategy of dialogue appropriate for the current context. This involved drawing public and private sector actors in to collaborate in their vision for a revitalized downtown area, demonstrating their organizational capacity and their own worth as contributors to the revitalization effort. This was also the way government participation was encouraged in the Morocco case, requiring similar levels of patience and persistence. Years of neglect were remedied by community-led innovation that showed government how it could deliver services efficiently and effectively.

In several cases, an astute use of the media was a key element of community strategies to get the attention of government and the public at large. Sometimes the media was used to embarrass the government, sometimes to remind government of its obligations, and sometimes to showcase community achievement as a way of attracting government or private sector attention. As the landless and neglected indigenous people in the Philippines case discovered, local government is keen to be associated with initiatives that have attracted positive media attention.

As appropriate forms of decentralized governance involving citizens in decision-making as a right (and a responsibility) are worked out, collaborative models of engagement will continue to emerge. However, creating political space for citizen participation can be just 'participatory window dressing.' What these cases suggest is that to take advantage of newly created political space, and the promise of collaboration, the experience of active citizen engagement in associations that are able to mobilize support for their cause is a distinct advantage (Fung and Wright, 2003). Not only does this experience put muscle behind political voice, but also provides protection against efforts to co-opt or to sabotage. SEWA's role in the partnership with the Gujarat government benefited initially from this experience, and its sense of collective identity has enabled it to stand its ground and survive without the partnership when the relationship faltered.

At the crux of this discussion on rights and responsibilities is an equation (Gaventa, 2004). On one side is the capacity of people to organize, to stay connected and informed and to advance their interests. On the other side is the capacity of local institutions in both private and public sectors to respond and collaborate. On both sides of this equation, imperfections exist, but these cases draw attention to communities that have found ingenious ways to align their own efforts with a sometimes very small opportunity that over time is enlarged through collaboration with public and private agencies. As such, they challenge a common perception that 'self-help' is an excuse for 'don't help', and unravel 'the paradox of assisted self-help' (Uphoff, 1986, in Hulme, 2000).

Implications for practice

While the authors of the cases in this book have highlighted citizen-driven initiative and local leadership, they have not shied away from acknowledging the important role that NGOs, local government and donor agencies can make at strategic turning points in the community's history. Building on insights drawn from the case studies, the following discussion explores some of the lessons and implications for development practitioners attempting to support or stimulate citizen-driven initiative.

We have seen that as communities shift from organizing for survival to organizing to meet opportunity, key individuals or institutions have played an essential role linking communities to information and other resources, and offering them strategies to maximize the possibilities. These individuals and institutions have been located both inside and outside the community, or are individuals that bridge that 'inside-out' divide. While appreciative of past success and achievement, they are the purveyors of opportunity, helping people to re-evaluate risk and uncertainty, and the trade-offs of effort and reward. They inspire hope and the possibility of mitigating risk through collective effort. They are trusted and build on trust within the community; and many of the cases go into some depth about how those relationships of trust are extended and deepened both within the community and beyond it. When such trust has been violated (as has been the case historically in many instances with respect to government or NGO services), efforts to rebuild that trust take time.

The spark that ignites change does not usually start in large community meetings, but rather in small pockets of enthusiasm, that gradually 'infect' others. Discovering and encouraging the kind of broad-based leadership of many (rather than a few) social entrepreneurs, managers, and mediators among older and younger generations, women and men, is all part of the process. By showing their strengths, not hiding them, the focus of community building is on reinvigorating these strengths and capacities through renewed action at the community level. Through that action, community relationships of trust are widened and strengthened. And from that basis of strength, assistance or 'investment' from outsiders, such as NGOs or government can be responsive rather than directive, and will reinforce rather than undermine community capacity.

When NGOs get involved in these cases, they sometimes respond to community-wide initiative, and sometimes deliberately get involved with particular marginalized groups to help build capacity and a sense of community, as evident in the case of Myrada. Here, 'investment' took the form of investing in the poorest groups, helping to strengthen their capacity to build financial assets, and helping to shift attitudes in the wider community about their potential as contributors to village life. In this setting, where caste distinctions are entrenched, community building began at the associational level, through SAGs, but over time these marginalized groups were able to move into the mainstream and gain acceptance and recognition in the wider community. The NGO role in this instance was to address social inequality head on, but through demonstrating to the wider community and external agencies the potential of those once marginalized by caste and gender.

In the Ethiopia, Philippines, and Kenya cases, NGOs used an asset-based methodology in an effort to rekindle community initiative and stimulate the community-driven process featured in the other cases. The methodology includes tools that help communities identify assets and opportunities. Some of these are adaptations of conventional PRA tools, but others are designed specifically to affirm community assets, skills and experience, and generate ideas for building the local economy. It is important, however, that an ABCD approach does not become co-opted and applied 'tyrannically' (Cooke and Kothari, 2001) as a means of extracting information by outside agencies, instead of catalysing citizen-driven initiative. In fact, the approach is fundamentally not about mapping or drawing up lists, but about community organizing, motivated by an awareness of existing community power to act. The merit of using the tools must then be assessed on whether they stimulate organizing rather than solely generating information.

Beyond the use of tools, the approach requires a shift in organizational culture. In keeping with Easterly (2006), this culture encourages 'searchers' rather than 'planners,' a deep respect for existing capacities in communities, and flexibility to pace their assistance so that those capacities are strengthened rather than undermined by a rush to meet project deadlines.

For some development workers, old habits and attitudes may be hard to break. The example of REST in the Ethiopia case illustrates that it can be easier to get community members to appreciate their own assets, experiences and potentials than it is to get senior NGO staff to appreciate the capacities of community members.

A shift in NGO practice also requires a shift in the role and expectations of donors. For example, donor preoccupation with accountability for results has tended to bias donors in favour of supporting discreet service delivery projects with rigid time lines that have left little room for community initiative or little tolerance for unpredictability. The cases in this book are a reminder to take a longer term view, to take into account the multiple factors influencing change, to invest in experimentation, and to track the process and impact of innovative practice, combining community expertise with expertise drawn from outside. Smaller donors, for example, can offer strategic small scale financial support but more importantly they can donate time and introductions to networks that pave the way for community groups to access the advice and information they need to move forward, as in the case of Ikhala Trust in South Africa. Different models for community foundations offer a range of possibilities for combining community assets with donor investment, managed at the local level.

As for the implications for local government practice, it is clear from these cases that the experience of local government decentralization has so far been extremely varied. In some places, as indicated by Robinson (2007) and Conyers (2007), unrealistic assumptions about the potential for local government to deliver services has led to disappointment and frustration when expectations have not been met. This is borne out by most of the cases at some point in their history but is particularly true in the Kenyan case. Yet several of the case studies highlight some of the ingredients of positive outcomes of recent local government decentralization. These include political commitment (evident in the Brazil, Philippines, South Africa and India cases, for example), community organizing and its associated capacity to hold local government accountable (to varying degrees in the Brazil, India, Philippines, South Africa and Egypt cases), the availability of adequate financial resources (i.e. fiscal decentralization, as in the case of South Africa), the technical and managerial capacity in local governments (notably stronger in Brazil, the Philippines, South Africa and India), and creative models for co-production of services by community groups and local governments.

These creative models are evident in several of the cases. We have seen governments invest in community-built and managed affordable housing for seniors (Canada) or a Latino retail market (US). We have also seen governments at several levels respond to the need for wider marketing for promising new products such as organic rice (Philippines), bamboo furniture (Vietnam) or medicinal herbs (Ecuador). We have even seen a national government replicate a community innovation in technology to provide a cheaper form of electrification (Morocco). While we know that governments can support community-driven initiatives, the question is: can they also stimulate them?

For this to happen, a number of suggestions could be made. For example, noting that elected officials have typically been trained to work for the community rather than with the community, Gaventa (2004) suggests they may need help changing attitudes and behaviours so that they listen to and engage with local communities, and local citizens can be helped to understand rights, responsibilities and procedures and provided opportunities to learn skills of negotiation and collaborative leadership. Also, creative incentive schemes could be put in place to reward local government officials for responsiveness, and to reward community groups that demonstrate active citizenship and community spirit.

In some places, citizens are offered opportunities to collaborate with local governments in development planning (Philippines, Brazil, India, and South Africa most notably). However, these plans often turn out to be reflections of the priorities of higher levels of government. When this is the case, community participation is often equated with mobilizing community labour or materials (or 'counter-parting' to use the Philippines case term). And yet these local government development plans could be so much more. They could be opportunities for developing consensus on what activities should (and could) be provided by the state, and what activities should (and could) be initiated and undertaken by groups of citizens, and perhaps at some later stage be invested in, or supported by, the state.

Finally, as citizen-led initiatives grow in scale and quality there are often opportunities to link with private sector partners. For example, in the Jambi Kiwa case, a customer of the cooperative eventually became a joint venture partner, distributing Jambi Kiwa tea products in the Ecuadorian market. In the South India case, commercial banks agreed to deal directly with self-help groups. An increasing number of private sector actors may see opportunities for partnering with communities that are organizing themselves for larger scale production (such as those in the Philippines and Ethiopian cases) as a way of addressing the issue of corporate social responsibility and the security of their supply chains. However, as already discussed with respect to the Ecuador and Vietnamese cases, one of the main obstacles private firms will encounter in trying to encourage social enterprises to partner and grow with them is the fear by communities of losing control of not only their businesses but also of their larger social agendas. Whether 'triple bottom line' enterprises can accommodate these agendas or actively assist in their realization will be something to watch in the future.

Implications for policy

Paying attention to the historical context of a community's development, these case studies complement a large body of work on the role of assets and institutions in sustainable livelihoods. Particular emphasis has been on how the policy environment can facilitate asset-building among poor and vulnerable groups. Moser (2007), for example, drawing on a 26-year study of a slum community in Ecuador, outlines a trajectory that is reflected in several cases in this volume: initial reliance on community social capital for survival and solidarity, a turning point when households acquire title to land or housing, another leap when basic infrastructure and services are provided. As financial (savings) and other assets begin to grow and diversify, strategic decisions can be made to sustain and build livelihood – whether to invest in children's education, purchase consumables, invest in small enterprise, or build savings and social relationships for both security and opportunity. In order to ensure a sustained improvement in well-being. Moser then goes on to explore the difference between policies associated with social protection and policies associated with asset accumulation. While social protection policies are designed to minimize risk, asset accumulation policy focuses on 'how to strengthen opportunities and dilute constraints' for sustainable livelihoods, identifying the circumstances under which 'risk' is an opportunity, in the sense that people are devising forward-looking strategies about how to invest the assets that they have. One policy development challenge is therefore how to tailor and target the appropriate mix of policies to minimize risk or reduce vulnerability and yet offer opportunity for risk-taking in an entrepreneurial sense if local economies are to flourish. This is a dilemma that is picked up in the South Africa chapter in this volume, and addressed squarely in the Philippines case where municipal policies supporting organic agricultural production are key motivators for community organizing around sustainable livelihoods.

One example of how policy has lagged behind events on the ground is in the area of remittances. Several of the case studies in this book illustrate how a community's diaspora can be drawn into supporting community-driven initiatives. With global remittances now running at roughly USD300 billion annually (IFAD, 2007), there is an opportunity for policy-makers to encourage not just household to household transfers but also the flow of resources from diasporas to their home communities in the form of support for, and investment in, community development activities. The experience of the Migrant Savings for Alternative Investments (MSAI) programme in Jagna municipality in the Philippines, for example, illustrates 'the possibility of transforming overseas contract migration into an opportunity for place-based community economic development' (Gibson-Graham, 2005: 7).

Finally, in the area of local government decentralization, the policy implications are to promote the changes necessary to stimulate both active citizen participation and responsive local government. Mechanisms for local government responsiveness may need to be 'incentivized', as might creative ways of engaging groups in the community that tend to be excluded. For example, quotas for women and scheduled caste representation in local government have not only provided a role to aspire to for those who have been downtrodden, but also strengthen the role of people's institutions such as SAGs to provide space for community members to gain experience for leadership in local government.

In positioning citizen-driven development in the context of local government decentralization, these cases should inspire further research into the results of these efforts. For example, the World Bank's strategy of 'Community Driven Development' could be expanded from a focus on supporting local governments and community groups in building sustainable infrastructure to include investment in a much wider range of citizen-led initiatives such as agriculture, natural resource management and enterprise development. Of course as the Bank itself acknowledges 'Such investments bring community-driven projects squarely into the "grey" realm of defining the appropriate role of the public sector in promoting market-led sustainable development' (World Bank, 2007). It is here that the tussles at the community level in resolving who is responsible for community development are writ large for the enabling policy environment: reconciling the imperative of social protection and public service with the space for people in communities to identify appropriate institutional models for engaging with the market.

Conclusion

By their very nature, case studies are context-specific and resistant to 'grand theory', but they can, paradoxically, provoke us into thinking differently. The people in the communities profiled in this collection remind us that they have skills and capacities that they can mobilize for change, the evidence being in stories of survival, struggle, sustained collective effort and a sense of community that has stayed afloat in the changing currents running through community life. They are powerful in their recognition of their own strengths, and in their motivation to make use of them, as new opportunities or crises arise. Their social connectedness is the bedrock of collective over individual effort. There is a 'master narrative' of collective consciousness. They have leadership that personalizes deeply held values and principles that reinforce identity with the common good. People in these communities are not naïve, but sophisticated in their ability to innovate socially and technically, astute in their ability to identify opportunity and invite others to invest in them. Above all they have generative power, inspiring others with 'We are poor, but we are many!' 'We can do something for ourselves,' and rejecting relationships that cast them as deficient. As Kretzmann observes, we should not seek ways to replicate these as models, but to remove the obstacles to their proliferation (personal communication, 2007), so that different expressions of active citizens in active communities can flourish. As outsiders and insiders, we need to educate ourselves about the 'unpolished diamonds,' not assume we know, and we should expect others to do no less.

References

Conyers, D. (2007) 'Decentralisation and service delivery: Lessons from Sub-Saharan Africa', in *IDS Bulletin*, 38(1): 18–32.

Cooke, B. and Kothari, U. (2001) *Participation: The new tyranny?* Zed Books, London.

Easterly, W. (2006) *The white man's burden: How the west's efforts to aid the rest have done so much ill and so little good*, Penguin Press, New York.

Fung, A. and Wright E.O. (2003) *Deepening democracy: Institutional innovations in empowered participatory governance*, Verso, London.

Gaventa, J. (2004) 'Towards participatory governance: Assessing the transformative Possibilities' In S. Hickey and G. Mohan (eds.), *Participation: From tyranny to transformation? Exploring new approaches to participation in development*, Zed Books, New York.

Gibson-Graham, J.K. (2005) 'Surplus possibilities: Postdevelopment and community economics', *Singapore Journal of Tropical Geography*, 26(1): 4–26

Goetz, A.M. and Gaventa, J., et al (July 2001) 'Bringing citizen voice and client focus into service delivery' *Working paper 138*, Institute of Development Studies, Brighton, UK.

Hulme, D. (January 2000) 'Protecting and strengthening social capital in order to produce desirable development outcomes', *Social Development Department, SD SCOPE Paper No. 4*, Institute for Development Policy and Management, University of Manchester, Manchester, UK.

International Fund for Agricultural Development (2007) *Sending money home: Worldwide remittance flows to developing countries.* Available from http://www.ifad.org/events/remittances/maps/ [Accessed 9 November 2007]

Moser, C. (ed.) (2007) 'Asset accumulation policy and poverty reduction', in *Reducing global poverty: the case for asset accumulation*, Brookings Institution, Washington, DC.

Pretty, J. (2001) 'Saving our small farms and rural communities' in J. Mander and E. Goldsmith (eds), *The case against the global economy and for a turn towards localization*, 2nd edn, pp. 277–288), Earthscan, London.

Robinson, M. (2007) 'Introduction: Decentralising service delivery? Evidence and policy implications' *IDS Bulletin* 38(1): 1-17.

Tapia, M., Underwood, C. and Jabre, B. (September 2003) *Emerging leadership in the Near East: Case studies from Egypt, Jordan, Lebanon and Palestine* (Working Paper), Johns Hopkins Bloomberg School of Public Health/ Center for Communication Programs (CCP), Ford Foundation and Save the Children Federation, The Johns Hopkins University, Baltimore, MD.

World Bank, The (2007) *Community driven development.* Available from: http://go.worldbank.org/24K8IHVVS0 [Accessed 30 January 2008].

Index

Lightning Source UK Ltd.
Milton Keynes UK
UKOW031418290413

209938UK00003B/27/P